AMERICA
UNITE OR DIE

D1602203

AMERICA
UNITE OR DIE
HOW TO SAVE OUR DEMOCRACY

Douglas E. Schoen
& Carly Cooperman

Regan Arts.

Regan Arts.

First Regan Arts paperback/hardcover edition, November 2021

LIBRARY OF CONGRESS CONTROL NUMBER: 2021910967

ISBN 978-1-68245-189-2 (eBook)
ISBN 978-1-68245-188-5 (TP)
ISBN 978-1-68245-190-8 (HC)

Interior design by Beth Kessler, Neuwirth & Associates
Cover design by Richard Ljoenes
Cover image by Richard Ljoenes

Printed in the United States of America

Table of Contents

Introduction   1

1 / Loss of Trust in America's Institutions   59

2 / Schoen-Cooperman Research Survey:
      Public Perceptions of Government   127

3 / The Divided States of America   147

4 / A History of Populism   193

5 / The Threat of Political Extremism   233

6 / Russia, China, and the New Cold War   265

7 / Centrist Reforms to Reunite Us   301

8 / Conclusion   401

Notes   429

Afterword   501

Introduction

American democracy—the defining characteristic that has made the United States a magnet for immigrants from around the globe, the leader of the free world, and a model for other nations—is under fire as never before and is threatened with possible extinction. This endangers the foundational rights and freedoms of every American under the Constitution, as well as our national security as we compete on the world stage with our authoritarian adversaries China and Russia.

Over the course of American history our democracy has been threatened from abroad—first by the British Empire and later by Nazi Germany and Imperial Japan, the Soviet Union and then Russia, and most recently Communist China and Islamist terrorism. In *The End of Democracy? Russia and China on the Rise, America in Retreat*, published in 2020, one of us (Douglas Schoen) described the serious danger these two powers pose to America, to global human rights, and to the future of democracy.[1]

Today, the most dangerous threat to our democracy comes not from a foreign adversary but from within, as the radical left gains strength in the Democratic Party and the radical right ascends in the Republican Party. These diametrically opposed forces, moving further and further apart, are threatening not just our democracy but our most fundamental institutions and values. We close our eyes to this grave danger at our peril. Democracy is not just a system of government. It is a system of liberty-affirming values that enshrine minority rights in addition to majority rule. It makes government the servant of the people and not the other way around—unlike in many countries around the world. The Bill of Rights in the Constitution says that freedom of speech and of the press, the right to protest, freedom of religion, the rights of those accused of crimes, and other rights are fundamental to our democracy.

Yet extremists on the left and right are now more focused on reshaping America to conform to their own values than on preserving the traditional democratic values that affirm our freedoms and rights. They have no patience for hearing the other side. They are so convinced of the rightness of their own beliefs that they want to suppress whoever disagrees with them. If they had their way, they would put America on a path that could eventually replace democracy with authoritarianism.

Alarmingly, the United States is more divided and less united today than at any time since our nation split in two during the Civil War. We have forgotten the warning Benjamin Franklin gave the American colonies in 1754 when he published the first American political cartoon in his newspaper, the *Pennsylvania Gazette*. The cartoon was a call for the British colonies to unite to fight as allies in the French and Indian War. It was later revived during the Revolutionary War calling on the new American states to unite to fight for independence from Great Britain. It pictured a snake cut into pieces, with a caption on the bottom stating "JOIN, or DIE."[2] Many people believed at the time that a snake cut into pieces could grow back to life if its parts were joined together before sunset. So Franklin's message was clear—the colonies, which later became states, could not survive unless they united.

Founding Father and former Virginia governor Patrick Henry expressed a similar sentiment in his last public speech in 1799 when he said: "United we stand, divided we fall. Let us not split into factions which must destroy that union upon which our existence hangs."[3]

And Abraham Lincoln famously said in 1858 in a speech to the Illinois Republican Convention: "A house divided against itself cannot stand. I believe this government cannot endure, permanently half slave and half free.... It will become all one thing, or all the other."[4] The unity of the nation and abolition of the evil of slavery were achieved—but only after the Civil War, when scholars now believe as many as 750,000 people died.[5] The total population of the United States was only about 32 million at the time—less than a tenth of our population today.[6] One symbol of national unity was reflected in the way Americans referred to their nation. Before the Civil War they said "the United States are" but after the war they said "the United States is," reflecting the view that the U.S. is a singular entity and not simply an alliance of separate states.

Fast-forward to February 2021, when a new Zogby Poll® found that 46 percent of likely voters believe that another civil war will erupt in our country. There was not much difference between Republicans and Democrats on the question, with 49 percent of Republicans and 45 percent of Democrats saying a second civil war is likely.[7] "It's quite astounding that nearly half of voters think we are headed for bloodshed!" a news release announcing the poll says. "Are we really close to citizens hurting each other on a large-scale basis? The violence that happened from both sides of the political spectrum the last year is significant. Violent protests in cities across the country during the summer, White supremacists, hate crimes on the rise, and tensions between two political parties have put the country on the brink."

America reunited in 1865 at the close of the Civil War, but right now we simply don't know whether we can reunite again after the bitter divisions fueled by both the far left and the far right during Donald Trump's presidency. Things have gotten so bad that many Republican officials won't criticize extremists on the right for fear of angering that faction of their party, while many Democratic officials won't criticize the far left for fear of angering their party's radical wing. The extremist tail is wagging the mainstream dog.

For example, when the U.S. House of Representatives voted 232–197 on January 13, 2021, to impeach then-president Trump for a second time on a charge of "incitement of insurrection" for his role in the deadly January 6 attack on the U.S. Capitol by his supporters—after he urged them to march on the Capitol and fight to overturn former vice president Joe Biden's election victory—only 10 Republicans voted to impeach.[8] At Trump's impeachment trial in the Senate the following month, only seven of the 50 Republican senators voted for his conviction, along with all 48 Democrats and the two independents who caucus with Democrats. The 57 votes for a guilty verdict fell short of the 67 votes needed to convict Trump on the incitement charge.[9]

In another example, when the House voted 230–199 on February 4, 2021, to remove Rep. Marjorie Taylor Greene (R-GA) from congressional committees, only 11 Republicans joined Democrats in supporting the measure.[10] Greene had endorsed the extremist QAnon movement; embraced wild conspiracy theories that were blatantly false, including some that were anti-Semitic and Islamophobic; liked a Facebook comment endorsing shooting House Speaker Nancy Pelosi (D-CA) in the head; and claimed school shootings were secretly staged by government actors. She disavowed some of these views shortly before the House vote, but not all of them. She continued sending fundraising emails almost daily saying Trump had actually won the presidential election and was fraudulently deprived of victory.

Crucially, Greene continued to have the support of Trump, who heaped praise on her. That clearly put her in the good graces of her House GOP colleagues and some Republican donors. In fact, Greene announced in early April 2021 that she raised an extraordinary $3.2 million in campaign donations in the first quarter of the year—a record amount for a House freshman in an off-year election quarter—with 98 percent of the donations coming in at less than $200. The astonishing cash haul was evidence of the level of extremism many Republicans have embraced. ". . . I have been the most attacked freshman member of

Congress in history," Greene tweeted in announcing her fundraising success. "The political ruling class fears the people because it's the people that can take away what they love most. Power. Because it's power that brings them everything else. I am one of the people and the people are with me, and I will always be with them. WE are just getting started!"[11]

It should have been obvious to every House Republican that Greene is a fringe figure who has no place in their party, but many feared voting against her would anger Trump and his millions of supporters. Brian Robinson, who advised Greene's primary opponent, John Cowan, said Greene "is not representative of the national party" but "does represent a segment of the party. I would imagine though that next year in some competitive primaries, where candidates are seeking the support of the most conservative voters, that you will see some people trying to get her endorsement in the primary and then try to never mention it in the general."[12]

On the Democratic side, many in the party neglected to denounce rioting that broke out in cities across the nation in the spring and summer of 2020 and also seemed to condone the Defund the Police movement—a movement based on demonization of police departments by the far left. This illustrates how many elected officials in both parties refused to risk alienating their extremist fringes.

Further, Democratic officials in several cities shifted funds needed by law enforcement to protect communities into social programs of unproven value in enhancing public safety. New York City mayor Bill de Blasio and the city council agreed in June to cut about $1 billion from the city's $6 billion police operating budget.[13] Los Angeles followed suit in November with a $150 million budget cut for its police department.[14] Overall, twenty-four of the fifty largest cities in the U.S. cut their police budgets for 2021, Bloomberg News reported in January 2021, although in some cases cuts came as the result of overall city budget reductions due to the coronavirus pandemic. Police budget reductions that Bloomberg News reported included an 11.2 percent cut in Seattle,

33.2 percent in Austin, 14.8 percent in Minneapolis, and 8.8 percent in Denver.[15]

The Defund the Police movement grew out of understandable anger over the May 25, 2020, death of George Floyd, a Black man killed as he lay on the ground handcuffed and not resisting arrest while White Minneapolis police officer Derek Chauvin knelt on his neck for over nine minutes.[16] Chauvin was fired and eventually convicted in April 2021 of second-degree murder, third-degree murder, and second-degree manslaughter for his crime. Three other officers were charged with aiding and abetting second-degree murder and second-degree manslaughter in Floyd's death, which was captured on video. The Minneapolis City Council voted unanimously in March 2021 to approve a $27 million civil settlement with Floyd's family over his killing. Minneapolis mayor Jacob Frey said the murder of Floyd caused a "century-in-the-making reckoning around racial justice that struck Minneapolis like a thunderbolt" and reverberated around the world.[17] Cell-phone and body camera footage of Floyd's murder made it impossible for officers to convince anyone he died under different circumstances, as they initially tried to do, and has sometimes happened in other police-involved killings in which officers were never charged or acquitted of criminal charges.

An estimated 15 to 26 million people joined in protests around the U.S. against Floyd's murder and against police killings of other Black people as well, calling for racial justice. The protests, under the slogan "Black Lives Matter," peaked on June 6 when they were held in 550 places across the U.S.[18] Most protesters were nonviolent and most were not members of the radical Black Lives Matter group, but simply adopted the slogan. A minority of people turning up at the protests engaged in rioting and looting, set stores and cars on fire, and attacked police in some cities. Some of the biggest protests and worst rioting took place in Minneapolis; New York City; Portland, Oregon (lasting for a hundred consecutive nights); Washington; Chicago; Kenosha, Wisconsin (where a seventeen-year-old White youth was charged with killing two protesters); Philadelphia; and Rochester, New York.[19] Police were accused by some on the right of not doing enough to stop the rioting, and by others on the left of responding too aggressively and violently.

The protests and rioting that broke out after Floyd was killed were about far more than the tragic and unwarranted death of one man in police custody. They were a reaction to hundreds of years of racism that began when the first African slaves were brought to America in chains in 1619, the immoral and barbaric enslavement of Black people that continued until the end of the Civil War in 1865, and the systemic racism and discrimination that followed and still lingers today, although in diminished form.

The protests and riots were also a reaction to the big gaps that still divide Black and White Americans—in earnings, family wealth, educational attainment, homeownership, imprisonment, unemployment, and by other measures. As a group, Blacks are worse off than Whites in all these areas, although some African Americans have reached the pinnacle of wealth, education, and professional success—most notably Barack Obama, who was elected and reelected as president of the United States and has become a multimillionaire since leaving office. We will discuss the urgent need to rectify these many centuries of discrimination later in this book, along with ways to bring Americans of all ethnicities together as one united people.

The riot sparked by Trump at the U.S. Capitol was a much more serious problem than the riots in many American cities months earlier, because the attack on the Capitol was an attack on our democracy. We understand the concerns of those on the right who believe that those on the left have, when it has suited them, been willing to put our democratic values and public safety at risk for political purposes. We endanger the very foundations of our society if we condemn only the violence and lawbreaking committed by our political opponents, but fail to condemn it when committed by our political allies. Without question, the rioting and violence in our cities and in the Capitol were both wrong. But the lawless mob that invaded our Capitol put our democracy in jeopardy.

The murder rate rose following police budget cuts and new restraints on the ability of police to protect their communities after the spring and summer urban riots. Some experts said the COVID-19 pandemic also played a role in boosting the murder rate, while reducing some other crimes because people were spending more time at home. The *Washington Post* reported that in 2020 the U.S. "has experienced the largest single one-year increase in homicides since the country started keeping such records in the 20th century, according to crime data and criminologists."[20] The *Post* said on the last day of 2020 that the U.S. experienced a 20.9 percent increase in killings for the first nine months of the year. The newspaper quoted University of Missouri criminologist Richard B. Rosenfeld as saying that "the increase tends to occur in nearly every city at the very end of May and the first day in June," shortly after George Floyd was killed. "During a period of widespread intense protest against police violence, it's fair to suppose that police legitimacy deteriorates, especially in those communities that have always had a fraught relationship with police," Rosenfeld said. "That simply widens the space for so-called street justice to take hold, and my own view is that is a part of what we are seeing."

Vox reporter German Lopez pointed out that "The surge [in murders] is from a relatively low baseline. It comes after decades of drops in murders and crime more broadly in the US, and the total number of murders is still far lower than it was for much of the 1990s and before. But that's one reason the surge is alarming . . . "[21]

Updating the impact of the Defund the Police movement, Fox News reported in April 2021 that it analyzed the impact of shifting funds from police departments to social services programs, as some cities have done. Fox said it found that "such cuts have led some departments to lay off officers, cancel recruiting classes, or retreat from hiring goals. As police departments were left to make do with shrunken budgets and less support, some big cities have seen sometimes drastic upticks in murders and other violent crimes."[22]

Fox reported the following statistics to illustrate the impact of police budget cuts: In Portland, Oregon, where the police budget was cut by $16 million in July 2020, homicides rose by almost 271 percent between then and February 2021 compared with the same period a year earlier. In New York City, murders rose almost 12 percent and shootings rose 40 percent from January 1, 2021, to March 21, 2021, compared with the same period a year earlier, after the city cut $1 billion from the police budget. In Los Angeles—where the city council cut $150 million from the police budget—homicides rose 38 percent in 2020 and 28 percent in 2021 as of March 13, while rapes and robberies decreased. In Minneapolis, where the police budget was cut in July 2020, homicides rose 49 percent between July 22, 2020, and March 28, 2021. Total violent crime in Minneapolis over the same period rose 22 percent from the same period a year before, hitting 3,692 crimes.

The spike in crime in many cities prompted a backlash against announced police budget cuts. In Minneapolis, for example, the city council voted in February 2021 to reverse plans to cut the police budget and instead added $6.4 million in funding to hire dozens of additional officers. Many officers quit, retired early, or remained on leave following the George Floyd killing, leaving the department with two hundred fewer officers available to work than in most recent years. Since Floyd's death, "some residents have begged city leaders to hire additional officers, saying they're waiting longer for responses to emergency calls amid a dramatic uptick in violent crime," the *Minneapolis Star Tribune* reported.[23] There were reports of deliberate police slowdowns in some cities in response to what officers perceived as lack of community support.

In addition, Texas Republican governor Greg Abbott called on the state legislature in late January 2021 to bar cities from cutting their police budgets, in reaction to the city of Austin slashing its police budget by about a third. "Texas is a law-and-order state, and we are going to keep it that way," Abbott said.[24] On a national level, Attorney General Merrick Garland used the Senate confirmation hearing on his nomination to make clear where he and President Biden stand on the issue. "President Biden has said he does not support defunding the police and neither do I," Garland said in February 2021.[25]

While any fair-minded person would acknowledge that systemic racism has afflicted America since colonial times, when slavery denied African Americans all human rights, it's simply inaccurate to portray the vast majority of police officers today as racist criminals. A small percentage of officers are clearly guilty of wrongdoing and should be prosecuted to the fullest extent the law allows, but the vast majority do a good job protecting people of all races in the communities they serve.

The truth is that while cities should weed out the bad cops and eliminate unnecessary use of force by police, defunding the police hurts Black Americans far more than Whites, because Blacks are far more often the victims of crime. For example, while Black people made up about 13 percent of the U.S. population in 2019, they accounted for 53 percent of murder victims in the nation that year. A total of 7,484 of the 13,987 people murdered in the nation were Black that year.[26]

In *USA Today* in July 2020, Heather Mac Donald of the Manhattan Institute wrote that "The African American community tends to be policed more heavily because that is where people are disproportionately hurt by violent street crime.... Nationally, African Americans between the ages of 10 and 34 died from homicide at 13 times the rate of white Americans, according to researchers from the Centers for Disease Control and Prevention and the Justice Department."[27] Mac Donald added: "Though they also want improved quality of policing, the percentage of Black respondents in a 2015 Gallup poll who wanted more police in their community was more than twice as high as the percentage of white respondents who said the same."

Wall Street Journal columnist Jason Riley, who is Black, wrote in February 2021 that we should "stop pretending that policing is a bigger problem than violent crime in poor black neighborhoods. In 2019, there were 492 homicides in Chicago, according to the *Sun-Times*, and only three of them involved police."[28]

No American of any race should be mistreated by police. But at the same time, no American should be victimized by crime. Yet increased crime is the inevitable result of programs that defund and demonize police, because defunding makes the police less effective in protecting us all. All Americans want to be safe. So, from a political as well as a public policy point of view, Democrats need to take a position as the pro–public safety party if they want to avoid major election defeats. We need improved policing and an end to police brutality—not less policing. Republicans shouldn't attack legitimate police reforms as "defunding the police."

At the same time, Democrats and Republicans need to acknowledge that crime is far from the only issue facing African Americans. Black people also deserve far more from the government to help them close the gaping prosperity gap with Whites. We must provide increased funding for improved schools in low-income neighborhoods, improved and expanded job training programs, more and larger college scholarships, expanded low-income housing programs, improved health care, and more. Importantly, this additional funding and assistance should not be focused on race. It should instead focus on helping people who need help the most, such as those living in poverty, the unemployed, and those with low levels of educational attainment.

Since Black people are disproportionately represented in all categories of disadvantaged Americans, targeting assistance based on need will disproportionately benefit them. At the same time, targeting assistance based on need will not leave out people of other races equally deserving of government assistance. Basing assistance strictly on race only breeds resentment and further divides Americans—the opposite of what needs to happen.

In addition, if we are to ever succeed in reunifying the American people, Republican and Democratic elected officials must do the right thing and hold their own supporters accountable for their actions— especially actions that result in violence. That means more Republicans in Congress should have condemned Trump and voted to impeach and convict him for undermining our democracy with his obstinate refusal to admit Biden defeated him in a free and fair election, and for inciting the riot at the Capitol. It also means far more Republicans should have joined Democrats in stripping Marjorie Taylor Greene of her House committee assignments. And it means Democratic officeholders should not have been reluctant to condemn the Antifa movement rioters who burned and looted stores and engaged in other instances of violence and lawbreaking in many American cities in the spring and summer of 2020.

The polarization dividing the American people has not been as severe as it is today since the Civil War.[29] We must work to tamp down the flames of this dangerous division and not allow it to grow if we want to ensure the survival of the United States as a united and democratic nation.

HOW DID WE BECOME SO DIVIDED?

Throughout much of the twentieth century, the Democratic Party was center-left and the Republican Party was center-right. There were moderate and even conservative Democrats (many from the South) holding local, state, and national office. There were moderate and even liberal Republicans (such as Senator Jacob Javits of New York) in office as well. In addition, some conservatives were elected from liberal states (such as Conservative Party senator James Buckley in New York) and some liberals were elected from conservative states (Democratic senator George McGovern in South Dakota). We had "big tent" parties able to accommodate ideological diversity, each anchored in the sensible center.

Times have changed. Today, the Democratic Party has moved further left, and the Republican Party has moved further right than ever before, widening the divide between them. Views that were once considered beyond the pale—such as the embrace of socialism and the Defund the Police movement on the left, and conspiracy theories about the Deep State and voter fraud on the right—have now entered the mainstream of each party. Democratic liberals and Republican conservatives who rose to leadership positions in government in earlier generations would in many cases be too moderate to win a primary within their own party today. Ideological purity and rigidity are now praised in both parties as strength, while a willingness to compromise is attacked as weakness. Instead of treating political opponents as adversaries to be respected, millions of Americans now view them as enemies to be despised.

In his speech nominating President Barack Obama for a second term at the 2012 Democratic National Convention, former president Bill Clinton said that "though I often disagree with Republicans, I actually never learned to hate them."[30] Clinton then gave a realistic assessment of the need to compromise and work with political opponents: "When times are tough and people are frustrated and angry and hurting and uncertain, the politics of constant conflict may be good. But what is good politics does not necessarily work in the real world. What works in the real world is cooperation." Political combat has escalated to the point that working with opponents to enact legislation is no longer an accepted practice by the most extreme partisan lawmakers and their followers.

Writing in the *New York Times* in April 2021, Nate Cohn described the animosity between Democrats and Republicans as "sectarianism"—a term usually used to describe animosity between different religions or sects within religions. "The two political parties see the other as an enemy," Cohn wrote. "It's an outlook that makes compromise impossible and encourages elected officials to violate norms in pursuit of an agenda or an electoral victory." [31]

When Henry Clay—who served as Speaker of the House, a senator, and secretary of state—was called "the Great Compromiser" for landmark legislation he shepherded to enactment in the first half of the nineteenth century, the title was considered a compliment, although he also faced his share of critics.[32] Today many would consider the title an insult and it could be hurled against a candidate by a primary opponent in a thirty-second TV attack ad. This rejection of compromise by far too many citizens and elected officials must change. It is emblematic of the inability of our government to deal effectively with many of the enormous challenges America faces today.

Without compromise, little gets accomplished. This is illustrated by Rep. Alexandria Ocasio-Cortez's failure to achieve anything legislatively in Congress. A survey issued in March 2021 by the Center for Effective Lawmaking, which is run by the University of Virginia and Vanderbilt University, found that none of the twenty-one substantive bills Ocasio-Cortez introduced in the House in the 2019–2021 session became law, or were even acted on in a committee. As a result, the center ranked her as one of the least effective members of Congress— No. 230 out of 240 Democratic House members.

The *New York Post* reported that a "Democratic insider" said of Ocasio-Cortez that "legislation was never her focus. It was media and narrative." The newspaper quoted another Democrat it did not identify as saying: "Tweeting is easy, governing is hard. You need to have friends. You need to understand the committee process, you need to be willing to make sacrifices. Her first day in Congress . . . she decided to protest outside Nancy Pelosi's office."[33] Protest movements have a long and important history in the United States, with many of the successful ones resulting in the enactment of new laws. But the American people have always expected lawmakers to use their posts to actually make new laws or change old ones, not simply to protest in demonstrations, in news media appearances, or more recently on social media.

Right now, America is at a crossroads: We can follow the path of "the Great Compromiser" Clay and heed President Biden's call in his inaugural address to end our "uncivil war," or we can follow the path of those on the far left and the far right who refuse to compromise. If we take this second path, we will remain divided into two Americas—hating, attacking, and demonizing those who differ with us politically and seeing our government paralyzed by partisan gridlock. The future of our country and our democracy depends on which path we follow.

Biden's call for unity in his inaugural address was inspiring. Yet as of August 13, 2021, he had signed fifty-four executive orders and thirty presidential memoranda directing federal agencies to take or stop an action involving public policy or management. The orders and memoranda have the same effect, but the memoranda are not required to be published and the president does not have to issue a budgetary impact statement.[34] "As a practical matter, the memorandum is now being used as the equivalent of an executive order, but without meeting the legal requirements for an executive order," Portland State University professor Phillip. J. Cooper wrote in his 2014 book, *By Order of the President: The Use and Abuse of Executive Direct Action.*[35] Since the executive orders and memoranda do not require approval by Congress, they enable the president to take action unilaterally. This eliminates any need for the president to seek bipartisan compromise from Congress or even approval from lawmakers in his own party, giving presidents a way to do an end-run around Congress to take action.

Aside from allowing presidents to act without ending what Biden called "our uncivil war," the executive orders and memoranda have less lasting power than laws. They can be overturned by the president who issues them and by any subsequent president—unlike laws that can only be repealed by Congress, or overturned by the courts if found to be unconstitutional. More than 13,700 executive orders have been issued by presidents since George Washington took office in 1789, according to the American Bar Association.[36] While they are an effective way of breaking gridlock, they hardly promote bipartisan (or even intraparty) unity and are, by definition, anti-democratic. America's founders created Congress and the federal court system in the Constitution because they wanted a system of checks and balances to limit the power of the president. All-powerful kings and dictators rule by decree; presidents should work with Congress to enact laws. We're not advocating eliminating executive orders and memoranda, but we'd like to see them used far less frequently by presidents of both parties.

In another move to act without getting Republican support, Biden won congressional approval for his $1.9 trillion coronavirus response and economic stimulus bill early in his term with only Democratic votes. The budget measure was passed under a seldom-used process called reconciliation, meaning it needed only a simple majority of 51 votes rather than the 60 votes required to stop a filibuster.[37] With fifty Democrats in the Senate and Vice President Kamala Harris able to vote to break ties, this gave Democrats a way around the filibuster and removed the need to compromise with Republicans.

Yet in fairness to Biden's moves to get around Republican opposition, the GOP seemed more interested in obstructing his legislative proposals than working out compromise measures with him and Democrats in early 2021. Senate Minority Leader Mitch McConnell of Kentucky made this clear when the Senate's top Republican said in May 2021: "One hundred percent of my focus is on stopping this new administration."[38] Compromise requires both sides to make concessions, but this willingness was lacking among both Democrats and Republicans in Washington.

Properly used, the filibuster can be an important tool to encourage the Senate to support centrist bipartisan compromise legislation and add stability to our laws. If far-left or far-right legislation is approved by a bare majority of 51 votes with support of only one party, it might be repealed after the next election if party control of the Senate shifts. However, legislation approved by a bipartisan majority of 60 or more is far more likely to be more acceptable to the minority party and be left in place when the minority party becomes the majority party, as will inevitably happen at some point.

It is unlikely that extremist legislation can win the support of 60 senators. Even when one party holds 60 or more seats, a majority of that size is likely to have members with a range of positions—from moderate to very conservative on the Republican side, and from moderate to very progressive on the Democratic side. When neither party holds 60 seats or more, an extremist proposal stands almost no chance of approval. As Senator Joe Manchin (D-WV) said in 2019, the filibuster gives the minority party "the ability to stop crazy stuff."[39] The 60-vote requirement of the filibuster always frustrates the majority party because it keeps members of that party from accomplishing all they want. But the requirement is always treasured by the minority party. Since Democrats and Republicans are each in the majority and in the minority at different times, it's not surprising that the views of some people on the filibuster change. When he was in office, President Trump urged then-Senate Majority Leader McConnell to get rid of the filibuster to push the Trump agenda through the Senate. McConnell refused, knowing his party would be in the minority in the future, as happened in 2021.

When Democrats captured control of the Senate in the 2020 election by the slimmest possible margin, many clamored to abolish the filibuster. Since no Republicans were likely to vote to get rid of the filibuster and reduce their party's power, abolishing the filibuster could only take place if every Democratic senator and Vice President Harris voted for the change. That doesn't look like it will happen. Senator Kyrsten Sinema (D-AZ) and Senator Manchin have both opposed ending the filibuster, and other Democrats have indicated reluctance to end it. In fact, the *Washington Post* reported in March 2021 that only about 20 percent of Senate Democrats are committed to eliminating the filibuster, which has been around since 1805.[40]

In an op-ed published in the *Washington Post* in April 2021, Manchin stated unequivocally that he will never vote to abolish the 60-vote requirement. "The filibuster is a critical tool to protecting that input and our democratic form of government," Manchin wrote. "That is why I have said it before and will say it again to remove any shred of doubt: There is no circumstance in which I will vote to eliminate or weaken the filibuster."[41]

Manchin indicated in interviews with NBC and Fox News in March 2021 that he might be open to requiring what is called a "talking filibuster," in which a filibuster could last only for as long as members stayed on the Senate floor and kept speaking.[42] Manchin co-sponsored a Senate rule change in 2011 that would have "required that Senators who wish to filibuster a bill must actually take the floor and make remarks," a news release from his office said, but the measure failed.[43] Currently, a single senator need only refuse to join in giving unanimous consent to having a bill voted on by the Senate to trigger the requirement for a 60-vote supermajority needed to pass a bill under filibuster rules. Importantly, President Biden has also said he supports bringing back the "talking filibuster."

We agree with Manchin on the need to preserve the filibuster to encourage bipartisan compromises in the Senate, and we favor requiring the "talking" form of the filibuster to make it harder to invoke so it is used less frequently. The filibuster should work like the airbag in your car—something deployed under urgent circumstances, but only in rare cases. This was true in the past, but no longer. Senate records show that from the 1917–1918 session through the 1969–1970 session, votes were held to end filibusters anywhere from zero to seven times per session. The number of votes to end filibusters then increased markedly, peaking at 298 times in the 2019–2020 session.[44]

Unwillingness to compromise by members of both parties is a disturbing sign of how dysfunctional our politics and our government have become. The inspiring words of the Pledge of Allegiance—that America is "one nation, under God, indivisible"— are sadly no longer true. We have become two nations, deeply divided—not just in Congress and in political campaigns, but in our everyday lives. The left and right inhabit separate bubbles, not talking to each other, not interacting. In some cases friendships are breaking up, parents and their adult children are facing strained relationships, and couples are divorcing over political disagreements.

In addition, more and more often, Republicans and Democrats are quite literally living apart. For example, the *Wall Street Journal* reported in November 2020: "If it seems like political divisions have sharpened in recent years, it may be because an increasing number of Americans are living in red and blue bubbles. Surveys from Pew Research Center have found 'ideological silos' now common on both the left and right, and 'consistently' conservative and liberal Americans are more likely than ideologically mixed Americans to say it is important to them to live in a place where most people share their political views."[45]

And in an earlier *Wall Street Journal* article, the newspaper reported in September 2019: "Republicans and Democrats not only represent different kinds of places. They represent two very different slices of the American economy. In Democratic House districts, college degrees and professional jobs are plentiful—and the economy is thriving....Republican House districts hold a growing share of jobs in low-skill manufacturing, agriculture, and mining—sectors that often do not require college degrees and which offer lower pay."[46]

The physical separation between Democrats and Republicans is combined with a drop in friendships, romantic relationships, and family ties bridging the political divide. NPR reported in October 2020: "Jocelyn Kiley, associate director of research at the Pew Research Center, said political polarization is more intense now than at any point in modern history. Nearly 80% of Americans now have 'just a few' or no friends at all across the aisle, according to Pew. And the animosity goes both ways." A poll by the Public Religion Research Institute shows about 80 percent of Republicans believe the Democratic Party has been taken over by socialists, while about 80 percent of Democrats believe the Republican Party has been taken over by racists.[47]

TWO DIFFERENT MEDIA ECOSYSTEMS

Similarly, *New York* magazine reported in 2018: "Many people with divergent [political] perspectives from their partners have not been able to make it work in the Trump era. A Reuters/Ipsos poll completed in early 2017 found that in the months following Trump's election win, 13 percent of 6,426 participants had cut ties with a friend or family member over political differences. This past summer, another survey of 1,000 people found that a third declared the same."[48]

One cause of this estrangement is that Americans on the right and on the left are inhabiting two different information ecosystems. Left-wing and right-wing media present very different versions of reality as a result of their story selection, presentation, and commentary. Consumers of right-wing media, for example, were led to believe that a Deep State—a secret cabal of sinister government bureaucrats—was trying to frame Trump with false accusations and that Trump was the victim of massive voter fraud in the 2020 election. Consumers of left-wing media were led to believe the exact opposite. There is no longer a shared reality we can all agree exists.

While Trump was president, Democrats tuned in to MSNBC and CNN. The two cable networks both aired frequent attacks against Trump and dropped any pretense of objective news reporting, becoming left-wing alternatives to the right-wing Fox News. CNN had once prided itself in being a straight news organization and claimed to be "the most trusted name in news," although polling did not back up that boast.[49] But CNN found ratings success by becoming the anti-Trump network, devoting increasing amounts of time to partisan rants by anchors excoriating Trump.[50] Fox News experienced great success with conservatives, but toward the end of Trump's term, the even more pro-Trump Newsmax and One America News Network (OAN) saw big jumps in viewership. Conservative and liberal news websites both grew in popularity over Trump's term, with people seeking out news from sources that reinforced their worldviews.

Polarization between Americans on the left and right accelerated during the 2016 election campaign and has kept growing ever since, reaching new heights in the 2020 campaign and its aftermath.

Democrats began an opposition movement to Donald Trump as soon as he won the 2016 presidential election—more than two months before he took office. We saw massive demonstrations around the nation denouncing him on January 21, 2017—just one day after he was inaugurated. The Women's March in Washington and at least 652 other locations around the nation protesting Trump attracted somewhere between 3.3 and 5.2 million people. An analysis published by the *Washington Post* called it "likely the largest single-day demonstration in U.S. history" up to that point.[51] Radical leftists seized control of the leadership of the marches, with anti-Semites, socialists, and others far out of the American mainstream taking prominent roles.

Trump opponents called themselves "the resistance"—the same name freedom fighters in Europe used when battling Nazi Germany during World War II. The implication was none too subtle: In the eyes of the left, Trump and his supporters were the embodiment of evil. The resistance took heart when Special Counsel Robert Mueller and a small army of prosecutors and FBI agents spent from May 2017 to March 2019 investigating allegations that Trump and his 2016 election campaign colluded with Russia to defeat Democratic presidential candidate Hillary Clinton. However, the Mueller probe ended by concluding there wasn't sufficient evidence to charge Trump or his campaign with conspiracy and said that, as a sitting president, Trump could not be charged with obstructing justice under Justice Department guidelines. Democrats were outraged. Republicans were thrilled. Americans remained divided as ever.

The Democratic-controlled House of Representatives impeached Trump in early 2020 on charges of obstruction of justice and abuse of power in connection with his call pressuring the president of Ukraine to provide damaging information about Democratic presidential candidate and former vice president Biden. Trump was acquitted in a Senate trial, thanks to Republicans standing behind him in partisan solidarity. The only Republican voting to convict the president was Senator Mitt Romney of Utah, the unsuccessful GOP presidential nominee in 2012.[52]

On the Republican side, Trump devoted his presidency to catering to his far-right base. He made little effort to appeal to moderates and virtually no effort to appeal to progressives. He stoked divisions on an almost daily basis with angry tweets and verbal tirades against his opponents. He attacked the news media and freedom of the press. Instead of trying to work with Democrats in Congress, Trump blasted and insulted them, calling House Speaker Pelosi "Crazy Nancy" and then-Senate Minority Leader Chuck Schumer (D-NY) "Cryin' Chuck."[53] And Trump couldn't accept criticism or ever say he made a mistake. He brushed off even the most legitimate attacks against him as lies and "fake news." He said he was "a very stable genius"[54] and the greatest first-term president in American history.

INSURRECTION AT THE U.S. CAPITOL

The partisan feuding and fighting came to a head with an unprecedented attempted coup attempt staged against democracy itself to overturn Trump's 2020 election loss. One part of the coup attempt was an attack on the U.S. Capitol on January 6, 2021, when thousands of rioters stormed the building after they had been summoned to Washington by President Trump to demand Congress give him another four-year term in office—despite his clear election loss.[55] Trump called the gathering the "Save America Rally," tweeting: "Big protest in D.C. on January 6. Be there, will be wild!"[56] At the rally near the White House, Trump lawyer Rudy Giuliani called for "trial by combat."[57]

Trump had been saying for months that because he was so enormously popular and had accomplished so much, the only way he could possibly be defeated in his reelection bid would be if the election were rigged. His most fervent supporters believed this absurd claim as an article of faith. In a fiery seventy-minute speech to thousands of supporters at the rally, Republican Trump attacked his own vice president, Mike Pence, for refusing to block congressional recognition of Democrat Biden's victory in the November election.[58] Pence had no legal power to overturn the election result and stop Biden from becoming president, but Trump falsely claimed Pence could do so and stirred his supporters to a fever pitch of anger.

Denouncing his election defeat as the result of fraud (despite no evidence of that) carried out through complex and implausible conspiracies involving both Democratic and Republican state and local officials around the nation, Trump told his supporters: "Now it is up to Congress to confront this egregious assault on our democracy. And after this, we're going to walk down, and I'll be there with you.... We are going to the Capitol."[59] Trump added: "We will fight like hell, and if you don't fight like hell, you're not going to have a country anymore." But as his adoring fans set off on their fateful march to the Capitol, Trump reneged on his pledge to go with them and instead went back to the White House to watch their attack unfold on TV.

The protesters who turned into rioters forced their way into the Capitol by breaking windows and doors and attacking badly outnumbered law enforcement officers. The rioters stormed the rotunda and eventually invaded the House and Senate chambers and much of the Capitol. President Trump watched this nightmare unfold on TV as if he were an ordinary citizen viewing an exciting show he had no control over, rather than acting like a leader with the power and responsibility to try to stop the attack.

After hours went by, the president finally responded to calls by aides to do something besides watching TV. He posted a video on Twitter in which he asked the mob to leave peacefully, yet still reiterated discredited conspiracy theories about the "stolen" election. In the video, Trump directed his remarks to the rioters and opened by saying: "I know your pain. I know you're hurt. But you have to go home now."[60] The president added: "We have to have peace. So go home. We love you. You're very special." Twitter later deleted the video and joined with Facebook, Instagram, Snapchat, and other social media platforms to ban Trump from further posts because of his inflammatory comments.

Five people died in the riot and about 140 law enforcement officers were injured.[61] Four law enforcement officers later committed suicide.[62] Congress reconvened once order was restored and certified the victory of Biden and Senator Kamala Harris of California—the first woman, first Black person, and first person of South Asian descent to serve as vice president. However, eight Republican senators and 139 GOP House members supported at least one objection to the Electoral College vote count in the early morning hours of January 7, 2021—just hours after the riot at the Capitol ended. Nevertheless, the will of the American voters was upheld and our democracy survived.

As bad as the Capitol assault was, it was just one part of President Trump's efforts to stay in power. He also pressured officials in several states—including on a long phone call with Georgia officials that was recorded and later made public—to turn his election losses into victories. Trump ordered dozens of lawsuits filed on his behalf alleging voter fraud and all manner of irregularities, but state and federal courts—including the Supreme Court—tossed out his legally weak claims more than sixty times. And Trump allegedly considered firing the acting attorney general so he could use the Justice Department to help him stay in power.[63]

Fox News, Newsmax, and OAN amplified Trump's lies, claiming that election fraud caused his defeat. When Fox finally acknowledged the reality of Trump's loss, Trump attacked the network that had loyally promoted him and urged his followers to desert Fox for Newsmax and OAN. Many did—temporarily ending Fox's reign as the most-watched cable TV network and sending Newsmax and OAN ratings soaring.[64] Without any evidence, some Trump followers claimed Dominion Voting

Systems had altered results from its voting machines to change millions of Trump votes to Biden votes. Dominion then filed a $1.3 billion defamation lawsuit against Trump attorney Sidney Powell in January 2021 in response to her making this claim in media appearances.[65] Dominion filed a similar lawsuit against Trump lawyer Rudy Giuliani, also seeking more than $1.3 billion.[66]

In addition, Dominion sued MyPillow Chief Executive Mike Lindell as well for more than $1.3 billion in damages, saying he defamed the company with baseless claims of fraud carried out with its voting machines. In March 2021, Dominion filed a lawsuit seeking at least $1.6 billion in damages from Fox News, saying the cable news channel "recklessly disregarded the truth" and aired false accusations of election fraud against Dominion because "the lies were good for Fox's business." Fox, Powell, Giuliani, and Lindell all fought the lawsuits. A Fox spokesperson said the news channel was "proud" of its 2020 election coverage, calling it "in the highest tradition of American journalism."[67]

In asking that the suit against her be thrown out, Powell's attorneys argued that her claims of election fraud by Democrats—which she had referred to as "the greatest crime of the century if not the life of the world"—were so absurd that they should not be accepted as true. The attorneys said Powell's statements were hyperbolic because they were part of a political campaign and "reasonable people would not accept such statements as fact but view them only as claims that await testing by the courts through the adversary process."[68] Yet, in fact, millions of loyal Trump supporters—including many of those who attacked the Capitol   sincerely believed the lies they were told by Powell, Giuliani, Lindell, and Trump himself on Fox News and elsewhere claiming that Trump actually was reelected.

On top of this, more than 4,000 lawyers signed an open letter attacking Trump's baseless election fraud lawsuits, stating: "President Trump's barrage of litigation is a pretext for a campaign to undermine public confidence in the outcome of the 2020 election, which inevitably will subvert constitutional democracy. Sadly, the President's primary agents and enablers in this effort are lawyers, obligated by their oath and ethical rules to uphold the rule of law." The letter called on "all lawyers and bar associations to publicly condemn this conduct [by Powell, Giuliani, and other Trump attorneys] and bar [association] disciplinary authorities to investigate it."[69]

Dominion was not alone in filing a lawsuit regarding false media reports about vote tallies in the 2020 election. Smartmatic—a company that provided voting machine technology for Los Angeles County and foreign countries—filed a $2.7 billion defamation lawsuit on February 4, 2021, against Fox News, three of its TV opinion show hosts (Maria Bartiromo, Lou Dobbs, and Jeanine Pirro), and Trump attorneys Giuliani and Powell, accusing them of falsely saying the company fraudulently manipulated voting machines.[70] Fox denied wrongdoing but canceled Dobbs's long-running program on the Fox Business Channel the day after the lawsuit was filed.

All these developments show how far apart Americans on the right and left have grown over the Trump years in power. At the most extreme ends, many of the most fervent Trump supporters believe President Biden got to the Oval Office as the result of election fraud, and that he and Democrats are socialists or communists who want to destroy the free-enterprise system, destroy religious institutions, confiscate guns, impose crippling tax increases, and take away our fundamental freedoms. On the other end of the spectrum, many far-left Democrats believe Trump and Republicans are racists who hate minorities and immigrants, favor environmental policies that will result in a planetary catastrophe, want to replace public schools with private ones, break laws and take unconstitutional actions as they please, and are focused on imposing policies to benefit the richest Americans and themselves.

Both these opposing views are exaggerated. But even in toned-down form, these differing perceptions of reality illustrate the depth of the division today between neighbors, coworkers, and even within families.

The truth is that, despite the name of our country, the people of the United States are far from united in these tumultuous times. The left and the right share the blame for this deep division.

Americans have never been united by a single religious faith, ethnic heritage, or race. With the exception of Native Americans, we are a nation of immigrants from every corner of the world, whether our ancestors arrived on U.S. shores hundreds of years ago or we arrived only recently. But we have been united throughout most of our history by a Big Idea—an idea that has made it possible for our extraordinarily diverse nation to become what our Latin motto *e pluribus unum* says we are—"out of many, one." The Big Idea is a civic faith that has become America's secular religion: a faith in democracy and the values it enshrines. A faith that we can cast ballots for candidates of our choice, that those ballots will be counted fairly and accurately, and that we will be governed by men and women we select to lead us at the local, state, and national level. A faith in the stirring words of the Declaration of Independence: "We hold these truths to be self-evident, that all men are created equal, that they are endowed by their Creator with certain unalienable Rights, that among these are Life, Liberty and the pursuit of Happiness.— That to secure these rights, Government are instituted among Men, deriving their just power from the consent of the governed."[71]

Polling shows that a large majority of Americans—85 percent—believe that our nation's founding ideals are freedom, equality, and self-governance and 73 percent believe these ideas provide a good foundation for bringing people together and unifying the nation, pollster Scott Rasmussen reported in March 2021. But only 53 percent of voters think most Americans believe in those ideals, Rasmussen found. And only 34 percent of voters believe the federal government supports those ideals—a sign of disillusionment and distrust in government. Rasmussen said this is consistent with other polling showing that 59 percent of voters view the federal government as a special interest group that primarily looks out for its own interests. Rasmussen said Democrats and Republicans hold markedly different views on these issues. While 57 percent of Republicans believe the federal government doesn't support America's founding ideals, 49 percent of independents and only 24 percent of Democrats hold this view. Rasmussen said the negative views by Republicans are due in part to the fact that the Democrat Biden is president.[72]

Free and fair elections are the centerpiece of self-governance and democracy. In authoritarian states like Russia and China, elections are a sham, with the ruling party deciding who can run and making sure the candidate the party favors wins.

In Russia, for example, President Vladimir Putin won't let term limits written into law stand in the way of his continued rule with an iron fist. He has been Russia's unquestioned ruler since 2000, including a stint as prime minister from 2008 to 2012 when he switched jobs with Dmitry Medvedev to get around term limits. In April 2021 Putin signed a bill into law altering term limits and allowing him to continue as president if he is reelected in 2024 and 2030 until 2036.[73] It's a safe bet that Putin will be reelected if he runs again. Russian officials claimed Putin won a landslide victory with 76 percent of the vote in 2018, while his nearest competitor in a multicandidate field allegedly got only 12 percent. The main opposition leader, now-imprisoned Alexei Navalny, was barred from even running. The BBC reported: "Video recordings from polling stations showed irregularities in a number of towns and cities across Russia. Several showed election officials stuffing boxes with ballot papers....During polling day, independent election monitoring group Golos reported hundreds of irregularities."[74]

Chinese president Xi Jinping won an even more lopsided victory than Putin when his nation's rubber-stamp parliament, the National People's Congress, voted 2,959–2 (with three abstentions) to remove the two-term limit on the presidency in 2018, effectively allowing Xi to remain president for life.[75]

Every election—whether free and fair like those in the U.S. or rigged like in Russia and China—produces one winner and one or more losers. We have both labored long and hard for outstanding political candidates who lost their races, and we know from personal experience that losing isn't easy—especially for the unsuccessful candidates themselves. Intense and painful feelings of rejection and dejection are common and understandable. Yet until now, every losing U.S. presidential candidate and the vast majority of losing candidates for lower-level offices have faced the grim reality of defeat, conceded, and wished the winning candidate well. The losers have understood they had a patriotic duty to do this. But, unlike past unsuccessful presidential candidates, Donald Trump has never conceded defeat. "We will never give up, we will never concede," Trump told his supporters at the rally near the White House shortly before they invaded the Capitol and launched their riot.[76] All signs point to him sticking to this pledge.

With his incessant attacks on the fairness of our elections and unsubstantiated claims of voter fraud and rigged election results over many months, Trump attacked not just Joe Biden or imagined Republican as well as Democratic supposed conspirators he believed were opposed to his reelection. The Republican president attacked democracy itself. And he wants us to believe that all the institutions of all levels of government around the country, including those controlled by Republicans, worked together not to keep the sitting leader in power—as has happened in Russia and China—but to remove him. This is simply not credible.

The truth is that Trump attempted to mount a coup to stay in power. He was stopped by honest judges in courts across the nation, along with elected and appointed government officials from both political parties who stood up for the rule of law. By their actions, they upheld the vow of President Abraham Lincoln in the Gettysburg Address, delivered during the Civil War, when he said that "government of the people, by the people, for the people, shall not perish from the earth."[77]

A PATH FORWARD

We have written this book to lay out a path forward from the abyss that nearly swallowed our democracy, threatening to replace "government of the people, by the people" with authoritarian rule. The fate of our nation hangs in the balance. Our democracy must be saved before it is too late.

Biden made it clear in his first speech as president of the United States that he clearly understands the need for the American people to renew our faith in democracy. In his inaugural address he said: "Today we celebrate the triumph not of a candidate, but of a cause, the cause of democracy. "[78]

The attempted coup Trump ignited, culminating in the horrific mob attack on the Capitol that turned into an insurrection to stop Congress from counting the electoral votes, sealed his defeat. To stop this from ever happening again, Americans must come together to support a Great Awakening of our civic faith in American democracy, comparable to the religious revival known as the Great Awakening that swept the British colonies in America in the 1730s and 1740s.

The late New York Democratic governor Mario Cuomo called Election Day democracy's "high holy day." He recognized the importance of democracy as our civic religion. Whether we are Democrats, Republicans, or independents, we must all agree on the urgent need to restore our faith in American democracy or risk the almost unthinkable prospect of having our cherished rights and freedoms replaced by dictatorial rule and tyranny. And we must view ourselves as co-religionists with a shared faith in democracy. Sure, Americans have disagreements with each other on many issues. But we must not differ from each other in our fundamental belief in our system of government and in our Constitution, which functions as our civic Bible. Adopting this view leads us to look at political opponents as adversaries but not enemies, and supports the traditional view that politics is the art of compromise.

The goal of those on the left and those on the right should be to forge cooperation with our fellow Americans to solve the problems facing our nation. If we do this, we can accomplish great things. Democracy, after all, is what made America great in the first place and what will keep America great—as long as we preserve it. But if our goal is confrontation rather than cooperation, fostering demonization and hatred of our opponents—and destroying democracy if necessary to keep our side in power—we are doomed to division and failure. Before Democratic pollster and political consultant Pat Caddell—our longtime friend and colleague—died in 2019, he said that the United States was in a "pre-revolutionary moment." Had he lived to witness the divisions of today, we believe he would have called this a "revolutionary moment." He would have been right.

We are not alarmists, nor have we ever been alarmist in our decades working as political consultants. However, the insurrection at the Capitol by Trump supporters showed us that the very foundation of our democracy is in danger today. September 11, 2001, sounded an alarm bell showing us that foreign terrorists could attack us in our homeland. January 6, 2021, must sound an alarm bell to show us we are vulnerable to domestic terrorists who masquerade as patriots. Just as the threat of international terrorism didn't disappear after the September 11 attacks on America, the threat of domestic terrorism didn't disappear after the January 6 attack on our Capitol. The attack has deep roots going back decades.

We must learn from history. The danger to our democratic system of government didn't begin with Donald Trump. Trump was a symptom, not the catalyst, of the ailments that have crippled our nation. Democrats and Republicans have both contributed to this crisis that has been brewing for decades. If we simply blame Trump for all of our country's current problems, we will be overlooking the very real, worsening, and systemic threats America faces from extremists in both political parties.

Most Americans had lost faith in the American Dream long before Trump descended the escalator at Trump Tower to announce his presidential bid in June 2015. Poll after poll shows that approval ratings for the federal government were at all-time lows, even though most voters usually cast ballots to reelect their own representatives and senators in the House and Senate. In a 2007 study that our firm conducted for the Aspen Institute, we found that only one in four Americans believed that the American Dream was still "alive and well," with 90 percent of Americans agreeing that the American Dream is harder to achieve than ever before. Further, in a 2010 study that our firm conducted of 1,000 likely voters, 68 percent of Americans felt that politicians did not care about their interests. And a shocking 2011 Rasmussen Reports poll revealed that 69 percent of Americans believed that the government no longer had the consent of the governed.[79] In 2014, two-thirds of Americans felt that the government was too large and powerful, according to a Gallup poll.[80]

The following issues, discussed at length in this book, are the most dangerous forces corroding the foundations of American democracy:

- A political class that has lost touch with mainstream America
- Public loss of trust in the institutions of democracy
- The rise and mobilization of extremism on the right and left threatening violence
- The rise of social media, websites, and cable TV news that splinters audiences and creates alternate realities
- Inequality of opportunity that creates a two-tiered society of haves and have-nots
- Anti-democratic regimes ruling China and Russia that threaten freedom around the world

THE OUT-OF-TOUCH POLITICAL CLASS

Self-preservation is one of the most powerful drivers of all human behavior. Politicians are driven by this just as we all are. Any candidate who wants to win an election must raise money (unless he or she is wealthy and can self-fund) and win the support of special-interest groups to be competitive. As a result, candidates and their staffs pay far more attention to people and groups that can help them get elected with funding, volunteers, endorsements, and other forms of support than they do to ordinary citizens. This has a profound impact on the actions politicians take, and the impact is not good.

"Power is the ultimate aphrodisiac," former secretary of state Henry Kissinger said, and he was right.[81] The lure of power draws people to seek elective office, often with the best of motives to improve the lives of their constituents. But because exercising power brings such gratification to elected officials and would-be officials, all too often they alter their behavior and positions on issues to support the interests of the donors and groups they need to get and hold onto power, rather than supporting the public interest.

On the national level, members of the U.S. House of Representatives and Senate live in a rarefied atmosphere. Unlike the rest of us, they don't just have to follow the law—they can change laws and write new ones. They can spend billions of dollars in taxpayer funds on programs and projects. Their reality is made up of government-funded staff members at their beck and call, government-funded travel, reporters publicizing their actions and views, crowds cheering at campaign rallies, and lobbyists currying their favor for support of legislation. This is heady stuff that would make anyone feel special, important, and powerful. All this is even truer for the president and vice president. So elected officials want to hang onto the power and prestige of their offices by keeping their approval ratings in polls high and planning year-round for their next election campaigns. This is particularly true for House members, whose terms last only two years.

Elected officials live in a world apart from average American. They regularly interact with each other and are often insulated from the problems of greatest concern to ordinary citizens. While our political system frequently doesn't work for most Americans, it usually works well for members of government. In fact, the system works so well that members of Congress seeking reelection won in 96 percent of their races in the 2020 elections, making a mockery of the claim that average citizens have a good chance to defeat incumbents.[82] In 38 states, all members of Congress who sought reelection in 2020 won their November races. This is why many have called our current political system an incumbent protection plan.

Because many state legislatures have drawn boundaries for congressional districts to favor one party or the other, and because some states are heavily blue or red, many members of Congress are more worried about facing opponents from their own parties in primaries than they are about general election contests. This has the unfortunate effect of pushing many Republicans running for office further to the right and many Democrats seeking office further to the left to avert or win primary challenges. The result is a more polarized Congress, with fewer lawmakers willing to move to the center and make necessary compromises for government to operate effectively. This often leads to gridlock.

Another factor that impacts election contests is campaign spending on behalf of candidates by political action committees known as super PACs. A 2010 Supreme Court decision allowed the creation of super PACs, which can spend unlimited amounts of money to support candidates, but are barred from coordinating with campaigns and from making contributions directly to candidates. There is no limit on what an individual, corporation, or group can donate to these super PACs. Some super PACs do not disclose their donors. They have been used by industries to support candidates favoring industry interests over the public interest. But other super PACs actually encourage moderation in politics by supporting moderate and centrist candidates and focus on public policy issues.

We are proud to have conducted work for nearly a decade for one—the Independence USA PAC created by Michael Bloomberg.[83] This super PAC supports candidates and referenda, and focuses on issues including gun laws, the environment, and education policy. Independence USA (IUSA) has a record of supporting pragmatic candidates on both sides of the aisle—as well as independent candidates—who exhibit a willingness to work in a bipartisan fashion on important causes.

While IUSA supported Democrats and Republicans in 2016 as it focused on backing candidates who supported gun safety reform, it moved to support only Democrats in 2018, as Republicans under President Trump had all but abandoned any efforts to address issues in a bipartisan fashion. We were especially proud to work on Independence USA PAC's successful effort in the 2018 U.S. House elections. Independence USA helped the Democrats win control of the U.S. House by backing twenty-four moderate Democratic candidates, and twenty-one out of those candidates won—including fifteen women.

In addition to their work at the federal level, Independence USA PAC also has a record of helping pass policies at the state level. They have worked to advance state-level gun safety reforms, education reform, and nonpartisan public health reforms like bans on e-cigarettes. Further, they have backed necessary clean air measures—like limits on carbon pollution from power plants—in states across the country, including Florida, Michigan, and Wisconsin.

The late Jesse Unruh, who served as the Democratic speaker of the California state assembly in the 1960s when California was a swing state, was quoted as saying: "Money is the mother's milk of politics."[84] Candidates have needed a lot more "milk" in recent years, as the cost of election campaigns has soared. In fact, the Center for Responsive Politics estimates that spending on the presidential and congressional races in 2020 totaled nearly $14 billion, including nearly $6.6 billion on the presidential election—up dramatically from about $2.4 billion on the 2016 presidential election.[85] These spending levels have led many

Democratic and Republican candidates to welcome spending on their behalf by super PACs.

The disconnect between problems facing ordinary Americans and the priorities of politicians was on clear display in 2020. Republicans and Democrats locked horns attempting to pass a second relief package in the face of rising COVID-19 infection rates and increasing lockdowns that sent unemployment soaring and shuttered many restaurants, theaters, retail stores, and other businesses. It was a bad time for inaction. The coronavirus pandemic was worsening but Democrats and Republicans couldn't reach a crucial compromise. The unwillingness of Democrats to spend less than they wanted and Republicans to spend more than they wanted to provide desperately needed help to the American people caused untold suffering.

Congress finally passed another round of $900 billion in coronavirus relief in December 2020, after the election, and Trump signed it into law December 27 after threatening a veto.[86] The House and Senate then passed President Biden's proposal for $1.9 trillion in coronavirus relief in March 2021 and Biden signed the bill into law. But not a single Republican supported the emergency aid request, even though 70 percent of U.S. adults polled by the Pew Research Center said they support the funding—including 41 percent of Republicans and 94 percent of Democrats.[87]

The failure of the House and Senate to reach bipartisan agreement on Biden's $1.9 trillion in emergency funding to battle COVID-19 and help the American people was alarming. It illustrates how members of Congress too often fail to prioritize middle-of-the-road compromise over partisan intransigence. We frequently hear Democrats and Republicans boast that they will fight for victory over their opponents, rather than saying they will reach across the aisle to actually win approval of beneficial legislation. Most of us want legislators to legislate, not to simply fight, fight, and fight some more about almost everything—often without accomplishing much of anything.

Sometimes it feels like the American people are being treated like children stuck between two arguing parents, with Mom and Dad each claiming to be the better parent. Seeking support from their children, each of the feuding parents makes a promise about what he or she will do the next day to make the kids happy—a trip to the zoo or an outing to an amusement park. But because Mom and Dad can't stop arguing, the kids stay home all day, watching them yell at each other.

LOSS OF TRUST IN AMERICAN INSTITUTIONS

In a poll conducted by CNN in 2014, just 13 percent of respondents said that they trusted the government to do "what is right, always or most of the time." A similar Pew Research Center Poll in 2019 found the figure had increased slightly to 17 percent.[88] In the current political climate, these numbers are hardly surprising, but the 2014 figure was an all-time low. This was a dramatic change from earlier years. The first Pew National Election Study to ask about trust in government was conducted in 1958 and found that 73 percent of Americans said they trusted government to do what is right "just about always" or "most of the time." The percentage of Americans trusting government to do what is right then dropped dramatically in Pew polls to 28 percent in 1979 and then rose and fell in the years since, peaking at 55 percent in October 2001 as the result of a patriotic surge following the September 11, 2001, terrorist attacks.

What happened to so weaken our trust in government?

After President Franklin Delano Roosevelt and Congress expanded the federal government enormously under the New Deal to pull America out of the depths of the Great Depression and deal with massive unemployment, Americans began expecting more and more help from Uncle Sam. Social Security, unemployment insurance, public housing—and years later Medicare, Medicaid, food stamps, the War on Poverty, and more programs—were woven together into a social safety net. Uncle Sam was viewed by many Americans as the trusted "good guy," there to help those in need. The role of government in the everyday lives of Americans then continued to grow. Americans were arguably more united in support of our government than ever before or since during World War II, when the nation mobilized and made enormous sacrifices to battle Nazi Germany, Fascist Italy, and Imperial Japan. We remained largely united in the 1950s under President Dwight Eisenhower, the World War II supreme Allied commander in Europe.

Then came the tumultuous years of the 1960s and 1970s. America was rocked and our people were divided by many things, including the civil rights struggle by Black Americans against centuries of racial discrimination; the unpopular Vietnam War that spawned a massive antiwar movement; the women's rights and gay rights movements; a sharp rise in illegal drug use; the countercultural revolution by millions of young people; the assassinations of President John F. Kennedy, Senator Robert F. Kennedy, Martin Luther King Jr., and others; urban riots that swept the nation after Dr. King's murder; growing crime; and the Watergate scandal that led President Richard Nixon to resign in disgrace. Many of these developments shook the faith of Americans in their government. The candidates who ran for president and those who made it to the White House in the following decades promised to improve things. But in many cases, instead of building up our faith in government, they stressed the limitations of government and became critics of government, undermining our faith in it.

Some examples:

Democratic president Jimmy Carter said in his 1978 State of the Union Address: "We need patience and good will, but we really need to realize that there is a limit to the role and the function of government. Government cannot solve our problems, it can't set our goals, it cannot define our vision."[89]

Republican president Ronald Reagan, who took office in 1981, fostered a view that rather than being helpful, government actually was harmful. Many of his supporters bought into his claims that government was bloated, wasteful, inefficient, and a threat to our freedoms. In his first Inaugural Address Reagan famously said: "In this present crisis, government is not the solution to our problem; government is the problem."[90] He made the same point in a 1986 news conference when he said: "The nine most terrifying words in the English language are: 'I'm from the government and I'm here to help.'"[91] As columnist E. J. Dionne wrote in the *Washington Post* in 2019 discussing that remark by Reagan: "…the sentiment behind it remains one of the most destructive forces in our politics." The Republican president turned President Franklin Roosevelt's faith in big government on its head, beginning a demonization of government that has continued and grown far worse in the years since, particularly during the term of President Trump.

In 1992, Arkansas governor Bill Clinton ran for president as a "New Democrat," championing a "Third Way" that would reconcile party differences and encourage bipartisanship. After winning with only 43 percent of the popular vote to nearly 38 percent for President George H. W. Bush (with billionaire businessman H. Ross Perot trailing with 19 percent), Clinton moved to the center. In an effort to burnish his centrist credentials and pick up Republican support, Clinton's most memorable line from his 1996 State of the Union Address was: "The era of big government is over."[92] President Clinton launched what became known as the National Partnership for Reinventing Government, headed by Vice President Al Gore, as another initiative to showcase his centrist views. The goals of the program were to improve government by making it run more like a business, reduce government regulations on business, and shrink the federal workforce. A total of 426,200 federal jobs were eliminated under the program, officials said, but many federal employees were replaced by private sector contractors, sometimes getting higher salaries. In fact, some federal employees became contractor employees to continue working for the government.[93]

Clinton won bipartisan support for largely responsible budgets and oversaw the longest economic expansion in American history up to that point. It was not until Clinton's impeachment almost two years into his second term for his false statements denying his sexual relationship with a White House intern that he retreated from his position of "triangulation" between the parties. Partisan gridlock returned.

Democratic president Barack Obama told members of Congress in his State of the Union Address in 2013: "The American people don't expect government to solve every problem," and said new initiatives he was proposing wouldn't add to the deficit. "It's not a bigger government we need but a smarter government that sets priorities." But that wasn't enough for Senator Marco Rubio of Florida, who delivered the Republican response to the president's address. "More government isn't going to help you get ahead," Rubio said, sounding like Reagan. "It's going to hold you back. More government isn't going to create more opportunities. It's going to limit them."[94]

As the belief of many Americans in government's ability to provide solutions to their problems continued to erode, businessman and reality TV star Donald Trump sought to intensify anti-government beliefs years before he announced his presidential candidacy. Trump painted a conspiracy-based picture of politicians as corrupt, incompetent, and not working for the interests of the American people. He attacked the legitimacy of America's first Black president, Barack Obama, with a series of lies that had no basis in reality. The Big Lie Trump helped spread was to question whether Obama—who was born in Hawaii and proved it by releasing his birth certificate—was actually born outside the U.S. and was therefore ineligible under the Constitution to serve as president. This lie, which did not originate with Trump, became known as "birtherism." Trump's ability to manipulate the media to get attention for his wild and baseless charges was on full display with his success in generating heavy news coverage of birtherism, previewing the success he would have in the 2016 presidential campaign.

The developments recounted above and many others make it easy to see why the trust many voters were willing to give the political class and the federal government had eroded to dangerously low levels by 2016. As a result, a significant portion of the electorate was in the market for something different—an outsider who would fix the problems caused by the insiders in the political class, the proverbial man on a white horse who could ride to America's rescue. In past years successful wartime military leaders filled this role. In 2016, Trump filled the role for millions of voters. Yet after Trump's election, the federal government continued to be dominated by partisanship and gridlock, with limited and exceptional moments of bipartisan cooperation. This had been the case for years. Since the federal government has consistently failed to deliver bipartisan solutions to the American people, it is easy to understand why a majority of Americans believe their government no longer represents their interests.

When citizens lose faith in their system of government to fix the problems they face, they turn to non-systemic alternatives and candidates who promise to take a radically different approach. Trump benefited from this on the right, while on the left Senator Bernie Sanders of Vermont—a self-described democratic socialist who caucuses with Senate Democrats—benefited by mounting strong challenges for the 2016 and 2020 Democratic presidential nomination, although he fell short of the prize. The original four radical-left Democratic House members in the Squad—Representatives Alexandria Ocasio-Cortez, Rashida Tlaib, Ayanna Pressley, and Ilhan Omar—also benefited from voter alienation with mainstream candidates after they were first elected in 2018 and then reelected in 2020, as the Squad expanded to six members. Yet the policies espoused by the extremists on both sides of the aisle are so far out of the mainstream that they have little chance of picking up support from the rival political party.

On top of this, some of the extremist positions taken to score ideological points have turned out to be disastrous. For example, coauthor

Douglas Schoen wrote in an op-ed published by Fox News in 2019 that the anti-business hostility of Ocasio-Cortez led her to oppose plans by Amazon to build a second corporate headquarters in her New York City congressional district.[95] As a result, Amazon canceled plans to build the headquarters, which it said would have created over 25,000 jobs with an average annual salary of over $150,000, possibly increasing to 40,000 jobs within fifteen years. New York governor Andrew Cuomo and New York City mayor Bill de Blasio—Ocasio-Cortez's fellow Democrats—had worked long and hard courting Amazon to bring the project to New York. The Schoen op-ed called the Amazon cancellation "a catastrophic loss for the city, New York state, and the metropolitan region" and pointed out that "Amazon's cancellation of its plans to come to New York is a loss not only for those like Ocasio-Cortez who want to redistribute wealth, but also for those who want to grow wealth and expand the economic pie for hundreds of thousands, if not millions, of Americans."

A major reason we believe Americans must be united in embracing a fundamental faith in democracy is because elections are the fairest way of settling our differences justly and peacefully, and of incentivizing our leaders to act in the public interest and respect our rights—or face defeat at the ballot box. Majority rule is far from perfect, and elected officials make plenty of mistakes and sometimes engage in deliberate wrongdoing. But elections hold them accountable. And our acceptance of election results—even when we strongly oppose the winning candidate—gives us a way of settling our differences without physically attacking those we disagree with.

The five deaths suffered as a result of the January 6, 2021, attack on our Capitol, followed by suicides of four law enforcement officers who were there, were bad enough. But this death toll pales in comparison with the deaths in the Civil War. That's an extreme example of political violence, of course, but if enough people view elections as illegitimate, we can't predict what awful consequences will follow.

Our democracy protects all factions. As former British prime minister Winston Church said in 1947: "No one pretends that democracy is perfect or all-wise. Indeed it has been said that democracy is the worst form of government except for all those other forms that have been tried from time to time."[96] America has a proud heritage of peaceful protests, and they are protected by the First Amendment of the Constitution. Dr. Martin Luther King Jr. and other civil rights leaders led many nonviolent protests that brought about long-overdue changes in law. Protests of an earlier generation gained women the right to vote, and later changes were sparked by protests against the Vietnam War, for LGTQ rights, and on behalf of many other causes. But we need to be clear and all agree that violence and terrorism in the name of any political cause—no matter how just its supporters believe the cause to be—cannot be considered acceptable in a democratic society.

For the sake of our country's future, Republicans and Democrats need to denounce violence by their supporters as well as by their opponents. We don't want to see more riots and another attack on our democratic institutions by anyone, whether on the right or on the left.

SOCIAL MEDIA, WEBSITES, AND CABLE TV NEWS

One of the most memorable comments by the late senator Daniel Patrick Moynihan (D-NY) was: "Everyone is entitled to his own opinion, but not to his own facts."[97] One of the most memorable comments by Kellyanne Conway, counselor to President Trump, came in 2017 when she was interviewed by Chuck Todd for the NBC program *Meet the Press*.[98] She described blatantly false comments by White House press secretary Sean Spicer exaggerating the size of the crowd at Trump's inauguration as "alternative facts." "Wait a minute," Todd responded. "Alternative facts? Alternative facts? Four of the five facts he uttered . . . were just not true. Alternative facts are not facts; they're falsehoods." Indeed they are. And unfortunately, Spicer's lie early in the Trump administration was a preview of all the lies to come from the administration in the next four years. The different views expressed by Moynihan and Conway illustrate one of the causes of the deep divisions in American society today and one of the reasons our democracy is endangered. Americans don't accept a common set of facts. This is why it sometimes seems as if those on the left and those on the right are living on two different planets, believing in two different realities.

One reason for this view of facts as relative rather than absolute is the explosion of information sources now available to the American people and people around the world. This is a profound difference from what was the case five decades ago. The audience for news has been segmented into much smaller groups, like a pizza divided into many small slices, so that the American people are getting many different versions of news telling them what they want to hear, sometimes spreading "alternative facts."

In the 1970s, TV news was available on morning programs, the evening news around dinnertime, and on local newscasts at the end of primetime. TV news was carried on no more than four channels in most communities—the local ABC, CBS, and NBC affiliates, along with a PBS newscast that drew far fewer viewers. Local stations reported news of their communities, and relied on network news divisions for morning and evening news programs. Audiences for the thirty-minute network evening news shows were huge, dwarfing the audiences those programs draw today.[99] Walter Cronkite, top-rated anchor of the *CBS Evening News* from 1962 to 1981, typically attracted 25 million to 30 million viewers. In 1980, more than 42 million viewers typically watched either the CBS, ABC, or NBC evening news programs.

Radio news was available throughout the day, but usually just in five-minute segments at the top of the hour. The only source of more in-depth news for most people was the local newspaper. While the *New York Times, Washington Post, Wall Street Journal*, and a few other newspapers had their own reporters covering national and international news, most papers relied on one or two wire services—the Associated Press and United Press International—to cover news outside their circulation areas. The same AP or UPI stories dealing with national and international news appeared in most newspapers. The newspaper, TV, radio, and wire service journalists weren't perfect, of course. They sometimes made honest mistakes. They sometimes ignored important stories and focused on the sensational or trivial to boost ratings or circulation. But in general, they tried as best as they could to be objective, keeping opinion out of news stories and confining it to newspaper editorial pages.

And then a media revolution began—a revolution as profound as the change from horse-drawn carriages to gasoline-powered cars. On June 1, 1980, CNN, the Cable News Network, began broadcasting as the first twenty-four-hour all-news TV station. Many Americans—including many journalists—thought the concept was ridiculous and would fail. CNN was derisively called Chicken Noodle News and at first drew tiny ratings. (It wasn't even available in most American homes.) But CNN gradually grew its audience and launched a sister station called Headline News (now HLN) in 1982. Competing cable news channel CNBC (focusing on business news) launched in 1989, and direct competitors MSNBC and Fox News launched in 1996.

Fox quickly staked out a spot as the source of news for conservatives, focusing on right-wing opinion shows that made no pretense at objectivity. MSNBC became the source for news from a left-wing perspective. CNN started out trying to be more centrist, but moved left and became openly hostile to President Trump during his term in the White House. The lower-rated One America News Network began in 2013 and Newsmax TV launched in 2014, with both positioning themselves to the right of Fox News.

Social media and narrowly focused websites became a major source of news, often aggregated from newspaper and broadcast websites. Google launched in 1998, Facebook began in 2004, and Twitter and

YouTube were both started in 2006. Many individuals with no journalism training began posting comments about the news and starting blogs on social media filled with opinion and rumors that turned out to be inaccurate. Newspapers started websites and saw big drops in readership of their print editions and in advertising revenue. The number of daily newspapers published in the United States dropped from 1,748 in 1970 to 1,279 in 2018. Newspapers cut their staffs by thousands of reporters and editors.[100]

All these changes mean that today individuals can choose to reside in their own news environments, giving them vastly different views of what is important and accurate. Republicans tend to watch Fox News, with some tuning in to the even more far-right Newsmax and OAN, and read conservative websites. Democrats turn to MSNBC and CNN and liberal websites. A Quinnipiac Poll released January 11, 2021, shows the dramatic difference in perceptions by Republicans, Democrats, and independents. The poll found that 73 percent of Republicans believed Trump's assertions that there was widespread voter fraud in the 2020 election in which Biden defeated Trump. But only 36 percent of independents and a mere 5 percent of Democrats believed there was widespread voter fraud in the election.[101] How can Americans hope to agree on anything if we can't agree on basic facts? This problem isn't going away, and poses one of the greatest challenges to uniting Americans with a revival of our faith in democracy.

INEQUALITY OF OPPORTUNITY

"It was the best of times, it was the worst of times," Charles Dickens wrote in the opening paragraph of his novel *A Tale of Two Cities*, published in 1859.[102] New York governor Mario Cuomo latched onto the "Tales of Two Cities" theme in his most famous speech—his eloquent keynote address at the 1984 Democratic National Convention.[103] Cuomo said President Reagan's vision of America as "a shining city on a hill" was an accurate description of our country for the affluent and well educated, but did not describe conditions facing the millions of Americans struggling just to get by. The New York governor said that "this nation is more a tale of two cities than it is just a shining city on a hill." He spoke of "another part to the shining city, the part where some people can't pay their mortgages, and most young people can't afford one; where students can't afford the education they need, and middle-class parents watch the dreams they hold for their children evaporate."

Cuomo then adapted his frequent reference to "the family of New York" to a national audience, saying all Americans are tied together and those at the top of the economic ladder have a responsibility to lend a hand to those on the lower rungs. He said: "We believe we must be the family of America, recognizing that at the heart of the matter, we are bound one to another; that the problems of a retired school teacher in Duluth are our problems; that the future of the child—that the future of the child in Buffalo is our future; that the struggle of a disabled man in Boston to survive and live decently is our struggle; that the hunger of a woman in Little Rock is our hunger; that the failure anywhere to provide what reasonably we might, to avoid pain, is our failure."

Mario Cuomo's words ring true today. We can't expect all the people locked out of the "the shining city on a hill" to fully embrace our democratic system if they feel perpetually left behind and denied just treatment. This was a common feeling—though for very different reasons—among the protesters for racial justice in American cities in the spring and summer of 2020 and the insurgents who attacked the Capitol on January 6, 2021. It is the call for change from the aggrieved. If we are to restore faith in our civic religion of democracy we must make democracy work for all Americans, whether the Black family worried about police brutality and systemic racism, or the White family worried about unemployment caused by American companies offshoring jobs to countries where labor is cheaper. This is easier said than done, of course, but it remains one of the greatest challenges facing our democratic system.

There can be no doubt that inequality of opportunity remains a major problem today. For example, most people of color have far lower incomes and net worth than White Americans. People without a college education earn far less than those with college degrees. One illustration of this is a 2020 report by the Brookings Institution titled "Examining the Black-White Wealth Gap." It states: "A close examination of wealth in the U.S. finds evidence of staggering racial disparities. At $171,000, the net worth of a typical white family is nearly ten times greater than that of a Black family ($17,150) in 2016. Gaps in wealth between Black and white households reveal the effects of accumulated inequality and discrimination, as well as differences in power and opportunity that can be traced back to this nation's inception. The Black-white wealth gap reflects a society that has not and does not afford equality of opportunity to all its citizens."[104]

Educational attainment is also a major factor dividing the haves and have-nots in America. The U.S. Bureau of Labor Statistic reported that among young people graduating from high school in 2019, 89.9 percent of Asian Americans were enrolled in college in the fall semester, compared with 66.9 percent of White high school graduates, 63.4 percent of Hispanic graduates, and 50.7 percent of Black graduates.[105] And this doesn't even take into account the lower high school graduation rates among Black and Hispanic students. This educational attainment gap is intolerable and more must be done to close it.

Even when educational attainment is equal, the wealth gap persists between White families and minorities. Writing in Axios in June 2020, Dion Rabouin reported: "On average, Black households in the U.S. with heads who have completed a college degree have less net worth than white households headed by someone with less than a high school education."[106] And in the coronavirus pandemic raging across much of the world as we write this, people of color and those without college degrees are experiencing the greatest economic pain because they are disproportionately represented among those who can't work from home. The children of people struggling economically are also having the hardest time learning remotely when in-person learning in schools has been suspended due to the pandemic. They don't have the same access to computers as children from more affluent families, they often live in crowded conditions not conducive to remote learning, and they can't get as much help from less-educated parents with their schoolwork.

In his 1951 poem "Harlem," Langston Hughes wrote about the consequences of Black people being denied equal opportunity. Yet the poem can be interpreted to apply to any group that feels cheated and denied justice from our democratic system. The poem ponders what happens to the deferred dreams of African Americans and suggests that they may dry up "like a raisin in the sun" or *"explode."*[107]

ANTI-DEMOCRATIC REGIMES IN CHINA AND RUSSIA

Up to now we've discussed internal threats to American democracy and the need for a Great Awakening to renew the civic faith of our own citizens in our democratic system. But only about 4 percent of the world's population lives in the U.S. We can't close our eyes to threats from the rest of the world.

The September 11, 2001, terrorist attacks understandably focused America's attention on Islamist terrorism and led directly to the U.S. invasion of Afghanistan, where al-Qaida leader and 9/11 mastermind Osama bin Laden was based and protected by the Taliban government. U.S., British, and allied Afghan forces toppled the Taliban regime in three months and a U.S. raid killed bin Laden in his hideout in Pakistan in 2011. President Trump unwisely agreed to pull all U.S. troops out of Afghanistan (except for a small contingent guarding the U.S. Embassy in Kabul) by May 1, 2021. President Biden delayed this withdrawal until the end of August 2021, and America's NATO allies pulled out their troops as well in response to the U.S. action. The troop withdrawals emboldened the Taliban and sapped the morale of the Afghan government. The Afghan military offered little or no resistance as Taliban forces seized control of every major city in Afghanistan in an 11-day blitzkrieg, capturing Kabul on August 15, 2021 and consolidating their control over the nation. Biden criticized Trump for the original withdrawal agreement, and Trump criticized Biden for withdrawing in August despite the failure of the Taliban to adhere to promises they made in the peace agreement. Trump even said that Biden should "resign in disgrace for what he has allowed to happen in Afghanistan" and for mishandling other issues. In addition, Trump said if he were still president, all would be well. "We were not going to let people get slaughtered," the former president told the *New York Post* after the Taliban seized power. "I had a relationship with the Taliban where they knew they weren't allowed to do this." As always, Trump refused to accept any blame for his own failings, and did not point out that he had earlier criticized Biden for not withdrawing all U.S. troops by May 1, 2021.

Other than partisan sniping and attacks against each other, neither Trump, Biden—nor other Republicans and Democrats—could offer a coherent response to the disastrous fall of Afghanistan. What the world saw instead was a divided America with no sense of purpose and no distinctive agenda, leaving the U.S. weakened in the eyes of our allies and adversaries. If any issue called for bipartisan agreement it should have been America's response to the September 11 terrorist attacks and the war on terrorism waged by two Republican and two Democratic presidents. Yet even on this major issue of national security, partisan arguments erupted as politicians showed more interest in fighting each other than the terrorist threat. In truth, presidents and members of Congress in both parties deserved to share the blame for the debacle in Afghanistan. They could not offer any sense of what our country stands for on the international stage or domestically. The world was not wrong in sensing that the U.S. left Afghanistan hurriedly and in chaos, just as we left South Vietnam in 1975. Both our defeats in Vietnam and Afghanistan reflected a failed enterprise that demonstrated a weakened national resolve. Both U.S. defeats also showed a decline in American influence, prestige and stature, and a complete abdication of leadership and direction.

America should not have disgracefully abandoned our Afghan allies to the tyranny of the Taliban's brutal rule. Women and girls will be especially hurt, deprived of the chance for an education, the opportunity to hold jobs, and subject to rape euphemistically labeled as "arranged marriages." America's strategic position around the world and our competition against our adversaries Russia and China will suffer as well, as nations view the U.S. as being disloyal to our friends and fearful of standing up to our enemies. Just as America maintains military forces in Germany, Japan, South Korea and other nations around the world, we should have maintained a residual force in Afghanistan to advise and support that nation's military so it could continue protecting the Afghan people and keeping the Taliban from once again turning Afghanistan into a base for international terrorism. Sadly, 20 years of war and the deaths of 2,448 members of the U.S. military and 3,846 U.S. contractors in the conflict served only to delay a Taliban victory, not to prevent it. America is less safe as a result.

After invading Afghanistan to respond to the September 11 attacks, America took its focus off that nation and invaded Iraq in March 2003, overthrowing the regime of Saddam Hussein in April. Fighting has continued for years against forces opposed to the U.S.-backed government. But by the summer of 2021 only 2,500 American troops were in Iraq helping the nation fight the remnants of the Islamic State terrorist group. Biden announced in late July 2021 that U.S. forces would end their combat mission in Iraq by the end of the year. However, he said some will remain to advise and train Iraqi forces—a wiser course than our abandonment of Afghanistan.[108]

Unfortunately, American presidents don't have the ability to deal with hotspots in only one region of the world. They must juggle multiple and often unexpected crises. Since 2001 America has stationed in troops in Afghanistan, Iraq, and other areas of the Middle East—and sought to stop Iran from developing nuclear weapons. And presidents have tried since 1948 to forge an Israeli-Palestinian peace agreement in the same region, to no avail. But at the same time, our two most powerful foreign adversaries, China and Russia, were hard at work seeking to undermine democracy around the world. China and Russia are run by dictatorial regimes with no use for democracy. The two nations have aggressively expanded unchecked as neo-colonialists, supported rogue nations like North Korea and Iran, and worked to undermine Western democracies. While President Trump refused to believe it, the U.S. intelligence community concluded unanimously that Russia interfered in the 2016 American presidential election to help elect Trump and later concluded that Russia interfered in our 2020 election in an unsuccessful effort to help Trump get reelected.

China has risen in the last few decades from an impoverished developing country to become a military and industrial power with no tolerance for internal opposition. The communist regime has a long record of human rights abuses, free-trade violations, and neo-colonial offenses. While adopting limited free-market reforms to boost its economy, Chinese leaders have rejected any move toward democratic reforms.

But rather than see China as the adversary and threat that it is, successive U.S. presidents of both parties have sought in vain to build friendly ties to the communist government in the hope that China's economic liberalization would gradually lead to political liberalization. This began with President Richard Nixon's historic one-week visit to China in 1972, ending the hardline policy of trying to isolate the regime. America and China established diplomatic relations in 1979 and the U.S. stopped recognizing the anti-communist government on Taiwan as

China's government. But instead of then standing up to China's aggressive undermining of democratic values, American presidents acquiesced time after time in the hope of finding common ground.

More than any president in recent history, President Trump took an aggressive stance against the rising military and economic power. But despite his adversarial rhetoric, Trump didn't challenge China substantively beyond imposing tariffs. For example, the Trump administration overlooked China's egregious human rights violations in Hong Kong and against its Uyghur Muslim population in the Xinjiang region. What message does that send to fledgling democracies around the world struggling against authoritarianism? Hong Kong protesters carried American flags and posters of Lady Liberty, but the Trump administration sat by and did nothing as Beijing crushed their democracy movement.

Trump took an aggressive stance against Beijing with regard to its mishandling and cover-up of the COVID-19 outbreak. Intelligence reports point to the fact that China knew about the virulence and deadliness of the novel coronavirus at the end of December 2019, but continued to downplay the seriousness of COVID-19 and the ease with which it was spread by people. We don't know for certain, but if China had shared all it knew about the outbreak with the world early on it might have sharply limited the toll of death and illness caused by this new disease around the world. It wasn't until January 20, 2020, that Chinese health officials admitted the novel coronavirus could be transmitted between humans. Chinese medical professionals refused to share virological data with U.S. vaccine laboratories, and on occasion purposely destroyed evidence. All the while, China was buying massive quantities of personal protective equipment for its own medical workers, creating the dire shortage of PPE that the rest of the world would soon experience.[109] In February 2020, Trump halted flights between the U.S. and China. The move was heavily criticized as xenophobic and racist, but was soon adopted by most countries.

While the U.S. and countries around the world struggled to contain the pandemic, China succeeded because of the harsh lockdown restrictions it imposed and enforced. The World Health Organization said China imposed a "unique and unprecedented public health response [that] reversed the escalating cases."[110] The *New York Times* reported in February 2020 that some 760 million Chinese—more than twice the entire U.S. population—were confined to their homes and said: "China has flooded cities and villages with battalions of neighborhood busybodies, uniformed volunteers, and Communist Party representatives, to carry out one of the biggest social control campaigns in history."[111] China was able to quickly contain the pandemic and was the only national economy in the world to actually grow in 2020.

The United States, and indeed the rest of the Western world, must rethink the nature of our relationship with China. To be sure, we take the risk of losing trade opportunities, escalating the conflict in the Pacific, and alienating a powerful adversary. The alternative, however, is to sit by while an authoritarian nation hostile to our founding ideals undermines and deceives its way to becoming the premier superpower in the world. Chinese power and influence are growing at an alarming rate, and we need to do something about it.

While dealing with the Chinese threat to democracies, the Biden administration must keep a close eye on Russia as well. Russia today poses less of a threat than the Soviet Union before it broke up, but the Russians still have the second-largest nuclear arsenal in the world, behind only the U.S., along with a powerful military. Russian president Vladimir Putin called the 1991 breakup of the Soviet Union "the greatest geopolitical catastrophe" of the twentieth century in a speech in 2005 and said in 2018 that he would reverse the breakup if he could.[112]

Presidents Bill Clinton and George W. Bush welcomed former Soviet satellites into NATO, angering Putin. President Obama's Russia policy was nothing short of incompetent. Obama imposed economic sanctions on Russia, which in turn closed diplomatic channels. But the Obama administration did nothing to curb Russian colonialism in Syria and Ukraine, aside from denouncing it. The shocking lack of response only served to embolden Russia's aggression and accelerate its expansion efforts.

Finally, Trump's outward indifference to Russian misdeeds—including Russian interference in our elections and its brutal crackdown in Ukraine—rendered his weak substantive policies ineffective. By abandoning Syria to Putin without pressure on other fronts, like cybersecurity, the Trump administration carried out the most ineffective Russia policy in our memory.

On their own, Russia and China each stands as a major threat to the United States. Together, they stand to imperil the cause of democracy worldwide. The Russia-China axis already exists in all but name, and President Biden has an obligation to stand up to the two powerful nations in support of democratic ideals.

CHALLENGES FACING BIDEN

President Biden took office on January 20, 2021, facing multiple serious challenges: the COVID-19 pandemic and the need to dramatically speed up vaccinations against the disease; the economic hardships and massive unemployment caused by business closures to battle the spread of the coronavirus; the need to reverse Trump policies that Biden campaigned against; and the need to convince millions of Americans that he defeated Trump fair and square and is a legitimate president, despite Trump's refusal to concede defeat and continued baseless claims that Biden was elected as a result of fraud. These are among the greatest challenges any new president has ever faced.

None of the forces that threaten the foundations of our democracy were created by Trump. In fact, the opposite is true. The Trump presidency and everything that came with it, including the January 6, 2021, insurrection, was the logical culmination of decades of disastrous and compounding political failures by both parties. The rise of a political class that has lost the trust of citizens and refuses to stand up to bad actors at home and abroad has led us to this. It was these trends that made it possible for Trump to be elected president in 2016 and created the conditions that ignited the most serious divisions and insurrection since the Civil War. Worst of all, none of these forces will go away on their own. If we fail to take effective action, they will intensify.

We fear that growing numbers of Americans will lose faith in our system, leading them to reject America's founding ideals in exchange for radical solutions like those advanced by Trump on the right and Senator Bernie Sanders and Representative Alexandria Ocasio-Cortez on the left. This could embolden domestic extremists and our foreign adversaries alike and create the conditions under which democracy collapses by insurgency or external pressure, or more likely both.

Is it too late to save our democracy? We don't think so. At least not yet. Nevertheless, America faces immediate, systemic, and existential threats, and our democracy is in peril. This book will discuss these threats and suggest what to do about them. Additionally, this book is a call to action for the Biden administration. The Biden presidency could be the most important in our nation's history. It must reverse the decline of faith in our democracy by the American people. This will be a tall task for a president who only 58 percent of Americans initially accepted as the legitimate winner of the 2020 presidential election.[113]

How should Biden move forward? In a poll that our firm, Schoen Cooperman Research, conducted following his election we found that 62 percent of respondents answered that Biden's victory was a "mandate for centrist policies," compared to only 28 percent who said it was a mandate for progressive policies.[114] These findings tell us that if Biden and the Democrats who control the House and Senate by very slim margins enact unpopular progressive legislation and if Biden issues far-left presidential executive orders, they will further anger an already furious electorate. In this scenario, the outcome could be historic losses for Democrats in the 2022 midterm elections. In other words, if Biden and Congress move too far left, they will make millions of voters feel left behind. Republicans want to convince voters that the Democrats are wild-eyed socialists embracing radical policies that will destroy rather than enhance the American Dream. If the GOP succeeds in painting the 2022 midterm election as a contest between the party of Lincoln and the party of Lenin, Democrats can say goodbye to their congressional majorities.

Most of us don't appreciate what we have until we lose it. We take our democracy for granted because it is all we have known in America during our lifetimes. But nothing lasts forever. If we fail to renew our national faith in democratic government and the values it encompasses, we risk losing it, as hard as that may be for many people to believe today. We have written this book to sound an alarm against those on the right and left who would threaten our legacy of democracy by their desire to impose their own views on our nation in undemocratic ways. Our goal is to preserve our democracy for all generations to come, and recover from the divisions that threaten its future.

1 / LOSS OF TRUST IN AMERICA'S INSTITUTIONS

American democracy is facing an existential crisis of historic proportions. Millions of our citizens no longer have faith and trust in our core institutions and values, including our system of government, our educational system, big business and capitalism, the news media, law enforcement, our commitment to racial equality, our health care system, and our traditional religious institutions. Most Americans still trust the military, but that trust has dropped sharply since 2018.

The optimism that generations of Americans have embraced since colonial times, expecting better days ahead even when times are hard, has been replaced for millions of people by feelings of pessimism. The belief in the American Dream of upward mobility—that someone can go from rags to riches, climbing the economic ladder from the bottom rungs—is nowadays often dismissed as a fantasy. We can't ignore this crisis if we want to keep our democracy from imploding.

The trust and optimism crisis has been worsening for decades. It is rooted in the failure of the institutions above and the people who lead them to respond to the needs of the American people in times of rapid change, and in almost nonstop partisan battles. Instead of focusing on solving problems, far too many politicians are focusing on the next election and on denying the opposing party credit for accomplishing anything significant. The old saying that "politics is the art of com-promise" has become sadly outdated. Many politicians and their most committed supporters and donors now consider compromise and mod-eration signs of weakness and insufficient ideological fervor. Many consider fighting more important than legislating.

Too few lawmakers embrace the view of then-representative Deb Haaland (D-NM) who in her first term beginning in 2019 built a record of bipartisanship. "I couldn't agree more that collaboration is import-ant," Haaland said during the Senate confirmation hearing on her nom-ination by President Biden to become interior secretary. "I was the highest-rated freshman in Congress on bipartisan collaboration....I feel like the people of New Mexico sent me to Congress to get work done and that's exactly what I've done."[1] Our democracy would be in much better shape if more lawmakers shared the attitude of Haaland, who was confirmed in March 2021 to become secretary of the interior and the first Native American to serve in a president's cabinet.

Democracy only works when most citizens believe in it and trust their leaders to be true public servants. Democracy fails when leaders become a corrupt elite out to game the system for their own advantage. When citizens who work hard and play by the rules believe they have no shot at the American Dream—or conclude that the American values, identity, and the principles they grew up with are vanishing—a giant question mark hangs over the future of our democracy. The urban riots of the spring and summer of 2020 that broke out amidst largely peaceful protests calling for racial justice—along with the right-wing insurrection at the Capitol on January 6, 2021, to keep Donald Trump in the White House—might be only the beginning of the troubles that await us.

Don't just take our word for it when we say American democracy is endangered. In a report published in early 2021, Freedom House (a nonprofit and nonpartisan organization) raised alarm about the weak-ening of democracy around the world—including in the United States. "The parlous state of U.S. democracy was conspicuous in the early days of 2021 as an insurrectionist mob, egged on by the words of outgoing president Donald Trump and his refusal to admit defeat in the November election, stormed the Capitol building and temporarily disrupted Congress's final certification of the vote," the report states. "This capped a year in which the administration attempted to undermine accountability for malfeasance, including by dismissing inspectors general responsible for rooting out financial and other misconduct in government; amplified false allegations of electoral fraud that fed mistrust among much of the U.S. population; and condoned disproportionate violence by police in response to massive protests calling for an end to systemic racial injustice."[2]

The Freedom House report said the U.S. was one of 73 nations out of 195 the organization studied that became less free in 2020. Freedom House dropped America from its list of nations with the strongest democracies and instead ranked the U.S. with countries known for weak institutions and corruption. The report received little notice in the U.S. media, but we should all pay attention. If we don't take action, our democracy could become even more endangered.

Unfortunately, instead of working together to strengthen our democracy and to help it recover from the trauma of the 2020 election and the insurrection at the Capitol, Democrats and Republicans in Congress are doing all they can to undermine each other—and hurting the American people in the process. Lawmakers are acting like two teams of rowers in the same boat working against each other—each rowing in the opposite direction. Because they can't agree on which way to go, they prevent the boat from making any progress. This has left millions of Americans on both the left and right disappointed, disillusioned, disgusted, and distrustful of our nation's government and many of society's major institutions. As a result of these deep divisions, American democracy is in dire straits.

Making things even worse is the sad truth that divisions in Congress are mirrored by the divisions among the American people. As President

Biden said in his inaugural address, we are engaged in an "uncivil war."[3] We are divided from each not just by political party affiliation, but by economic class, race, ethnicity, religion, sexual orientation, geography, educational level, and other factors. Too often, we see each other as members of a particular group rather than as fellow Americans. One of the few ideas finding broad support among the American people is that the elite are exploiting everyone else and—as the old saying goes—the rich get richer and the poor get poorer.

Even when a majority of the American people are in agreement on issues, bitter partisan divisions among citizens and lawmakers often stand in the way of effective government action. For example, following two mass shooting in March 2021—one claiming the lives of eight people (including six Asian American women) in the Atlanta area, and a second in Boulder, Colorado, in which ten people were murdered—a *USA Today*–Ipsos poll found that 65 percent of Americans believe gun control laws should be stricter, down from 78 percent in a Gallup poll in 1972. But the gap between Democrats and Republicans on this issue in the 2021 poll was enormous. While 90 percent of Democrats favor tougher gun laws, only 35 percent of Republicans do.[4] Democratic support in 2021 was about the same as it was in a poll two years earlier, but Republican support for more gun control dropped substantially from 54 percent two years earlier.[5]

This widening of the gap on the gun issue between Democrats and Republicans illustrates how divisions between Americans are growing at a time when they need to be shrinking. Republican members of Congress—understanding full well that they could be attacked in primaries for supporting almost any new gun controls—are largely opposed to any new firearms legislation. As a result, there is virtually no chance that such legislation could receive the necessary 60 votes needed for passage in the Senate to overcome a GOP filibuster.

In order to take some small steps to reduce gun deaths, President Biden announced six executive actions he was taking in April 2021.

One action will require all parts in kits that are used by consumers to assemble so-called "ghost guns" to have serial numbers, making it possible for the guns to be traced if they are used in crimes. The unassembled parts of the "ghost guns" would be classified as firearms for the first time, subjecting buyers to background checks. Another action will more strictly regulate a stabilizing brace that turns a pistol into a rifle with a short barrel. Such a brace was used in the mass shooting in Boulder. The president also said the Justice Department will publish model "red flag" legislation that state legislatures can consider passing to enable family members and police to petition a court to remove guns temporarily from people who may present a danger to themselves or others. However, stronger gun control measures that Biden would like to see—including a national red flag law, a ban on assault rifles, closing background check loopholes for gun purchases, and taking away protections gun manufacturers now have against lawsuits—would require congressional approval. Biden acknowledged that "much more needs to be done." He said: "Gun violence in this country is an epidemic, and it's an international embarrassment."[6]

In an analysis on the CNN website shortly after seven mass shootings in seven days (including the ones in the Atlanta area and Boulder) took place, reporter Zachary Wolf wrote: "These sad truths about mass shootings in the U.S. are self-evident: In a country with easy access to guns, there will be mass shootings....Lawmakers will talk about making it ever-so-slightly more difficult for people to buy guns. They will fail to do anything about it."[7] Wolf's article quoted Representative Cynthia Lummis (R-WY) explaining Republican opposition, even in the wake of new mass shootings: "Every time that there's an incident like this, the people who don't want to protect the Second Amendment use it as an excuse to further erode Second Amendment rights," Lummis said. "I no longer believe the goal of people who want to erode our rights, little by little, is to just affect or tweak our rights. I now believe that their ultimate goal is to abolish our rights."

However, despite Republican claims, Democrats couldn't repeal the Second Amendment of the Constitution—which the courts have ruled allows gun ownership—even if they wanted to. The amendment states, in its entirety: "A well-regulated Militia, being necessary to the security of a free State, the right of the people to keep and bear Arms, shall not be infringed."[8] To adopt a new amendment or repeal an amendment to the Constitution requires a two-thirds vote by both the U.S. House and Senate, followed by ratification by legislatures or conventions in three-fourths of the states (38 states). There is zero chance that repealing the Second Amendment could get this level of support.[9]

According to the Gun Violence Archive, 43,541 people were killed by guns in the United States in 2020—19,385 in homicides and accidents, and 24,156 by suicide. Another 39,429 people were wounded by guns in 2020.[10] Surveys from the Pew Research Center, Harvard University, and Northeastern University have found that about 40 percent of Americans say they or someone in their household owns a gun. In addition, the Small Arms Survey, based in Switzerland, reports that while the U.S. has only about 4 percent of the world's population, Americans possess about 40 percent of civilian-owned guns in the world. The survey estimates that Americans own 393 million guns—meaning the number of guns in the U.S. exceeds the population of 331 million.[11] A Gallup poll found that in 2020, 42 percent of Americans said they had a gun in their home, down from 51 percent in 1982.[12]

The large number of guns in America makes it clear that gun violence will unfortunately claim some lives every year, no matter what Congress does. But common sense tells us that reasonable new restrictions on guns—such as requiring background checks for all gun purchases and a ban on assault weapons, on top of existing restrictions—will save lives without infringing on the rights of law-abiding Americans to own guns.

Democrats need to acknowledge that millions of Americans want to own guns and have a right to do so. Pew found in a 2017 survey that 67 percent of gun owners said a major reason for gun ownership is protection, while 38 percent cited hunting, 30 percent cited sport shooting, 13 percent cited gun collections, and 8 percent said they owned guns for their jobs.[13] Republicans need to accept the fact that government will not repeal the Second Amendment, confiscate all guns, or take away all our liberties if laws are changed to do a more effective job keeping guns out of the hands of people at risk of committing murder and other crimes. After all, we have speed limits on our roads, require drivers and passengers to wear seat belts in vehicles, and outlaw drunk driving—but that hasn't led to government confiscation of cars and trucks. The fact that the two sides continue to be unable to come together to agree on any new reasonable gun regulatory measures is a testament to the dysfunction of our political system.

Sadly, political combat today has escalated from a boxing match with rules and a clear ending to become a never-ending knife fight where anything goes. We see this most vividly in former president Trump's incessant repetition of the Big Lie that he won the 2020 presidential election, even though state and federal courts tossed out this baseless claim when they dismissed more than sixty Trump campaign lawsuits. Yet a Suffolk University/USA Today poll of 1,000 people who voted for Trump found that "Three of four, 73 percent, say Biden wasn't legitimately elected. . . . Six in 10, 62 percent, say congressional Republicans 'should do their best to stand up to Biden on major policies, even if it means little gets passed.'"[14] By April 2021, a Reuters-Ipsos poll showed that the number of Republicans who believe that "the 2020 election was stolen from Donald Trump" stood at 58 percent—still a majority.[15]

If this attitude prevails among GOP members of the House and Senate, we can expect Democrats to pay the next Republican president back when the shoe is on the other foot. This is a recipe for congressional gridlock to become a permanent affliction, except during the occasional times when the same political party controls the White House, the House of Representatives, and a 60-vote supermajority in the Senate to block filibusters (assuming the filibuster survives efforts by some Democrats to end it).

In Congress, Democrats have pulled out all the stops to attack Trump and Republicans. Many Democrats accused Trump of colluding with Russia to win the 2016 presidential election and were enthusiastic supporters of the nearly two-year probe of that claim by Special Counsel Robert Mueller, which ended with a report saying there was insufficient evidence to prove a criminal conspiracy. House Democrats later impeached Trump twice and Senate Democrats voted to convict him twice on other issues (the second time after his term had ended), but he was acquitted because most Republican senators supported him in his trials and refused to convict him.

Some Democratic members of Congress have hurled angry charges, including condoning racism and violence, at Republicans. For example, after House Minority Leader Kevin McCarthy (R-CA) refused to strip far-right extremist Rep. Marjorie Taylor Greene (R-GA) of her committee assignments, Democratic Rep. Alexandria Ocasio-Cortez of New York responded on MSNBC in late January 2021: "There are no consequences in the Republican caucus for violence. No consequences for racism. No consequences for misogyny. No consequences for insurrection. And no consequences means that they condone it. It means that that silence is acceptance."[16] House Democrats wound up removing Greene from her committee assignments in an unprecedented action. This only intensified the bitterness between Democratic and Republican House members.

While President Trump was in office, Rep. Maxine Waters (D-CA) called on people to harass members of the Trump administration. She said on MSNBC in June 2018: "I have no sympathy for these people that are in this [Trump] administration who know it's wrong for what they're doing on so many fronts . . . these members of his Cabinet who remain and try to defend him, they won't be able to go to a restaurant, they won't be able to stop at a gas station, they're not going to be able to shop at a department store. The people are going to turn on them."[17]

The name-calling and threats by Democrats against Republicans and by the left against the right—and vice versa—seem to grow in ferocity with each passing year. In the 2020 election campaign, each side conjured up horrific visions of disaster that would befall the nation if the other side was victorious. But rather than elevating themselves to be more appealing to voters than candidates of the other party, Democrats and Republicans have made millions of voters distrust and detest both parties. This reinforced the view of many Americans that elected officials from both parties have failed to address the needs of the American people.

DISTRUST IN GOVERNMENT

A Pew Research Center poll conducted in July and August 2020 found that only 2 percent of Americans said they trust the federal government to "do the right thing" just about always, while 18 percent said they trust the government to do so most of the time. The combined 20 percent figure is the lowest point in more than a decade of Pew surveys.[18] The same poll found that 57 percent of Americans said they feel frustration toward the federal government, 24 percent said they feel angry toward government, and only 18 percent said they are basically content. In addition, 59 percent said government should do more to solve problems, but 39 percent said government is doing too many things that should be done instead by individuals and businesses. Since the federal government can't do more and less at the same time, a lot of people are destined to be upset however the government acts.

In addition, polling by Gallup over the years has shown a steep drop in the amount of confidence Americans have in our nation's governmental institutions, including Congress, the presidency, and the Supreme Court. In 2020, 42 percent of Americans had "a great deal or quite a lot" of confidence in Congress, down from a high point of 68 percent in

1975. In 2020, just 39 percent of Americans had "a great or quite a lot" of confidence in the presidency, down from a high point of 72 percent in February 1991 (a spike due to America's success in the First Gulf War) and 50 percent in October 1991. In 2020, 40 percent of Americans expressed "a great deal or quite a lot" of confidence in the Supreme Court, down from a high point of 56 percent in 1988.[19]

In a poll conducted in March 2021 among 2,200 U.S. adults, Morning Consult reported that Congress is the least-trusted government institution, with only 42 percent of Americans expressing trust in the legislative branch. However, the trust level differed dramatically among Democrats and Republicans, with 57 percent of Democrats but only 31 percent of Republicans saying they trusted Congress. Since Democrats controlled both the House and Senate, it's not surprising in our polarized times Congress was trusted less by Republicans. The same poll found that 53 percent of Americans said they trusted the U.S. government overall, but again there was a big partisan split, with 60 percent of Democrats but only 34 percent of Republicans saying they trust the federal government.[20] Republican trust dropped 33 points since mid-October 2020 when Donald Trump was president.

The collapse of Americans' faith in government is a multigenerational story. The Vietnam War and the Watergate scandal were the twin events of the 1960s and early 1970s that shattered Americans' trust in their government. In 1964, a Gallup poll found that 77 percent of Americans trusted the federal government to do what was right just about always or most of the time. After Watergate and the Vietnam War, that proportion plummeted 50 points to just 27 percent, but rebounded back to 44 percent in the 1980s and 54 percent by the end of Bill Clinton's presidency in 2001.

From today's perspective, even the diminished trust numbers of the Vietnam-Watergate era look like a comparative golden age. For more than thirty years—from 1972 to 2004—on average, 69 percent of Americans expressed a great deal or a fair amount of trust in the government to deal with foreign affairs and 62 percent said the same about the government's capacity to deal with domestic issues, Gallup reported. In the summer of 2020, Gallup found that just 48 percent of Americans expressed this level of trust in the government to deal with foreign affairs and 41 percent said the same about the government's ability to handle domestic affairs.[21]

Today's lack of trust stems from the government's failure to solve problems in a hyper-partisan environment. In the wake of the September 11, 2001, terrorist attacks, public faith in Congress and the presidency rose to ten-year highs, only to be squandered by President George W. Bush's administration, which misled the American public about Iraq's chemical and nuclear weapons capabilities and invaded Afghanistan and Iraq. President Obama came into office pledging to unite the country, but the country was badly divided when he left. As then-freshman senator Ben Sasse (R-NE) said in his first Senate speech in 2015: "The people despise us all . . . because we're not doing the job we were sent here to do."[22]

Unsurprisingly, when Republicans control the government—particularly the White House—self-identified Republicans display higher levels of trust in the institutions of government. The same is true for Democrats when their party controls the White House. In 2013, when Obama was president, 34 percent of Democrats trusted the government "to do what is right" just about always or most of the time, while less than 11 percent of Republicans expressed such confidence in the federal government. During Trump's presidency this flipped, and 28 percent of Republicans expressed trust, while but only 12 percent of Democrats trusted the government all or most of the time.[23]

In a more recent example, the 2020 Pew poll discussed above found Democrats and Republicans sharply divided on the question of the U.S. government's handling of threats to public health, coming at a time when the coronavirus pandemic was sweeping across the world during the final summer of the Trump presidency. While 70 percent of Republicans said the federal government was doing a somewhat good or very good job on public health, just 17 percent of Democrats said this. It was as if Democrats and Republicans were living in two different nations, experiencing two different realities regarding not only the pandemic but other issues as well. Uniting people across such a vast partisan divide of perceptions is an extraordinarily difficult task.

"When hardly anyone from the party opposite the president trusts the government, governance becomes all but impossible," University of North Carolina political science professor Marc Hetherington wrote on the Brookings Institution blog in September 2015. "It is this group who must make sacrifices to support the president on an issue. Such ideological sacrifices require trust."[24]

The public's distrust in government is also reflected in a September 2018 Harris poll showing that three out of four likely voters thought members of Congress served their leaders and not their constituents. Nearly nine out of ten believed America won't find solutions to its biggest problems until Republicans and Democrats work on compromises.[25] Yet, elected officials of the two parties are drawing farther apart instead of moving to the center to reach compromise solutions.

In 2015, the late pollster Patrick Caddell—along with Republican National Committee veteran Bob Perkins and communications consultant Scott Miller—found that 86 percent of all voters believed "political leaders are more interested in protecting their power than in doing what's right for the American people." And 83 percent said they believed "the country is run by an alliance of incumbent politicians, media pundits, lobbyists, and other interests for their own gain." Over two-thirds agreed that "the real struggle for America is not between Democrats and Republicans but mainstream America and the ruling political elites."[26] Unfortunately, many Americans today agree with the assessment of former House Speaker Newt Gingrich (R-GA), who in 1995 said that "you can't trust anybody with power."[27]

Clearly, elected officials need to do a better job showing voters they can be trusted to put the best interests of the nation and the American people ahead of their own self-interests. In other words, show they are truly public servants.

DECREASING OPTIMISM

Since 1928, the Optimist International service clubs have been conducting speech contests for high school students on the importance of optimism.[28] A friend of ours still vividly recalls competing in his local club's contest in 1967 on the topic each student was given that year: "Patriotic Citizenship Needs Optimism." Optimism, he said back then, was necessary to unite the American people to work together to build a better future. That was true then and it is still true today.

Unfortunately, American optimism has been eroding for years, just as has the trust of the American people in our government. In the American Values Survey released in October 2020, the Public Religion Research Institute called the United States "a house divided and fragile." The survey found that 67 percent of Americans believed the U.S. was "heading in the wrong direction" and only 32 percent said the country was headed in the right direction. However, the views of Americans varied enormously based on their political affiliation in the closing months of the Trump administration. Some 66 percent of Republicans said the country was moving in the right direction under Trump, but only 26 percent of independents and just 10 percent of Democrats shared this optimistic view.[29]

A Pew Research Center poll released in March 2019 was headlined "Looking Ahead to 2050, Americans Are Pessimistic About Many Aspects of Life in U.S."[30] When asked what they thought the U.S. would be like in 2050, 73 percent of Americans predicted that the income gap between the rich and poor would grow wider, 57 percent said people sixty-five and older would have a lower standard of living, and 83 percent said most people would have to work into their seventies to be able to afford retirement. In addition, 59 percent said the condition of the environment would worsen. Some 92 percent said robots and computers will definitely or probably do much of the work now performed by people and 69 percent said this would be a bad thing. Some 76 percent said this increased automation would increase the inequality between the rich and poor, and 66 percent said the increased automation would be unlikely to create many new and better-paying jobs for people.

Following Joe Biden's election as president, an *Economist*-YouGov poll published in February 2021 showed Biden voters in the 2020 presidential race had a dramatically more optimistic outlook on the world than Trump voters. Some 77 percent of Biden voters—but only 21 percent of Trump voters—agreed with this optimistic statement: "It's a big, beautiful world, mostly full of good people, and we must find a way to embrace each other and not allow ourselves to become isolated." In stark contrast, 66 percent of Trump voters—but only 11 percent of Biden voters—agreed with this pessimistic statement: "Our lives are threatened by terrorists, criminals and illegal immigrants, and our priority should be to protect ourselves."[31]

One reason contributing to the loss of optimism could be that the American middle class is shrinking. According to the Pew Research Center: "The share of American adults who live in middle-income households has decreased from 61 percent in 1971 to 51 percent in 2019. This downsizing has proceeded slowly but surely since 1971, with each decade thereafter typically ending with a smaller share of adults living in middle-income households than at the beginning of the decade....From 1971 to 2019, the share of adults in the upper-income tier increased from 14 percent to 20 percent. Meanwhile, the share in the lower-income tier increased from 25 percent to 29 percent."[32]

Pew also reported in February 2020 that income inequality was increasing in the United States and that "the wealth gap between America's richest and poorer families more than doubled from 1989." Pew said that in 2018 the top-earning 20 percent of American households earned 52 percent of all U.S. income. The organization's polling shows that 78 percent of Democratic and Democratic-leaning voters said there was too much income inequality in the nation, but only 41 percent of Republicans held that view.[33]

The growing pessimism about our nation's future feeds into a related view held by more and more of our citizens that the American Dream is dead. This is an ominous development for our democracy. The dangerous downward spiral of American optimism must be reversed.

THE VANISHING AMERICAN DREAM

The United States is a nation of immigrants drawn from every country on Earth with the dream of building better lives for themselves and for their children. With the exception of Native Americans and enslaved Africans brought here in chains, the rest of us are either immigrants ourselves or can trace our ancestry to immigrants who chose to leave their home countries and families in search of what we now call the American Dream. The American Dream has been defined in different ways over the years, but its essence says that the U.S. is a land of endless possibilities. It says that no matter who you are, where you were born, where your parents came from, or whether you were born rich or poor, you can find success and advance with hard work—and your children can advance even further.

Historian James Truslow Adams popularized the term "American Dream" in his 1933 book, *The Epic of America*, in which he defined it as a "dream of a land in which life should be better and richer and fuller for everyone, with opportunity for each according to ability or achievement.... It is not a dream of motor cars and high wages merely, but a dream of social order in which each man and each woman shall be able to attain to the fullest stature of which they are innately capable, and be recognized by others for what they are, regardless of the fortuitous circumstances of birth or position."[34]

We know this vision of the American Dream was more aspirational than realistic for much of our history. The Constitution permitted the immoral institution of slavery to exist until 1865, and even after emancipation America allowed legalized discrimination to continue against Black people for another hundred years—while illegal discrimination remains with us today. We know that Native Americans were forced off their lands and didn't become U.S. citizens until 1924. And we know that women didn't gain the right to vote until 1920 and are still fighting for equality. Nevertheless, despite all the barriers that existed and that still exist for the advancement of some groups, the American Dream was an idea that brought millions of people to our shores.

Sadly, in recent years, polls have shown that fewer Americans than ever believe the American Dream still exists, and even fewer believe that it is within their reach. For example, a YouGov poll published in July 2020 found that just a narrow majority of 54 percent of U.S. adults think the American Dream is something they can personally achieve, while only 51 percent believe most people living in the U.S. can achieve it.[35] Only 45 percent of Black Americans believe they can achieve the American Dream and just 43 percent believe most Americans can achieve it. The same poll showed that 37 percent of Americans believe the American Dream is less attainable now that it was for past generations, while only 29 percent believe it is more attainable.

Perhaps nothing captures the essence of the American Dream and why so many immigrants came to the U.S. better than the poem "The New Colossus" written in 1893 by Emma Lazarus and placed on the pedestal of the Statue of Liberty in 1903. The poem says in part:

> Give me your tired, your poor,
> Your huddled masses yearning to breathe free,
> The wretched refuse of your teeming shore.
> Send these, the homeless, tempest-tost to me,
> I lift my lamp beside the golden door!

An important part of the American Dream is the expectation that children will earn more than their parents. However, that is becoming increasingly less likely. Stanford University researchers reported in December 2016 that while 90 percent of children born in the 1940s grew up to earn more than their parents, only 50 percent of children born in the 1980s were earning more than their parents. The study compared the household incomes of children at age thirty with the household incomes of their parents at the same age, adjusting for inflation, taxes, wealth transfers, and changes in household size. It was one of the most comprehensive studies ever done on income between generations and was based on a combination of Census Bureau data and anonymized Internal Revenue Service records. "One of the defining features of the American Dream is the ideal that children have a higher standard of living than their parents," said Professor Raj Chetty, a coauthor of the Stanford study. "We assessed whether the U.S. is living up to this ideal, and found a steep decline in absolute mobility that likely has a lot to do with the anxiety and frustration many people are feeling, as reflected in the [2016] election."[36]

The Great Recession (discussed in more depth later in this book) that began in December 2007 played a significant role in eroding the optimism of the American people and our belief in the American Dream, because it had such a devastating economic impact. The Federal Reserve reported in 2012 that the middle class suffered the largest loss of wealth and income due to the economic downturn, with low-income Americans suffering as well.[37]

In fact, the median American family had no more wealth in 2010, after the financial crisis and Great Recession ended, than it had in the early 1990s. Reporter Binyamin Applebaum explained this in the *New York Times* in June 2012, writing: "A hypothetical family richer than half the nation's families and poorer than the other half had a net worth of $77,300 in 2010, compared with $126,400 in 2007, the Fed said....Median family income fell to $45,800 in 2010 from $49,600 in 2007. All figures were adjusted for inflation."[38]

Wealthy Americans recovered most fully from the Great Recession. Between 2000 and 2016, high-income families increased their median net worth by 33 percent. In the same period, middle- and low-income families saw their net worth plummet by 20 percent and 45 percent, respectively, the Pew Research Center reported in January 2020.[39] Millions of Americans suffering a major financial blow were less optimistic and lost faith in the American Dream. In a study by Pew in 2015, Americans were asked if climbing the income ladder or financial stability was more important. Some 92 percent desired mere financial stability.[40] If these people were already on firm financial footing with secure and well-paying jobs, more would be concerned with income growth. The fact that the vast majority said they simply wanted financial stability showed that many were just struggling to stay afloat and be able to pay their bills.

Both Republican and Democratic politicians understand that millions of voters want to see the American Dream made real once again. But instead of coming up with centrist policies that would draw support from a majority of voters to breathe new life into the American Dream, extremists in each party are embracing increasingly radical programs that are polar opposites.

Democrats want to expand government to fund expensive programs designed to reduce income inequality, combat climate change, and accomplish many other progressive goals. These programs would need to be funded with massive deficit spending (like President Biden's $1.9 trillion American Rescue Plan to respond to the coronavirus pandemic) or tax increases that could slow economic growth and job creation.[41] Democrats also want to impose costly new government regulations on business, such as more than doubling the minimum wage to $15 an hour over four years (which the Congressional Budget Office estimates would eliminate 1.4 million jobs but also lift 900,000 people out of poverty); sharply cutting greenhouse gas emissions; and giving employees increased benefits.[42] However, increased regulations will slow the economic recovery from the coronavirus pandemic, raise energy prices, and impede job creation.

Republicans want to reduce the size and role of government (curtailing the ability of government to operate beneficial programs); cut taxes (forcing either big federal budget cuts, greater deficit spending, or more likely both); allow more fossil fuel production (worsening climate change); and severely limit government regulations (reducing the protections such regulations offer to the environment, workers, consumers, and others). They contend that this would unleash the private sector to create jobs and spark economic growth.

As far apart as these different political philosophies and proposed solutions to our problems are, compromise would be possible if both sides were willing to stop letting their quest for the perfect be the enemy of the good, and if they would stop trying to score political points by attacking members of the other party year-round. Such compromise has happened throughout American history, especially in times of crisis. Compromise like this—balancing the costs and benefits of policy choices—would be good for the American people and help restore their sense of optimism and faith in the American Dream. But unfortunately, most of our federal elected officials show little sign of embracing this commonsense notion.

DISTRUST IN OUR EDUCATION SYSTEM

Education has long been considered the surest pathway to achieving the American Dream. But educational opportunities are far from equal for all Americans. Because a large chunk of school funding comes from property taxes, school districts with large concentrations of low-income students are often starved for cash and operate with crowded classrooms in substandard buildings. While middle-class and wealthy students—who typically go to well-funded public or private schools—have a high rate of graduation from high school and college, low-income students and students of color (with the exception of Asian Americans) do not.

Public confidence in public schools has fluctuated over the years. According to Gallup, in 2020, some 41 percent of Americans had a great deal or quite a lot of confidence in public schools, down from a high point of 62 percent in 1975.[43] This clearly indicates that most Americans believe that schools, like much of government, are failing to do as good a job as they should.

Low-income students often face many hurdles to academic success. These include such things as living in single-parent homes and having less-educated parents—and in some cases parents who speak little English—who are unable to help them with homework or guide them through the college application process. In addition, many low-income students must care for younger siblings while their parents are at work because childcare isn't affordable, and must take after-school jobs as soon as they are old enough in order to help support their families. This takes time away from studies and prevents the students from participating in extracurricular activities that often teach valuable skills and strengthen college applications.

Low-income students are also less likely to have access to computers and high-speed internet connections at home—an especially serious problem when the coronavirus pandemic replaced classroom education with remote learning. In addition, these students are far less likely to participate in educationally enriching experiences like visits to museums, travel around the nation and abroad, and costly after-school lessons and tutoring. Children from minority groups are disproportionately low-income and concentrated in financially strapped school districts. This is reflected in high school dropout rates. According to the National Center for Education Statistics, in 2018 the overall high school dropout rate was 5.3 percent. But it was 9.5 percent for Native Americans, 8 percent for Hispanics, 6.4 percent for Black students, 4.2 percent for Whites, and 1.9 percent for Asian Americans.[44] Similar gaps were found in the percentage of adults who had a bachelor's degree or a higher-level degree, the U.S. Census Bureau reported. In 2019, 18.8 percent of Hispanics, 26.1 percent of Blacks, 40.1 percent of non-Hispanic Whites, and 58.1 percent of Asian Americans twenty-five and older held four-year college degrees.[45]

When looked at strictly in terms of income, a report issued in 2018 by the Pell Institute for the Study of Opportunity in Higher Education and the Alliance for Higher Education and Democracy found that in 2016 some 78 percent of students who had recently left high school and came from the top 20 percent of the wealthiest families went on to attend a two-year or four-year college. The figure for students from families with the lowest 20 percent of incomes was only 46 percent going on to higher education. The same report found that 58 percent of students from the wealthiest families were likely to graduate with a bachelor's degree by age twenty-four, compared with only 11 percent of students from the lowest-income families. The report also found federal financial aid to low-income students under the Pell Grant program had failed to keep up with rapidly rising college costs. While Pell Grants covered 65 percent of average college costs in the 1974–1975 school year, they covered only 25 percent of such costs in the 2016–2017 school year.[46]

Very few Americans had college degrees for most of our nation's history, but the number of degrees skyrocketed after World War II when the G.I. Bill gave veterans grants for college tuition and job training programs.[47] In addition, a Census Bureau report issued in 1984 concluded: "College attendance to maintain a draft deferment most likely caused an increase in college enrollment rates among young men in the 1960's, and the elimination of the draft in the early 1970's probably had some negative impact on enrollment rates in succeeding years."[48] In 1940, only 5.5 percent of men and 3.8 percent of women had completed four years or more of college. By 2019, the college completion rate figures rose to 35.4 percent of men and 36.6 percent of women.[49] As a result of the increased number of college graduates in the job market, a college degree is now required for many more jobs than in decades past and is the ticket to higher paying jobs.

A major problem colleges need to tackle is improving the graduation rate of their students. Only 41 percent of students in four-year colleges earn their bachelor's degrees within four years.[50] The graduation rate rises to 62 percent after six years (59 percent for men and 65 percent for women), the National Center for Education Statistics reported in 2020.[51] In two-year colleges, 33 percent of full-time students who enrolled in 2015 earned associate degrees within three years, 15 percent transferred to other schools in that time period, 11 percent remained enrolled in their original schools, and 41 percent dropped out, the NCES found.[52] While the goal of achieving 100 percent graduation rates for all colleges is likely impossible, more must clearly be done to help students succeed and graduate in a timely manner.

As more and more American jobs not requiring a college degree are replaced by automation and computers, or outsourced to other nations where workers earn far lower wages, the percentage of jobs requiring college degrees is sure to grow in coming years. Even many of the jobs not requiring college degrees will inevitably demand more specialized skills, requiring high schools and community colleges to improve their vocational education offerings to prepare students to fill these jobs.

Higher earning potential is a major reason growing numbers of young people are going on to college. The Federal Reserve Bank of New York reported in June 2019 that the average college graduate in recent years earned about $78,000 a year, compared with $45,000 for the aver-age high school graduate—a $33,000 difference.[53] Wages will rise over time and most likely so will the earning gap between college grads and those with just a high school diploma. But even not factoring in these inflationary increases, someone earning an extra $33,000 annually with a college degree over the course of a forty-five-year career would collect nearly $1.5 million more than a high school graduate. And, of course, many college graduates earn far higher salaries than $78,000 annually.

Over six in ten respondents in a 2020 poll said that the escalating costs of higher education make the American Dream less realistic.[54] The cost of tuition and room and board has far outpaced real wage increases and inflation, leaving low- and moderate-income students hard-pressed to afford a college education if they are unable to secure adequate financial aid. In addition, for years there has been a widening gap between SAT scores and economic circumstances; students in households making over $120,000 annually achieve far higher SAT scores than students in households making less than $20,000 annually.

In 2020, total student debt in the U.S. amounted to $1.7 trillion. That represents an average of $37,691 for each of the 45.3 million Americans with student debt. In the last decade, student debt has more than doubled and is growing six times faster than the U.S. economy.[55] "We've never had a historical era where so much debt was taken out at an early age," said Diana Elliott, research manager for financial security and mobility at Pew.[56] This amount of debt taken on early becomes a burden for many years.

The student debt problem creates a gloomy picture for the prospects of achieving another milestone of the American Dream: homeownership. The average age of first-time homeowners increased from twenty-nine in the 1970s and 1980s to thirty-two in 2018.[57] Owning a home is a critical aspect of the American Dream, and its significance on the American psyche cannot be understated. It is no surprise, then, that six in ten millennials in November 2020 no longer believed the American Dream is achievable.[58] When these young Americans look toward such a dismal future, how can we blame them for being pessimists?

All these statistics show how the failings of the American education system are increasing the loss of faith in the American Dream and our democracy that is spreading among many Americans. The situation worsened as many schools and colleges shut their doors and switched to virtual learning in the spring of 2020 and throughout much of the 2020–2021 academic year due to the coronavirus pandemic.

While eliminating in-person classes had a positive effect in reducing the spread of COVID-19, it had a negative impact on student learning, socialization, and mental health. The closing of schools and childcare centers was also harmful to families, forcing many parents (usually mothers) to leave the workforce to be with their children at home, reducing family income. While no precise figure exists for how many parents left the workforce due to school and childcare center closings, between February and September 2020 an estimated 900,000 mothers and 300,000 fathers left the U.S. workforce, according to economist Ernie Tedeschi, writing in the *New York Times* in October 2020.[59]

If we are to restore American optimism, fulfill the promise of the American Dream, and give the American people renewed faith in our democracy, Democrats and Republicans must work together to improve the quality of our public schools, particularly in areas with large numbers of low-income and minority students. Both parties must work together to make college affordable and increase the college graduation rate, and to improve vocational education for students not going on to college. This is essential to build a better future and prepare the next generation for the jobs of tomorrow. It is also the right thing to do, fulfilling the obligation of one generation to prepare the children they brought into the world to take the baton and build a brighter and better future for America in the years ahead.

DISTRUST IN BIG BUSINESS AND CAPITALISM

The American people have long had a love-hate relationship with big business and the capitalist system.

On the one hand, the private sector has been the mighty engine that has powered our economy and brought most Americans relative prosperity and a high standard of living when compared with people around the world. People need jobs to support their families, and as the old saying goes, you can't have employees without employers. This gives workers a vested interest in seeing their employers prosper. "After all, the chief business of the American people is business," President Calvin Coolidge said in 1925. "They are profoundly concerned with producing, buying, selling, inventing and prospering in the world."[60]

On the other hand, employers—particularly big businesses—have long been demonized in popular culture as greedy and uncaring, exploiting workers, eliminating American jobs through automation and offshoring, and caring little about the environment or the best interests of society. The labor union movement arose to give workers greater power to demand higher wages, shorter hours, safer working conditions, health insurance, and pensions. Unions made great gains in these areas, playing a crucial role in creating the middle class. For example, between 1945 and 1970, unionized manufacturing workers more than tripled their weekly earnings.[61]

Socialist and communist movements pitched themselves as alternatives to capitalism. While a few unions and far-left politicians in the U.S. embraced socialism over the years, socialists never were able to create a major political party. Communist candidates fared even worse. The most successful Socialist Party candidate for president was Eugene V. Debs, who ran for president five times and had his best election performance in 1912, when he won 6 percent of the popular vote but no electoral votes.[62] Samuel Gompers, who led the American Federation of Labor (now part of the AFL-CIO) from its founding in 1886 until his death in 1924, opposed socialism and fought for more rights for workers within the capitalist system.[63]

Advocates of President Franklin Roosevelt's New Deal argued that the reforms it instituted were necessary to block socialism and communism from taking hold in America during the Depression. Roosevelt was vehement in denying he was a socialist or communist. In accepting the Democratic nomination in 1936 for his second term in the White House, Roosevelt framed his New Deal programs as benefiting "the many thousands of small business men and merchants who sought to make a worthy use of the American system of initiative and profit."

But while not attacking capitalism by name, Roosevelt attacked the "economic royalists" of big business, comparing them to the British royalty that the American colonists rebelled against to establish our independent nation. He said that "the economic royalists carved new dynasties. New kingdoms were built upon concentration of control over material things. Through new uses of corporations, banks, and securities, new machinery of industry and agriculture, of labor and capital—all undreamed of by the [founding] fathers—the whole structure of modern life was impressed into this royal service."[64]

The vast majority of liberal Democratic politicians in the years after Roosevelt have been equally careful to reject socialist and communist labels, considering them too unpopular among voters. Donald Trump and his supporters labeled Joe Biden and other Democrats as socialists numerous times during the 2020 election campaign. Trump said that "a vote for any Democrat in 2020 is a vote for the rise of radical socialism and the destruction of the American Dream."[65] However, all candidates in the 2020 Democratic presidential primary except Senator Bernie Sanders of Vermont, who proudly calls himself a democratic socialist, rejected the socialist label. Representative Alexandria Ocasio-Cortez of New York was elected as a Democrat but also calls herself a democratic socialist.

It's a testament to the loss of faith in the American system and the American Dream that socialism and capitalism were equally popular in a Gallup poll of young Americans in 2019, while capitalism remained more popular among older generations. In the poll, 50 percent of people ages 18 to 39 had a positive view of socialism, while the other half had a favorable view of capitalism. Among those 40 to 54, only 39 percent had a positive view of socialism, while 61 percent had a positive view of capitalism. And among people 55 and older, positive views of socialism fell to 32 percent of Americans, while 68 percent had a positive view of capitalism.[66] Many people become more conservative as they grow older, but only time will tell if the young people now voicing support for socialism will hold the same view in future decades. A lot may depend on whether the feuding Democrats and Republicans stop fighting long enough to act to improve the U.S. economy to make it clear that the American Dream can be achieved again within our capitalist system.

Another sign of Americans' disillusionment with capitalism is the low confidence they have in big business. A Gallup poll in 2020 found that only 19 percent of Americans had a great deal or quite a lot of confidence in big business—a sharp drop from the 34 percent who expressed that view in 1975. In contrast, an impressive 75 percent of Americans expressed a great deal or quite a lot of confidence in small business in 2020, the highest number since Gallup began polling on that institution in 1997. In addition, 31 percent of Americans expressed a great deal or quite a lot of confidence in organized labor in 2020, down from a high of 39 percent in 1977.[67]

One reason for the low opinion many Americans have regarding big business and capitalism could be that the wages of workers haven't risen as fast as their productivity. Since the late 1970s, the growth in real wages as a function of worker productivity has slowed considerably. While each worker's average output has more than doubled since 1980, worker earnings adjusted for inflation have only increased by about 50 percent.[68] Businesses are seeing revenues rise and keeping their costs of doing business low to maximize profits.

In addition, in the wake of the 2008 financial crisis and resulting government bailouts of the auto and financial industries, many Americans lost faith in banks and financial institutions for their role in causing the crisis. A Gallup poll found that in 2020, 38 percent of Americans had a great deal or quite a lot of confidence in banks—up from a low of 21 percent in 2012, not long after the financial crisis and Great Recession, but far below the peak of 60 percent recorded in 1979.[69]

The financial crisis, which we will discuss later in this book in more detail, prompted the federal government to bail out Wall Street and big business but not ordinary citizens whose homes were taken from them in foreclosure proceedings and who suffered in other ways as well. This solidified the view of many Americans that big businesses that were considered "too big to fail" were getting special treatment they didn't deserve. A major characteristic of the American Dream is that it is supposed to be something every citizen can aspire to. When many people conclude the dream is only achievable for big businesses and the rich, our democracy is in trouble.

The Great Recession that lasted from December 2007 to June 2009 hit young people particularly hard, shaking their faith in our democratic system. According to a 2018 report by Federal Reserve Bank of St. Louis, the combined wealth of millennials (people born between 1981 and 1996) was 34 percent lower than it would have been had the financial crisis never occurred. The report said this puts millennials at serious risk of becoming a "lost generation," or one that never makes more than their parents. Generation X (born between 1965 and 1980) was hit the hardest wealth-wise, but was able to recover. However, millennials were early in their careers in the Great Recession or were in school, and entered an abysmal job market with huge student debt, made worse by low wages. Since the Great Recession forced many older Americans to delay retirement or come out of retirement as they watched their savings shrink, an already weak job market became even more saturated.

Older millennials, who had recently joined the ranks of homeowners, were hit hardest by the foreclosure crisis. Banks had been using extremely low standards for loan eligibility and allowing people in their twenties to take out large mortgages with minimal down payments. When the real estate market crashed, these buyers were the first to lose their homes. As Mark Muro, a senior fellow and policy director at the Brookings Institution, explained: "Older millennials were squarely hammered."[70] As a result, trust in banks was low. In a 2018 survey of over

30,000 Americans, only 28 percent said they trusted banks to be "fair and honest."[71] And 25 percent said they did not save any or very much money using banks or credit unions.[72] Financial institutions, especially banks, must respond to these widespread fears—but all private businesses will have to take steps to address the crippling lack of public trust they receive.

When citizens distrust big business as well as government, and when support for socialism grows among the young, America is headed for a troubled future. Ignoring this serious problem will not make it magically disappear.

DISTRUST IN THE NEWS MEDIA

Former President Trump denounces any news report that reflects poorly on him as "fake news"—even if it is incontrovertibly accurate—and continues to falsely claim he won the 2020 presidential election. Since beginning his campaign for the 2016 Republican presidential nomination he has frequently demonized the media—repeatedly attacking journalists as "dishonest people," "enemies of the people," "scum," "slime," and "sick people"—and questioning their loyalty to the United States.[73] In doing so, he has succeeded in increasing distrust in the news media, especially among his supporters. This endangers our democracy because it prevents the American people from operating under one set of objectively correct facts.

A Gallup poll in September 2020 found that only 10 percent of Republicans said they had a great deal or a fair amount of trust in the media to report the news "fully, accurately and fairly." The comparable figure for independents was 36 percent, and for Democrats it was an overwhelming majority of 73 percent.[74] The March 2021 poll by Morning Consult mentioned above found the same dramatic difference. Overall, 48 percent of Americans said they trusted the news media "a lot" or "some," but the figure for Republicans was only 19 percent, compared with 57 percent for Democrats.[75] The huge gap in trust in the media between people of different political persuasions widened dramatically beginning in 2016, during Trump's run for the presidency. In 1999, the three groups were much closer in the amount of trust they placed in the media. Back then 52 percent of Republicans, 53 percent of independents, and 59 percent of Democrats had a great deal or a fair amount of trust in the news media, Gallup found.

The differing degrees of confidence in the media explain the differing perceptions of reality between Trump supporters and opponents. A Pew poll published January 13, 2021—a week before Trump left office—found that 40 percent of people who voted for him in 2020 believed that he "definitely" won the election and 36 percent said he "probably" won. "Only 7 percent of Trump voters concede that Biden definitely won the 2020 election, while another 15 percent say he probably won," Pew reported. "Biden voters nearly unanimously believe their candidate won."[76]

America has only one president at a time. The president doesn't need the support of all Americans, but if he isn't even recognized as the legitimate leader of the country by millions of citizens it becomes an enormous challenge to govern and unite the nation. Trump's repeated false claims that he won the 2020 election and that Biden is not the legitimate president have misled the former president's supporters and are a major obstacle to getting Americans to accept the fact that Biden is leading our country as the result of a free and fair election. Trump's false claims were accepted as gospel truth by the insurrectionists who invaded the Capitol on January 6, 2021, after he summoned them to Washington to rally on his behalf to "stop the steal." Trump's Big Lie continues to motivate followers of the QAnon conspiracy theory, White supremacists, and others on the right to oppose Biden and Democrats on just about everything.

The former president's unprecedented refusal to admit he lost the election fair and square has left an open wound on our democracy that may not heal for a long time. If Trump runs for president in 2024, he will deepen the wound, and if he is the GOP nominee and loses it's a safe bet that the he will falsely claim he really won by a landslide and is once again the victim of a rigged election. If this happens we can only hope that better security will be in place to stop another deadly attack on the Capitol, and that Congress and the courts will again uphold our democracy.

While no other U.S. presidential candidate has so stubbornly refused to admit defeat, plenty of elected officials and candidates for federal, state, and local offices have joined Trump in criticizing the media throughout American history. President George Washington complained about being "buffeted in the public prints by a set of infamous scribblers."[77] Although Thomas Jefferson had been a champion of press freedom before he became president, he changed his tune after he assumed our nation's highest office and was criticized in newspapers. "Nothing can now be believed which is seen in a newspaper," President Jefferson wrote in a letter to journalist (and later U.S. senator) John Norvell in 1807. "Truth itself becomes suspicious by being put into that polluted vehicle."[78]

And in the last century, President Harry Truman wrote a scathing letter to *Washington Post* music critic Paul Hume, after Hume wrote a negative review of the president's daughter Margaret's singing performance at Constitution Hall in Washington in 1950. "It seems to me that you are a frustrated old man who wishes he could have been successful," Truman wrote. "Some day I hope to meet you. When that happens you'll need a new nose, a lot of beefsteak for black eyes, and perhaps a supporter below!"[79]

All politicians would love to get nothing but adoring praise from every news organization covering them on a daily basis, but that day will never come. That's because the relationship between politicians and journalists is, by its nature, adversarial. The job of journalists is not to present politicians in the most favorable possible light, ignoring their shortcomings, false statements, and wrongdoing. The job of journalists is to be skeptical, demand proof of claims, and report both positive and negative news about the people they cover. This can be challenging when reporters face the threat of losing access to sources if they report negative stories. Reporters also work to get both sides of the story, meaning they will seek out critics of the people and actions they report on to give opposing views.

"I've never worked for a politician who thought they got good press," Joe Lockhart wrote in an op-ed published by CNN in March 2021. Lockhart served as White House press secretary for President Clinton from 1998 to 2000, press secretary for the 1984 presidential campaign of former vice president Walter Mondale, and worked on the presidential campaigns of Michael Dukakis in 1988 and President Jimmy Carter in 1980.[80] His comment on the Democrats he worked for is true for just about all politicians. Unhappiness with media coverage is widespread among people running for office in both parties.

For example, President Biden is certainly not happy about news stories about his son Hunter's business dealings, which are being investigated by federal prosecutors at this writing. Hillary Clinton would no doubt have wished the media never covered the FBI investigation of her use of a personal email account and server for State Department business when she was secretary of state. And New York governor Andrew Cuomo couldn't be pleased with stories that broke in the *New York Times* in February 2021 in which women alleged he had sexually harassed them, leading to his resignation six months later after a slew of additional negative news stories and a highly critical investigatory report by the state attorney general. The three are all Democrats. Republicans in addition to Trump get upset when they are the subject of these negative news stories. Examples include Representative Marjorie Taylor Greene's angry response to criticism of her embrace of wild QAnon conspiracy theories, and the complaint by Rep. Matt Gaetz (R-FL) that allegations of sexual misconduct against him were politically motivated.

Nevertheless, while just about all politicians have at times criticized the media, Trump's criticism stands out for being extraordinarily harsh, broad, sustained, and hyperbolic. Trump's attacks on the media are not just complaints about inaccuracies or bias involving specific stories or reporters. Rather, they are an assault on the very concept of a free press and its ability to report any negative news and criticism of him. "It's frankly disgusting the press is able to write whatever they want to write," Trump said in October 2017, criticizing the basic premise of the Constitution's First Amendment that guarantees freedom of the press. "People should look into it." And later that month he tweeted: "Network news has become so partisan, distorted, and fake that licenses must be challenged and, if appropriate, revoked. Not fair to public!"[81] CBS News *60 Minutes* correspondent Lesley Stahl said Trump told her off-camera in 2016 why he so ferociously attacks the news media. "He said, 'you know why I do it? I do it to discredit you all and demean you all so when you write negative stories about me, no one will believe you,'" Stahl said in 2018.[82]

No one—including journalists—claims the news media never make mistakes and never show bias. And in very rare cases journalists have lost their jobs for knowingly and deliberately concocting what can legitimately be called "fake news." For example, *Washington Post* reporter Janet Cooke won a Pulitzer Prize for a story published in 1980 about an eight-year-old heroin addict that was beautifully written—but turned out to be a work of fiction. When her hoax was exposed, she resigned, her career in journalism ended, and the *Post* returned the Pulitzer. "What I did was wrong," Cooke said in a 1996 interview with *GQ* magazine. "I regret that I did it. I was guilty. I did it, and I'm sorry that I did it. I'm ashamed that I did it."[83] The Cooke scandal prompted news organizations to tighten the standards and do more fact-checking. That was a positive step, although similar scandals followed at the *New York Times*, the *New Republic, USA Today*, and *Rolling Stone* magazine.

More recently, the news media have opened themselves to criticism—and to increasing distrust from the public—because many news organizations have abandoned past standards of at least trying to be objective and strictly factual. Cable news channels have clearly chosen ideological sides. Fox News and rivals Newsmax and One America News Network are firmly siding with Trump and Republicans, and their schedules are filled with opinion shows. CNN and MSNBC are firmly in the Democratic camp, and their news shows are filled with opinion as well. This is a money-saving strategy in addition to one driven by the desire for high ratings, because it is much cheaper to have people sitting in a studio (or at home in front of computer cameras during the COVID-19 pandemic) opining on the news than it is to send reporters and camera crews around the world to cover the news.

In addition, talk radio is filled with opinion, usually right-wing, and people calling in don't need to be paid. While well-reasoned and calmly stated opinion presentations are informative, they can be boring. The way for TV and radio to boost ratings is to air more extreme and inflammatory opinions, filled with sharp attacks on the other side. This can be entertaining, but it increases divisions among the American people and lowers credibility of the media.

Republicans are generally skeptical of liberal media, and Democrats are generally skeptical of conservative media. For example, a Pew Research Center poll released in January 2020 found that Republicans and Democrats had sharply different views about which news organizations they trust. Fox News was trusted by 65 percent of Republicans (including voters leaning Republican), but only 23 percent of Democrats (including voters leaning Democratic). In contrast, only 23 percent of Republicans said they trusted CNN, compared with 67 percent of Democrats. MSNBC was trusted by just 18 percent of Republicans, compared with 48 percent of Democrats. The *New York Times* was trusted by only 15 percent of Republicans, but 53 percent of Democrats. The major broadcast TV networks all received far greater trust from Democrats than Republicans.[84]

While all the major cable news channels employ reporters in Washington, New York, California, and in a few other U.S. and foreign bureaus—and send reporters around the nation and around the world to cover major news stories—the bulk of cable news programming consists of interviews and discussions conducted by anchors, who make it crystal clear what their own opinions are on many stories. Most viewers gravitate to the news channel that best suits their ideological tastes, meaning that depending on what channel they watch they get very different versions of the news. As a result, we no longer have a shared reality the way Americans did in years past when the three network evening news programs took a similar approach to their thirty-minute (including commercials) newscasts. In addition, the right-wing cable news channels criticize the accuracy and bias of the left-wing channels on the air, and left-wing channels do the same for the channels on the right. These attacks erode viewer trust in all the news media even further.

On top of this, millions of Americans now get their news primarily from websites, social media, and talk radio programs. Pew reported in January 2021 that a survey showed that 86 percent of U.S. adults get news sometimes or often from a smartphone, computer, or tablet connected to the internet. Pew found that the comparable figures for other media are 68 percent from TV, 50 percent from radio, and 32 percent from print publications.[85] In July 2020, Pew examined in greater detail the sources where Americans say they primarily get their political news. The breakdown was: news websites or apps—25 percent; social media—18 percent; cable TV—16 percent; local TV—16 percent; broadcast network TV—13 percent; radio—8 percent; print publications—3 percent; and no answer—1 percent.[86]

While there are plenty of mainstream and reputable news organizations posting stories on social media and on their own websites, a significant amount of "news" on Facebook, Google, other social media platforms, and on websites is posted by non-journalists and special interest groups and is filled with errors, exaggerations, and other deficiencies. The 2020 Pew study cited above on where Americans get their political news found that people who rely the most on social media for political news are "less likely to follow major news stories" and "less knowledgeable about these topics." Before the advent of the internet you had to work for a newspaper, magazine, broadcast station, or network to widely distribute news. Now anyone can tweet or post on other social media sites, even if they have no commitment to truth and accuracy and know nothing about journalistic standards. On top of this, non-journalists anonymously post comments routinely on social media sites and websites and call in to talk radio shows. When readers realize that many of these posts and calls are not credible, it hurts the credibility of all media, eroding public trust.

The three top newspapers in the U.S.—the *New York Times*, the *Wall Street Journal*, and the *Washington Post*—are all thriving with large staffs and many readers paying for online and print subscriptions. However, most other U.S. newspapers are struggling with sharply reduced staffs and less ability to cover the news than they had years ago. The internet destroyed the old business model of newspapers, as many readers stopped paying for printed newspapers and read news for free on the web. Advertisers left printed papers for the web as well. Growing numbers of newspapers are now charging for access to their stories online and are seeking compensation from Facebook and Google, which link to newspaper content and benefit from billions of dollars in advertising revenue. But most newspapers are in bad financial shape.

Writing about a lawsuit in federal court seeking compensation for newspapers from the social media giants, *Washington Post* media columnist Margaret Sullivan said in February 2021 that "more than 2,000 local newspapers have shuttered since 2004."[87] Pew reported several dismal statistics about the decline of U.S. newspapers in February 2020, including the following: In 2018 circulation figures for printed daily newspapers dropped to the lowest level since recordkeeping began in 1940, falling to about 28.6 million on weekdays and 30.8 million on Sundays—a reduction of 8 percent and 9 percent respectively from 2017; newspaper advertising revenue plummeted 62 percent from 2008 to 2018, falling from $37.8 billion to $14.3 billion; and newsroom employment dropped by 47 percent from 2008 to 2018, falling from 71,000 people to 38,000.[88]

Newspapers aren't the only news organizations cutting staff. In 2020, a record 16,160 newsroom jobs at newspapers, magazines, websites, and broadcast stations and networks were eliminated in the U.S., according to a January 2021 report by the outplacement firm Challenger, Gray & Christmas.[89] Media organizations across the board lost advertising revenue due to the coronavirus pandemic. Cumulatively, job cuts at all types of news organizations from 2008 through 2020 (including the 16,160 cited above) totaled 91,905.

Print, broadcast, and website journalists today also have more to do than they did in the past and face new pressures. Many are expected to devote significant time to posting on Twitter and Facebook because an estimated 3.8 billion people around the world use social media, according to a report published in January 2021 by We Are Social.[90] Growing numbers of journalists are doing podcasts. TV and radio stations and networks all have websites, so reporters frequently have to produce written reports and update them as well as broadcast stories. With fewer reporters, editors, and photographers on the job and more to do, it is inevitable that the quality and accuracy of the news stories that journalists produce suffers, further eroding public trust in the media.[91]

DISTRUST IN LAW ENFORCEMENT

Public trust in law enforcement hit a record low in 2020, with only 48 percent of Americans expressing a great deal or quite a lot of confidence in police, a Gallup poll conducted from early June to mid-July found.[92] This was the lowest level since Gallup began polling on this question in 1993. (The highest level of confidence in the police was reached in 1996, when it hit 60 percent.[93]) Confidence in police dropped five points from 2019 to 2020 in the wake of the May 25, 2020, police killing of George Floyd, an unarmed and handcuffed Black man who died as Minneapolis police officer Derek Chauvin knelt on his neck for over nine minutes. Chauvin was convicted of second- and third-degree murder and second-degree manslaughter in April 2021 for killing Floyd, after his trial was televised by cable news networks in the high-profile case.

Floyd's killing and other killings of Black people by police set off a wave of protests against police misconduct and demanding racial justice. The protests took place in over 1,700 cities across the U.S. and in many other countries, and in some cities turned into riots over the course of the spring and summer. Four police officers were fired and charged in Floyd's death. In addition to Chauvin, who was the first officer to stand trial, fired officers Thomas Lane, J. Alexander Kueng, and Tou Thao were charged with aiding and abetting second-degree murder and manslaughter.[94]

Outrage at the police killings of Black people and long-standing complaints about discriminatory treatment of African Americans by police are responsible for a sharp divide in confidence in law enforcement officers between Blacks and Whites, and between Democrats and Republicans. Gallup found that confidence in police actually rose by seven points in 2020 from 2019 among Republicans, hitting an overwhelming majority of 82 percent. But among Democrats there was a six-point drop from 2019 in 2020, with just 28 percent expressing a great deal or quite a lot of confidence in police. There was also a large confidence gap regarding police between Blacks and Whites, with 56 percent of Whites but only 19 percent of Blacks expressing a great deal or quite a lot of confidence in police in 2020. On top of this, a Pew survey released in July 2020 showed that 89 percent of Republicans believe police treat people of different races equally—far fewer than the 10 percent of Democrats who hold that belief.[95]

A later poll by ABC and the *Washington Post* found that differences in views of police persisted based on political affiliation and race. Pollsters asked Americans if they agreed with the statement that "the country should do more to hold police accountable for mistreatment of Black people." Overall, 60 percent agreed. But when broken down by party and by race, the differences were enormous. Some 85 percent of Democrats, 58 percent of independents, and just 31 percent of Republicans agreed that police should be held more accountable for mistreating Black people. Some 83 percent of Black people, 67 percent of Hispanics, and 53 percent of Whites wanted to see greater police accountability.[96]

The huge confidence gap in police along political party and racial lines illustrates how badly divided Americans are from each other, as if we are living in separate worlds with different realities. Closing this gap will be an enormous challenge for police departments and elected officials, but it needs to be a high priority. The divide was illustrated when the U.S. House passed the George Floyd Justice in Policing Act on March 3, 2021, by a vote of 220–212. The bill would create a national database to track police misconduct, ban some types of no-knock search warrants, ban police chokeholds, ban religious and racial profiling, and make it easier to hold police officers accountable in civil and criminal court for misconduct.[97] Only two Democrats voted against the bill, and only one Republican voted for the measure. However, the Republican—Rep. Lance Gooden of Texas—said he had accidentally hit the wrong button and would submit a correction to this vote. President Biden supports the legislation, but the House bill is unlikely to win approval in the Senate without substantial changes, because it would need 60 votes to overcome a Republican filibuster.

The characterization of the policing bill by Democrats and Republicans could not be more different. "To make our communities safer, we must begin by rebuilding trust between law enforcement and the people they are entrusted to serve and protect," the White House said in a statement. "We cannot rebuild that trust if we do not hold police officers accountable for abuses of power and tackle systemic misconduct—and systemic racism—in police departments." But Republicans countered that the policing legislation would weaken the ability of police to protect the public. Representative Kat Cammack (R-FL) told Democrats during the House debate on the bill: "You say this is a reform bill, and I say that's BS. Your own conference members have been advocating for the defunding of our local police officers, calling them names I cannot and will not repeat here today." House Majority Leader Steny Hoyer (D-MD) responded: "It would be an irresponsible policy to defund the police and we are not for that.…You can say it, over and over and over again. It will be a lie, no matter how well it serves your political purposes."

As long as Democrats and Republicans use police reform as an issue to attack each other, nothing will be accomplished. That would be an unfortunate lost opportunity. New attention was focused on law enforcement reform after Derek Chauvin was convicted of murdering George Floyd. *Washington Post* columnist Marc A. Thiessen came up with a good suggestion, writing soon after Chauvin's conviction: "The guilty verdicts in the Derek Chauvin trial give President Biden a once-in-a-presidency opportunity to deliver on his promise of unity and bipartisanship. To seize it, he should immediately call Sen. Tim Scott (R-SC) and offer to work with him to pass bipartisan police reform legislation."

Scott, "a Black man who had experienced police discrimination," introduced a bill called the Justice Act shortly after Floyd was killed in 2020, designed as a bipartisan measure incorporating some Democratic proposals, Thiessen explained. The conservative columnist wrote that Scott's bill "incorporated a number of Democratic proposals into his legislation, including making lynching a federal hate crime, creating a national policing commission to conduct a review of the U.S. criminal justice system, collecting data on police use of force, barring the use of chokeholds by federal officers, withholding federal funds to state and local law enforcement agencies that do not similarly bar chokeholds and withholding funds to police departments that fail to report to the Justice Department when no-knock warrants are used."[98]

Unfortunately, Democrats attacked the Scott bill as not strong enough and made no attempt to use it as the basis for compromise legislation in 2020. Senator Dick Durbin (D-IL), who is now the Senate majority whip, called the Scott bill a "token, halfhearted approach" but later apologized for use of the word "token" after Scott said he was offended.[99] House Speaker Nancy Pelosi (D-CA) said the Scott bill was "trying to get away with murder, actually. The murder of George Floyd." Pelosi refused to apologize after the Senate Republican Communications Center tweeted that she "owes Senator Scott an apology for these disgusting comments." Pelosi responded that "our bill does something, theirs does nothing."[100]

But in fact, the Scott bill did something—several important things, actually. It simply didn't go as far as Democrats wanted. By definition, compromises don't allow either side to get everything it wants. In an encouraging sign, Representative Karen Bass (D-CA) reopened negotiations on police reform legislation with Scott shortly after Chauvin's conviction. "We now know that this bill must be done, it must be enacted into law," Pelosi said in April 2021, sounding very different from her comments in 2020. She said she was open to changes in the House bill, but the compromise must be "meaningful." Negotiations were continuing as of June 2021.[101]

We discussed the Defund the Police movement in the introduction to this book and pointed out President Biden's opposition to cutting police funding. We also noted that while elected Democrats in some cities have voted to cut police budgets in the wake of the George Floyd killing, this action has coincided with crime rates increasing. In addition, defunding police is politically unpopular. The Pew survey from July 2020 mentioned above found that 73 percent of Americans believe funding for law enforcement should either stay the same or be increased, and only 26 percent want to see police funding cut.[102]

A Gallup Poll published in July 2020 found that only 15 percent of Americans support eliminating police departments, with support for abolition of the departments coming from just 12 percent of Whites, 20 percent of Hispanics, 22 percent of Blacks, and 27 percent of Asian Americans. Broken down by political party, 27 percent of Democrats, 12 percent of independents, and just 1 percent of Republicans favored eliminating police departments. Asked if they favored reducing police department budgets and shifting the money to social programs, 47 percent of Americans agreed with that idea. The breakdown was: 41 percent of Whites, 49 percent of Hispanics, 70 percent of Blacks, and 80 percent of Hispanics. On a partisan basis the percentages supporting shifting money from police to social programs were: 5 percent of Republicans, 12 percent of independents, and 27 percent of Democrats.[103]

A more recent poll for *USA Today*, conducted by Ipsos and published in March 2021, found: "Support to redistribute police department funding has decreased among Americans since August after a summer of protests had erupted across the country against racial injustice and police brutality.... While some believe defunding the police is a call to get rid of law enforcement completely, many activists behind the slogan intended to make a more nuanced argument for police budgets to be steered toward community social programs so officers were less often required to take on roles better suited to social workers. Only 18 percent of respondents supported the movement known as "defund the police," and 58 percent said they opposed it."[104]

Republicans are eager to characterize Democrats as anti-police and anti-public safety radicals whose reckless actions will send crime rates soaring and endanger the lives of the American people, and they hope to convince the public that Democrats who embrace the Defund the Police movement are proving that this characterization is accurate. This Republican effort drew strength from the views of some prominent Democrats supporting cuts in police funding, although not supporting the complete elimination of police departments. The *New York Times* reported in June 2020: ". . . Democratic Party officials are expressing broad support for significantly reallocating funds away from police departments. . . . Interviews with 54 Democratic National Committee members, convention superdelegates, and members of a criminal justice task force convened by Mr. Biden and Senator Bernie Sanders found a near-unanimous sentiment that local governments should redirect more money toward social services, education, and mental health agencies."[105]

Clearly, reforming the police is an essential step to weed out officers who are abusive, engage in excessive force, and target people for illegal discrimination based on their race, ethnicity, religion, or other factors. Democrats and Republicans should use the House policing bill and its Senate counterpart as vehicles to work out a compromise set of reforms both sides can agree on. As we saw when rioters attacked the U.S. Capitol, police heroically put their lives on the line to protect the rest of us, and sometimes suffer grievous injuries and death while doing so. We must not let the small minority of bad actors among them overshadow the good work the vast majority of officers perform.

DISTRUST IN AMERICA'S COMMITMENT TO RACIAL EQUALITY

When then-senator Barack Obama gave a speech on race at the National Constitution Center in Philadelphia in March 2008 during his campaign for the presidency, he stated correctly that the Constitution "was stained by this nation's original sin of slavery."[106] Obama pointed out how the immoral institution that was permitted to continue under America's founding document was a direct contradiction to a Constitution that proclaimed the "ideal of equal citizenship under the law . . . [and] liberty and justice." He added: "What would be needed were Americans in successive generations who were willing to do their part—through protests and struggle, on the streets and in the courts, through a civil war and civil disobedience and always at great risk—to narrow that gap between the promise of our ideals and the reality of their time."

Obama, of course, went on to become America's first and so far only Black president. It was an historic achievement and seemed to many to be a fulfillment of Dr. Martin Luther King Jr.'s famous "I Have a Dream" 1963 speech at the Lincoln Memorial in Washington where he talked about his four children living in a nation where they would be judged by the content of their character and not by the color of their skin.[107]

But although Obama convinced millions of Americans not to judge him by the color of his skin, he wasn't a miracle worker. He couldn't erase the four-hundred-year legacy of slavery and discrimination against African Americans and wipe out racial disparities and racism. These long-standing scars on our nation's claims to equality unjustly limit access to the American Dream. The pent-up grievances they created were major factors in the protests seeking racial justice across America following the brutal murder of George Floyd in Minneapolis on Memorial Day in 2020.

Thankfully, America has come a long way since our early days when Africans were enslaved and didn't receive even the most basic human rights, followed by another century of legally permitted racial discrimination. Black Americans were denied jobs, admission to segregated schools and housing, voting rights, equal justice, and much more for generations long after slavery ended. But despite progress made with the passage of civil rights legislation in the mid-twentieth century and advances since then, racism has not disappeared. As we discussed earlier, Black Americans still lag woefully behind Whites in terms of family income and wealth, educational attainment, homeownership, and other measures of achieving the American Dream.

In addition, the Pew Research Center reported that in 2018 Black Americans made up 33 percent of the sentenced prison population, even though they accounted for only 12 percent of the nation's total population.[108] Yet as bad as that statistic on imprisonment is, Black imprisonment fell by 34 percent from 2006 to 2020—a hopeful sign.

In March 1968—exactly forty years before candidate Obama's speech on race at the Constitution Center—a presidential commission issued a landmark report following riots by Black people that broke out in over 160 American cities in the summer of 1967.[109] The worst riots were in Detroit (where forty-three people died) and Newark, NJ (where twenty-six died). The presidential commission was officially called the National Advisory Commission on Civil Disorders, but became known as the Kerner Commission after its chairman, Illinois Democratic governor Otto Kerner. The report's chilling conclusion made headlines: "Our nation is moving toward two societies, one black, one white, separate and unequal."

The Kerner Commission report "argued that the riots were caused in large part by poor neighborhood conditions and limited labor market options facing Black Americans as a consequence of racism and rampant discrimination in housing and labor markets." Marcus Casey and Bradley Hardy of the Brookings Institution wrote in 2018. "Although the report's authors believed in full integration as the long-term solution, they argued that more immediate relief was possible through large-scale, targeted government investment in housing, education, and employment programs, and more robust social insurance programs."[110]

There has been a great deal of progress in the fight against racial discrimination since the Kerner Commission report was issued, with the opening of many new opportunities to African Americans. Yet in the twenty-first century, relations between White and Black Americans have grown worse, Gallup found in its polling.[111] Asked about the state of relations between White and Black Americans, 46 percent of Whites and 36 percent of Blacks said relations were very good or somewhat good in 2020, Gallup found. In surveys since 2002, the percentage of Whites characterizing relations as very good or somewhat good hit a high of 75 percent in 2007, and the percentage of Blacks saying this peaked at 70 percent in 2002 and 2003. This is a disturbing trend.

In a similar question, people were asked in 2020 how satisfied they are with the way Black people are treated in the U.S. Some 41 percent of Whites, 39 percent of Hispanics, but only 21 percent of Blacks said they were very or somewhat satisfied with the treatment Black Americans receive.

A poll published in September 2020 by the University of Massachusetts Lowell Center for Public Opinion showed that White and Black Americans had dramatically different views on the extent of racial discrimination against Blacks today. While 48 percent of Whites said Blacks are treated less fairly than Whites by police, 73 percent of Blacks held that view. And while 41 percent of Whites said Blacks and Whites are treated equally when applying for jobs, only 7 percent of Blacks held that view. Some 41 percent of Whites believe both races have the same educational opportunities, but only 10 percent of Blacks hold that view.[112] The differences in views on all these issues by race is profound.

The recommendations of the Kerner Commission hold up remarkably well after more than a half-century. They deserve a fresh look today to see how they can be updated as needed and implemented by government at all levels and by the private sector to make America's commitment to equal opportunity for all a reality and not just a slogan. We need to throw open the gates to the American Dream to everyone in this country, regardless of race—and regardless of ethnicity, gender, religion, sexual orientation, gender identity, or any other factor people have no control over.

But while creating equal opportunity for all is vital, creating equal outcomes for all is an impossible task and goes against the American Dream. The American Dream says we should all be able to rise as far as our hard work and talents will take us and be judged on our individual merits. That requires clearing the obstacles that stand in front of the success of some Americans, such as being born into a low-income family, living in substandard housing, being raised by a single parent, or facing racial or other types of discrimination. And the American Dream requires that government provide help to those who need it through social safety net programs, such as unemployment assistance, Social Security, Medicare, Medicaid, the Affordable Care Act, the Supplemental Nutritional Assistance Program (SNAP), and low-income subsidized housing assistance.

Crucially, the American Dream also requires equal educational opportunities for children from low- and moderate-income families and from every race and ethnicity, which means governments must increase funding to improve the quality of substandard schools and make charter schools available to more students. College scholarships and low-interest student loans also need to be increased substantially to make college affordable for all who want to go and can gain admittance. But even if we do all these things, not everyone in America will have an equal outcome in life. We won't all be millionaires. We won't all be corporate executives, doctors, or lawyers. We won't all send our children to Ivy League universities. No society—including in socialist and communist nations—has ever guaranteed that all citizens will have equal outcomes in life. If Democrats insist on equal outcomes, which they refer to as "equity," they will not only be seeking the impossible; they will drive voters unwilling to endorse a system of strict racial and other quotas into the arms of Republicans. President Biden, Vice President Harris, and many others are embracing equity. "Never has a modern U.S. president emphasized the concept [of equity] quite as much as Biden has, nor used it to signal such a clear focus on achieving racial justice," Bloomberg City Lab reported in February 2021.[113] When she was running in 2020, Kamala Harris said that equity refers to equitable treatment, which means "we all end up at the same place." She said, "There's a big difference between equality and equity."[114]

Republicans and Democrats both face challenges when it comes to the issue of their commitment to racial equality.

Republicans have largely written off getting more than a small percentage of the Black vote. Too many are still pursuing the Southern strategy developed by President Richard Nixon of appealing to White voters who feel threatened by Blacks and other minorities. This has led to the unfortunate rise of White nationalism on the Republican fringe, as manifested at a march and rally by neo-Nazis in Charlottesville, Virginia, in August 2017. Marchers with torches chanted "Jews will not replace us" and shouted "Heil Hitler," while speakers said "we must secure the existence of our people and a future for White children."[115] The rally ended in the death of an anti-Nazi protester and the injury of nineteen others when a White nationalist drove his car into them.

In addition, White nationalists were also among the rioters who broke into the U.S. Capitol on January 6, 2021. Black Capitol Police officers said the rioters repeatedly yelled racist slurs at them. BuzzFeed News quoted one officer as saying, "I got called a n——15 times today."[116] This isn't to say the majority of Republicans are racists. But when Black voters see racists embracing Trump and the Republican Party, they are understandably repelled and lose trust in Republicans.

Republicans need to come to grips with the fact that the Census Bureau predicts that non-Hispanic Whites will make up just under 50 percent of the U.S. population by 2045 and an even smaller percentage in later years. That means the GOP needs to become more inclusive and welcoming to Blacks, Hispanics, and Asian Americans if Republicans hope to have a long-term future on the national political stage.[117] In the 2020 presidential election, polling by the Associated Press of 110,000 people in the days leading up to and on Election Day showed that Donald Trump failed to win a majority of the support from any of these minority groups—a bad sign for Republicans in future balloting.[118]

The AP poll found that only 8 percent of Black voters, 28 percent of Asian American voters, and 35 percent of Hispanic voters cast ballots for Trump. Together, these people of color made up 22 percent of voters in 2020—a percentage sure to grow in future elections. Trump was supported by 55 percent of White voters, but even though Whites cast 74 percent of ballots in the election, that wasn't enough to reelect him.

Yet, instead of trying to capture the support of more voters of color by advocating policies that will benefit them, Trump and many Republicans have doubled down on their strategy of appealing to aging White voters—including those who long for the days when Blacks and a much smaller Hispanic population were largely stuck in low-paying jobs and not competing for their fair share of prosperity and the American Dream. *Washington Post* columnist Dana Milbank described this losing GOP strategy this way in a column published in March 2021: "The Republican Party's dalliance with authoritarianism can be explained in one word: race. Trump's overt racism turned the GOP into, essentially, a White-nationalist party, in which racial animus is the main motivator of Republican votes. But in an increasingly multicultural America, such people don't form a majority."[119]

Explaining why she believes Trump didn't get more Black votes in 2020, *USA Today* columnist Suzette Hackney wrote in November 2020 that "certain broad issues—racial injustice, economic inequality, voter suppression, law enforcement bias, educational access, health care—resonate with Black Americans," but Trump's positions on all these issues went against the prevailing position among Blacks.[120]

Democrats have the good fortune of doing well with Black voters and other voters of color. Their challenge is to maximize turnout of minority voters at the polls—while Republicans want to minimize it. This is why House Democrats passed legislation on March 3, 2021, to make voting easier. No Republicans voted for the bill, called the For the People Act, and only one Democrat opposed it. The measure requires automatic voter registration, expands early and mail-in voting, weakens state laws mandating that voters produce identification at the polls, makes it harder to purge voter rolls, and restores the right to vote to people convicted of felonies who have completed their prison sentences. It also imposes new campaign finance and lobbying rules and aims to end partisan gerrymandering of congressional districts.

However, strong Republican opposition and the opposition of Democratic senator Joe Manchin of West Virginia in the Senate will make it virtually impossible to pass the bill there with the 60 votes needed if the filibuster rule remains in effect in the chamber. "The right to vote is sacred and fundamental—it is the right from which all of our other rights as Americans spring," President Biden said in support of the For the People Act. "This landmark legislation is urgently needed to protect that right, to safeguard the integrity of our elections, and to repair and strengthen our democracy."[121]

But as *New York Times* contributing opinion writer Christopher Caldwell pointed out in an essay published in June 2021, the For the People Act offers "not an expansion of voting rights but a relaxation of voting regulations."[122] Voting rights expanded when constitutional amendments allowed freed slaves, women, and people ages eighteen, nineteen, and twenty to vote. In contrast, the For the People Act would legalize many of the steps states took to make voting easier during the height of the coronavirus pandemic, allowing more voters to cast absentee ballots. Caldwell makes a strong argument in favor of going back to pre-pandemic rules that limited absentee voting to guard against voter fraud, but also calls for enacting some ideas in the For the People Act, such as making Election Day a national holiday and backing up votes cast on machines with paper ballots in case recounts are needed. He also points out that the Democratic legislation is designed primarily to increase voting by groups likely to cast ballots for Democrats, while Republican efforts that are supposedly designed to root out voter fraud are really designed to limit voting by people likely to support Democrats. Thus, rather than being about civil rights or preventing fraudulent voting, the whole dispute over the bill is largely an attempt to gain a partisan advantage at the polls through the legislative process, despite the rhetoric each side is employing.

If Democrats and Republicans are willing to compromise they could pass a bill that preserves the most beneficial elements of the For the People Act—particularly those designed to reform partisan congressional redistricting and campaign financing. But they seem to be on a collision course that will keep compromise legislation from being enacted.

Another challenge Democrats face in working to increase trust in America's commitment to racial equality is dealing with attacks from Republicans who are seeking to paint the Democrats as radicals who want to defund the police, support left-wing rioters, unfairly charge police with wrongdoing if they use force to protect the public from dangerous criminals, and discriminate against Whites to curry favor with Black people. As noted earlier in this chapter, Biden has come out against defunding the police and many Democratic elected officials have criticized riots that erupted during protests of the killing of George Floyd and other Black people in 2020, while also noting the legitimate problem of police misconduct.

However, as we have noted, some far-left Democrats—including Representative Alexandria Ocasio-Cortez—have called for defunding the police and criticized police conduct in a number of cases. In fact, Ocasio-Cortez was upset that New York City's plans to cut $1 billion from its police department did not go far enough. She complained that some funds were simply being transferred to other city departments where they could be used to pay for police, such as diverting money from the police to the city's Education Department to pay to keep police in schools. "Defunding police means defunding police," Ocasio-Cortez said in a statement in June 2020. "It does not mean budget tricks or funny math. It does not mean moving school police officers from the NYPD budget to the Department of Education's budget so the exact same police remain in schools."[123]

Notably, Ocasio-Cortez did not complain about the presence of police in the U.S. Capitol complex during the January 6, 2021, riot. In fact, in an Instagram Live video she said she feared for her life as she hid in an office building near the Capitol, even though rioters never entered that building.[124] If Capitol Police are defunded, there will be fewer officers to protect Ocasio-Cortez and other lawmakers. Instead, the Capitol Police are expected to get a bigger budget and add more officers.

Democrats need to make clear that they strongly support racial equality and want to fund and support programs to provide equal opportunity to all. They need to support reform of police departments, but not defunding. By taking these positions, they will meet the legitimate needs of people of color stuck at the bottom of the economic ladder without going to radical extremes that will strengthen Republican opposition. And Democrats need to make clear that they support these steps with actions, not just rhetoric. They did this convincingly by voting to approve Biden's proposed $1.9 trillion coronavirus relief bill in March 2021. The measure, which Biden signed into law, provides the greatest benefits to low-income Americans with children—including many Black and Hispanic families. It will lift 13 million families out of poverty, researchers for the Columbia University Center on Poverty and Social Policy concluded.[125]

In another move to show his support for racial equality, on his first day in office President Biden signed the Executive Order on Advancing Racial Equity and Support for Underserved Communities Through the Federal Government. In the order, Biden states: "Equal opportunity is the bedrock of American democracy, and our diversity is one of our country's greatest strengths. But for too many, the American Dream remains out of reach. Entrenched disparities in our laws and public policies, and in our public and private institutions, have often denied that equal opportunity to individuals and communities....It is therefore the policy of my Administration that the Federal Government should pursue a comprehensive approach to advancing equity for all, including people of color and others who have been historically underserved, marginalized, and adversely affected by persistent poverty and inequality. Affirmatively advancing equity, civil rights, racial justice, and equal opportunity is the responsibility of the whole of our Government."[126]

Democrats and Republicans may never have identical views on exactly how to eliminate racism and promote equality for all, but they ought to be able to agree that doing so must be a priority and find common ground to get the job done. Instead of emphasizing conflict, confrontation, and our differences, both parties need to start emphasizing cooperation and conciliation, and agree that as Americans we share a common identity and destiny.

Former National Basketball Association star forward Charles Barkley, who is Black, expressed this view when he criticized politicians in both parties for fanning the flames of racial division. Speaking during the CBS Sports broadcast of the Final Four NCAA men's basketball tournament in April 2021, he said: "Man, I think most White people and Black people are great people. I really believe that in my heart, but I think our system is set up where our politicians, whether they're Republicans or Democrats, are designed to make us not like each other so they can keep their grasp of money and power."[127]

As we have mentioned, the late New York Democratic governor Mario Cuomo often spoke of "the family of New York," united despite the different races and ethnicities of the diverse population.[128] We need to look at our country as the family of America and recognize that it is in our mutual self-interest to work together and overcome prejudices that have divided us for far too long. We need to view ourselves as brothers and sisters in the American family, even though we are not all identical. Plenty of liberals and conservatives have worked on this important issue, giving us a good foundation to build upon.

On the left, Heather McGhee—board chair of the racial justice organization Color of Change and former president of the progressive think tank Demos—persuasively argues that racial discrimination is harmful to people of all races and society as a whole in her 2021 book, *The Sum of Us: What Racism Costs Everyone and How We Can Prosper Together*.[129] In an interview on the NPR program *Fresh Air* in February 2021, McGhee criticized what she called "this zero-sum idea that progress for people of color has to come at the expense of white people. But that zero-sum idea is a lie. It's a lie that has been aggressively sold, I believe, to white Americans by people who are very vested in the economic status quo and in keeping the concentration of wealth and power very narrowly held." Her point was that by looking at society through an economic lens rather than a racial lens it is clear that many of the initiatives that would benefit struggling Black families—like lowering the cost of a college education, raising the minimum wage, and making health care more available and affordable—would actually benefit more White Americans than Black Americans. So, rather than letting the wealthy class divide other Americans by race, it is important for the poor and middle class to unite for their mutual benefit.[130]

"I don't think the facts bear out the idea white people benefit from the kind of racism that we have today and that people of color are the only people who are harmed," McGhee said in an interview with Vox in 2016. "I'm very patriotic because I believe if America is exceptional it's because of the great diversity of our people, and I believe it's time for a new story about who we are as a country that says our diversity is our greatest asset."[131]

On the right, the late Jack Kemp was a champion of fighting racism and poverty and opening the door to the American Dream wider. Kemp was a professional football player who went on to serve as a Republican in the U.S. House representing Western New York from 1971 to 1989, secretary of the Department of Housing and Urban Development for four years under President George H. W. Bush, and the unsuccessful GOP vice presidential nominee in 1996. He called himself a "bleeding-heart conservative" and said friendships he developed with Black teammates in his years as a professional football player made him a strong advocate of racial equality, civil rights legislation, and efforts to help people escape poverty. "This is my way of redeeming my existence on Earth," he once told a reporter. "I wasn't there with Rosa Parks or Dr. King or John Lewis. But I am here now and I am going to yell from the rooftops about what we need to do."[132]

Kemp advocated for costly government programs to help the Black community, including enterprise zones—areas in low-income inner cities where businesses would get tax breaks and government would invest in infrastructure improvements to create jobs. Many states created such zones, which brought Kemp praise from Democrats. "I watched him interact in poor communities with so clearly a love of people, and a fierce idea of equality," said Senator Cory Booker (D-NJ). The senator said Kemp's "compassion, engagement and comfort" were clear when he met with Black people and Hispanics.[133] Kemp also favored allowing welfare recipients to keep 85 percent of their public assistance payments even if they got jobs (to remove a disincentive to work), affirmative action, and funding to enable public housing residents to buy their apartments. But these ideas and other parts of what Kemp wanted to become a Republican War on Poverty were repeatedly shot down during his tenure as HUD secretary by White House Budget Director Richard Darman as being too expensive and impractical.[134]

While some of his positions sounded like they came from a Democrat, Kemp was a staunch conservative best known for his advocacy of supply-side economics, which contended that big tax cuts would pay for themselves by stimulating economic growth. That view proved popular with Republicans and President Reagan, and Kemp won approval of his legislation cutting income taxes by 25 percent over three years. But his 1988 campaign for the GOP presidential nomination never got off the ground and he collected only thirty-nine delegates. Nevertheless, he showed that a Republican conservative could be what we would call today a committed racial justice warrior. Had Kemp made it to the White House, the state of race relations might be very different today. If Republicans want to become competitive for the Black and Hispanic vote, they would do well to take a fresh look at his ideas and join with Democrats to make the fight for racial equality a bipartisan effort.

DISTRUST IN THE MILITARY

Most Americans still have trust in the U.S. military, but the number has been dropping. The 2021 Reagan National Defense Survey found that 56 percent of Americans had a great deal of trust and confidence in our military, but that was down dramatically from 70 percent in 2018. Every demographic group saw double-digit drops in its military trust. There was a strong split by party, with 70 percent of Republicans expressing a great deal of trust and confidence in the military, but only 48 percent of Democrats and 47 percent of independents.[135]

Alarmingly, the people with the lowest levels of trust in the military were young men and women under 30—the very people the military needs to fill its ranks in our all-volunteer armed forces. Only 38 percent of those under 30 said they had a high degree of trust and confidence in the military, compared with 58 percent of those 30 to 64, and 69 percent of those over 65. In addition, less than half of Black Americans—44 percent—said they had a high degree of trust and confidence in the military.

One worrisome development that may be contributing to the loss of trust in the military is that some active-duty military members and veterans are members of extremist groups. "The vast majority of those who serve in uniform and their civilian colleagues do so with great honor and integrity," Defense Secretary Lloyd Austin said in a memo he issued in April 2021. "But any extremist behavior in the force can have an outsized impact." Austin's memo announced new screening and training to keep extremists out of the military, help identify those already in the military, and prepare service members returning to civilian life to resist efforts of violent hate groups to recruit them.[136] Some current and former military members were among the rioters who attacked the U.S. Capitol. Their weapons and combat skills make them attractive to groups interested in violent extremism.

DISTRUST IN OUR HEALTH CARE SYSTEM

The Affordable Care Act (also known as Obamacare) has proven to be an extremely divisive law, drawing high levels of distrust and disapproval from Republicans. Signed into law by President Obama in 2010, the act was designed to enable millions of Americans without health insurance to get coverage at a price they could afford.

The law made more Americans eligible for Medicaid, which provides health insurance to Americans with low incomes. It created health insurance exchanges that provided access to federally subsidized health insurance. It barred insurance companies from denying people coverage or charging them more due to their preexisting medical conditions. And it allowed children to remain covered by their parents' health insurance until age twenty-six, among other provisions. The law also said all health insurance plans had to cover specific "essential health benefits" and to cover certain preventive services at no charge to patients, and required everyone to be covered by health insurance (a requirement later removed). Under President Biden's $1.9 trillion American Rescue Plan passed by Congress in early 2021 to respond to the coronavirus pandemic, federal health insurance subsidies were increased and made available to those with increased incomes.[137]

Democrats hailed the enactment of the Affordable Care Act as a historic achievement and one of Obama's greatest accomplishments. Republicans ceaselessly attacked the complex law, which was difficult for many Americans to deal with when it came to selecting the right health insurance coverage (especially during its early rollout when there were problems with the Affordable Care Act website). GOP members of Congress and Trump mounted court challenges to the law and succeeded in weakening some provisions. But they tried and failed many times to repeal the law in Congress. Congressional Republicans and President Trump promised repeatedly to come up with a replacement for the Affordable Care Act that would be far superior—but never did.

A Gallup poll released in December 2020 found that 55 percent of Americans overall approved of Obamacare, but the difference in the approval rate by political party was stunning. While an overwhelming 94 percent of Democrats approved of the law, 57 percent of independents approved of it, and a mere 13 percent of Republicans approved of the law.[138] This was clear evidence that ten years of repeated attacks on Obamacare by Republicans worked in convincing party loyalists it was terrible. Even though many Republicans benefited by the law, they had a number of misconceptions about it, stoked by attacks from Trump and other GOP elected officials.

As the COVID-19 pandemic hit the U.S. and the world, Democrats and Republicans were also sharply divided in their trust in medical scientists and all scientists as a whole. A Pew Research Center poll published in May 2020 found that 53 percent of Democrats said they had a great deal of confidence in medical scientists, but only 31 percent of Republicans did. Similarly, 52 percent of Democrats had a great deal of confidence in all types of scientists, compared with only 27 percent of Republicans.[139]

Republicans and Democrats also responded very differently to the COVID-19 pandemic. The Pew Research Center reported in March 2021 that its polling showed that "the biggest takeaway about U.S. public opinion in the first year of the coronavirus outbreak may be the extent to which the decidedly nonpartisan virus met with an increasingly partisan response. Democrats and Republicans disagreed over everything from eating out in restaurants to reopening schools, even as the actual impact of the pandemic fell along different fault lines, including race and ethnicity, income, age, and family structure.... No country was as politically divided over its government's handling of the outbreak as the U.S. was in a 14-nation survey last summer."[140]

Republicans followed the lead of President Trump in downplaying the health threat of the coronavirus and taking fewer precautions against the spread of the disease. Pew polls from March 2020 through February 2021 consistently showed a huge partisan gap when voters were asked if the pandemic was a major threat to the health of the U.S. population. In February 2021, 82 percent of Democrats but only 41 percent of Republicans—exactly half as many—called COVID-19 a major health threat.

Another Pew poll released in March 2021 showed a similar partisan gap in acceptance of vaccinations against the deadly disease. While a strong majority of 83 percent of Democrats said they plan to get or had already received one of the coronavirus vaccines, only a slim majority of 56 percent of Republicans said they had been vaccinated or planned to get vaccinated. A Monmouth University poll in April 2021 confirmed this result. Only 5 percent of Democrats said they likely will never get the vaccine to protect themselves against COVID-19, but that grew to 22 percent for independents and jumped to 43 percent of Republicans.[141] This disturbing lack of vaccine acceptance means that far more Republicans than Democrats are putting themselves at risk of becoming seriously ill, infecting others, and dying from COVID-19. From a public health standpoint, if almost half of Republicans continue to decline to be vaccinated, the pandemic will continue and the chance of new variants arising that may be more resistant to vaccines will grow.[142]

What is particularly ironic about the reluctance of so many Republicans to be vaccinated against COVID-19 is that the accelerated development of the vaccines against the disease in record time is one of President Trump's greatest accomplishments. Logically, Trump ought to be one of the biggest cheerleaders for the vaccines and should be playing a major role in urging all Americans—and particularly his supporters—to get vaccinated as soon as possible. Trump himself was hospitalized with a serious case of COVID-19 and his wife, Melania, contracted a milder case of the disease, while their teenage son tested positive but was asymptomatic.[143] Donald and Melania Trump were quietly vaccinated against COVID-19 before moving out of the White House—but not on camera. Word of their vaccinations did not come until weeks later.

After much pressure, the former president recommended in March 2021—two months after he left office—that people get vaccinated, but with a caveat that people were free to decline the inoculation. "I would recommend it," Trump said in an interview aired on Fox News. "And I would recommend it to a lot of people that don't want to get it and a lot of those people voted for me, frankly. But again, we have our freedoms and we have to live by that and I agree with that also. But it is a great vaccine. It is a safe vaccine and it is something that works."[144]

Unfortunately, while Trump was president, he held superspreader events at the White House and campaign rallies around the country where large numbers of people did not wear masks and were not socially distant, disregarding the advice of his own administration's health officials. Many White House staff members contracted COVID-19, as did people who attended Trump campaign events. Trump rarely wore a mask in public and ridiculed presidential candidate Joe Biden for wearing a mask and not holding large campaign rallies.[145] Sadly, unsuccessful 2016 Republican presidential contender Herman Cain died of COVID-19 after he was diagnosed with the disease just days after he attended a Trump campaign rally in Oklahoma in the summer of 2020.[146]

In fairness, we need to note that while many Democratic elected officials strongly criticized Trump and Republicans for not doing enough to slow the spread of the coronavirus, few objected to the COVID-19 risks of the racial justice protests that spread across the U.S. in the wake of the May 2020 killing of George Floyd. Surveys indicated that somewhere between 15 million and 26 million people participated in these protests over the spring and summer. Social distancing was often impossible at the crowded protests, and while many protesters wore masks, significant numbers did not.[147] It's clear that Trump supporters and racial justice protesters, despite their many differences, believe strongly and sincerely in the importance and righteousness of their very causes—and both groups have their right to peaceably assemble and protest protected by the Constitution. But the coronavirus pays no heed to why people gather together, any more than raindrops have the ability to select who they will land on. Social distancing, wearing masks, and taking other precautions should be matters of public health—not politics.

Democratic officials feared raising alarms about spreading the coronavirus in the racial justice protests, lest they offend Black Lives Matter supporters and others taking part in the protests, along with protest sympathizers watching on TV. And many Republican governors prioritized political loyalty to Trump and a desire to boost their state economies over public health, imposing far less stringent precautions against the spread of COVID-19 than Democratic governors.

South Dakota Republican governor Kristi Noem hosted a crowded Fourth of July celebration at Mount Rushmore in 2020 attended by Trump and about 3,700 mostly unmasked people seated in folding chairs tied together with zip ties—making social distancing impossible.[148] Noem then boasted at the 2020 Republican National Convention and at the Conservative Political Action Conference in February 2021 about how little she had done to protect South Dakotans from COVID-19. "For those of you who don't know, South Dakota is the only state in America that never ordered a single business or church to close, we never instituted a shelter-in-place order, we never mandated that people wear masks," Noem told the cheering crowd at CPAC, casting her decision to ignore public health guidelines as a badge of honor in a bold defense of American liberty. She is now considered a possible contender for the 2024 Republican presidential nomination.[149] However, one thing Noem couldn't brag about was her state's coronavirus death rate. On a per capita basis, sparsely populated South Dakota ranked eighth in the nation for COVID-19 deaths in April 2021, with per 219 deaths per 100,000 residents.[150] Pretending there is no connection between South Dakota's lack of precautions against the coronavirus plague and its relatively high death toll is absurd.

Other Republican governors who had partially closed down their states rushed to lift mask mandates and otherwise reopen in early 2021 against the advice of health officials in the Biden administration and sometimes in their own states. For example, Texas governor Greg Abbott fully reopened his state with no capacity restrictions on businesses and facilities on March 2, 2021, and lifted a state mask mandate on the same day.[151] "With the medical advancements of vaccines and antibody therapeutic drugs, Texas now has the tools to protect Texans from the virus," Abbott said in a news release. "We must now do more to restore livelihoods and normalcy for Texans by opening Texas 100 percent. Make no mistake, COVID-19 has not disappeared, but it is clear from the recoveries, vaccinations, reduced hospitalizations, and safe practices that Texans are using that state mandates are no longer needed." In early April 2021, Abbott and Florida Republican governor Ron DeSantis became the first governors to sign executive orders barring state agencies and many business from requiring their employees to be vaccinated against COVID-19.[152]

President Biden responded to the Texas reopening with a sharp attack on the decision, fanning the flames of the partisan battle. "Texas—I think it's a big mistake," Biden said at the White House. "We are on the cusp of being able to fundamentally change the nature of this disease because the way in which we are able to get vaccines in people's arms. The last thing—the last thing—we need is Neanderthal thinking in the meantime."[153] That's not exactly a response that could be expected to prompt Abbott to reconsider.

By mid-August 2021, the CDC reported that 169 million people in the U.S. had been fully vaccinated against COVID-19, accounting for 51 percent of the nation's population.[154]

It speaks to the sad state of the deep divisions in our country and the lack of trust in our bedrock institutions that the battle against a deadly virus has become the center of a political dispute and name-calling. This is a far cry from the near universal acceptance that greeted the then-experimental polio vaccine in 1954. In the worst year of the polio epidemic in 1952 the disease infected more than 58,000 people, paralyzed about 21,000, and killed over 3,000 in the U.S.—most of them children. Terrible as this toll was, it is far smaller than the nearly 37 million people infected and 623,000 tragically killed by COVID-19 in the U.S. as of mid-August

2021, fueled by the spread of the more contagious and more deadly delta variant of the coronavirus.[155]

Looking back at the discovery of the polio vaccine by Dr. Jonas Salk, *Time* magazine reported in 2015 that "the only fear most parents felt was that it wouldn't become widely available fast enough to save their kids." To build public confidence in the vaccine, Salk first tested it on himself, his wife, and their children. They all successfully produced polio antibodies without getting sick. Soon the vaccine was given to nearly 2 million schoolchildren in a clinical trial and when it proved safe and effective it was approved for widespread use in 1955.[156] The anti-vaccine movement that is posing such a challenge to acceptance of the COVID-19 vaccine and other vaccines today had not yet emerged.

If Salk had patented the polio vaccine, he could have made as much as $7 billion. But he chose not to do so because he wanted the vaccine distributed around the world as widely and cheaply as possible. "He is still remembered as a saintly figure—not only because he banished a terrifying childhood illness, but because he came from humble beginnings, yet gave up the chance to become wealthy," Jennie Rothenberg Gritz wrote in the *Atlantic* in 2014.[157] In his 2006 book, *Polio: An American Story*, author David M. Oshinsky wrote that development of the vaccine was greeted with jubilation around the nation and Republican president Dwight Eisenhower fought back tears in a White House ceremony honoring Salk. "I have no words to thank you," President Eisenhower told Salk. "I am very, very happy."[158] How different our times of national disunity and division are today—and how sad.

President Trump and others have compared our battle against COVID-19 to a war. But the only war to take a deadlier toll on our nation was the Civil War, which grew out of our nation's divisions. In World War II, which united Americans like nothing since, an estimated 418,500 American military members and civilians died—roughly 204,000 less than have died of COVID-19 in the U.S. at the time of this writing.[159] Democrats and Republicans had their differences in the World War II years, of course, and elected officials and military leaders made mistakes that cost American lives, just as President Trump and some governors of both parties did in the war against the coronavirus. But American leaders in the 1940s stood shoulder to shoulder—joined with our Allies that were under attack—to fight the forces of Nazi Germany, Fascist Italy, and the Japanese Empire. It is both disappointing and dangerous that partisan divisions have been a factor in our battle to defeat COVID-19, weakening our ability to form a united front against the killer virus that strikes Democrats, Republicans, independents, socialists, communists, and everyone else with equal force.

DISTRUST IN RELIGIOUS INSTITUTIONS AND VALUES

Religion has played an important role in American life since colonial times. Many of the earliest European settlers in what became the United States came here to escape religious persecution. The Puritans established the first free schools in British America and opened Harvard College as the first college in the colonies in 1636, named after the Reverend John Harvard, who left his personal library and half his estate to create the college. Much of the focus of early schools was on religious instruction, and Harvard and the eight other colleges that were established before America's independence trained many young men for the ministry.[160] In addition, the Declaration of Independence has a firm grounding in religion, justifying independence based on "the laws of Nature and of Nature's God" and saying all men "are endowed by their Creator with certain unalienable Rights" and that the declaration has "a firm reliance on the protection of divine Providence."[161]

In more recent times, religious institutions played an important role in the civil rights struggle in the last century. In fact, some of the leading figures in the movement for racial equality—most notably the Reverend

Dr. Martin Luther King Jr.—were members of the clergy. Most White Evangelicals moved to align themselves with the Republican Party since the 1960 presidential election, partly out of prejudice against John F. Kennedy running on the Democratic ticket to become our first Roman Catholic president and partly out of prejudice against Black people fighting for equal rights. The late Reverend Jerry Falwell Sr. became a powerful right-wing figure when he founded the Moral Majority in 1979. The Reverend Pat Robertson ran unsuccessfully for the 1988 Republican presidential nomination and remains chairman of the conservative Christian Broadcasting Network.[162]

Religion has generally spread a message encouraging consideration for and cooperation with others—although at times religion has been used to demonize some fellow Americans, such as gay people and minorities. Just about all of us heard the golden rule growing up: "Do unto others as you would have them do unto you." This basic rule for morality is rooted in the words of Jesus in the Sermon of the Mount: "All things whatsoever ye would that men should do to you, do ye even so to them." The Hebrew Bible has a similar instruction: "Whatever is hurtful to you, do not do to any other person."[163] Other religions preach the same message. While many people who identify with religions fail to follow this guidance—and even though religion has sparked long-running conflicts around the world—religion has always provided a moral underpinning for American government and society, and for many Americans.

However, the role of religion is lessening in the United States, and public trust in traditional religious institutions and values is dropping. Gallup polling asking Americans to rate the importance of religion in their own lives found that 75 percent said it was very important and 20 percent said it was fairly important in 1952. But by 2020 the percentage saying religion was very important had dropped to 48 percent and the percentage saying it was only fairly important had increased to 25 percent.[164] Gallup found that in 1957 some 62 percent of Americans said religion can answer all or most current problems, but that dropped to 46 percent in 2018.[165]

The confidence of Americans in the church or organized religion has been measured by Gallup in polling since 1973. It peaked in 1975 when 68 percent of Americans said they had a great deal or quite a lot of confidence in organized religion, but fell substantially to 42 percent in 2020.[166] At the same time, the number of Americans who identify with the nation's dominant religion of Christianity shrank and the number of people saying they are religiously unaffiliated grew. A Pew Research Center survey conducted in 2018 and 2019 reported that 65 percent of Americans described themselves as Christians—down from 77 percent in the previous decade. Some 26 percent of Americans said they were religiously unaffiliated (atheists, agnostic, or "nothing in particular") in 2018–2019, up from 17 percent in 2009. The percentage of Americans who said they identify with non-Christian faiths increased slightly in 2018–2019 to 7 percent, up from 5 percent in 2009.

The percentage of Christians was highest for the oldest Americans and lowest for young adults in 2018–2019, Pew found. This could indicate we should expect a further drop in identification with Christianity in the years ahead and that most Americans could eventually be unaffiliated with any religion. The Pew survey found that among the generation born between 1928 and 1945, 84 percent said they were Christian, just 10 percent were unaffiliated, and 4 percent belonged to non-Christian faiths. Among baby boomers (born between 1946 and 1964), 76 percent said they were Christian, 17 percent were unaffiliated, and 6 percent belonged to non-Christian faiths. Among Generation X (born between 1965 and 1980), 67 percent said they were Christian, 25 percent were unaffiliated, and 6 percent belonged to non-Christian faiths. And among millennials (born between 1981 and 1996), just 49 percent said they were Christian, 40 percent were unaffiliated, and 9 percent belonged to non-Christian faiths.

The lessening role of religion in American life is accompanied by a lessening of a belief in traditional religious values. For example, the Centers for Disease Control and Prevention reports that in 2018, nearly 40 percent of births in in the U.S. were to single mothers.[167] Polling by Gallup found that in 2001 some 42 percent of Americans thought it was morally wrong for an unmarried man and woman to have a sexual relationship, but the figure dropped to 27 percent by 2020. The high rate of births out of wedlock is bad news for children. Research has shown that children from single-parent homes are less likely to go to college, earn less during their working years, and are more likely to become involved with gangs and crime. In addition, children who grow up in homes with two married parents see their chances of falling into poverty decrease by 82 percent.[168]

The loss of religious faith by millions of Americans and their widespread loss of faith in our democracy and other foundational institutions and values is leaving many of our citizens feeling unmoored and alienated. This contributes to the unfortunate increase in the number of Americans embracing extremist ideologies like White supremacy and groups like QAnon on the right, and socialism on the left.

It is long past time for Democrats and Republicans in elected office to put our national interest above their partisan interests and come together in the sensible center to develop practical solutions to the serious problems confronting the United States. If the most important job of elected officials is to get reelected and never do anything to endanger their reelection prospects, they need to find another line of work. Their most important job should be serving their constituents and the American people. They need to stop trying to score political points by obstructing and demonizing each other like warring factions and accept that patriotism is more important than partisanship. If elected officials refuse to do these things, they are endangering the very survival of our democracy and they need to be defeated at the ballot box.

2 / SCHOEN-COOPERMAN RESEARCH SURVEY
Public Perceptions of Government

It is clear that voters are losing faith in their leaders, in their institutions, and most of all, in their democracy. A national poll conducted by our firm, Schoen-Cooperman Research, in April 2021 sheds light on this trend.

The findings of our survey—which was conducted among a nationally representative sample of eight hundred likely 2022 midterm election voters—paint an alarming picture of the current state of American politics.

Our survey conclusions illuminate the urgency and necessity of political and electoral reform in order to safeguard democracy for future generations. Simply put, American democracy is at risk, and these findings should be taken as a call to action by our leaders, politicians, and elected officials.

In order to gain a full and complete understanding of voters' perceptions of government and their declining trust in the system, our survey probed several areas of focus, which provide the organizational basis for the following chapter:

- The Current Mood of the Country vis-à-vis our Political System, Elected Officials, and Political Polarization
- The January 6 United States Capitol Riot

- Black Lives Matter Protests in the Summer of 2020
- New Elections and Voting Laws in Georgia and Around the United States
- The Future of the Country
- Potential Solutions to the United States' democratic crisis

THE CURRENT MOOD OF THE COUNTRY VIS-À-VIS OUR POLITICAL SYSTEM, ELECTED OFFICIALS, AND POLITICAL POLARIZATION

With regard to current attitudes, most voters believe they live in a divided and polarized country in which untrustworthy, self-interested, and out-of-touch politicians are loyal to their own extreme partisan interests and donors, do not care about voters, and fight with one another instead of solving major problems.

Indeed, by more than a 3-to-1 margin (65 percent to 20 percent), voters believe American politics have gotten worse. Likewise, overwhelming majorities believe the country has become more divided (79 percent) rather than less divided (5 percent); and more polarized (62 percent) rather than less polarized (9 percent). (See Table 1.) And nearly three-quarters (74 percent) say that this current political partisanship in Washington, D.C. makes our country weaker.

Table 1. Views on the Evolution of American Politics in Recent Years	
Position	% Likely Voters
[The U.S. has become] more divided.	79%
[Politics in America have] gotten worse.	65%
[The U.S. has become] more polarized.	62%

SCHOEN-COOPERMAN RESEARCH SURVEY / 129

In addition, overwhelming majorities of voters agree with statements which collectively portray America as a country that is more divided than ever (91 percent agree) where elected officials put political interests and donors first (90 percent agree) and fight rather than address our major problems (89 percent agree). To that end, voters also feel that Washington D.C., has become all about partisan fighting and bickering (79 percent agree) and thus, also believe most elected officials are out of touch with average Americans (79 percent agree). (See Table 2.)

Table 2. Statement Agreement: Current State of American Politics	
Statement	% Likely Voters Agree
The country is more divided than ever before.	91%
Elected officials put their own political interests and donors first over the average American who elected them.	90%
I am frustrated because all elected officials do is fight rather than address our major problems.	89%
Washington D.C. is all about partisan fighting and bickering.	79%
Most elected officials are out-of-touch with average Americans.	79%

While voters overwhelmingly favor compromise over ideological purity, they believe politicians make decisions in their own best interests and for political reasons, rather than based on what is best for their constituents.

Indeed, voters overwhelmingly feel that the federal government makes decisions based on political reasons (73 percent), rather than based on what is right (19 percent). (See Chart 1.)

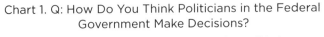

Chart 1. Q: How Do You Think Politicians in the Federal Government Make Decisions?

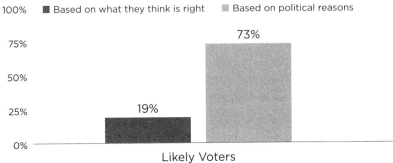

However, a majority of voters want elected officials to compromise and work with one another to accomplish things (67 percent), rather than stay true to their ideology (24 percent). (See Table 3.)

Table 3. Trade-off: Compromise vs. Ideology	
Position	% Likely Voters
Elected officials should compromise and work across the aisle to accomplish things.	67%
Elected officials should stay true to their ideology, even if it's harder to address problems.	24%

Further, majorities of voters in both parties prefer compromise over staying true to political ideology, though Democrats are more likely to prefer compromise than are Republicans (72 percent to 56 percent). (See Table 4.)

Table 4: Trade-off: Compromise vs. Ideology		
Position	% Democrats	% Republicans
Elected officials should compromise and work across the aisle to accomplish things.	72%	56%
Elected officials should stay true to their ideology, even if it's harder to address problems.	21%	29%

Our politicians' self-serving behavior has led to a concerning decline in trust in government, particularly among young Americans, which bodes poorly for the future of our democracy.

According to an April 2021 Harvard/Ipsos poll among young Americans (18 to 29), two-thirds (66 percent) trust the federal government to do the right thing only some of the time or never, while 32 percent trust the federal government to do the right thing all or most of the time.[1]

Further, the same Harvard/Ipsos poll reveals that majorities of young Americans agree that elected officials seem to be motivated by selfish reasons (68 percent), and agree that [their] government does not represent the America [they] love (55 percent).

To that end, according to an AP/NORC poll from February 2021, just 16 percent of U.S. adults believe democracy is working extremely well or very well in the U.S., while 38 percent say it's working somewhat well and 45 percent say it's working not too well or not well at all.[2]

And while many in the media and elsewhere are quick to blame Donald Trump for the current political polarization in America, our April 2021 survey reveals that a majority of voters believe our country's problems predate Trump (53 percent).

Ultimately, our (SCR's) findings also show that political polarization in America is at crisis levels—we have reached the point where voters fear violence and distrust their elections.

Indeed, nine-in-ten voters are concerned that political violence will increase in the U.S. (See Chart 2.)

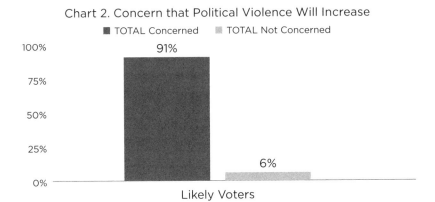

Chart 2. Concern that Political Violence Will Increase

And just one-half of voters are confident in the electoral system, while 44 percent are not. (See Chart 3.)

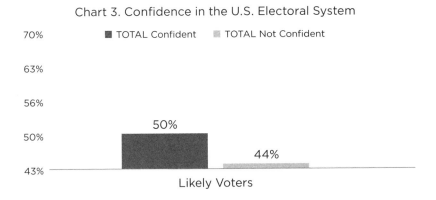

Chart 3. Confidence in the U.S. Electoral System

Notably, our survey found that there is a wide disparity by party in terms of confidence in the electoral system. While more than three-quarters of Democrats (76 percent) are confident in the U.S. electoral system, close to seven-in-ten Republicans (69 percent) are *not* confident. (See Chart 4.)

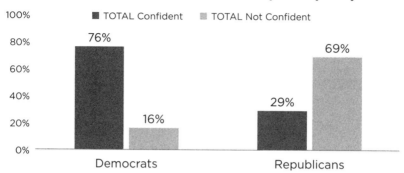

Chart 4. Confidence in U.S. Electoral System by Party

Moreover, voters are worried that the current levels of political polarization in America pose an actual threat to our country's survival.

Strong majorities agree that the current polarization in the U.S. hurts our ability to address our most pressing domestic and national security crises (84 percent); and the most dangerous threat to our democracy comes not from a foreign adversary, but within the U.S. from the radical right and left (79 percent).

To that end, voters also feel that political polarization has become so extreme that their personal relationships have suffered. More than one-third say they have had a falling-out with friends as a result of differing political views (35 percent), while approximately one-quarter say relationships with family members have been strained as a result of differing political views (26 percent).

THE JANUARY 6, 2021, U.S. CAPITOL RIOT

Our survey asked respondents a series of nuanced questions about the U.S. Capitol riot on January 6 when a mob of pro-Trump supporters stormed the U.S. Capitol to protest the certification of Joe Biden's Electoral College victory.

While seven-in-ten voters oppose the January 6 riot, voters are split over whether they believe the riot was a protest that got out of hand (46 percent) or an attack on our democracy (47 percent). (See Table 5.)

Table 5. Trade-off: Attitudes Toward January 6th U.S. Capitol Riot	
Position	% Likely Voters
It was a protest that got out of hand.	46%
It was an attack on our country and our democracy.	47%

Notably, while a strong majority of Democrats (67 percent) believe the Capitol riot was an attack on our country and democracy, a similar majority of Republicans (64 percent) believe it was a protest that got out of hand. (See Table 6.)

Table 6: Trade-off: Attitudes Toward January 6th U.S. Capitol Riot by Party		
Position	% Democrats	% Republicans
It was a protest that got out of hand.	28%	64%
It was an attack on our country and our democracy.	67%	26%

Further, close to three-quarters of all likely voters (73 percent) are concerned that another such attack could happen. (See Chart 5.)

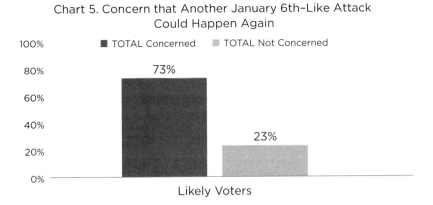

Chart 5. Concern that Another January 6th–Like Attack Could Happen Again

Notably, there is a clear recognition that January 6 did not occur in a vacuum, and that the attack actually speaks to a larger truth about loss of trust in our political system, as well as the threat of political disinformation in twenty-first-century American society.

Majorities of voters surveyed agree that, while the Capitol riots were the immediate consequence of Donald Trump's supporters refusing to accept the results of the election, the attack speaks to a larger loss of trust in our political system (71 percent agree) and demonstrates the issue of rampant disinformation in our politics (65 percent agree). (See Table 7.)

Table 7. Statement Agreement: January 6th U.S. Capitol Riot	
Position	% Likely Voters Agree
While the Capitol riots were the immediate consequence of Trump's supporters refusing to accept the results of the election, they demonstrate the larger issue of loss of trust in our political system.	71%
While the Capitol riots were the immediate consequences of Trump's supporters refusing to accept the results of the election, they demonstrate the larger issue of rampant disinformation in our politics.	65%

Accordingly, an overwhelming majority of voters say that political disinformation poses a very or somewhat serious threat to the survival of our democracy (85 percent), and six-in-ten say it poses a very serious threat. Of course, the U.S. Capitol attack was ignited by rampant political disinformation about the 2020 election results.

BLACK LIVES MATTER PROTESTS IN THE SUMMER OF 2020

Our survey probed respondents on their attitudes toward police misconduct generally and in light of the summer 2020 Black Lives Matter racial justice protests, which took place in the aftermath of George Floyd's death at the hands of Minneapolis police. Though the January 6 U.S. Capitol riot was clearly a more serious threat than the Black Lives Matter protests, we find that there is clear polarization of Americans on both of these anti-systemic issues and challenges.

While there is a clear recognition by voters that police reform is necessary, Americans are split over their support for the summer 2020 Black Lives Matter protests, and a majority actually believe the protests were counterproductive.

With regard to police misconduct, nearly three-in-four voters surveyed believe police misconduct is the most, a very, or a somewhat serious problem (72 percent).

Yet voters are split over approval for the Black Lives Matter protests last summer (48 percent approved, 47 percent disapproved). (See Chart 6.)

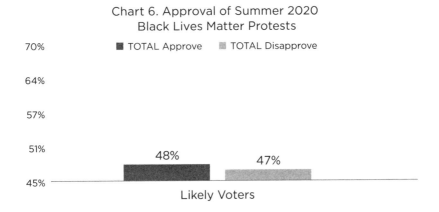

Chart 6. Approval of Summer 2020 Black Lives Matter Protests

To that end, there is a sharp party-line divide over approval of the Black Lives Matter protests. While more than three-quarters of Democrats (78 percent) approve of the protests, a similar share of Republicans (76 percent) disapprove. (See Chart 7.)

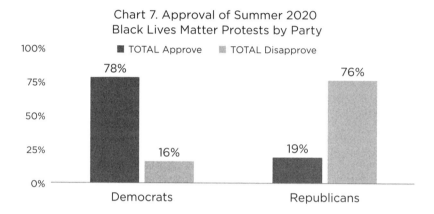

Chart 7. Approval of Summer 2020 Black Lives Matter Protests by Party

Moreover, a majority of voters believe the protests were actually inappropriate and became counterproductive (52 percent), rather than being necessary to drive police reform (40 percent). (See Table 8.)

Table 8: Trade-off: Attitudes Toward Summer 2020 Black Lives Matter Protests	
Position	% Likely Voters
The protests were inappropriate and became counterproductive.	52%
The protests were necessary to drive police reform.	40%

Our survey's conclusions that America is divided over support for the Black Lives Matter movement is supported by additional public opinion polling. An April 2021 UMass Amherst/WCVB poll asked a thousand Americans nationwide whether they support the goals of Black Lives Matter, and found that less than half of Americans (48 percent) said they somewhat or strongly support the movement's goals. Further, 46 percent said they were either neutral on the subject (14 percent) or somewhat or strongly opposed the movement's goals (32 percent).[3]

Further, Civiqs has been asking about support for the Black Lives Matter movement for almost four years in a tracking poll. According to their assessment, never have a majority of white Americans supported the movement. Support for the movement peaked at 43 percent last June, just after George Floyd's death, but since then, White Americans' support for the movement has dropped to 37 percent.[4]

NEW ELECTIONS AND VOTING LAWS IN GEORGIA AND AROUND THE U.S.

Our survey sought to understand likely voters' attitudes toward the voting laws passed in the state of Georgia in March 2021. Notably, we found that a majority of likely voters believe these laws are fair (56 percent to 35 percent). (See Chart 8.)

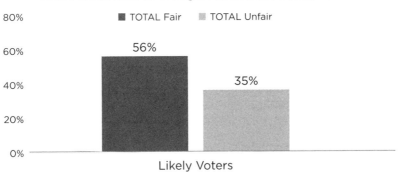

Chart 8. Fairness of Georgia March 2021 Voting Laws

Accordingly, voters favor the law (52 percent to 38 percent). (See Chart 9.)

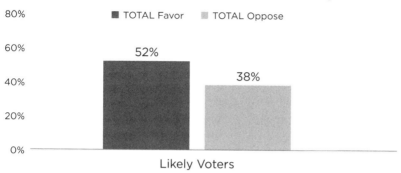

Chart 9. Favor/Oppose Georgia's March 2021 Voting Laws

Support for Georgia's new voting laws falls on party lines. While close to eight-in-ten Republicans (78 percent) favor the new voting laws, a majority of Democrats (57 percent) oppose them. (See Chart 10.)

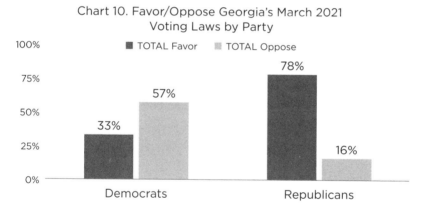

Chart 10. Favor/Oppose Georgia's March 2021 Voting Laws by Party

Yet, when presented with a trade-off on the issue—meaning voters were given both Democratic arguments against the law and Republican arguments for the law, and asked to indicate which argument comes closer to their view—likely voters were more evenly divided on the issue.

In the trade-off, likely voters are split over whether new laws like Georgia's are needed to restore confidence in elections (45 percent) or are politically motivated and designed to disenfranchise minorities (44 percent). (See Table 9.)

Table 9. Trade-off: New Voting Laws	
Position	% Likely Voters
New election and voting laws are needed to restore confidence in elections and actually expand voter access.	45%
New election and voting laws are politically motivated and designed to make it more difficult for poorer voters and people of color to vote.	44%

THE FUTURE OF THE COUNTRY

In terms of America's future, voters demonstrate some degree of optimism. However, this slight optimism is overshadowed by voters' negative overall outlook on the future of the country vis-à-vis political polarization and disinformation in our politics.

By more than a two-to-one margin (68 percent to 31 percent), likely voters surveyed believe the government can still get big, positive things done. Likewise, by a two-to-one margin, they believe our best days are ahead of us (54 percent) rather than behind us (26 percent). Furthermore, likely voters are optimistic (50 percent) rather than pessimistic (42 percent) about the future of our country. (See Chart 11.)

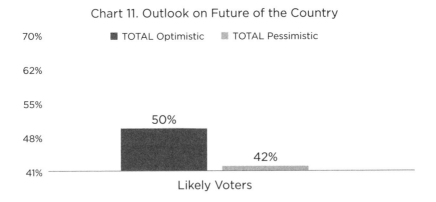

Chart 11. Outlook on Future of the Country

There is a notable divide between Democrats and Republicans in terms of their outlook on the future of the country. While nearly three-quarters of Democrats (73 percent) are optimistic about the future of the country, a majority of Republicans (63 percent) say they are pessimistic. (See Chart 12.)

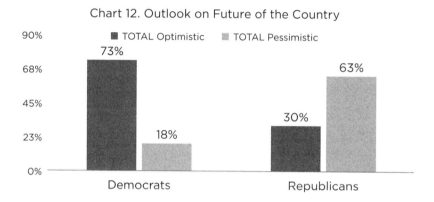

Chart 12. Outlook on Future of the Country

Yet, a majority believe we will become more divided (56 percent), while only one-in-six believe we will become less divided (17 percent). Moreover, voters are overwhelmingly concerned about political extremism going forward (86 percent). (See Chart 13.)

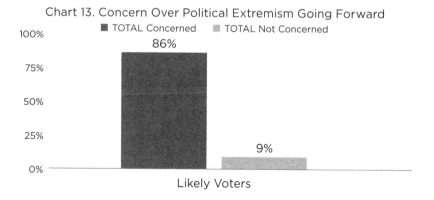

Chart 13. Concern Over Political Extremism Going Forward

Furthermore, we find that a plurality is equally concerned about extremism from the right and the left (47 percent). (See Chart 14.)

Chart 14. Concern Over Political Extremism Going Forward

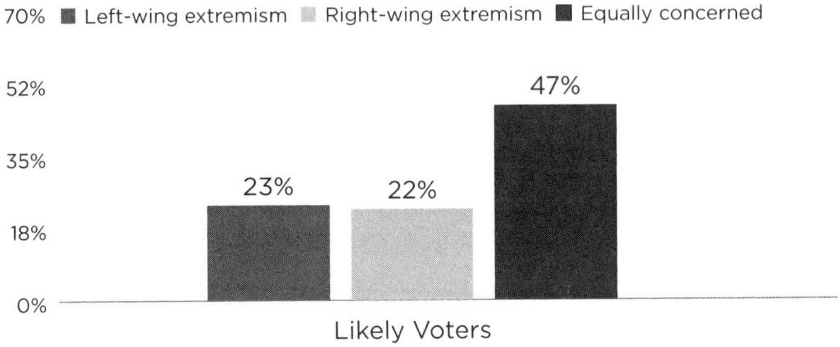

70% ■ Left-wing extremism ▧ Right-wing extremism ■ Equally concerned

Likely Voters

Voters also have a grim outlook on the endurance and survival of American democracy. A majority believe U.S. democracy is at risk of extinction (55 percent), and less than a quarter believe its survival is secured (23 percent). Likewise, three-quarters of likely voters believe U.S. democracy needs a complete overhaul or major reform in order to survive. (See Table 10.)

Table 10. Outlook on Future of U.S. Democracy	
Position	% Likely Voters
U.S. democracy is at risk of extinction.	55%
U.S. democracy's survival is secured for future generations.	23%

POTENTIAL SOLUTIONS TO THE UNITED STATES' DEMOCRATIC CRISIS

According to the February 2021 AP/NORC survey, more than eight-in-ten Americans think factors such as a fair judiciary, liberties defined by the Constitution, the ability to achieve the American Dream, and a democratically elected government are important aspects of the country's identity.[5]

Yet, it is clear that the country has strayed far from these principles, and thus far from its identity. There is an urgent need for long-term political reforms to make our democracy freer, fairer, and more functional.

Our survey found that likely voters overwhelmingly support democratic reforms aimed at achieving this goal. The reforms—which will be discussed in greater detail later in this book—fall into three major categories: campaign reforms to increase transparency; reforms to the Supreme Court to maintain the court's legitimacy; and changes to our voting system to make elections fairer. (See Tables 11–13.)

First, there is strong support for campaign reforms to increase transparency and decrease the potential influence of special interests when individuals run for public office.

More than seven-in-ten likely voters favor increasing disclosure by lobbyists of their contacts with members of Congress (75 percent) and banning all federal employees and elected officials from going to work as lobbyists for at least two years after they leave federal service (71 percent). There is also strong support for requiring all candidates for federal office to release their last five years of state and federal income tax returns (73 percent) and mandating that all candidates elected to federal office divest from ownership of any companies and place all investments in a blind trust (71 percent).

Table 11. Support for Reforms to U.S. Political System	
Reform	% Likely Voters Support
Encourage bipartisan groups of lawmakers to work together.	81%
Increase disclosure by lobbyists of their contracts with members of Congress.	75%
Require all candidates for federal office to release their last five years of state and federal income tax returns.	73%

Table 11. Support for Reforms to U.S. Political System	
Reform	% Likely Voters Support
Increase public education efforts on the safety of vaccines in general and the coronavirus vaccine in particular.	73%
Require all candidates elected to federal office to divest from ownership of any companies and place all investments in a blind trust.	71%

Second, likely voters want reforms to the Supreme Court that would preserve the court's legitimacy and independence from other branches of government.

We find that close to seven-in-ten voters favor a constitutional amendment to set the size of the Supreme Court at nine justices to prevent court packing (69 percent); require a vote by the full Senate on Supreme Court and other judicial nominees within ninety days of their nomination (68 percent); and prevent the Judiciary Committee from being able to block a nominee from coming to the floor (68 percent).

Reforms to the Supreme Court are necessary to ensure that the court can no longer be used as a political weapon by either party, which has led voters to distrust the court. According to a Harvard/Ipsos poll from April 2021 among young Americans (18 to 29), half (51 percent) trust the Supreme Court to do the right thing only some of the time or never, while 47 percent trusts the court to do the right thing all or most of the time.[6]

Table 12. Support for Reforms to U.S. Political System	
Reform	% Likely Voters Support
Ban all federal employees and elected officials from going to work as lobbyists for at least two years after they leave federal service.	71%

Table 12. Support for Reforms to U.S. Political System	
Reform	% Likely Voters Support
Proposing a constitutional amendment to set the size of the Supreme Court at nine justices to prevent court packing.	69%
Require a vote by the full Senate on Supreme Court and other judicial nominees within 90 days of their nomination and preventing the Judiciary Committee from being able to block a nominee from coming to the floor.	68%
Include third-party candidates in Presidential debates.	68%
Require social media companies to steer users to news stories giving both sides of issues.	64%
Awarding Electoral Votes for President by each candidate's percentage of the vote, rather than winner-takes-all.	61%
Implemening instant runoff voting, which allows voters to rank their choices and ensures that the winner has support from at least 50% of voters.	61%
Creating nonpartisan redistricting commissions in each state for US Congress and state legislatures.	60%

Lastly, likely voters favor reforms that would make our elections and voting system fairer, less partisan, and more open to third-party and independent candidates. There is a clear desire to move away from our current voting system, which allows two parties to dominate, locks independent candidates out of the system, and often forces voters to choose the "lesser of two evils."

Table 13. Support for Reforms to U.S. Political System	
Reform	% Likely Voters Support
Include third-party candidates in Presidential debates.	68%
Require social media companies to steer users to news stories giving both sides of issues.	64%
Awarding Electoral Votes for President by each candidate's percentage of the vote, rather than winner-takes-all.	61%
Implemening instant runoff voting, which allows voters to rank their choices and ensures that the winner has support from at least 50% of voters.	61%
Creating nonpartisan redistricting commissions in each state for US Congress and state legislatures.	60%

Majorities of likely voters favor reforms that would include third-party candidates in presidential debates (68 percent); award electoral votes for president by each candidate's percentage of the vote, rather than winner-takes-all (61 percent); and implement instant runoff voting, which allows voters to rank their choices and ensures that the winner has support from at least half of voters (61 percent).

Further, six-in-ten also support the creation of nonpartisan redistricting commissions in each state for U.S. Congress and state legislatures (60 percent) in order to end gerrymandering.

To that end, there is support for reforms aimed at decreasing partisanship. Voters favor changes that would encourage bipartisan groups of lawmakers to work together (81 percent); increase public education efforts on the safety of vaccines in general and the coronavirus vaccine in particular (73 percent); and require social media companies to steer users to news stories giving both sides of issues (64 percent).

Now, it is clear that our elected officials and leaders need to heed these findings and act on political and electoral reforms to make our democracy freer, fairer, and one that is actually by and for the people.

3 / THE DIVIDED
STATES OF AMERICA

President Biden began his term of office on January 20, 2021, as the leader of the Divided States of America. About the only thing that united the American people was a loss of faith in our democratic system and our government—a government that is paralyzed by partisan sniping and gridlock much of the time, and too often more concerned with the welfare of insiders in the political class than with the welfare of the American people.

Joe Biden won the 2020 presidential election by a comfortable margin in the Electoral College—defeating President Trump 306–232—and won 51.4 percent of the popular vote to 46.9 percent for Trump.[1] But in an unprecedented move, Trump said repeatedly that he will never concede defeat, and continued to falsely claim Biden won as the result of fraud and was therefore an illegitimate president. Millions of Trump's supporters believed him, even though every one of the more than sixty Trump lawsuits seeking to overturn his election defeat was rejected by courts.

The deep divisions among the American people were reflected in Congress. The Senate seated in 2021 was evenly split after Democrats won two runoff elections in Georgia in January, with 50 Republicans and 50 Democrats. Vice President Kamala Harris's ability to cast tie-breaking votes gave Democrats the narrowest possible majority. And Democrats held a slim 222–211 majority in the House of Representatives. Even in the early days of 2021, lawmakers and their most ardent backers were talking about the 2022 election and whether Democrats would keep their majorities or surrender them to the GOP. This was not at all conducive to bipartisan cooperation to serve the American people.

Biden spent the first weeks of his administration taking executive actions to reverse many of Trump's policies on the federal response to the coronavirus pandemic, high unemployment, energy, the environment, climate change, immigration, foreign policy, national security, and other areas. Democrats rejoiced, but those on the far left said Biden was not doing enough. Many Republicans continued mourning Trump's loss and the reversal of his policies, and criticized Biden for doing too much.

In his inaugural address, Biden called for unity and gave a sober and accurate assessment of the challenges he faced: "Few periods in our nation's history have been more challenging or difficult than the one we're in now," Biden said. "A once-in-a-century virus silently stalks the country. It's taken as many lives in one year as America lost in all of World War II. Millions of jobs have been lost. Hundreds of thousands of businesses closed. A cry for racial justice some four hundred years in the making moves us. The dream of justice for all will be deferred no longer. A cry for survival comes from the planet itself. A cry that can't be any more desperate or any more clear. And now, a rise in political extremism, white supremacy, domestic terrorism that we must confront and we will defeat. To overcome these challenges—to restore the soul and to secure the future of America—requires more than words. It requires that most elusive of things in a democracy: Unity. Unity."[2]

Indeed, unity is desperately needed—but the demand for the elusive quality far exceeds the supply. It will be a monumental challenge—and perhaps an impossible dream—for Biden to unite the American people at a time of hyper-partisanship that is frustrating both Republicans and Democrats. It remains a tall order to expect millions of Trump followers who sincerely believe Biden stole the presidency to unite behind him. Disunity and congressional dysfunction are thinning the ranks of members of Congress seeking reelection. Four senators and thirty-six House members (twenty-nine Republicans, ten Democrats, and one Libertarian) didn't seek reelection in 2020.[3] In announcing in January 2021 that he wouldn't seek reelection in 2022, moderate Republican senator Rob Portman of Ohio said his frustration over the "partisan gridlock" preventing Congress from taking action to solve problems facing the nation was a factor prompting him to end his Senate career. "We live in an increasingly polarized country where members of both parties are being pushed further to the right and further to the left, and that means too few people who are actively looking to find common ground," Portman said.[4] "This is not a new phenomenon, of course, but a problem that has gotten worse over the past few decades." He's right.

Most voters don't intensely follow every new development in politics and government. They simply want—and deserve—an effective government that can tackle the major problems America faces, which at the start of Biden's term were the coronavirus pandemic and the soaring death toll and economic devastation it has brought about. If government continues to fail to deliver solutions to these and other major problems and the agents of gridlock succeed, Americans will only get angrier and their faith in democracy will be eroded further. That would take our country down a dangerous road and could lead to the election of members of Congress and a president who would cause greater harm to our democratic system. This would leave our democracy even more imperiled.

When we talk about the division of our country into two Americas we are not just referring to the partisan divide separating Democrats from Republicans. There is also a class divide. On one side we have the political class—the affluent elite of politics, business, special-interest groups, and the media. They exert oligarchical influence on our system of government and benefit from it. On the other side is everyone else.

Pollster Scott Rasmussen developed three survey questions in 2010 to determine whether a person is a member of the political class or mainstream America that the political class is supposed to serve. The questions, which reveal much about the nature of this elite group, are:

1. Generally speaking, when it comes to important national issues, whose judgment do you trust more, the American people or America's political leaders? *Those in the mainstream say the American people, but those in the political elite say political leaders.*

2. Some people believe that the federal government has become a special-interest group that looks out primarily for its own interests. Has the federal government become a special-interest group? *Mainstreamers say yes, but the political elite say no.*

3. Do government and big business often work together in ways that hurt consumers and investors? *Mainstreamers say yes, but the political elite say no.*

Based on exhaustive research, Rasmussen determined that only 7 percent of Americans make up the political class. Importantly, the responses to his survey questions did not depend on party affiliation in either the mainstream or the political elite. In other words, mainstreamers were Republicans, Democrats, and independents, as were the elite making up the political class.

Michael Lind discussed the common characteristics of the political class transcending political party differences in a 1995 article in *Harper's* magazine.[5] He concluded that "the closer you come to the centers of American politics and society, the more everyone begins to look the same . . . the people who run big business bear a remarkable resemblance to the people who run big labor, who in turn might be mistaken for the people in charge of the media and universities. They're the same people...most of the members of the American elites went to one of a dozen Ivy League colleges or top state university.... They talk the same. They walk the same."

Coauthor Douglas Schoen defined the political class this way in his book *Hopelessly Divided: The New Crisis in American Politics and What it Means for 2012 and Beyond*: "The political class includes Republicans, Democrats, and independents. Genuine policy differences exist among them but are less important than their shared goals and outlooks, perhaps the most important of which is the conviction that they are the people best suited to run America's government, to make political decisions, and to affect social change. They differ on specifics, but they all agree that 'ordinary' Americans possess neither the talent nor the temperament to make these decisions. In short, the political class has essentially co-opted and subverted the American democratic system for its own gain."[6]

The current system works for the political class. In most cases its members haven't been thrown out of work by the coronavirus pandemic, their investments continue to grow in the stock market, and they hold onto their places of power and influence. While they believe they are the best and the brightest and know what's best for the rest of America, they remain disconnected from ordinary Americans. Many are sincerely motivated to improve the lives of our people, but they are also motivated to preserve the status quo and their own power and privileges.

Too often, politicians forget that their top goal should not be getting elected and reelected. Their top goal should be making America a better place as a result of their government service—even if doing so causes them to lose the next election. The most frequently quoted line from President John F. Kennedy's 1961 inaugural address is: "And so, my fellow Americans: ask not what your country can do for you—ask what you can do for your country." We should admire those stirring and beautiful words not just as grand rhetoric, but as guidance to live by. This is particularly true for elected officials, whose job is to put country ahead of self. Regrettably, many do not.

PROFILES IN COWARDICE

When he was a senator, Kennedy won a Pulitzer Prize for his 1956 book, *Profiles in Courage*, which tells the story of eight U.S. senators who took courageous stands and as a result were criticized and saw their popularity plummet. Unfortunately, profiles in courage are hard to find in Congress today.

Most Republicans praised and supported Donald Trump during his four years in the White House despite his mismanagement of the presidency and the country, repeated lies, incessant attacks on his opponents that further divided America, and false claims that he defeated Biden in the presidential election. And most continued to support him after he incited the insurrectionist riot at the Capitol, opposing his impeachment and conviction. The loyalty most GOP members of the House and Senate continued to express for Trump after he left office was a profile in cowardice. It may have been primarily motivated by fear that he would support primary challenges against them if they turned on him. But whatever the motivation, their refusal to get off the Trump train was bad news for all of us who want to see Democrats and Republicans work together to govern on a bipartisan basis and restore the faith of the American people in democracy.

Former representative Richard Gephardt (D-MO), who served as House Majority Leader from 1989 to 1995 and House Minority Leader from 1995 to 2003, said in January 2021 that the refusal of many Republicans to accept Trump's election loss is a threat to democracy.[7] "The majesty of democracy is that the losing side . . . is willing to grudgingly put up with the result because they believe it was fair—or fair enough—and that their voice was heard," he said. "They just didn't win on that vote; they will have a chance another day to turn it around." Speaking of the January 6 insurrection, Gephardt said: "I have never been in my whole life as worried as I was on that day . . . about whether or not we could survive as a democracy. I think we are as divided and in danger of losing the democracy as we were in 1860."

On the Democratic side, many members of Congress are afraid to criticize radical positions advanced by left-wing extremists like Senator Bernie Sanders and Representatives Alexandria Ocasio-Cortez, Ilhan Omar, Rashida Tlaib, and Ayanna Pressley. These positions include socialism, sky-high soak-the-rich tax increases, the extraordinarily impractical and expensive Green New Deal, Medicare-for-all, harsh and one-sided criticism of Israel, the Defund the Police movement, and a $15 minimum wage that would be devastating to small businesses still reeling from shutdowns due to the coronavirus pandemic.

Why are Republican elected officials so afraid to criticize their party's right wing, and Democratic officials so afraid to criticize the left wing of their party?

Commenting on the fear by Democrats, *New York Times* columnist Thomas Edsall wrote: "Bold progressive stands may be risky in general elections, but recent research suggests that policy radicalism pays off in primaries . . . voters in primary elections prefer candidates who are willing to take more extreme positions."[8] Edsall quoted University of Pennsylvania political scientist Yphtach Lelkes, who has studied voter preferences in primaries, as saying: "In fact, moderates are punished for their policies [in primaries]. . . . If we are to decrease affective polarization in the United States, we need politicians that are politically moderate. Unfortunately, voters prefer politicians of their own party that are politically extreme. This incentivizes extreme political candidates, which will only exacerbate current tensions." This is a major flaw of the primary system, which we discuss in greater depth later in this chapter.

More lawmakers need to follow President Kennedy's advice and focus on what they can do for our country. By doing so they would exhibit profiles in courage, putting their belief in democracy and our Constitution ahead of partisan considerations and reelection concerns. We could then see a Congress able to break out of gridlock and work effectively to tackle the major challenges facing the American people, resolving differences through compromise. Unfortunately, Congress is not doing this today. On top of this, too often we are seeing traditional American values—including our faith in democracy—abandoned by political combatants on the far left and far right. This is not only unwise for the future of our nation; it's bad politics.

For generations, conventional political wisdom dictated that embracing traditional values and appealing to centrist voters was the key to winning general elections. Indeed, Biden's reputation as a centrist was a key to his general election victory. But once Biden became president he began giving in to pressure from the left wing of the Democratic Party on a host of issues that could hurt Democrats in the 2022 congressional elections and hurt him in 2024 if he seeks reelection. Our leaders have long touted the values that made America great. They need to start doing so again in both word and deed to begin healing our deep divisions. We're talking about values that appeal to all Americans, not just those on the extreme ends of the political spectrum. And these are the values candidates need to win elections.

"I want an America that values the freedom and the dignity of the individual," Bill Clinton said as a presidential candidate in September 1992 in a speech at the University of Notre Dame.[9] "All of us must respect the reflection of God's image in every man and woman. And so we must value their freedom, not just their political freedom, but their freedom of conscience in matters of philosophy and family and faith." The remark sparked criticism because Clinton was talking about abortion rights at a Catholic university, but he couched his argument in traditional American values in an effort to make it more acceptable. And responding to Republican claims that Democrats had abandoned "family values," Clinton said: "I want an America that does more than talk about family values. I want an America that values families." It was a clever move of political jujitsu, turning the Republican argument against the party. Clinton was wise not to cede "family values" to the Republican Party as an important issue.

In a letter to visitors to his presidential library written after he left the White House, Clinton commented on what should be the value of public service accepted by all sides, writing: "Public service is a noble calling, and doing the people's business is a solemn trust."[10] He added that during his years in government he asked himself a question "that every representative of the people must strive to answer: 'How can my actions help improve the life of the people I serve and the future of our children?'" The question is one our elected leaders should continue asking today if they sincerely want to work for the interests of the American people rather than simply preserve their power.

Clinton was elected and reelected in large part because he was able to win support from centrist voters as well as those on the left. But he suffered a major setback in the 1994 midterm elections when Republicans captured control of majorities in the House and Senate. Coauthor Douglas Schoen then became Clinton's pollster. Clinton responded to the bad news of the midterm election losses by stressing values and moving to the political center to take on the role of "New Democrat."[11] He adopted the Republican goal of balancing the federal budget, said religious expression was allowed in schools, criticized violence in the media, and took other actions designed to appeal to moderates and even some conservatives. Clinton cast himself as a moderate protecting the nation from far-right extremist Republicans, and the repositioning worked as his popularity rose and he was reelected in 1996.

Unfortunately, if Democrats continue moving left they are unlikely to nominate a truly centrist presidential candidate in the foreseeable future. That's bad news for Democrats if Republicans nominate a less divisive candidate than Trump who can appeal to moderate voters unhappy with the leftward drift of Biden and Democrats in Congress. Throughout most of our history, presidential candidates seen as members of the extreme right or left have lost. This was true of Republican senator Barry Goldwater in 1964 and Democratic senator George McGovern in 1972, for example. While Goldwater and McGovern were badly defeated in their presidential races, their positions on the far right and far left of their parties at the time accelerated the divide between

Democrats and Republicans. Millions of Americans became increasingly disillusioned in subsequent decades by worsening government dysfunction and escalating political warfare between Democrats and Republicans.

We have now arrived at the point where Democrats almost reflexively oppose most proposals Republicans favor, and vice versa. It's as if partisans on both sides are taking their direction from Marx—Groucho Marx—who sang in the 1932 Marx Brothers movie *Horse Feathers*: "I don't know what they have to say, it makes no difference anyway, whatever it is, I'm against it!"[12] Groucho's song was funny. The constant partisanship that has paralyzed Congress is not.

Endless battling between Democrats and Republicans in Washington as each party moves further left or right has been a major factor contributing to the public's disillusionment with democracy itself. Because politicians are unable to work together to respond to the challenges facing the American people, millions of citizens feel left out of the American Dream. These Americans are Republicans and Democrats, Whites and people of color, old and young. They share feelings of alienation and grievance, although for different reasons.

Millions of Americans have not only lost faith in democracy; they have turned against their fellow citizens and our democratic system itself. Desperate for change, many of them turned to Donald Trump and his populist appeals, helped elect him president in 2016, and supported him in 2020 as well. Others turned to self-described democratic socialist senator Bernie Sanders—Trump's polar opposite in many ways—as Sanders unsuccessfully sought the Democratic presidential nomination in 2016 and 2020. Many of the Trump and Sanders supporters didn't simply want incremental change. They wanted big and bold changes to a democratic system they believed was not working.

Another reason for the growing loss of faith in democracy by many Americans is growing economic inequality. As the Economic Policy Institute reported in 2018: "Income inequality has risen in every state since the 1970s and, in most states, it has grown in the post-Great Recession era. From 2009 to 2015, the incomes of the top 1 percent grew faster than the incomes of the bottom 99 percent in 43 states and the District of Columbia. The top 1 percent captured half or more of all income growth in nine states. In 2015, a family in the top 1 percent nationally received, on average, 26.3 times as much income as a family in the bottom 99 percent."[13]

Income inequality has long been a major reason for the loss of faith in governments and a cause of revolutions around the world. The French Revolution, the Russian Revolution, and the communist revolutions in China, Cuba, and elsewhere are examples of this. In fact, the battle against income inequality was at the very root of communism. This was spelled out clearly by Karl Marx and Friedrich Engels in *The Communist Manifesto*, published in 1848.[14] "Workers of the world unite! You have nothing to lose but your chains!" is the popular English translation of the final exhortation in *The Communist Manifesto*.

The line from *The Communist Manifesto* later became the motto of the Soviet Union and other communist nations. And while Donald Trump is certainly no communist, it's easy to spot the similarity in his exhortation to Black voters: "You're living in poverty, your schools are no good, you have no jobs, 58 percent of your youth is unemployed—what the hell do you have to lose?" Trump asked in 2016.

For all the talk you hear about American exceptionalism, there is no reason to believe that Americans respond differently than people around the world to economic inequality and worsening economic conditions that spark hopelessness. This is happening as we write this during the coronavirus pandemic. This hopelessness endangers the system of government in power—in America's case, our democratic system.

Many people feared a communist revolution would come to America in response to the Great Depression until President Franklin Delano Roosevelt and the Democratic Congress enacted a host of new programs to create jobs and fight poverty. This was followed by the massive mobilization for World War II that filled the ranks of the U.S. armed forces with 16.5 million men and women and created jobs in factories manufacturing the weapons and munitions of war. We would be naive not to believe that economic inequality poses a threat to democracy at home and abroad today.

President Kennedy said in his inaugural address in 1961: "If a free society cannot help the many who are poor, it cannot save the few who are rich." Kennedy was speaking about both domestic and international conditions. He and other Democrats of his day who were concerned with the spread of communism were big proponents of the need to make fighting economic inequality a big part of the war of ideas that pitted capitalism against communism.

As foreign policy columnist James Traub pointed out, writing about Senator Hubert Humphrey (D-MN) who later served as vice president under President Lyndon Johnson and was in the vanguard of this group: "Figures like Humphrey, who came to be known as 'Cold War liberals,' argued that the struggle against Soviet totalitarianism could be won only if the United States proved that democracies could deliver social justice more effectively than communism could."[15]

In our day, growing economic inequality fuels movements on both the left and right seeking drastic change in our system of government. It certainly played an important role in Trump's 2016 election victory, powered by alienated voters who saw him as a welcome change agent. It also boosted Bernie Sanders's presidential campaigns and the campaigns of Democrats who ran for Congress as socialists.

As our economy continues its shift from jobs reliant on manual labor requiring little education to an economy more dependent on a skilled and educated workforce, we see factory jobs lost to automation or exported to other countries that provide cheap labor. American workers without college degrees feel increasingly left behind. And as opportunities for women and minorities grow, some White men feel abandoned. At the same time, some Black Americans and other Americans of color feel targeted by police brutality, voter suppression efforts, and other forms of racial discrimination. The coronavirus pandemic that has killed hundreds of thousands of Americans, destroyed millions of jobs, shuttered businesses, and crippled our economy has made things worse for everyone. All these factors have combined to endanger the future of our democracy. They played a role in the insurgent riot on the U.S. Capitol on January 6, 2021, and in the protests seeking racial justice that sparked rioting in American cities during the summer of 2020.

FEUDING AND FIGHTING

As if fighting between Democrats and Republicans isn't bad enough, members of each party are battling each other as well, as moderate Republicans try to keep their party from moving too far right and moderate Democrats try to keep their party from moving too far left. The intraparty feuding was more intense on the Republican side at the end of Trump's term in office and the beginning of Biden's term.

On the GOP side, Trump loyalists attacked the ten Republican House members who voted with Democrats on January 13, 2021, to impeach Trump for a second time. Representative Liz Cheney, the third-ranking member of House Republican leadership, came under the strongest attack for her support of impeachment after she said of Trump's conduct regarding the Capitol riot: "There has never been a greater betrayal by a President of the United States of his office and his oath to the Constitution."[16] Cheney was blasted by Representative Matt Gaetz (R-FL) who flew to her home state of Wyoming on January 28, 2021, to launch a campaign to defeat her in a primary in 2022. In a fiery speech, Gaetz lashed out at several members of the political class that he himself belongs to—including the Senate GOP leader and one of his party's former presidential nominees.[17] "The truth is that the establishment in both political parties have teamed up to screw our fellow Americans for generations," Gaetz said in his denunciation of the political class. "The private insider club of Joe Biden, Mitch McConnell, Mitt Romney, Nancy Pelosi, and Liz Cheney, they want to return our government to its default setting: enriching them."

Gaetz called Cheney—daughter of former Republican vice president Dick Cheney—"a Beltway bureaucrat turned fake cowgirl that supported an impeachment that is deeply unpopular in the state of Wyoming." However, despite the attacks on Cheney from fellow House Republicans, she initially survived an effort by some to remove her from her leadership post. The *New York Times* reported that GOP members in the House voted 145–61 to keep her in her leadership post on February 3, 2021.[18]

In addition, dozens of members of the traditional GOP establishment—many of them critics of Trump—pulled out their checkbooks to support Cheney in her 2022 reelection bid. In the three-month period after she voted to impeach Trump, Cheney collected nearly $1.6 million in campaign contributions, the *Washington Post* reported. That's a significant sum for an election in Wyoming, the least-populous state in the nation with only about 580,000 residents and low-priced rates for the broadcast, print, and web advertising so vital to any campaign. Donors to Cheney included five Republican senators, among them two attacked by Gaetz—Senate Minority Leader Mitch McConnell of Kentucky and Senator Mitt Romney of Utah. Ten current and former House members, including former Speaker Paul Ryan of Wisconsin, also donated to Cheney. House Minority Leader Kevin McCarthy (R-CA), who is close to former President Trump, was conspicuously absent from the list of Cheney donors.[19]

McCarthy later turned against Cheney after she continued to attack Trump's false claim that he won the 2020 presidential election, and kept up her criticism of the former president for his role in the riot and insurrection at the Capitol by his supporters. McCarthy joined a majority of Republican House members who cast a voice vote May 12, 2021, that removed Cheney from her position as House Republican Conference chair.[20] That didn't stop Cheney from giving a series of TV interviews that week continuing her attacks on Trump. She told ABC News that "I regret the vote" she cast for Trump in the 2020 presidential election and criticized Republicans who selected Rep. Elise Stefanik (R-NY)—a Trump supporter endorsed by the former president—to replace Cheney as conference chair. "I think it's dangerous. I think that we have to recognize how quickly things can unravel," Cheney told ABC. "We have to recognize what it means for the nation to have a former president who has not conceded and who continues to suggest that our electoral system cannot function, cannot do the will of the people."[21]

Gaetz also got into a feud with Rep. Adam Kinzinger (R-IL), who joined Liz Cheney in voting to impeach Trump. After Kinzinger announced he was forming a new political action committee to campaign against House Republicans who supported Trump's false claims of fraud in the presidential election, Gaetz tweeted on February 10, 2021: "My response: F---ing bring it. Adam needs PACs to win election. I don't."[22] Gaetz's political future is now uncertain, because at this writing he was under federal investigation involving allegations of sex trafficking (including of a seventeen-year-old girl), illegal drug use, and public corruption.[23] Gaetz has denied any wrongdoing and said he has been targeted as part of a political attack.

Cheney and Kinzinger further angered Republicans loyal to Trump, who dominated the House GOP caucus, when the two agreed to be appointed by Speaker Nancy Pelosi to serve on a House select committee investigating the January 6 insurrection at the Capitol. House Republican Leader Kevin McCarthy sought to put five other Republicans on the panel, but Pelosi blocked two of them—Representatives Jim Jordan of Ohio and Jim Banks of Indiana—because they were among Trump's staunchest defenders and had made statements saying he bore no responsibility for the attack on the Capitol. McCarthy said Pelosi's action rejecting his appointees was "an egregious abuse of power" and withdrew all five of his selections from the committee. But the presence of Cheney and Kinzinger on the committee deprived Republicans of the talking point that the panel was made up only of partisan Democrats out to frame Trump. McCarthy said Republicans would conduct their own separate investigation of the January 6 attack, which was virtually certain to absolve Trump of any responsibility for sparking the insurrection. Democrats and some Republicans had earlier sought to create an independent nonpartisan commission to investigate the events of January 6, but Senate Republicans used the filibuster to prevent a vote on the commission. Pelosi then turned to the House panel as fallback to conduct the investigation of the insurrection.

Former president Trump used his first speech since he left office—a high-profile address to the Conservative Political Action Conference on February 28, 2021—to join in the Republican civil war, reading off the names of Republican House members who voted to impeach him and Republican senators who voted to convict him and calling for their defeat in primaries. This was the equivalent of a warning shot fired at Republican candidates around the country: Failing to support Trump could incur his wrath and lead him to back a primary opponent. In this way, Trump remains a force in the Republican Party even out of office. His impact is bound to grow should he become a candidate for the 2024 Republican presidential nomination.

As for the Democrats' internal civil war, moderates blamed those on the far left for Democratic losses of House seats in the 2020 election and warned against radical positions becoming more popular in the party. The two sides squared off for over three hours in what was supposed to be a private conference call three days after the election, but news organizations reported on their comments. Moderate representative Abigail Spanberger (D-VA) sharply criticized left-wing Democrats for their support of defunding the police and socialism, CNN and the *Washington Post* reported. Democratic representatives Marc Veasey of Texas and Debbie Muscarsel-Powell of Florida made similar remarks.[24] "If we are classifying Tuesday as a success from a Congressional standpoint, we will get [expletive] torn apart in 2022," Spanberger said, according to CNN. "The number one concern in things that people brought to me in my [district] that I barely re-won was defunding the police. And I've heard from colleagues who have said 'Oh, it's the language of the streets. We should respect that.' We're in Congress. We are professionals. We are supposed to talk about things in the way where we mean what we're talking about. If we don't mean we should defund the police, we shouldn't say that."

"We want to talk about funding social services, and ensuring good engagement in community policing, let's talk about what we are for," Spanberger added. "And we need to not ever use the words 'socialist' or 'socialism' ever again. Because while people think it doesn't matter, it does matter. And we lost good members because of it." That brought a rejoinder from far-left representative Alexandria Ocasio-Cortez on Twitter: "You can't just tell the Black, Brown, & youth organizers riding in to save us every election to be quiet or not have their reps champion them when they need us . . . Esp. when they're delivering victories." Representative Rashida Tlaib backed up fellow Squad member Ocasio-Cortez, saying some House Democrats are only interested in appealing to suburban White voters. "To be real, it sounds like you are saying stop pushing for what Black folks want," the *Post* quoted Tlaib as saying.

All this political sniping between Republicans and Democrats and within each party doesn't augur well for any hopes of getting them to work together on legislation to benefit the American people. Our elected representatives need to stop viewing the running of government as a zero-sum game, in which one party's victory can only come at the expense of the other party's loss. If they want to narrow the gaping divide between the political class and the rest of the American people, our elected officials must focus on making government work for ordinary Americans. If campaigns for elections are perpetual—with campaigns for the next election beginning the day the last election ends—little will ever get accomplished. While elections are zero-sum games in which no candidate wins unless the opposing candidates lose, government will not work and our democratic system will become paralyzed if compromise is rejected in favor of constant fighting and endless campaigning.

THE FAILURE OF THE POLITICAL CLASS

The increasing disillusionment of Americans with our government and their declining faith in the political class has been documented in numerous public opinion surveys over decades. A good measurement of this disturbing drop is the American National Election Study jointly run by the National Sciences Foundation, the University of Michigan, and Stanford University. In 1956, about 27 percent of Republicans, 31 percent of Democrats, and 42 percent of independents said they believe "people like me don't have any say in what the government does."[25] By 2015, the numbers believing they had no say in government jumped to about 49 percent of Republicans, 50 percent of Democrats, and 55 percent of independents. The same survey asked if "quite a few of the people running the government are crooked." In 1960, about 21 percent of Republicans, 28 percent of Democrats, and 23 percent of independents answered "yes." By 2011, the percentage of people believing many people running government are crooked had more than doubled to about 69 percent of Republicans, 59 percent of Democrats, and 70 percent of independents. This is a stinging indictment of America's leaders.

In 2004, the late political scientist Samuel Huntington examined scholarly studies that documented the growing divide between the political elite and popular opinion.[26] He found that in the 1970s there was 75 percent consistency between public opinion and government policy. However, the consistency steadily declined after that. In the 1980s, it was 67 percent. In the early 1990s, it was down to 40 percent, dropping to 37 percent by the end of the decade. How does a system of government supposedly adhering to the "will of the people" stray so far from the views of the people it represents?

According to a study conducted by the Public Religion Research Institute, in 2016: "More than six in ten (61 percent) Americans say neither political party represents their views anymore. Dissatisfaction with America's two major parties has risen significantly since 1990, when fewer than half (48 percent) of Americans believed neither political party represented their views."[27] In a survey our firm conducted of 1,000 likely voters in 2010, 68 percent of respondents agreed with the statement "the Political Class doesn't care what most Americans think," with only 15 percent saying politicians care about the views of their constituencies.[28] In a 2019 survey, 34 percent of Americans cited government as a "major problem" that the nation is facing.

In addition, a Gallup poll in January 2021 gave House Speaker Nancy Pelosi an approval rating of 44 percent, while Senate Republican Leader Mitch McConnell had an approval rating of just 22 percent among all voters.[29] Congress as a whole received an approval rating of 25 percent in the same poll—up 10 points from a poll just a month earlier. The rise in approval came after three major developments: the riot at the Capitol, enactment of coronavirus relief legislation, and Democrats capturing majority control of the Senate.

Together, these surveys and others show that our political system doesn't have the confidence of the majority of the American people. This endangers the survival of our democracy, because without faith in the very idea of our system of government, citizens look to radical alternatives rather than solutions within the system. For the far right this can mean attacking the Capitol and rioting to overthrow our democracy, believing in crazy QAnon conspiracy theories, and denying the fact of Trump's election loss. For the far left this can mean justifying urban riots as a response to the very real problem of systemic racism, calling for capitalism to be replaced by socialism, and calling for defunding the police.

THE POLARIZED STATES OF AMERICA

Americans have been divided on major issues since colonial times. History professor David E. Shi points out that the American Revolution "was as much a brutal civil war fought between Americans ('Patriots' versus 'Loyalists') as it was a conventional conflict between American and British armies. Americans killed Americans in large numbers."[30]

Our divisions have persisted, peaking in the Civil War and continuing to this day. Millions of Americans can remember the civil rights struggle for Black Americans and the anti–Vietnam War movement that convulsed the nation in the second half of the twentieth century. And as we have pointed out, the bitter 2020 election, the insurrectionist attack on our Capitol, and gridlock in Congress have created a crisis today that threatens our very future as a democracy. We will always have disagreements, but we must not let those disagreements turn us into enemies of our fellow countrymen if we are to remain one nation. America has healed from our past divisions, but we can't just assume this will happen again.

Because we can't even agree on the same set of facts, our debates on major issues like immigration, climate change, racial justice, gun control, abortion, and more leave many Americans so far apart that our differences seem irreconcilable. For example, Trump and many of his supporters view unauthorized immigration as a threat to American sovereignty—a scourge allowing our country to be flooded with rapists and other violent criminals, illegal drugs, disease, low-wage workers who take American jobs, and people who draw welfare payments for years. This led Trump to prioritize building a wall on our border with Mexico and to take harsh actions against people he referred to as "illegal aliens." But many Democrats view these same people—who they call "undocumented" rather than "aliens"—as members of hardworking families fleeing dangerous conditions. These Democrats also believe more legal immigrants will strengthen our economy and our nation by taking jobs now going unfilled, paying taxes, sometimes serving in our armed forces, and sometimes going to college or sending their children to college and making important contributions to our society, while many Republicans see them as a burden and unwilling to assimilate.

With such dramatically different views of the immigration issue— and other issues as well—agreement via compromise is difficult. This is especially true when each side demonizes the other not just as holding different views, but as evil and motivated by bad intentions. Yet there are some hopeful signs that bridging the divide between Americans of different political views is not an impossible dream.

We can draw some encouragement from Steve Corbin, a professor emeritus of marketing at the University of Northern Iowa. He wrote in the *Des Moines Register* in February 2020 that a nonpartisan organization called More in Common conducted a national poll that found 50 percent of Republicans and 48 percent of Democrats believe that the other party is misguided, but think it's worthwhile trying to find common ground.[31] Corbin wrote that the survey found "only 8 percent of Americans can be called die-hard Democrats (Progressive Activists) and 25 percent are hard-core Republicans (Devoted Conservatives and Traditional Conservatives). This combined 33 percent of the population are in a cult of their own thinking, vehemently opposed to the other party's values and would vote for the devil if that were 'their' candidate." Thankfully, most Americans are not in these groups holding extreme views, although it is troubling to see they make up a third of the population.

When the political class works to mobilize one faction of Americans against another, it may win short-term victories but will cause long-term problems for our nation. Yet too often, members of the political class focus their attention on winning approval of legislation in Congress, imposing or repealing government regulations, or winning an election campaign. What will be the long-term consequences? The political class often leaves that question for another day.

Money plays a huge role in our system of government and politics. Candidates running for office need more and more money every election cycle to mount winning campaigns, as the cost of advertising and other expenses soars. And whenever one candidate raises lots of money, his or her opponent must try to raise lots as well to remain competitive. Spending big bucks on a campaign is far from a guarantee of victory, but spending too little sharply increases the chances of defeat. Beyond the outsize influence of political money, the destructive forces shaping government gridlock and political polarization include partisan redistricting (gerrymandering), which has reduced the competitiveness of our elections, and the broken party primary process, which tends to punish candidates for being moderate pragmatists. These realities have made America less democratic and thus have bred anger toward the government.

On top of this, there have been two great failures in recent years that have shaken the faith of the American people in our government and spurred a growing desire for alternatives outside the political system. These were the stock market crash and resulting subprime mortgage crisis of 2007–2008 that led to the Great Recession, and the bungled federal response to the COVID-19 pandemic.

Let's now take a deep dive into each of the major trends in our politics and government that have steadily pushed our flawed system to the verge of collapse.

CAMPAIGN FINANCE

In his 2013 book, *The Future: Six Drivers of Global Change*, former vice president and unsuccessful 2000 Democratic presidential nominee Al Gore wrote that "American democracy has been hacked" and said Congress "is now incapable of passing laws without permission from the corporate lobbies and other special interests that control their campaign finances."[32]

Money has always been the lifeblood of campaigns. Campaigning without money is like trying to get a plane get off the ground without fuel. And today the need for cash to fuel campaigns has never been greater. In the 2020 election cycle, almost $14 billion was spent on the presidential, House, and Senate races. That's more than twice the amount spent four years earlier. Small-dollar donations accounted for 22 percent of the total donations made to Democratic and Republican candidates in the 2020 cycle.[33] Most of the small donations come from people passionately committed to political causes, both on the far left and the far right. These small donors tend to respond to extreme appeals that demonize the other side, and warn of disastrous consequences if the opposing party candidate is elected. This incentivizes both Democrats and Republicans to ramp up their attacks on opponents with hyperbolic and sometimes inaccurate charges, further exacerbating polarization.

New York University constitutional law professor Richard H. Pildes wrote in an opinion piece for the *Washington Post* in February 2020 that small donors contributing to campaigns "tend to be more ideologically extreme" than other Americans.[34] "Academic studies show that individual donors cluster at the 'very liberal' or 'very conservative' poles of the ideological spectrum, with few in the middle," Pildes wrote. "The distribution of non-donors is more even across the spectrum: 45 percent of non-donors describe themselves as moderates, compared with 16 percent of donors. Unlike many business groups, which traditionally have contributed across the political spectrum to buy access, most individual donors give for ideological reasons. And small donors are at least as ideologically extreme as other individual donors—perhaps more so. Research also show that more ideologically extreme legislators raise a greater proportion of their money from individual donors than other candidates."

Significantly, most of the cash donated to congressional candidates doesn't come from constituents. In the U.S. Senate race in South Carolina in 2020, Democrat Jaime Harrison raised almost 95 percent of his nearly $132 million from out-of-state contributions.[35] He lost to Republican senator Lindsey Graham, who received 91 percent of his $109 million from outside the state. In another example, almost all the money spent on the two U.S. Senate races in Georgia won by Democrats Jon Ossoff and the Reverend Raphael Warnock in runoff elections January 5, 2021, came from outside the state. As the *Hill* reported: "Together, the candidates and their supportive outside allies have pumped more than $830 million into the two races, an unheard-of sum that rivals totals spent in presidential campaigns of just a few decades ago."[36]

Two important political fundraising vehicles are PACs (political actions committees) and super PACS. PACs have existed since 1944, when the first one was created by a labor union (the Congress of Industrial Organizations) to raise funds to help reelect President Franklin Roosevelt.[37] Super PACs have only been around since a Supreme Court decision in 2010. As their name implies, the super PACs are a lot more powerful.

PACs are independent, tax-exempt, not-for-profit organizations that pool contributions from many donors and spend the donations to influence the outcome of an election. The committees became far more widespread after enactment of the Federal Election Campaign Act of 1971 (amended in 1974), which created contribution limits on political donations by individuals, businesses, and unions. Then the Campaign Reform Act of 2002 barred donations from corporations and unions altogether—but not from individual corporate employees and union members. PACs are limited to donating $5,000 to a candidate in an election cycle, $5,000 a year to another PAC, and $15,000 a year to a national political party committee. An individual can donate no more than $5,000 to a PAC.[38] These are significant amounts of money, but just a tiny fraction of the money super PACs can spend on behalf of candidates.

The 2010 Supreme Court decision *Citizens United v. Federal Election Commission* led to the creation of super PACs. In the decision, the high court overturned parts of the Campaign Reform Act of 2002. This decision, combined with the decision in *Speechnow.org v. FEC*, allows PACs that don't donate directly to candidates to receive unlimited donations from corporations, individuals, unions, and other groups for the purpose of "independent expenditures" like campaign advertising. Thus, the super PAC was born.

A super PAC may spend money on political ads, events, and other campaign expenditures on behalf of candidates. Since 2010, traditional political action committees have decreased in importance and super PACs have become one of the most influential forces in American elections. Super PACs enable donors to donate unlimited quantities of money to benefit candidates, since donors are capped at how much they can give directly to a candidate.

For example, business interests spent $4.6 billion to boost the candidacies of both Biden and Trump, with most of the money being spent on behalf of Biden. The majority of these donations were made in September and October 2021, when polling made it clear that Biden was ahead. Big donors often wait until the last possible moment to join the winning side, lest they waste money on the losing candidate.

As we said in the introduction to this book, some super PACs support candidates favoring industry interests over the public interest, while hiding the names of donors, but other super PACs support moderate candidates and work on public policy issues to promote the public interest. We are proud to say that our firm has worked for the Independence USA PAC (IUSA), created by former New York City mayor Michael Bloomberg, for nearly ten years.[39] This super PAC supports candidates and referenda, and focuses on issues including gun laws, the environment, and education policy.

Independence USA PAC has a successful track record of promoting bipartisanship by helping elect moderate candidates on both sides of the aisle, as well as independent candidates, and a record of accomplishment of passing pragmatic policies at both the federal and state level. Indeed, many state-level advances on gun policy, public health, and education policy have in large measure been made possible by Independence

USA PAC's support. IUSA has worked to advance state-level gun safety reforms as well as nonpartisan public health reforms, like bans on e-cigarettes. They have also backed necessary clean air measures—like limits on carbon pollution from power plants.

In 2016, IUSA focused a lot of its spending around gun control. It helped reelect Republican senator Pat Toomey in Pennsylvania, airing ads on his leadership on gun control legislation after the Newtown shooting, and helped unseat Republican senator Kelly Ayotte in New Hampshire, by running ads attacking her for voting against it.

In 2018, as Republicans in the era of President Trump had almost entirely abandoned a bipartisan approach on gun safety and virtually every other issue, IUSA moved to help moderate Democrats, and particularly focused on helping Democrats win control of the U.S. House of Representatives.

As mentioned in the introduction, we were especially proud to work IUSA's remarkably successful effort in the 2018 U.S. House elections, in which twenty-one out of twenty-four candidates backed by Independence USA won—including fifteen women.

The danger of donations influencing politicians drops if the general public and watchdog groups know who donates money to political candidates. Unfortunately, in the majority of outside spending (such as by super PACs), this information is not disclosed. According to the Center for Responsive Politics, "only 30 percent of outside spending comes from groups that fully disclose their donors, an all-time low."[40] For example, a "dark-money" group called One Nation contributed $62 million to the Senate Leadership Fund, helping Senate Republican Leader Mitch McConnell win reelection in 2020. Yet other PACs, like Independence USA PAC, strictly adhere to the letter of the law with regard to publicly disclosing their donors.

THE DANGEROUS POWER OF LOBBYISTS

Lobbyists take advantage of the clearly broken political campaign finance system to direct their clients to make campaign donations that will prove most useful. Before newly elected House members and senators even make it to Capitol Hill they are already indebted to these groups. This dynamic necessarily makes our nation less democratic. When politicians depend on big donors to be elected and reelected they give the donors access, talking with them at fundraising events and in meetings, and hearing what the donors are seeking in terms of legislation and regulatory changes.

Lobbyists and other big donors don't hand members of Congress and candidates briefcases full of cash in exchange for explicit promises to vote a certain way. That would be bribery and a crime. Instead, the interactions between funders and politicians are much more subtle. Suppose a politician says publicly that he favors tax breaks for the oil industry, justifying this because he says it benefits America's energy needs and creates jobs. The oil industry spends a lot of money to help the politician win the next election because it says he takes beneficial positions. But you can bet the candidate takes into account the financial benefit of supporting the oil industry, finds more time to spend with big-money donors, and is more attentive to their desires than to ordinary constituents. Ordinary constituents are far more likely to be directed to a call with a junior staffer to raise their concerns than to get a meeting with a member of Congress.

The enduring and growing power of lobbyists creates a pay-to-play dynamic between politicians and special-interest groups, where Congress represents the elite—and the rest of America is left disenchanted and betrayed. "Of the billions of dollars now spent every year on politics ... only a fairly small fraction is directly connected to electoral contests. The bulk of it goes to lobbying," political science professors Jacob Hacker and Paul Pierson wrote in their 2011 book, *Winner-Take-All*

Politics: How Washington Made the Rich Richer—and Turned Its Back on the Middle Class.[41]

The amount of money spent on lobbying is steadily increasing, and more industries are getting involved. For example, facing threats of increased government regulation, Google, Facebook, Amazon, Apple, and Microsoft spent a combined $61 million on direct lobbying costs in 2020.[42] These numbers tell a story: Lobbyists have a greater ability to influence policy than ever before. Members of the elite know this and use it to their advantage. According to the nonprofit and nonpartisan Center for Responsive Politics, total spending on lobbying federal agencies and Congress rose from $1.45 billion in 1998 to $3.49 billion in 2020. The number of Washington lobbyists increased from 10,417 in 1998 to 11,524 in 2020.[43] Common sense tells you that clients wouldn't be paying so many lobbyists that much money if the lobbyists didn't deliver results by influencing legislation and regulations.

Some lobbyists have worked for members of Congress and for the executive branch senior officials they are trying to influence—up to and including the president. For example, a *Wall Street Journal* article published in November 2020 was headlined "Washington Lobbyists Know Biden Well—as Their Former Boss." The article said: "Scores of Mr. Biden's former aides now on K Street [as lobbyists] represent hundreds of companies, trade groups, and foreign companies."[44] On the Republican side, CNBC reported in May 2018 that former Trump personal attorney Michael Cohen (who was later sentenced to prison and turned against Trump) was paid $600,000 by AT&T, $1.2 million by Swiss drug company Novartis, and $150,000 by a South Korean aerospace company for advice on dealing with the new Trump administration in 2017. The same article said: "In 2017 alone, 112 individual lobbyists from 34 different firms, including AT&T's in-house team, reported lobbying to advance the telecom giant's policy goals. Another 85 lobbyists representing 15 different firms disclosed that they had lobbied on behalf of Novartis."[45] This is a staggering number of lobbyists for just two companies.

In hiring the over 11,000 lobbyists in Washington, clients place a premium on people with personal connections to the president, important officials in his administration, and members of Congress. This is why Michael Cohen was able to collect so much money for making connections with the Trump administration when he was still in Trump's good graces. And it is why so many former Biden staff members from his days as a senator and as vice president are now lobbyists.

The term "revolving door" is used to discuss the frequent practice of people moving from government service to lobbying (where salaries are higher) and sometimes back onto the government payroll again. The skills and connections lobbyists have are valuable in government, and the skills and connections government employees have are valuable in lobbying. According to the Center for Responsive Politics, 466 former members of Congress have lobbied on behalf of corporations, unions, municipalities, and organizations.[46] Since the center's website—OpenSecrets .org—began profiling lobbying, Senate Republican Leader Mitch McConnell and Senate Democratic Leader Chuck Schumer have each had 57 staffers go through the revolving door. Congressional committee staff positions are prime targets for lobbyists when they become federal employees. Since Opensecrets.org started keeping track, over 600 staffers serving the Finance, Ways and Means, and Energy, and Commerce committees have either gone through the revolving door to K Street or entered congressional staffs from it.

The Center for Responsive Politics describes the revolving door this way: "Although the influence powerhouses that line Washington's K Street are just a few miles from the U.S. Capitol building, the most direct path between the two doesn't necessarily involve public transportation. Instead, it's through a door—a revolving door that shuffles former federal employees into jobs as lobbyists, consultants and strategists, just as the door pulls former hired guns into government careers. While officials in the executive branch, Congress, and senior congressional staffers spin in and out of the private and public sectors, so too does privilege, power, access and, of course, money."

Here's an example of the harmful impact the revolving door can have on Congress: In 2011, a "super committee" made up of House members and senators was formed to reach a deal on $1.2 trillion in proposed cuts to the federal budget.[47] Super committees were created with honest intentions: to reduce partisan bickering, temper extremist rhetoric, and get our government working again. The bipartisan committee, made up of six Republicans and six Democrats, was thought to be sufficiently isolated from the phalanxes of distracting lobbyists and special interests. It was a laudable plan, but it failed miserably. At the time, there were nearly a hundred registered lobbyists who had previously worked for one of the twelve committee members, and half of both Democrats and Republicans on the committee employed former lobbyists on their staffs. These revolving door regulars had represented special interest groups like defense contractors, public-sector unions, health care conglomerates, and others that had vested interest in the outcome of the committee's decision. With the presence of so many conflicting special interests, the panel unsurprisingly failed to reach a decision.

Lobbyists do more than direct campaign donations by their employers and clients. They are an important source of information to Congress and the executive branch, but their job is to share information favorable to the causes they advocate. In addition, lobbyists use highly sophisticated public relations and communications strategies and technology to influence public opinion to support the objectives of special interests. The nature of lobbying has changed, and with it the way politics is conducted. Increasingly, ordinary citizens are shut out of the democratic process. To a greater extent than most people are aware, lobbyists, special-interest groups, wealthy individuals, and political party leadership have enormous influence on major government decisions. For the majority of Americans already frustrated with an ineffective federal government, this is bad news.

Lobbyists are the bridge between special interests—Wall Street, labor unions, big business, advocacy groups, and state and local governments—and Congress and the executive branch. For example, some lobbyists seek stricter environmental regulations from the Environmental Protection Agency and stricter environmental laws from Congress, while other lobbyists seek exactly the opposite. The environmental lobbyist will discuss the pollution and climate change caused by the burning of fossil fuels, while the fossil fuels industry lobbyist will discuss jobs created and taxes paid by the industry. The opposing lobbyists will criticize the claims of the other side.

Lobbyists don't make up statistics and supporting facts that have no basis in reality, because they need to maintain their credibility. But they make a case for their side in the most favorable light possible, like opposing lawyers arguing a case in court and reaching different conclusions. And they make very different forecasts about what could happen in the future if their side wins or loses. On many occasions they actually write suggested legislation and regulations and provide those to members of Congress and executive branch officials, to make it as easy as possible for friendly lawmakers and regulators to give the lobbyists what they are seeking.

On top of using lobbyists as a source for information and proposed legislation, elected officials understand that taking a position favored by lobbyists can bring them campaign contributions from individuals and PACs, and "independent expenditures" from super PACs. Unions have long turned out volunteers to run phone banks, campaign door-to-door, and carry out other labor-intensive work in the run-up to elections. College students, retirees, and others also provide volunteer campaign manpower for candidates who embrace their causes. For example, in 1967, many college students opposed to the Vietnam War campaigned for antiwar candidates such as Senator Eugene McCarthy (D-MN), who unsuccessfully sought the Democratic presidential nomination. Senator Bernie Sanders's two presidential campaigns also attracted many young volunteers

Sometimes lobbyists cross the line from influence-peddling to outright lawbreaking. Lobbyist Jack Abramoff pleaded guilty in 2006 to conspiracy to bribe public officials, fraud, and tax evasion in a complex scheme in which he and his partner charged Native American tribes an estimated $85 million to lobby for government permission to establish casinos. A total of twenty-one people either pleaded guilty or were found guilty of criminal conduct in the scheme. Abramoff and other defendants were ordered to make a least $25 million in restitution of funds defrauded from Native American tribes and other clients. After serving almost four years in a federal prison, Abramoff wrote about the scandal in his 2011 book, *Capitol Punishment: The Hard Truth About Washington Corruption from America's Most Notorious Lobbyist.*[48] The Abramoff scandal shined a light on lobbying excesses, prompting lawmakers and lobbyists alike to be more careful. In 2007, Congress amended the Lobbying Disclosure Act in response. The first person charged with violating the amended law was none other than Abramoff, who pleaded guilty in 2020 to violating the law for work he secretly agreed to do in 2017 for the marijuana industry without registering as a lobbyist.[49]

Lobbying quickly evolved after the Abramoff scandal made news in 2006. The public blowback inspired creative and stealthy attempts by lobbyists and their clients to influence legislation and regulations. Lobbyists increased their efforts at "grassroots lobbying," which involves using members of the public to support their causes. For example, AARP and its lobbyists could work to mobilize senior citizens to write letters, send emails, make phone calls, and seek meetings with their elected representatives to lobby against reductions in Social Security benefits. Or in another example, proponents of opening a factory could mobilize people who might get jobs at the factory to seek needed zoning changes on the local level and overcome objections by environmentalists.

"Astroturf lobbying" is a related tactic, named for its artificial mimicking of grassroots lobbying. In these cases, lobbyists and public relations agencies create organizations supposedly representing ordinary citizens supporting legislation or a change in regulations. For example, suppose pesticide manufacturers are being criticized for making products dangerous to the environment. Lobbyists could create a new organization called Parents to Protect Our Kids representing people in low-income housing who say they need pesticides to protect their children from disease-bearing rat and roach infestations common in their apartments. A handful of mothers living in public housing could get training in how to talk to the media and lawmakers about their concerns. Public housing residents could then be mobilized to contact their representatives in Congress and post on social media. Such a campaign would have much greater impact than direct appeals by pesticide executives and could influence lawmakers and regulators. But in our fictional example, Parents to Protect Our Kids wasn't formed by parents—in truth, it was created and financed as a front for the pesticide industry.

If only the pressure from a legislator's constituents was organic rather artificial, our government would be much more responsive to the will of citizens and our nation would be much better off as a whole. As it is today, the general electorate is relinquishing control of legislative decision-making to special-interest groups and the political elite. Lobbyists are the medium through which the political class operates—the connective tissue. Silicon Valley, Wall Street, unions, corporations, single-issue groups, and defense contractors are just some of the more than 20,000 special-interest groups that have spent money to lobby the federal government in the past three decades.

In a show of dedication to "draining the swamp," President Trump issued an executive order in 2017 forbidding former White House employees from lobbying following their service. But just days before the end of his term, he rescinded the order. This will only worsen the situation in Washington as former Trump administration officials profit from their familiarity with the executive branch.

All in all, despite the checks against its power, lobbying continues to grow, modernize, and become more powerful. Reforms can slow this process, but one thing is clear: Ordinary citizens will continue to yield control over government officials to businesses and special-interest groups. If there is one dynamic empowering the political class, lobbying is it. If nothing is done, Americans will continue to lose faith in our government and democracy itself.

REDISTRICTING: THE INCUMBENT PROTECTION PLAN

Democratic and Republican elected officials are in complete agreement on one thing: They all want to be reelected or elected to higher office until they choose to retire. This drives them to seek support and campaign contributions from special interests, to devote enormous time and energy trying to generate favorable news coverage to boost their images, and to spend huge sums on their election campaigns. In addition, elected officials do everything they can to tilt the playing field to increase their odds of winning elections. One of the most powerful ways they do this is by redrawing districts for the U.S. House of Representatives and state legislatures every ten years in response to population changes.

Each state is represented by two U.S. senators who are elected statewide. But U.S. House and state legislative districts are based on population, which shifts from decade to decade due to births and deaths, and as people move out of some communities and into others. This requires district boundaries to be changed. States sometimes gain and lose U.S. House seats based on increases or decreases in their share of the U.S. population. As our population has risen, the number of people per House district has grown from about 34,000 following the 1790 census, to about 212,000 following the 1910 census, to about 710,000 following the 2010 census. It will reach about 761,000 as the result of the 2020 census.[50] The Apportionment Act of 1911 set the number of U.S. House seats at 435. In most states, state legislatures draw the district boundary lines, meaning that whichever political party controls the legislature and governorship can draw the districts (or both parties must reach agreement if different parties control each house of a legislature and governor's office).

If redistricting was based on nonpartisan principles it would be a straightforward process. State legislators or others in charge of redistricting would avoid splitting up political jurisdictions to the greatest extent possible and keep districts compact. For example, two counties and part of a third could be in one district. Or, in a big city, the district lines would divide the city into two or more contiguous parts. But that's usually not how redistricting works. In most states, districts are carved up in all sorts of strange shapes to make them safe for one party or another. Some of these decisions have been challenged in the U.S. Supreme Court as violating the constitutional requirement of one person, one vote. Other instances of redistricting have been challenged in court for being based on race.[51]

Redistricting is derisively known as gerrymandering, named after Elbridge Gerry, because when he was governor of Massachusetts from 1810 to 1812, the state legislature redrew state Senate district lines to favor his Democratic-Republican Party, including a bizarrely convoluted district that resembled a salamander. (Gerry went on to serve as the fifth vice president of the United States before dying in office in 1814.) Gerrymandering is alive and well, despite some court decisions overturning the most flagrant abuses.

The Supreme Court issued a major decision in 2019 allowing gerrymandering to continue. As the *New York Times* reported on June 27 that year: "The Supreme Court on Thursday ruled that federal courts are powerless to hear challenges to partisan gerrymandering, the practice in which the party that controls the state legislature draws voting maps to help elect its candidates.... The drafters of the Constitution, Chief Justice John G. Roberts Jr. wrote for the majority, understood that politics would play a role in drawing election districts when they gave the task to state legislatures."[52]

The political class has mastered the art of gerrymandering, hiring consultants with computer optimization programs. In some cases the voting power of the opposing party is diluted by splitting up its supporters into several districts. For example, if a county has a large majority of registered Democratic voters, it could be split between four congressional districts to give each district a Republican majority. In other cases, the opposite tactic is employed. One district could be drawn to have an overwhelming Democratic majority, leaving three neighboring districts as heavily Republican. This would most likely give Republicans three House seats, while Democrats would get one.

Partisan redistricting has clearly worked. Between 1990 and 2008, the number of "close-call" House elections—those determined by a margin of 51–49 percent or narrower—has declined by 37 percent. In 2003, in one of the most notorious redistricting battles in American history, Republicans in the Texas legislature gerrymandered the state's 32 congressional districts to go from 17–15 House seats in favor of Democrats to a 21–11 margin in favor of Republicans in the 2004 elections. Courts upheld the action, and other state legislatures became emboldened to take similar steps. As a result, many congressional districts are rarely competitive. In the 2018 midterm elections, Democrats had already secured 40 House seats before Election Day, simply because Democrats ran unopposed in those districts.

With so many districts where the deck is stacked through redistricting so that one party or the other is almost certain to win, it is difficult for general election voters to hold their representatives accountable. Instead, primaries usually determine who wins elections in such districts—but incumbents are unlikely to be defeated or even challenged in primaries. As a result, it is nearly impossible to defeat an incumbent in a favorably gerrymandered district unless the incumbent is tainted by a scandal or denounced by his or her own political party. For example, in the 2014 midterm elections, none of California's fifty-three U.S. House seats changed hands, and only two seats in Texas changed hands. Attacks on incumbents from within their own parties are unusual. The most prominent recent cases took place involving the ten House Republicans (most notably Rep. Liz Cheney of Wyoming) who voted to impeach President Trump shortly before he left office, and the seven GOP senators who voted to convict Trump on the impeachment charge after his term ended.[53] Trump attacked them all.

All this shows that while gerrymandering helps elected officials get reelected, it doesn't serve the public interest. We'd be better off if more House members were elected from districts with a mix of Republicans, Democrats, and independents. This would force candidates to take centrist positions that appeal to a broad range of voters, rather than rewarding the most polarizing candidates with election victories.

PROBLEMS WITH PARTY PRIMARIES

The Constitution doesn't say anything about political parties. George Washington was unanimously elected as our first president by the Electoral College. Political parties first appeared in 1800 and party leaders selected candidates to run for office.[54] Conventions began in the mid-1800s, controlled by party leaders and elected officials. Ordinary voters were left out of the process. Primaries began appearing in the Progressive Era between 1890 and 1920 to give voters a say in who the parties nominated for elective office. By 1916, twenty-five of the forty-eight states had primaries, but after World War I eight of those states abandoned primaries and returned to conventions. More primaries and nominating caucuses began after World War II and eventually spread to every state.

While state and national party political conventions are still held, in most cases they simply ratify selections made by primaries for state offices, the U.S. House and Senate, and the presidency.

Unfortunately, the primary system is deeply flawed. Moderate and pragmatic candidates willing to reach across the aisle to achieve positive change are at a disadvantage when competing in these intraparty contests. Because voter turnout in primaries is usually lower than in general elections and voters are more politically involved, Democratic primary voters are typically more liberal than Democrats overall, and Republican primary voters are typically more conservative than Republicans overall. As a result, primary voters often nominate candidates with a strong ideological bent. This makes moderates an endangered species in Congress, and the legislative branch is more polarized and paralyzed than in years past.

With the exception of a few brave senators and representatives, lawmakers today usually cast party-line votes on major legislation, with individual members in most cases afraid to break ranks. This doesn't serve the best interests of the American people. It encourages confrontation rather than cooperation between our elected representatives. To pass needed legislation to build a better future for the American people, we need lawmakers to spend less time feuding and fighting, and more time negotiating and compromising on centrist solutions to the problems we face. The current system contributes to the erosion of our faith in democracy, our civic religion.

Primaries don't necessarily produce the best candidates. On the presidential level, campaigning in states across the nation for many months becomes a test of endurance and fundraising ability for candidates. For most of the presidential elections of the past few decades, every candidate has been generally disliked by the majority of the electorate, with the exception of then-senator Barack Obama in 2008. For too long, our process has been to choose the lesser of two evils, or the "anyone but the other guy" candidate.

Because Democratic primary voters tend to favor candidates who are the most progressive (Biden was an exception to this tendency) and Republican primary voters tend to favor candidates who are the most conservative, this can hurt a party's chances of winning in the general election. For example, as we write this in 2021, Republicans are expressing concern that they could lose some U.S. Senate races in 2022 by nominating candidates who are strong Trump supporters. *New York Times* reporter Trip Gabriel explained this problem: "Strong state parties, big donors and G.O.P. national leaders were once able to anoint a candidate, in order to avoid destructive demolition derbies in state primaries. But in the Trump era, the pursuit of his endorsement is all-consuming, and absent Mr. Trump's blessing, there is no mechanism for clearing a cluttered primary field."[55] So while loyalty to Trump could boost the chances of candidates to win their primary races, it could hurt them in the general election by making it hard to get independent, Democratic, and even some moderate Republican votes.

As an indication of how closely divided the nation is now between Democrats and Republicans, since 1984 the winner of the presidency has not been determined by a double-digit margin in the popular vote. Candidates have sometimes won with pluralities rather than outright majorities, due to minor party candidates on the ballot. And in this century, two presidential candidates—George W. Bush and Donald Trump—were elected with Electoral College majorities despite losing the popular vote (in the 1800s, John Quincy Adams, Rutherford B. Hayes, and Benjamin Harrison were also elected president while losing the popular vote).[56]

One reason for the success of extremists in primaries and sometimes in general elections is that extremism can be exciting and entertaining. Moderation can come off as boring. Barry Goldwater and George McGovern both excited the extremes of their parties because they made bold stands and strayed far from the center. But they were too extreme to be elected president. When Donald Trump ran for president in 2016, he was aided by CNN President Jeff Zucker's decision to air many Trump campaign rallies live in prime time because the rallies got great ratings and were entertaining. Zucker is "a ratings whore," Preston Beckman, who was executive vice president for program planning at NBC, told the *New York Times*. "But it's one thing to be a ratings whore in prime time and it's another thing to be a ratings whore when it comes to news," said Beckman, who worked with Zucker at NBC.[57] Beckman is right: News should be looked at differently than entertainment. And not just by TV executives and journalists, but by the public as well. Donald Trump may have been a great ratings draw and an entertaining TV star on *The Apprentice*, but once in the Oval Office he proved he was miscast in the real-life role as commander in chief.

Just as the entertaining Donald Trump was the surprise winner of the Republican presidential primary and general election in 2016, Alexandria Ocasio-Cortez was the surprise winner of the Democratic primary and general election in her New York congressional district in 2018. Ocasio-Cortez defeated ten-term incumbent Rep. Joseph Crowley in the 2018 primary by capturing 57 percent of the vote.[58] Her socialism and embrace of radical policies are unpopular in most of the country, but in her heavily liberal congressional district, winning the Democratic party's nomination is a virtual guarantee of election. She won the 2018 general election with 78 percent of the vote and was reelected two years later with 74 percent of the vote.

Another shortcoming of the presidential primary and caucus system is that it gives enormous influence to two sparsely populated rural states holding the first presidential nominating contests every four years—Iowa and New Hampshire. Neither state matches the U.S. demographically. For example, 85 percent of Iowa's population is white, 6 percent is Hispanic, 4 percent is Black, 2 percent is Asian, and 2 percent is mixed race.[59] New Hampshire's population is 90 percent white, 3 percent Hispanic, 3 percent Asian, 2 percent Black, and 2 percent mixed race.[60] Candidates of color and people living in urban areas have complained that they get less attention from presidential candidates early in primary campaigns as a result.

In 2020, seven states and territories nominated candidates for president in caucuses, which are far less democratic than primaries. Voters usually must spend a good deal of time gathering with others in their communities at a specific time for the caucuses and must in many cases cast their votes publicly. Turnout is typically lower than in primaries. Recognizing these problems, the Democratic National Committee encourages states to use primaries rather than caucuses to nominate candidate. In 2020, nominating caucuses were held in Iowa, Nevada, American Samoa, North Dakota, Wyoming, Guam, and the Virgin Islands.[61] (Residents of territories don't vote in presidential elections, but they can vote in caucuses and primaries.)

Iowa plays a key role in nominations, despite its small population, because its caucuses are the first nominating contest, typically preceding the New Hampshire primary by a week. There is a saying that "there are only three tickets out of Iowa." For the most part, this has been true. Other than George H. W. Bush and Joe Biden, if a candidate doesn't finish in the top three in Iowa —"first class, business class, or coach" as the candidates say—then his or her nomination hopes are usually dashed. Very few candidates can raise enough funding to continue campaigning after exerting a titanic effort to win in Iowa and underperforming.

There is no perfect way of nominating candidates at the presidential, congressional, and state level, of course. But the political parties would be well served to examine alternatives.

GOVERNMENT FAILURES: THE GREAT RECESSION AND THE COVID-19 PANDEMIC

The issues we have discussed in this chapter—campaign financing, the power of lobbyists, redistricting, and the broken primary and caucus system used to nominate candidates—all weaken the relationship between elected officials and their constituents, and strengthen the power of special interests. This has played an important role in weakening the faith of millions of Americans in our democratic system and poses a danger to our democratic future. Two crises illustrate the failings of our current political system: the government response to the 2008 financial crisis and Great Recession, and the government response to the deadly COVID-19 pandemic of 2020 and 2021—causing both a health crisis and an economic crisis.

The Great Recession brought the self-serving nature of the Washington–Wall Street relationship into clear view for the American people. Millions of Americans lost their homes, jobs, and retirement savings to a crisis created by their government and Wall Street. But instead of seeing government come to their rescue, average Americans watched Washington—in an unusual display of bipartisanship—come to the rescue of big banks, corporations, and investors. The $700 billion Emergency Economic Stabilization Act bailing out the banks was unpopular. A *New York Times*–CBS poll five years after the bailout found "nearly six in ten Americans express disapproval of the 2008 bailout, and only about a third approve."[62] And while the bailout certainly stopped the downward spiral of our economy, it directed government help to some of the wealthiest corporations and individuals in the country. Ordinary Americans were left out of the closed-door negotiations.

The government bailout did nothing to hold any of those most responsible for the disaster accountable for their misdeeds. From the point of view of many average Americans hurt by the crisis—whether Democrats, Republicans, or independents—Wall Street had caused the crisis and then profited off of it. Senate Democratic Leader Chuck Schumer—who has long been attentive to New York–based investment banks because he represents the state—blocked some of the strictest proposed financial reforms from becoming law.[63] Following the financial crisis and Great Recession that it brought about, much of the political class was more enriched and empowered. The crisis betrayed the deep entanglement between Wall Street and Washington, sparking opposition from the left and right. Richard Fuld, Lehman Brothers' last CEO, left the failed company with a $72 million golden parachute.[64] There was no demand from Washington that he give it back. Franklin Raines, the disgraced CEO of Fannie Mae—which was bailed out by taxpayers at a cost of over $162 billion—resigned with a severance package valued at $240 million.[65]

On the left, the Occupy Wall Street movement called for radical wealth redistribution at the expense of Wall Street millionaires and billionaires. The response on the right was the Tea Party, which called for smaller government as the solution for the corruption of the political class. Coauthor Schoen wrote about the Tea Party movement extensively in his 2010 book with Scott Rasmussen, *Mad as Hell: How the Tea Party Movement is Fundamentally Remaking Our Two-Party System*.[66] We will discuss both movements extensively in a later chapter. The Occupy movement and the Tea Party, although originating from different sides of the political spectrum, offered non-systemic solutions to the question: How do you create a system that serves average Americans, not the elite?

The federal response to the COVID-19 pandemic was another crisis where the political class fell down on the job. President Trump admitted to author Bob Woodward in February 2020 that he deliberately downplayed the severity of the pandemic, claiming this was to avoid causing a panic.[67] From the beginning, Trump treated the pandemic as a political crisis rather than a health crisis, giving out false and contradictory information and blaming governors for problems in the response. Trump conducted pandemic briefings for the media himself, rather than letting medical experts speak freely. As deaths mounted, Trump repeatedly praised himself and the federal government for doing an outstanding job. The president continued to hold large gatherings that acted as superspreader events and rarely wore a mask. He even encouraged resistance to guidelines from his own administration that were intended to slow the spread of the disease—even after he was hospitalized with a serious case of COVID-19.

In March 2020, Congress passed and Trump signed into law a $1.76 trillion bipartisan bill called the CARES (Coronavirus Aid, Relief and Economic Security) Act that added $600 a week to unemployment insurance checks, gave most adults a $1,200 payment plus $500 per child, imposed a moratorium on evictions, and sent aid directly to small businesses, among other provisions.[68] However, parts of the bill added billions of dollars in tax breaks that benefited wealthy Americans. Allan Sloan listed these in an article published in June 2020 by ProPublica headlined: "The CARES Act Sent You a $1,200 Check but Gave Millionaires and Billionaires Far More."[69]

After the CARES act, however, Democrats and Republicans in Congress deadlocked on approving additional spending to help Americans with the economic and health impacts of the pandemic, which forced many business to close and sent unemployment soaring. It took another nine months before a second coronavirus stimulus bill worth $900 billion was passed in late December 2020—after the election.[70] Negotiations on the measure broke down before the election and Trump and House Speaker Pelosi stopped speaking with each other, instead trading insults in the media and on Twitter. President Biden proposed an additional $1.9 trillion coronavirus relief bill early in his term and the House and Senate approved the measure but with only Democratic votes. Biden signed the bill into law in March 2021.

The pain inflicted by COVID-19 did not strike all Americans equally. Many professionals were able to work from home. But low-income workers either lost their jobs (among them employees at restaurants, theaters, and stores closed to contain the pandemic) or had to endanger their health by continuing to go to their workplaces (such as supermarkets, food-processing facilities, and factories) to stay employed. The stock market soared despite the pandemic, conferring the greatest benefits on wealthy investors.

THE CHALLENGE AHEAD

The widening divide between the political class and the rest of America is the most corrosive force eroding the foundations of our democracy today. Millions of Americans make it clearer and clearer in every election that they detest their leadership because of issues of personal character (as with Donald Trump), or because candidates are too ideologically extreme (as with Senator Bernie Sanders when he sought the Democratic presidential nomination). Millions of us also make it clearer and clearer that we want members of Congress and the president to work together on centrist solutions to our problems, rather than to fight endlessly for far-left or far-right positions.

House Speaker Sam Rayburn (D-TX), who served in the House of Representatives from 1913 to 1961 (including seventeen years as Speaker) once said: "A jackass can kick a barn down but it takes a carpenter to build one."[71] Rayburn was a master dealmaker and negotiator who steered many pieces of landmark legislation to become law. He knew it was much easier to fight all the time and block legislation—to "kick down a barn"— than to be an effective lawmaker and get things done. And he was content to work quietly in the background without seeking publicity and boasting of his every achievement.

Unfortunately, many members of Congress don't reach across the aisle to compromise today because it's not in their best interest to do so. Washington is awash with elite money and the system keeps incumbents in power. Thanks to the combination of a broken campaign financing system, an ineffective party primary system, special-interest lobbying, and gerrymandering, lawmakers are no longer accountable to their constituents. Instead, they serve their financial sponsors and their party leadership to the detriment of ordinary Americans. More lawmakers need to follow Sam Rayburn's example, coming up with creative ideas to bridge differences with members of the other party. They need to be willing to lead and not simply follow public opinion polls and cower in fear that being reasonable and willing to compromise will bring them a primary opponent or otherwise end their political careers. And they need to focus on helping ordinary Americans rather than the political class.

Like Rayburn, President Biden has served in government for a very long time—in the Senate from 1973 to 2009 and as vice president from 2009 to 2017. And like Rayburn, Biden has long prided himself in being able to reach across the aisle to make deals with Republicans. Unlike Trump, Biden was not born into wealth. And unlike Trump, he understands how government works. We hope he will succeed where Trump failed in bridging the divide between right and left and between the political class and average Americans. However, unless Biden can make the political class accountable to mainstream Americans, the loss of faith in government and democracy will only continue to accelerate among the American people. Voters on both sides of the political divide will seek out alternatives—socialism, populism, even insurgency—until they find a government that serves them once more. Every American should wish Biden success in restoring our faith in our democracy and in making us a less divided and more united nation.

4 / A HISTORY OF POPULISM

Populism is a response to the needs and wants of ordinary people who feel they are ignored and treated unjustly by those in power. It embraces the rights, wisdom, and virtues of ordinary citizens and works to ensure their fair treatment from the rich and powerful. It seeks to change an unresponsive political system that elites on the left and right have long taken advantage of in many parts of the world. Like the word "popular," the word "populism" comes from the Latin word "populus," meaning "the people." In any democracy, popularity is essential to win elections. That's why pollsters—including our own firm—routinely ask voters about the popularity of candidates and policies before elections. Even in authoritarian states, leaders embrace populism and want their policies to be popular.

Populism has both positive and negative aspects.

On the positive side, populism can help the downtrodden deal with the challenges they face, climb the economic ladder, and have a shot at better days ahead. The graduated income tax, for example, is a populist mechanism to transfer wealth from the affluent to fund government programs that benefit the entire population, particularly people in the greatest need. The federal minimum wage, free public schools, government-subsidized state colleges and universities, Social Security,

Medicare, Medicaid, the Affordable Care Act, food stamps, public housing, and other social welfare programs are also populist programs. So are laws allowing workers to form unions, protecting people against racial and other types of discrimination, and protecting consumers from dangerous drugs and other products.

On the negative side, the rising tide of populism sweeping across America today can create an "us versus them" attitude dividing our population by ideology, race, ethnicity, religion, economic status, and in other polarizing ways. This type of populism can be not only anti-establishment. It can be anti-intellectual, anti-science, and in extreme cases even anti-reality. An example of this is the anti-vaccine movement endangering the health and lives of millions of Americans by prompting many people in 2021 to refuse to be vaccinated against the coronavirus that is responsible for the COVID-19 pandemic. Other examples are fringe groups like QAnon preaching wild conspiracy theories and calling for violent action against their opponents.

Unfortunately, extreme and divisive populism has become more widespread in recent years. It is sometimes exploited by opportunistic politicians who have found it politically beneficial to emphasize our differences rather than our commonalities. This type of extreme populism poses a clear and present danger to our national unity and well-being, and to the continued existence of the United States as a democracy. While populist movements on the left and on the right have arisen throughout American history, today they are flourishing on both ends of the political spectrum at the same time, sometimes eroding the faith of Americans in our democratic system of government.

In this chapter we will discuss populist movements and leading populists dating back to our nation's birth up to our recent past, because understanding yesterday's populism is essential to understanding the populism of today and the populism that might emerge in the future. We will examine the successes and failures of populists including Presidents Thomas Jefferson, Andrew Jackson, Franklin Delano Roosevelt, Ronald

Reagan, and Bill Clinton; unsuccessful presidential candidates William Jennings Bryan, Barry Goldwater, George Wallace, and H. Ross Perot; would-be presidential candidate Huey Long, who was shot to death before he could launch a campaign against FDR; and House Speaker Newt Gingrich and his Contract with America. We will also look at populist uprisings, focusing particular attention on the right-wing Tea Party movement and the left-wing Occupy Wall Street movement of the early twenty-first century, and look at how they paved the way for the populist movements of today.

In recent years populism brought us President Trump on the right. On the left it brought us Senators Bernie Sanders of Vermont and Elizabeth Warren of Massachusetts, along with Representative Alexandria Ocasio-Cortez of New York and other progressives. Populism was at the root of the insurrection at the Capitol by Trump loyalists seeking to overturn his election defeat, as well as the far-left movements of Black Lives Matter and the riots that hit U.S. cities in the spring and summer of 2020.

Both far-left and far-right populism have sparked a frighteningly high degree of alienation from our political system and have sometimes resulted in violence. The January 6, 2021, riot at the Capitol that claimed the lives of five people has quite appropriately received enormous attention, but it's important to understand that at least twenty-five Americans were killed in other political unrest in 2020, including the Black Lives Matter protests in the spring and summer and "patriot rallies" of Trump supporters.[1] These deaths make it clear that while the riot at the Capitol was more serious than the urban riots, since it was a direct attack on our system of government, it was one of many violent populist attacks and not an isolated event.

Populism is not new. In fact, it is older than America itself and was the foundation of the American Revolution—a revolt to end the rule of the far-off British king and create a nation ruled by elected representatives of the common man (or more precisely the common white man, since it would unfortunately be many years before women, Black people, and Native Americans gained voting rights). In a nutshell, populism emphasizes that it represents ordinary people who have been wronged by the wealthy and powerful elite. In *Mad as Hell*, Scott Rasmussen and Douglas Schoen said that "in a large sense, American populist movements across the centuries share a sense of moral decay, a suspicion of the conniving elite, an unshakable faith in the essential goodness of ordinary people, a disgust with a presumed business-government conspiracy, and a belief that the ordinary American has undergone a systemic betrayal by power-monopolizing institutions."[2]

Mad as Hell also points out that the defining difference between right-wing and left-wing populists is their proposed way of solving the problems facing the nation. For the right-wing populists, government is the problem, not the solution, just as President Reagan said. They want to shrink government, reduce regulations, and cut taxes to lessen the power of government over the citizenry. Left-wing populists take the opposite position, contending that a bigger government can benefit ordinary Americans by limiting the power of the elite. They favor higher taxes on the wealthy, tougher regulations on business, and expanded government programs to help workers, people with low incomes, minorities, and others not part of the elite.

Two professors who study populism—Cristóbal Rovira Kaltwasser of Diego Portales University in Chile and Cas Mudde of the University of Georgia and the University of Oslo—have described populism as "a thin-centered ideology that considers society to be ultimately separated into two homogenous and antagonistic camps, 'the pure people' versus 'the corrupt elite.'"[3]

Writing in the *Guardian* in February 2015, Mudde said: "Populism's black and white views and uncompromising stand leads to a polarized society—for which, of course, both sides share responsibility—and its majoritarian extremism denies legitimacy to opponents' views and weakens the rights of minorities. While left-wing populism is often less exclusionary than right-wing populism, the main difference between them is not whether they exclude, but whom they exclude, which is largely determined by their accompanying ideology (e.g., nationalism or socialism)."[4]

"Most successful American presidents, from Franklin D. Roosevelt to Reagan to Bill Clinton, have been populists to some extent," according to Geoffrey Kabaservice, author of *Rule and Ruin: The Downfall of Moderation and the Destruction of the Republican Party*. "But leaders of both parties also have been wary of populism's tendency to slide into demagoguery. History has shown that populists find it difficult to resist scapegoating minorities and outsiders, proffering simplistic and unrealistic solutions for complicated problems and destroying trust in every social or government institution other than the military and police."[5]

Comparing the populism of Bernie Sanders to Donald Trump's populism, Georgetown University history professor Michael Kazin told the *New Yorker* in early 2020: "Bernie's populism, of course, is left-wing populism, which speaks to or for a large majority—the 'ninety-nine per cent,' undifferentiated by race or ethnicity or national origin or religion—against the economic élite. A more right-wing populism, like Trump's, speaks to the white middle of the population against certain élites at the top, especially cultural élites and the media and former liberal governing élites."[6]

All American populist movements have been defined by their hostility toward elites, their distrust of government's relationship with business, and their anger directed against a broken system and how it disadvantages average American families. American populists for the past two centuries have been motivated by economic or social crises to wage war against the political class on behalf of the American people.

In his 2000 book, *Populism*, Paul Taggart made the case that every populist movement since the nineteenth century has had—at its core—a political, social, or economic rift. "The importance to U.S. populism of a sense of crisis has not changed," he wrote. "The particular crisis may well have changed, but the populist response has been remarkably consistent."[7] This is because crises draw public attention to the performance and failures of government. When government shortcomings draw more intense scrutiny, Taggart said populists can gather more support for their cause.

Mad as Hell says populism grows in times of crisis and that without a crisis of some sort, populism simply cannot exist. Crises that boost the growth of populism are often economic, such as the Great Depression of the 1930s and the Great Recession that hit the U.S. between 2007 and 2009. As we write this, the U.S. is immersed in the crisis of the coronavirus pandemic that has tragically killed hundreds of thousands of Americans, closed businesses and schools, and caused massive unemployment.

Reporter Marc Fisher pointed out in the *Washington Post* in February 2021: "Since ancient times, pandemics have spurred sharp turns in political beliefs, spawning extremist movements, waves of mistrust and wholesale rejection of authorities. Nearly a year into the coronavirus crisis, Americans are falling prey to the same phenomenon, historians, theologians and other experts say, exemplified by a recent NPR-Ipsos poll in which nearly 1 in 5 said they believe Satan-worshipping, child-enslaving elites seek to control the world."[8]

On top of the pandemic, the crisis of division in America is being worsened by populist former president Trump's refusal to stop his baseless claims that Democratic and Republican elites around the nation conspired to fraudulently award the presidential election to Joe Biden. The majority of Republican senators voted on February 13, 2021, to acquit Trump at his impeachment trial on a charge of inciting the insurrection at the Capitol, so although seven Republicans joined all fifty Democrats and independents in favor of conviction, Trump was found not guilty. Two-thirds of the hundred-member Senate—meaning sixty-seven senators—would have needed to vote for a conviction to return a guilty verdict. The acquittal means that unless Trump is convicted of a crime in court, he can choose to run for president again in 2024 as a candidate for the Republican nomination or as a third-party candidate—a development that would only intensify divisions among the American people.

In 2016, almost half of the electorate voted for Trump, who was described by the *Guardian* as an "archpopulist."[9] And while Trump lost his 2020 reelection bid, the 74.2 million votes he received gave him the second-highest vote total of any presidential candidate in history—topped only by Biden's 81.3 million votes.[10] Even in defeat, Trump maintains a large populist following, because he succeeded in portraying himself as the champion of the white working class. Pulling this off was a remarkable feat, since Trump was born the son of millionaire parents and is among the richest Americans. A CNBC poll taken in February 2021 showed that 89 percent of Americans without college degrees want him to remain in politics—the highest percentage of any group.[11] Many of these voters are members of the white working class that makes up a good chunk of the Republican base that fueled Trump's populist "Make America Great Again" movement.

Trump owes his remarkable rise to the Oval Office to his extraordinary talent for portraying a fictional version of himself as a populist hero, even though this bears little relationship to reality. He shot to stardom on *The Apprentice*—an unreal reality TV show—by pretending to be a brilliant businessman, and fostered the myth for decades through books ghostwritten for him, most notably *The Art of the Deal*, published in 1987. As the *New York Times* reported in October 2018: "The president has long sold himself as a self-made billionaire, but a *Times* investigation found that he received at least $413 million in today's dollars from his father's real estate empire, much of it through tax dodges in the 1990s."[12] In addition, the newspaper deflated Trump's claims in May 2019 that he was a business success.[13] The *Times* said Trump's tax records from 1985 to 1994, which it obtained, showed he reported an astounding $1.17 billion in business losses. The *Times* reported that "year after year, Mr.

Trump appears to have lost more money than nearly every other individual American taxpayer."

Of course, wealthy Democrats have been eager to cloak themselves in the populist mantle as well. Most recently, Senators Bernie Sanders and Elizabeth Warren were the two most competitive populist presidential candidates seeking the Democratic presidential nomination in 2020. Both denounced "millionaires and billionaires" with regularity on the campaign trail, and Warren promised so many times that she would "fight" for ordinary Americans that she sounded like an aspiring boxer. Yet Sanders had an estimated net worth of $3 million and Warren had an estimated net worth of $8 million in 2020, with both senators earning a big chunk of their wealth from books they wrote.[14] Populist president Franklin Delano Roosevelt—who launched Social Security, unemployment insurance, and other programs to help ordinary Americans in need—had an estimated net worth of about $67 million in 2019 dollars.[15] In fact, many presidents have been wealthy, but Trump tops the list of the richest with an estimated net worth of $2.5 billion, according to *Forbes* magazine.[16]

Sanders and Warren positioned themselves considerably to the left of Biden in the Democratic primary in 2020, just as Sanders staked a claim to the far-left lane when he ran unsuccessfully against Hillary Clinton and others for the Democratic presidential nomination in 2016. Sanders might have captured the 2020 nomination over Biden if Warren hadn't been in the race, taking away some of his supporters. If Sanders had become the Democratic nominee to challenge Trump, voters would have had to choose between a left-wing and a right-wing populist in the presidential election.

AMERICAN POPULISM'S EARLY HISTORY

Although the term "populist" didn't exist until the 1890s, Thomas Jefferson—principal author of the Declaration of Independence—arguably became our first populist president when he took office in 1801. He expressed populist sentiment when he said that "every government degenerates when trusted to the rulers of the people alone. The people themselves are its only safe depositories."[17] Additionally, Jefferson said: "I believe that banking institutions are more dangerous to our liberties than standing armies."[18] In his comments standing up for average Americans against the power of government and big banks, Jefferson clearly articulated a populist view.

The Declaration of Independence, which was primarily authored by Jefferson, can be viewed as a foundational statement of American populism, affirming the right of the people to self-government when it states: "We hold these truths to be self-evident, that all men are created equal, that they are endowed by their Creator with certain unalienable Rights, that among these are Life, Liberty and the pursuit of Happiness.—That to secure these rights, Governments are instituted among Men, deriving their just powers from the consent of the governed,—That whenever any Form of Government becomes destructive of these ends, it is the Right of the People to alter or to abolish it, and to institute new Government, laying its foundation on such principles and organizing its powers in such form, as to them shall seem most likely to effect their Safety and Happiness."[19]

Andrew Jackson, who served as president of the United States from 1829 to 1837, was another populist leader of our country. The father of the modern Democratic Party rose up against the entrenched elite—bankers, businessmen, and politicians. A hero of wars against Native American tribes and the War of 1812, he said he represented "the common man" against a "corrupt aristocracy."[20] Jackson would be called an anti-establishment candidate today. When he first ran for president in

1824 in a four-candidate race, Jackson won a plurality in the Electoral College, but fell short of the majority needed to win. The House of Representatives elected John Quincy Adams as president, even though he trailed Jackson in electoral votes, after unsuccessful candidate Henry Clay threw his support to Adams and Adams appointed Clay as secretary of state. Jackson and his supporters said he was denied the presidency because of a "corrupt bargain." Jackson's supporters then spent the next four years attacking the Adams administration as illegitimate and corrupt, and in the 1828 election Jackson easily defeated Adams. Jackson's slogan was pure populist: "Andrew Jackson and the Will of the People."[21] Donald Trump has called Jackson his "hero," and ordered a large portrait of Jackson hung prominently in the Oval Office near his desk. If Trump runs for president again in 2024, he could find inspiration from Jackson's comeback victory after losing the presidency to Adams four years earlier.

Bard College professor and *Wall Street Journal* columnist Russell Mead finds many similarities between the two populist presidents. "Trump's base remains Jacksonian," Mead told *Politico* in January 2018. "And Trump knows how to play to this base."[22] Trump "is not the second coming of Andrew Jackson," Mead added. "But there was such a hunger in America for a Jacksonian figure that people were willing to project a lot of qualities onto this sort of very unlikely Queens real estate developer who becomes the folk hero of Americans who hate New York and are suspicious of Big Business."

As the *Washington Post* pointed out: "Jackson, like Trump, was a wealthy man who gave voice to the frustrations and anger of working-class whites against moneyed interests."[23] When Trump visited Jackson's Tennessee plantation, the Hermitage, on the 250th anniversary of Jackson's birth, he said, "I'm a fan.... They say my election was most similar to his." A month later Trump said: "Andrew Jackson had a great history." Presidents James K. Polk, Franklin Pierce, and Abraham Lincoln also compared themselves to Jackson. And when populist president Franklin Roosevelt visited the Hermitage during the Great Depression, he said: "The more I learn about old Andy Jackson, the more I love him." Writing in the *Wall Street Journal*, Michael Barone said: "Jackson was not a 'spread the wealth' populist. On the contrary, he opposed the American System of John Quincy Adams and Henry Clay to have the government build roads and canals and other public works. He killed the central bank and paid off the national debt. Jackson argued that government interference in the economy would inevitably favor the well-entrenched and well-connected. It would take money away from the little people and give it to the elites."[24] The distrust of elites and big government has been a consistent quality of populist uprisings ever since.

Decades after Jackson, another leading American populist was William Jennings Bryan—the Democratic presidential nominee for president in 1896, 1900, and 1908. He preached the expansion of the monetary base to relieve Western farmers overburdened with debt from East Coast bankers. Bryan came to prominence as a young legislator riding the Free Silver wave of the late nineteenth century. The movement was precipitated by an act of Congress that said U.S. currency had to be backed by gold and could not be backed by silver—effectively shrinking the monetary base. Free Silver was a call for the reauthorization of the silver dollar. The opponents of Free Silver argued that silver currency would debase the dollar, which was pegged to the price of gold, and cause inflation. Out of context, the movement seems like an oddly specific economic disagreement to gain such popular support. However, because inflation essentially lightens the burden of debt, Free Silver represented the struggle between heavily indebted farmers and the wealthy East Coast bankers who were their creditors.

This movement attracted populists like Bryan, who denounced the business elite's treatment of ordinary Americans. A Populist Party was even created, and reached national recognition in the 1880s. In the 1890s, the United States was in the deep pit of an economic recession, and as usual, the crisis hit average Americans hardest. Bryan's message at the 1896 Democratic National Convention, which nominated him for president for the first time, became his most famous oration, known as the "Cross of Gold" speech.[25] It resonated with millions of hardworking and struggling Americans who believed they had been cheated by the elite. The speech had a distinctly populist message, saying that Americans with modest incomes were as important as the wealthy elite.

Bryan said in the speech: "The man who is employed for wages is as much a business man as his employer; the attorney in a country town is as much a business man as the corporation counsel in a great metropolis; the merchant at the cross-roads store is as much a business man as the merchant of New York; the farmer who goes forth in the morning and toils all day—who begins in the spring and toils all summer—and who by the application of brain and muscle to the natural resources of the country creates wealth, is as much a business man as the man who goes upon the board of trade and bets upon the price of grain; the miners who go down a thousand feet into the earth, or climb two thousand feet upon the cliffs, and bring forth from their hiding places the precious metals to be poured into the channels of trade are as much business men as the few financial magnates who, in a back room, corner the money of the world. We come to speak for this broader class of business men....What we need is an Andrew Jackson to stand as Jackson stood, against the encroachments of aggregated wealth."[26] Bryan concluded by saying, "You come to us and tell us that the great cities are in favor of the gold standard; we reply that the great cities rest upon our broad and fertile prairies. Burn down your cities and leave our farms, and your cities will spring up again as if by magic; but destroy our farms and the grass will grow in the streets of every city in the country.... You shall not press down upon the brow of labor this crown of thorns, you shall not crucify mankind upon a cross of gold."

While he never made it to the White House, Bryan's populism had an enormous impact on American politics and government by getting some populist ideas accepted as mainstream. For example, he successfully advocated for giving women the right to vote, the election of senators by citizens rather than by state legislatures, the eight-hour workday, creation of a graduated federal income tax, outlawing alcoholic beverages in what became known as Prohibition, and the creation of the U.S. Labor Department.[27] Even Republican president Theodore Roosevelt adopted some of Bryan's populist proposals. When Bryan helped Woodrow Wilson win the presidency in 1912, the new president named him secretary of state. Bryan helped win enactment of populist reforms at home and worked to keep the U.S. neutral in World War I. He resigned in 1915 to protest Wilson's actions favoring Britain and France in the conflict.

Bryan's influence continues to this day. "[Bernie] Sanders's most obvious antecedent was William Jennings Bryan," then-Fox News politics editor Chris Stirewalt wrote in February 2020, adding that "Sanders' secular religious zeal was nothing compared to Bryan's brand of Christian radicalism."[28] But neither Bryan nor Sanders ever became president, because their populism remained too far left to win a national election. Trump has also been compared to Bryan many times. Writing in the *New York Daily News* shortly after Trump was elected president in 2016, Woodrow Wilson National Fellowship Foundation President Arthur Levine said Bryan advocated an impossible dream: turning back the clock to an America centered on a farm-based economy at a time when the U.S. was becoming an industrial nation. Levine called Trump "the contemporary Bryan" who wanted to turn back the clock on the "economic, demographic, technological, and global transformation" that is changing the U.S. from an industrial economy into a digital information economy where Whites will no longer make up a majority of the population. "The problem is that, no matter how much we may want it, it's impossible to restore the past," Levine added. "That only happens in movies, novels, and at Disneyland."[29]

FROM THE DEPRESSION THROUGH THE 1970S

The Great Depression, which began with the stock market crash in October 1929, sparked the next populist wave. Soaring unemployment, and huge drops in business profits and tax collections, sent the U.S. economy and economies around the world into a tailspin. New York Democratic governor Franklin Delano Roosevelt easily defeated Republican president Herbert Hoover in the 1932 presidential election with a mandate from voters to take dramatic action to spark an economic recovery. FDR famously championed "the common man" against the financial and business elite, who he blamed for plunging the world into the Depression.

Roosevelt's rhetoric was as anti-elite and populist as any president. He denounced greedy "economic royalists" and said he was opposed by "business and financial monopoly, speculation, reckless banking, class antagonism, sectionalism, war profiteering.... Never before in all of our history have these forces been so united against one candidate as they stand today. They are unanimous in their hate for me, and I welcome their hatred."[30] Roosevelt launched the era of Big Government and created the social safety net of unemployment insurance, Social Security, and other programs, as we have discussed earlier.

Huey Long, who served as Louisiana's Democratic governor from 1928 to 1932 and then as a U.S. senator until he was assassinated in 1935, embraced more extreme populism than Roosevelt and was denounced by his critics as a demagogue and would-be dictator. He favored big increases in federal spending to stimulate the economy, a wealth tax, and wealth redistribution. Like Roosevelt, Long gained popular acclaim by his adept use of nationwide radio, a democratizing force and the most advanced form of instant communication at the time. He frequently criticized Roosevelt's New Deal as not progressive enough, and was preparing to run for the presidency as an independent in the 1936 election when he was shot to death. The *Atlantic* compared Long to Donald

Trump in a 2018 article headlined "When Demagogic Populism Swings Left."[31]

In the *Atlantic* article, Annika Neklason wrote: ". . . Long has one notable modern counterpart: Donald Trump. . . . Both men rose to national political prominence in the aftermath of a global financial crisis, with ethnic violence on the rise, automation putting workers' jobs in doubt, and autocratic leaders gaining political power worldwide. . . . And both, once in power, showed little concern for norms and standard legislative procedures when pursuing their goals."

Unlike William Jennings Bryan, Franklin Roosevelt and Huey Long were devoted to a set of policies. Bryan's policy platform did not define his political appeal as much as his anger against the elite and support of the common man. Bryan took advantage of populist fervor wherever it existed. At the start of his career, he rode the momentum of popular support from the Free Silver movement. When consensus was eventually reached in support of the gold standard for U.S. currency, Bryan abandoned Free Silver for the anti-imperialist movement, which gained widespread popular support in the early 1900s before World War I. Roosevelt and Long helped to define liberal populism in a way that still holds to this day. Like conservative populism, liberal populism blamed government for failing to protect the people's interests. However, where American right-wing populism views government as the inherent enemy of individualism and personal autonomy, left-wing populism attributes government's failures to powerful corporate and Wall Street elites who have hijacked government for their own personal gain.

All left-wing populists since Roosevelt and Long have supported a fundamental alteration of traditional capitalism to give the federal government greater control over the private sector and financial markets. These proposals, plus aggressive action against climate change, were embraced by all the major candidates seeking the 2020 Democratic presidential nomination. Bernie Sanders and Elizabeth Warren took positions on the most extreme left side of the group. Joe Biden and Michael Bloomberg campaigned as the major centrist candidates in the race. Biden won the party's nomination by presenting himself as the candidate best able to defeat Trump, while characterizing Sanders and Warren as too far left to win in the general election.

Right-wing populism developed decades after the left-wing variety. Senator Joseph McCarthy (R-WI) "proved to be the most dangerous populist demagogue of the twentieth century," University of Oklahoma history professor Steven M. Gillon wrote in an essay for History.com in 2019.[32] McCarthy used fear of communism to launch a witch hunt for communists in government beginning in 1950, highlighted by false claims and accusations that many Communist Party members were working in policymaking positions in the U.S. government. At the time, Americans were fearful of the rising tide of communism abroad. The end of World War II was followed in 1949 by the Soviet Union developing an atomic bomb and a communist victory in the Chinese Civil War. Soviet-backed communist North Korea invaded South Korea to launch the Korean War and American troops battled with allied nations to defend the South. Given these development, many Americans believed McCarthy. As chairman of the Senate Government Operations Committee, McCarthy held hearings to investigate supposed infiltration of government by communists and homosexuals, denouncing "egg-sucking phony liberals" for defending "communists and queers." Over 2,000 government employees lost their jobs because of McCarthy's investigations, which finally ended after his televised hearings investigating his claims of communists in the U.S. Army turned public opinion against him. The Senate censured him in 1955 for "inexcusable," "reprehensible," "vulgar and insulting" conduct "unbecoming a senator."[33]

In 1964, conservative senator Barry Goldwater (R-AZ) became the GOP presidential nominee by staging what amounted to a hostile far-right populist takeover of the Republican Party, trouncing the moderate wing led by New York governor Nelson Rockefeller. In addition to his moderate-to-liberal positions, a big obstacle for Rockefeller in competing against Goldwater was that Rockefeller was divorced and had remarried—a common occurrence today, but frowned upon by many conservative Republicans at the time.

According to Geoffrey Kabaservice, there were many similarities between Goldwater and Trump. "After presiding over a divided party convention, the prickly and headstrong Goldwater refused to pivot toward a more measured, level-headed 'presidential' posture," Kabaservice wrote in the *Guardian*."[34] Democratic president Lyndon Johnson portrayed Goldwater as a dangerous extremist who might lead the U.S. into a nuclear war, and defeated Goldwater in a landslide. Similarly, Democrats characterized Trump a dangerous extremist when running against him in 2016 and again in 2020 when Biden defeated him.

Another prominent populist politician was George Wallace, who became the voice of disaffected, segregationist Whites in the South. He was elected four times as a Democrat to serve as governor of Alabama in the 1960s, 1970s, and 1980s.[35] Wallace won national notoriety for a line in his 1963 inaugural address, saying he stood for "segregation now, segregation tomorrow, segregation forever." And in 1963 he tried to stop Black students Vivian Malone and James Hood from integrating the University of Alabama by standing in the doorway of an auditorium of the university to prevent the two from registering for classes. He finally stepped aside when ordered to do so by a general in the Alabama National Guard, which had been federalized by President John F. Kennedy.

Wallace ran unsuccessfully for the Democratic presidential nomination three times and ran in 1968 as the presidential candidate of the American Independent Party, winning 13.5 percent of the popular vote and carrying five southern states with 46 electoral votes. He came in third behind the victorious Republican candidate, Richard Nixon, and Democratic vice president Hubert Humphrey. Wallace knew he couldn't win, but hoped to throw the election to the House of Representatives by blocking Nixon and Humphrey from gaining an Electoral College majority and then bargaining to give his support to the candidate who would back off desegregation enforcement. Significantly, Wallace's strong performance as a third-party candidate helped convince Republicans to mount more aggressive efforts to win the support of working-class White voters, leading most southern states to move from the Democratic to the Republican column in subsequent elections. In fact, many Democratic elected officials became Republicans as a result of this party realignment.

Wallace made his last try for the White House in 1972, seeking the Democratic presidential nomination. But an assassination attempt left him paralyzed from the waist down. In his last race for governor in 1982, he said he had been wrong to support segregation and was elected with the support of Black voters, organized labor, and others. "We thought [segregation] was in the best interests of all concerned. We were mistaken," Wallace said. "The Old South is gone" but "the New South is still opposed to government regulation of our lives."[36] Wallace was still a populist, minus his past racism.

Right-wing populism also had a big impact in California in the 1970s, when 65 percent of state voters approved the anti-tax Proposition 13 in 1978.[37] The amendment to the California Constitution put new limits on property taxes that resulted in tax collections dropping by billions of dollars a year. Proposition 13 also said the California state legislature and local governments couldn't raise certain tax rates without the approval of a two-thirds majority of voters, rather than a simple majority. Subsequent efforts to modify Proposition 13 have failed at the ballot box, most recently in 2020.[38]

Looking back at the 1978 Proposition 13 approval in an article in August 2019, *Los Angeles Times* reporter John Myers wrote that it was "a primal scream from angry voters and became a symbol of their reluctance to pay more money for more government services."[39] Writing in the *New York Times*, Clyde Haberman said in October 2016: "In between

America's two most famous tea parties, the Boston affair in 1773 and the protest movement that arose in 2009, there was a referendum known as Proposition 13. Like the tea parties, it was rooted in an abhorrence of taxation (with or without representation). Like them, too, it had enduring consequences....For better or for worse, Proposition 13 inspired tax revolts in other states. In its wake, anti-tax firebrands rose to prominence."[40] Ronald Reagan, a former actor who served as California's governor from 1967 to 1975, jumped on the tax revolt bandwagon and rode it all the way to the White House.

LATE-TWENTIETH-CENTURY POPULISM

Ronald Reagan was a transformational populist president during his years in the White House from 1981 to 1989.[41] He cast himself as the champion of ordinary Americans by fighting to make government smaller rather than bigger, and by cutting federal regulations and taxes. This was a dramatic reversal from the expansion of government that had taken place since the days of President Franklin Roosevelt. Reagan's anti-government rhetoric laid the foundation for the Tea Party movement decades later. The small-government low-tax movement (discussed later in this chapter) paved the way for Donald Trump's election as president in 2016. However, Reagan's tax cuts helped increase the national debt by $1.85 trillion—a 186 percent increase.[42] That amount would be $3.9 trillion in 2021, adjusted for inflation.

Reagan was the heir to many of Barry Goldwater's policies and pushed the Republican Party to the right, diminishing the influence of moderate Republicans. What was termed the "Reagan Revolution" pushed some Democrats further to the left in response to Reagan's conservative policies, while others tried to move to the center. Because he was a former film and TV actor, Reagan was comfortable in front of the camera, came off as warm and friendly, and was able to stick to a script in speeches, giving him an appeal to independents and some moderate Democrats. He also surrounded himself with an excellent White House staff and had the discipline to follow good advice. This no doubt contributed to Reagan's success and landslide reelection victory in 1984, when he captured 59 percent of the popular vote and defeated former vice president Walter Mondale by a stunning Electoral College vote of 525–13. Democrat Mondale carried only his home state of Minnesota and the overwhelmingly Democratic District of Columbia.

In the 1992 presidential election, independent candidate and billionaire businessman H. Ross Perot seized the populist mantle, sharply criticizing the federal government and both Republican and Democratic politicians, saying they had failed the American people. He was unconventional and said that as an outsider he could reform the political system and make the government work for ordinary Americans. In many ways, he was a precursor to both the Tea Party and to Donald Trump. "Perot followed the populist model set down by William Jennings Bryan in his (unsuccessful) campaigns for the presidency in 1896, 1900, and 1908," Suzanne McGee wrote in an article for History.com in October 2020.[43] "Like Bryan, Perot reached out to working-class and middle-class Americans who felt ignored by the political establishments within both parties....Perot's insistence on 'taking the country back' and voters behaving like 'the owners of this country' brought a new sense of empowerment to Americans."

In his campaign, Perot espoused some liberal and some conservative positions. He favored the virtues of a small government, a balanced budget, a free market, higher taxes on the wealthy, protectionist trade policies, and social programs to benefit disadvantaged children. He said Americans would be better off by reducing the power and abuses of government. Perot's message included familiar mantras later embraced by Trump: a distrust of the elite (although he and Trump were both members), a denunciation of the failure of government to represent the average American, and a repudiation of the political class as out of touch with mainstream America. While Perot didn't use Trump's slogan of "drain the swamp" of Washington corruption, he expressed the same sentiment.

Perot won 19 percent of the popular vote (but no electoral votes) in the 1992 presidential election—more than any third party or independent candidate since Theodore Roosevelt in 1912. Republican president George H. W. Bush lost support because a recession was underway and because he broke his 1988 pledge of "read my lips, no new taxes" and raised taxes anyway. Bill Clinton won by positioning himself as a centrist New Democrat, capturing 43 percent of the popular vote and 370 electoral votes, to Bush's 37 percent of the popular vote and 168 electoral votes. Perot ran for president again in 1996 but performed poorly, capturing only 8 percent of the popular vote and again winning no electoral votes. The Perot movement had two major and immediate consequences on American politics, as both parties clamored to win the support of his constituency. On the left, President Clinton moved to the center and achieved Perot's goal of balancing the federal budget. On the right, Republicans won majority control of the U.S. House and Senate in the 1994 midterm elections with the help of their populist Contract with America, which embraced some of Perot's positions.

Then–House Minority Whip Newt Gingrich (R-GA) and Representative Dick Armey (R-TX) crafted the Contract with America as a campaign document saying what Republicans would do if they took majority control of both houses of Congress for the first time in four decades.[44] The ideas—including a balanced budget amendment to the Constitution, tax cuts, welfare reform, and changes in how government operates—came from the conservative Heritage Foundation think tank and from President Reagan's 1985 State of the Union Address and were selected because a majority of Americans polled favored them. All but two Republican House members and every other GOP congressional candidate signed the contract. Republicans gained fifty-four House seats and eight Senate seats in the election, and Gingrich became Speaker of the House. Republicans also made gains in governorships and state legislatures in what became known as the Republican Revolution.

The Contract with America was the most widely supported platform of populist ideals that the political elite had ever promised. In a larger sense, it represented a rethinking of the role of government in people's lives. It was essentially a new social contract in which ordinary Americans were put in the driver's seat and every GOP member of Congress was accountable to them. This was an exciting moment for the many Americans who were disillusioned with our government. Republicans were unable to enact all of the contract over opposition from Democrats and President Clinton. But they won approval for enough significant changes to move the U.S. to the right.

Gingrich "embraced the idea that voters want something to vote *for*, not simply a reason to vote against the other candidate or party," David Winston, the president of a strategic planning and survey research firm and former Gingrich staffer, wrote in 2014 in The Ripon Forum.[45] "The Contract was more doctrine than a communications message. It offered voters change that could actually happen and would work. It was a realistic, doable political document that served as an organizing principle for a radical change in campaign strategy." Writing in the Capitol Hill newspaper *Roll Call* in 2019, Winston said: "Gingrich was one of those rare political leaders whose vision and strength of personality could change not only the course of a nation but the lives of its people in direct and positive ways.... In their first two years, Republicans slowed the expansion of government and Clinton in his 1996 State of the Union famously acknowledged, 'The era of big government is over.' It was a remarkable moment for Gingrich and his caucus, leaving many in the press to comment that Clinton sounded more like a Republican."[46]

However, Winston wrote that House Republicans made a grave error in 1998 when instead of "running on this remarkable success" they focused attention on Clinton's sex life. They impeached Clinton for lying under oath and obstruction of justice in connection with a sexual harassment lawsuit filed against him by one woman and for lying about his sexual relationship with a White House intern. Instead of gaining twenty to thirty House seats as had been expected, Republicans lost five seats, because most voters opposed impeachment. With some Republicans seeking to replace him as Speaker, Gingrich resigned his House seat.

TWENTY-FIRST-CENTURY POPULISM

A common theme of both left-wing and right-wing populism is disillusionment with government, corporations, the media, the education system, and other institutions run by the elite. While the two branches of populism have very different sets of complaints, their decades-long drumbeat of grievances has contributed to growing divisions between Americans and a loss of faith by millions of people in our democratic system.

Over the course of American history, the populists we have discussed in this chapter—along with others—have all amplified the voices of citizens who feel shortchanged. The challenge our democracy faces today is to convince the American people that they can influence our institutions at the ballot box and within the system, rather than by turning to lawbreaking and violence. When people believe democracy no longer works to bring about change, we see dangerous developments like the insurrection at the Capitol.

To better understand the current state of the populist uproar, we must understand how it exploded on both sides of the ideological spectrum in 2010. In that year the Tea Party and the Occupy Wall Street movement gained national support as non-systemic alternatives to our established political, social, and economic system. Although both movements eventually petered out, the populist fervor they sparked continues. The Tea Party movement and Donald Trump drove right-wing populism in the second decade of the twenty-first century, aided by conservative media like Fox News and its more extreme TV and radio imitators, along with conspiracy groups like QAnon and those representing White nationalists. Left-wing populism was driven by Democratic elected officials and movements such as Occupy Wall Street, Black Lives Matter, and the loose coalition known as Antifa. The relationship between today's populist revolt and the movements of 2010 is similar to how World War II was a continuation of World War I with a "time-out" in the interwar period. Although each populist movement was different in its platform and message, they must be viewed as different manifestations of the same sentiments.

While the populist revolts that began in 2010 were deeply rooted in American history, their strongest trigger was the global financial crisis that set off the Great Recession, which hit the U.S. economy and economies around the world from 2007 through 2009 and continued to impact nations for years beyond. As we have learned from the past, economic crises result in a rise in extremism and populist movements that blame the elite for causing the crises. This happened once again after the Great Recession, which was sparked by a sharp drop in housing prices in the U.S. after years of rapid increases.

When the housing bubble burst it caused the value of home mortgage–backed securities to fall and sent shockwaves through Wall Street.[47] Financial markets were shaken further when Lehman Brothers, then the fourth-largest investment bank in the U.S., declared bankruptcy in September 2008. The Dow Jones Industrial Average dropped 4.5 percent in one day and in eighteen months it lost more than half its value, triggering massive losses for investors. Millions of Americans saw the value of their homes fall below what they owed on their mortgages. MarketWatch reported that 6.3 million families lost their homes to foreclosures from January 2006 to April 2016.[48]

The Great Recession sent unemployment soaring, doubling from 5 percent in December 2007 to a peak of 10 percent in October 2009, according to the U.S. Bureau of Labor Statistics.[49] The Census Bureau recorded 46.2 million Americans living in poverty, more than ever before.[50] Low- and moderate-income families were hit hardest. President George W. Bush signed the Economic Stimulus Act into law in February 2008 to give taxpayers rebates of $600 to $1,200, cut taxes, and increase loan limits for federally backed home mortgages. But that legislation didn't provide enough relief for hard-hit families.

With major banks and industries teetering on the edge of going out of business, Bush signed the Troubled Asset Relief Program (TARP) into law in October 2008, allocating $700 billion in federal funds to buy the assets of companies to keep them from shuttering. Adding to the TARP cash infusion, President Obama signed a $787 billion stimulus package into law soon after taking office in January 2009 that cut taxes further and funded new spending on infrastructure and other projects.[51] TARP and other measures that saved giant banks and corporations deemed "too big to fail" proved to be unpopular with average Americans, who often felt the government did not do enough to help them. A Reuters-Ipsos poll taken in 2013 found that "as many as 44 percent of those polled believe the government should not have bailed out financial institutions, while only 22 percent thought it was the right move. Fifty-three percent think not enough was done to prosecute bankers; 15 percent were satisfied with the effort," Reuters reported.[52]

There can be no question that the government bailouts—no matter how beneficial they were in preventing an even worse economic crisis and massive job losses—were the spark that lit the fuse of populist explosions that have erupted in subsequent years. While past populist movements have been on either the left or right, the new populism erupted on the right with the Tea Party and on the left with Occupy Wall Street at the same time. Writing in the *Financial Times* in August 2018 about the economic crash caused by the Great Recession, Philip Stephens said: "After a decade of stagnant incomes and fiscal austerity, no one can be surprised that those most hurt by the crash's economic consequences are supporting populist uprisings against elites."[53]

New York Times columnist Ross Douthat expressed a similar view years earlier in October 2010, writing: "Nothing in this election season, no program or party or politician, is less popular than the Troubled Asset Relief Program of 2008.... It was TARP that first turned Tea Partiers against Republican incumbents, and independents against Washington. It was TARP that steadily undermined Barack Obama's agenda, by making activist government seem like a game rigged to benefit privileged insiders."[54]

We'll never know if Donald Trump, Bernie Sanders, Elizabeth Warren, Alexandria Ocasio-Cortez, and other populists on the right and left would have amassed as much popular support as they did if not for the chain of events triggered by the financial crisis and the Great Recession. But all of the populists clearly used the loss of faith in our system of government created by the economic turmoil to fuel their rise.

THE TEA PARTY

There have been protests against taxation in America going back to colonial times. The most famous early protest took place on December 16, 1773, when American colonists angered by a tea tax imposed by the British Parliament (where the colonies had no representation) boarded three ships in Boston Harbor and dumped 342 chests of tea from the British East India Company into the frigid waters. The protest against "taxation without representation" has gone down in history as an important precursor to the American Revolution, where the colonies broke free of a government headed by a remote king and an elite ruling class, and created the democracy we are still fortunate to have today.[55]

Fast-forward almost 236 years to February 19, 2009. Republicans were complaining about President Obama's bailout plan to deal with the financial crisis that began near the end of President George W. Bush's term. A portion of the bailout, called the Homeowners Affordability and

Stability Plan, set aside $75 billion to help up to 9 million homeowners avoid foreclosure when they were unable to make their mortgage payments. Speaking from the floor of the Chicago Mercantile Exchange, CNBC commentator Rick Santelli said homeowners who were unable to make payments on high-risk mortgages were "losers" and attacked the Obama administration for wanting to help them avert losing their homes.

"The government is promoting bad behavior....I have an idea," Santelli said, shouting during a live-shot on the business network. "The new administration's big on computers and technology. How about this, president and new administration: Why don't you put up a website to have people vote on the internet as a referendum to see if we really want to subsidize the losers' mortgages? . . . President Obama, are you listening? . . . We're thinking of having a Chicago tea party in July, all you capitalists that want to come to Lake Michigan, I'm going to start organizing!"[56] Traders standing near Santelli cheered. His angry diatribe made news. Conservatives were already upset at Obama's bailout plan, and soon groups adopted the Tea Party name (later said to stand for Taxed Enough Already) and began organizing protests that spread like wildfire.[57]

The Tea Party wasn't an actual political party. It was a populist movement of people who believed government was too big and spent too much, collected too much in taxes, and imposed too many regulations on businesses, organizations, and individuals. Many people who joined Tea Party groups were owners of small businesses struggling to make a profit after spending much of their earnings on taxes and to comply with government regulations. The movement supported free markets, and wanted to end deficit spending and pay off the national debt. The Tea Party strongly opposed President Obama and his Affordable Care Act (better known as Obamacare), which congressional Democrats approved over strong Republican opposition. "The Tea Party reflects the values of Andrew Jackson: self-reliance, individualism, loyalty, and courage. Followers are suspicious of federal power, which is why they're such avid supporters of the Second Amendment," Kimberly Amadeo wrote in The Balance in December 2020. "They . . . [are] anti-elitist. They believe ordinary people are wiser than the experts and that seemingly complicated problems have simple solutions."[58]

The positions embraced by the Tea Party were, above all, manifestations of what its supporters abhorred most of all: Washington's unresponsiveness to their needs and desires. Describing the early days of the Tea Party, reporter Jeremy Peters wrote in the *New York Times* in August 2019: "Lawmakers accustomed to scheduling town hall meetings where no one would show up suddenly faced shouting crowds of hundreds, some of whom brought a holstered pistol or a rifle slung over the shoulder. One demonstrator at a rally in Maryland hanged a member of Congress in effigy. A popular bumper sticker at the time captured the contempt for the federal bailout of certain homeowners. 'Honk if I'm Paying Your Mortgage,' it said."[59]

The loss of faith in government expressed by Tea Party supporters was a widely held view among the American public, pollsters found. In an article in the *Christian Science Monitor* in April 2010, reporter Patrik Jonsson wrote: "A Pew poll in early March found 71 percent of Americans 'dissatisfied with the way things are going in the country today,' while a CNN poll showed that 56 percent of Americans are more than just discontented with Washington. Instead, that majority of respondents agreed that the government is 'so large and powerful that it poses an immediate threat to rights and freedoms of ordinary citizens.'"[60]

In a 2011 poll, Scott Rasmussen found that 45 percent of voters agreed with the statement: "The gap between Americans who want to govern themselves and politicians who want to rule over them is now as big as the gap between the American colonies and England during the eighteenth century." Of participants who identified themselves as supporters of the Tea Party, 84 percent agreed with the statement.[61] At one point in 2010, more voters said they aligned themselves with the Tea Party movement than either the Republican or Democratic Parties. The national breakdown of the Tea Party composition was 57 percent Republicans, 28 percent independents, and 13 percent Democrats, according to three national polls conducted by the Winston Group in 2010.[62] With such a composition, it is clear that the movement wasn't purely political. It was a response to an overwhelming frustration with government by millions of Americans with differing political loyalties.

At a Tea Party rally that coauthor Schoen attended in 2010, several attendees said they felt betrayed by President Obama. In the 2008 presidential election, Obama campaigned on two slogans: "Hope" and "Change We Can Believe in."[63] When Obama made it to the White House and Democrats captured control of the House and Senate, many people had high, unrealistic, and contradictory expectations about great things he would do to dramatically transform American society. Inevitably, complaints arose when Obama fell short. Some complaints focused on his bailout legislation in response to the financial crisis and the Great Recession, with critics saying he was doing too much to funnel assistance to Wall Street and big corporations and not enough for ordinary citizens. Other criticism focused on the Affordable Care Act, which some critics labeled "socialized medicine" that would reduce the quality of health care available to Americans.

By 2010, the Tea Party's meteoric growth made it arguably the most powerful movement in American politics. Some Republican candidates and members of Congress, along with candidates for state offices, said they were supporters of the movement. At its height, the Tea Party Caucus in the House had sixty members, and ten senators identified as Tea Party supporters. But rather than acknowledging the power of the Tea Party movement and attempting to reach agreement with its adherents on issues, most Democrats and much of the media consistently painted the movement as a radical fringe protest group.

Although Democrats incensed Tea Party supporters by denouncing them, many Republicans in Congress who said they supported the movement fundamentally misunderstood its purpose. The main impetus of the revolt was not specific policy platforms and fiscal responsibility. Such things could never sustain such an emotionally charged movement. The anger behind the Tea Party was directed at the inefficiency of government and the lack of representation that everyday Americans had felt for decades. While many congressional Republicans called for the tax and spending cuts supported by the Tea Party, they were so averse to compromise with Democrats that they only worsened the problem of government gridlock and made government more dysfunctional. This further angered Tea Party supporters.

In an essay published in the *National Review* in February 2021, Mario Loyola commented on the problems caused by Republican Tea Party supporters in Congress who made ideological purity a higher priority than passing legislation. "When I was on Senate staff in the final years of the Bush administration, a faction of die-hard ideological conservatives—soon to be known as the 'Tea Party'—had coalesced around Senators Jim DeMint of South Carolina and Tom Coburn of Oklahoma," Loyola wrote. "I called them the 'Alamo faction,' because they would rather go down in glorious defeat than compromise on any of their principles."[64] "Loyola . . . went on to criticize both the right and left for refusing to compromise and said this would lead more Americans to lose faith in our democratic system of government."

In earlier years, populist movements like the Tea Party prompted Congress and the president to implement small but real changes in the direction of government accountability and transparency. By failing to bridge their divisions to do this, Democrats and Republicans weakened public faith in our democratic system and worsened the divide between Americans on the right and left. In *Mad as Hell*, coauthors Rasmussen and Schoen suggested that the Tea Party could elect a president in the following decade.[65] It didn't take that long. Donald Trump seized the populist mantle of the angry outsider who could fix the broken and unresponsive government that sparked the creation of the Tea Party movement.

"Nobody knows the system better than me, which is why I alone can fix it," Trump said in his speech accepting the nomination for president at the Republican National Convention in July 2016. He added that "the problems we face now—poverty and violence at home, war and destruction abroad—will last only as long as we continue relying on the same politicians who created them in the first place."[66] Continuing to emphasize his populist stance advocating for the average American, Trump added: "Big business, elite media, and major donors are lining up behind the campaign of my opponent because they know she will keep our rigged system in place. They are throwing money at her because they have total control over everything she does. She is their puppet, and they pull the strings. That is why Hillary Clinton's message is that things will never change. My message is that things have to change—and they have to change right now. Every day I wake up determined to deliver a better life for the people all across this nation that have been ignored, neglected, and abandoned."

In the 2016 election, much of the Tea Party transformed into Trump's loyal base. Although we can never prove it, we postulate over 70 to 80 percent of the original Tea Party constituency voted for Trump, because his message and his personality perfectly captured the anger and sentiment of the movement. Today the Tea Party has faded in importance, transforming in many ways into the Trump Party, with supporters reorienting their goals to embrace the goals of the now-former president. As Jeremy Peters wrote in the *New York Times* in August 2019, "The ideas that animated the Tea Party movement have been largely abandoned by Republicans under President Trump . . . because after winning the White House in 2016, Republicans did what politicians have always done when they have the unlimited checkbook of the United States government. They spend, and voters are largely fine with it."[67]

Trump saw the populist wave of the Tea Party sweeping across America and cleverly rode it all the way to the White House in 2016, capturing the support of many voters in traditional Democratic constituencies. But his failure to deliver on all his promises cost him the support of voters outside his base in 2020, enabling Joe Biden to be elected president. A big part of the battle to win majority control of the House and Senate in 2022 and the White House in 2024 will center on which party and which candidates can lay claim to the populist cause and win the lion's share of votes from Americans who have lost faith in our democratic system.

OCCUPY WALL STREET

Just as the Tea Party set the stage for the right-wing populism epitomized by Donald Trump, the Occupy Wall Street movement that began in September 2011 was clearly the precursor to the far-left populism of Bernie Sanders, Elizabeth Warren, Alexandria Ocasio-Cortez, and others. The slogan of the Occupy movement was "We are the 99 percent," protesting the economic inequality that resulted in the concentration of wealth in the richest 1 percent of Americans while millions of Americans struggled to put food on the table and keep a roof over their heads.

The seeds of the Occupy movement were planted on July 13, 2011, when the radical Canadian magazine *Adbusters* called for an occupation starting September 17 (Constitution Day in the U.S.), "where 20,000 people flood into lower Manhattan, set up tents, kitchens, peaceful barricades, and occupy Wall Street for a few months."[68] In addition to posting this seemingly absurd proposal on its website, the magazine sent it to its email list. And then, amazingly, the idea went viral, with word spreading around the world via the internet and stories in the media.

The man behind the Occupy Wall Street campaign was Kalle Lasn, who fled the advancing Soviet Army when it entered his native Estonia as a young boy with his parents near the end of World War II. He spent a few years in German resettlement camps, grew up in Australia, and after graduating from college went to work for the Australian military writing computer code for war games. He then launched a market research firm in Japan and was radicalized on a trip to France by a left-wing student uprising in Paris in 1968.[69] Embracing radical politics, Lasn moved to Vancouver in Canada and founded *Adbusters*. The magazine attacked capitalism, global corporations, and consumerism, and worked to combat climate change. Inspired by the Arab Spring uprisings that overthrew governments in Egypt, Libya, Tunisia, and Yemen, Lasn said he came up with the idea of Occupy Wall Street with the goal of "achieving a soft regime change in the United States, of finding some way to tap into the revolutionary zeitgeist."

On September 17, 2011, about a thousand protesters gathered in Zuccotti Park in lower Manhattan and marched on Wall Street. In the next few days, Occupy movements spread to Chicago and San Francisco, where protesters marched on Federal Reserve Bank offices. More than 5,000 protesters staged a march October 1 in New York City and about 15,000 marched on the financial district there on October 5.[70] The protesters, whose huge numbers surprised even the organizers, camped out in the Zuccotti Park for seven weeks until they were eventually evicted in November. The Occupy movement gained national and international attention at lightning speed. Less than three weeks after the first protest was called, similar Occupy protests had popped up in 950 cities worldwide. Celebrities expressed their support for the movement. Occupiers began sit-ins in corporate headquarters, bank lobbies, other businesses, and universities. The protests were amplified with heavy media coverage.

Going well beyond the left-wing populist platforms of Huey Long, Franklin Roosevelt, and other Democrats, the Occupy movement called for dramatic wealth redistribution. It endorsed socialized medicine and drastic action against climate change. Much like the Tea Party, the supporters of the Occupy movement were disgusted and fed up with the relationship between corporations, banks, and the federal government. Like earlier left-wing populist movements, Occupy Wall Street favored expanding government to achieve its goals. But rather than expanding the existing government, many supporters of the movement wanted to replace the existing government with something revolutionary and new, because they had lost faith in the government and existing two-party system.

"Occupiers were angry at the state of the world in the wake of the 2008 financial crisis," Emily Stewart wrote in *Vox* in April 2019.[71] "They rejected the deep inequalities that capitalism had fostered....Occupy was the birthplace of some left-wing ideas that have gained mainstream traction....It animated the rise of Sen. Bernie Sanders (I-VT) ... and it is in ways responsible for some of the most prominent ideas in the Democratic Party right now."

The Achilles' heel of the Occupy movement was that it lacked a national leader and institutional structure. Occupy groups in different cities each headed in their own direction, operating like communes based on the consensus of members. Much of their time and energy was devoted to running their own encampments at the sites they occupied rather than to broader national policy goals. On top of this, many occupiers had not only lost faith in America's leaders, but in the idea of representative government itself. As a result, Occupy did not align itself with the Democratic Party in the same way the Tea Party aligned itself with the Republican Party.

While Occupy had the broad objectives discussed above, it did not have a detailed list of specific actions it wanted government to take and did not endorse candidates for elected office or deliver campaign contributions. As a result, while the Occupy movement had lasting influence on pushing Democrats leftward, it soon faded as a distinct organization. However, many supporters decided to work within the system and paved the way for present-day progressivism. Bernie Sanders, Elizabeth Warren, and other far left Democrats benefited from the backing of Occupy supporters.

THE FUTURE OF POPULISM

Since the rise of the Tea Party and the Occupy movements, people disillusioned with our government and the democratic system have been pulled in two different directions, with some embracing populism of the left and others embracing populism of the right. As a result, our nation is less united, with the political center shrinking and the far left and far right growing. Beyond the simultaneous economic and public health crises that America faces today with COVID-19, the current populist revolt on both ends of the political spectrum is sustained by a failure of governance and a resulting loss of faith in our institutions themselves. It will likely be with us for many years to come.

On the right, former president Trump has stated repeatedly that he will never concede defeat to President Biden in the 2020 election and has raised the possibility of running for the presidency again in 2024. He has also said he will work to defeat House and Senate Republicans who voted for his impeachment or removal when primaries are held in 2022. By sticking with his false claim that Biden is an illegitimate president occupying the White House as a result of fraud, Trump encourages GOP members of Congress to fight the Biden administration at every turn if they want to avoid primary challenges by more pro-Trump opponents. This is a recipe for continued confrontation and gridlock, and minimal cooperation and effective governance.

CNN commentator and *Washington Post* columnist Fareed Zakaria noted the seriousness of this problem in February 2021: "The current Republican congressional delegation includes people who insist the

2020 election was stolen, have ties to violent extremist groups, traffic in antisemitism and have propagated QAnon ideologies in the past. At the state level, it often gets worse.…Already, much of today's Republican Party has been permeated by extremism."[72]

On the left, progressive Democratic lawmakers are pushing Biden to fight hard to enact proposals that reject centrism and compromise with Republicans. These include raising the minimum wage from the current $7.25 an hour (last raised in 2009) to $15 an hour in stages by 2025, with annual increases after that tied to median hourly wage growth to keep up with inflation. The Democratic bill, which Biden supports, would also gradually eliminate the much lower subminimum wage of $2.13 an hour, which was last raised in 1991. Employees who collect over $30 per month in tips from customers—primarily waiters, waitresses, and bartenders—and teenagers employed for ninety days or less are covered by the subminimum wage and would see it phase out by 2027 under the Democratic bill. Some disabled workers are also covered by the subminimum wage and would see it phase out in 2025 under the bill.[73] Raising the minimum wage for all workers would boost the incomes of an estimated 32 million workers (60 percent of them women) according to the progressive Economic Policy Institute and the National Employment Law Project.[74] However, the big jump in the minimum wage would also wipe out 1.4 million jobs, according to a projection by the Congressional Budget Office.[75] Many small-business owners, such as those in the restaurant industry hard-hit by closures due to the coronavirus pandemic, say such a big increase could put them out of business.

In another example, progressives are also pushing Biden to move even more aggressively than he has to fight climate change by embracing the proposed Green New Deal to replace fossil fuels with renewable energy. This would eliminate jobs in the coal, oil, and natural gas industries but create new jobs to generate wind and solar power. Still, it's hard to imagine many workers and others hurt by the loss of existing energy jobs voting for Democrats. Biden made moves early in his administration in the direction of the Green New Deal by rejoining the Paris Climate Agreement, restricting fossil fuel production on federal lands, reversing Trump's relaxation of emissions regulations, canceling the Keystone XL oil pipeline from Canada, and proposing an infrastructure plan devoting billions of dollars to clean energy initiatives.[76]

With populists on the right pulling in one direction and populists on the left pulling in the opposite direction it will be difficult for members of Congress to coalesce around centrist compromise proposals to make government more effective and responsive to the needs of the American people. Yet it is precisely this lack of effectiveness and responsiveness that has fueled discontent with our democracy by millions of Americans of all political views, exacerbating our divisions.

The segmentation of the media further inflames our divisions. After Trump's election defeat, Fox News ratings dropped when Trump urged his supporters to watch the more pro-Trump Newsmax and One America News Network. Fox could have chosen to expand its news staff and increase news programming to better compete with MSNBC and CNN. Instead, Fox laid off nearly twenty news staffers from its website and replaced an hour of evening TV news with a new right-wing opinion show to double down on pro-Trump programming so it could better compete with the much smaller Newsmax and OAN.[77] On the left, MSNBC and CNN continued attacking Trump and his supporters, while giving the Biden administration sympathetic coverage. And social media and websites were filled with strong opinions on both sides of the political divide.

The point of summarizing the history of American populism in this chapter is to show that while populism's roots run deep, when it goes to the extreme left or extreme right it is fundamentally different, more dangerous, and more pervasive today than in the past. For the first time, right-wing and left-wing populism are flourishing at the same time. And instead of simply seeking reforms of our system of government that could win bipartisan support, many of today's populists and their supporters are seeking to throw out our current system and replace it with something dramatically different. In addition, partisans on the left and right are often treating those on the other side as enemies rather than political adversaries. The two opposing extremist branches of populism will only grow and pull Americans further apart unless we address their root causes and somehow get the American people to embrace cooperation over confrontation with fellow citizens. When millions of Americans on the left and right believe our democratic system is too dysfunctional and too corrupt to be reformed, our democratic system is in big trouble.

Our elected leaders must respond to this populist insurrection. To save our democracy, Republicans and Democrats in Congress will need to work with President Biden to make needed reforms to our system of government and enact legislation that improves the lives of the American people and that both left and right can accept. If the top priority of both sides is to demonize the other, deny their opponents credit for accomplishing anything, and focus on victory in the next election above all else, America is in big trouble. Never-ending election campaigns are a guarantee of never-ending partisan battles and government dysfunction.

When William Jennings Bryan criticized monopolies and trusts such as Standard Oil, Presidents Theodore Roosevelt, William Howard Taft, and Woodrow Wilson began trust-busting and worked with Congress to enact some of the progressive reforms that Bryan promoted. Huey Long made a name for himself by advocating massive federal spending, higher taxes on the rich, and wealth redistribution policies. He criticized President Franklin Roosevelt's New Deal as not progressive enough, and was expected to challenge Roosevelt for the 1936 Democratic presidential nomination before being assassinated in 1935. Roosevelt sought to win the support of Long's followers by incorporating some of Long's proposals into the Second New Deal. When Ross Perot garnered 19 percent of the popular vote in the 1992 presidential election by emphasizing the need for a balanced budget and protecting American jobs from outsourcing, President Clinton expanded his agenda to incorporate those issues and actually balanced the budget.

In contrast, millions of Americans believed that the grievances expressed by the Tea Party and Occupy Wall Street movements in 2010, which were shared by many Americans who never participated in the activities of either movement, went unanswered by our nation's elected leaders. Rather than recognizing the need for real reform, too many elected officials of both parties acted as if the protest movements were minor and transitory nuisances that could be ignored. Unfortunately, the crises that conceived these protest movements of the right and left have only grown worse.

Millions of Americans remain worried about globalization, economic stagnation, the challenges to our economy and national security posed by a resurgent China and Russia, a loss of trust in government, and a loss of faith in the American Dream. These crises will not just magically disappear, and in fact are more pressing than ever before. Republicans and Democrats in Washington must stop feuding and fighting and start responding. Our own government is not "too big to fail." The populist fervor will continue to dominate our politics until reform is made. Far too many Americans have already lost faith in our democracy. If we want to save it, we need to act now. Fortunately, the insurrectionists who stormed the Capitol at the beginning of 2021 were unsuccessful. And the spring and summer riots that broke out at widespread protests seeking racial justice largely stopped, although there were new protests and some looting in 2021 following additional police killings of unarmed Black people. All these events gave us a preview of what is to come if no reforms are made. We are in the endgame. Our government must change its ways.

5 / THE THREAT OF POLITICAL EXTREMISM

C alling a candidate for elective office an extremist—and making the charge stick—was once a political kiss of death. But as Democrats have moved leftward and Republicans have moved rightward, positions once embraced by only the extreme fringes of each party have gained many new adherents, driving the parties further apart.

When Senator Barry Goldwater won the Republican nomination for president at the party's 1964 national convention, he torpedoed his own candidacy by saying in his acceptance speech: "I would remind you that extremism in the defense of liberty is no vice. And let me remind you also that moderation in the pursuit of justice is no virtue."[1] President Lyndon Johnson and his fellow Democrats never let the American people forget that line, and used it to successfully attack Goldwater as too extreme to be president. The Democrats pilloried the senator from Arizona for his proposal to privatize Social Security and his opposition to the 1964 Civil Rights Act, along with his denunciation of President Franklin Delano Roosevelt's New Deal that had created a social safety net for people in need three decades earlier. Most devastating of all, Democrats portrayed Goldwater as a trigger-happy hawk who could start a nuclear war. The message to voters couldn't be more frightening: Vote for Goldwater and you and all your loved ones might be killed in the deadliest war in global history.

"The reaction [to Goldwater's comment on extremism] was swift and brutal," historian Lee Edwards wrote in a commentary for the Heritage Foundation in July 2019. "New York Governor Nelson Rockefeller, Goldwater's principal and very liberal rival for the Republican nomination, called the statement 'dangerous, irresponsible, and frightening.' Martin Luther King, Jr., saw 'dangerous signs of Hitlerism' in Goldwater's programs. NAACP secretary Roy Wilkins said a Goldwater victory 'would lead to a police state.'"[2]

Looking back at the 1964 campaign in an article in 2016, President Nixon's former White House Counsel John Dean (who turned against Nixon during the Watergate scandal) wrote of the impact of Goldwater's "extremism in defense of liberty" comment: "With a lot of help from political commentators and the news media, the Johnson campaign managed to portray Goldwater—one of the most liked members of the U.S. Senate by his colleagues across the political spectrum—into something of a madman, 'the village anarchist,' as one reporter put it, a political extremist who would take the country into a nuclear world war.... The news media took this line as proof positive that Goldwater was crazy."[3] Goldwater didn't even originate the line about extremism. It came from speechwriter Karl Hess.[4] President Johnson defeated Goldwater in a landslide, winning 61 percent of the popular vote and 486 electoral votes to just 52 for Goldwater. The Republican candidate won only five Southern states and his home state of Arizona.[5]

In 1972, Republican president Richard Nixon and his party firmly affixed the extremist label to Democratic presidential candidate Senator George McGovern of South Dakota. McGovern was the son of a minister and had been a bomber pilot in World War II, flying dozens of missions in Europe and earning the Distinguished Flying Cross after he crash-landed his plane when it was hit by enemy fire. He was certainly no pacifist. Reflecting on his wartime service years later, he said: "I believed in that war then; I still do. Hitler was an incredible monster."[6] But although he was a genuine war hero, Republicans portrayed McGovern as a radical extremist, based on his calls for a U.S. troop withdrawal from South Vietnam, abolition of the draft, amnesty for draft evaders, big cuts in military spending, and guaranteed jobs and a guaranteed income for all Americans.

Presidential historian Theodore H. White wrote in his book *The Making of the President 1972* that McGovern "frightened too many Americans." In McGovern's obituary in the *New York Times* in 2012, reporter David E. Rosenbaum wrote: "The Republicans portrayed Mr. McGovern as a cowardly left-winger, a threat to the military and the free-market economy and someone outside the mainstream of American thought." McGovern himself said in 2005: "I think they [voters] thought that Nixon was a strong, decisive, tough-minded guy, and that I was an idealist and antiwar guy who might not attach enough significance to the security of the country."[7] Nixon was reelected with 61 percent of the popular vote and carried forty-nine states in the Electoral College; McGovern carried only Massachusetts and the District of Columbia. The lopsided electoral vote was 521 for Nixon and only 17 for McGovern.[8]

Today, extremism has gone mainstream. Goldwater and McGovern might be considered moderates within their own parties if they were still alive. While the two men had very different political views, both put patriotism before party, risking their lives to serve their country as Army Air Force pilots in World War II and devoting themselves to what they saw as the nation's best interests in their years in the Senate. Both fully embraced the norms of democracy and—unlike Donald Trump—both conceded their election losses and didn't file dozens of lawsuits or summon their supporters to Washington to protest supposed election fraud. Neither man ever embraced the far fringes of the political spectrum or bizarre conspiracy theories.

When McGovern conceded on election night in 1972, he sent a telegram to President Nixon that read: "Congratulations on your victory. I hope that in the next four years you will lead us to a time of peace abroad and justice at home. You have my full support in such efforts. With best wishes to you and your gracious wife, Pat." Similarly, in Goldwater's concession telegram to President Johnson, he wrote: "Congratulations on your victory, I'll help you in any way I can toward achieving a growing and better America and a secure and dignified peace. The whole of the Republican Party will remain in that temper, but it also remains a party of opposition when opposition is called for. There is much to be done with Vietnam, Cuba, the problem of law and order in this country, and a productive economy. Communism remains our number one obstacle to peace and I know that all Americans will join with you in honest solutions to these problems."[9]

McGovern and Goldwater made the type of concession statements losing presidential candidates have made throughout American history. They didn't embrace the policies of their victorious opponents—no one expected them to—but they acknowledged the reality of their losses and sought to unite the nation after bitter election campaigns. Had Trump followed their example, the horrific and unprecedented attack on the U.S. Capitol would have never happened and America would be a more unified nation today.

We can only hope that no other unsuccessful presidential candidate ever turns out to be as sore a loser as Donald Trump. We won't be able to preserve our democracy or unite the American people if after every presidential election a mob supporting the losing candidate invades the Capitol when electoral votes are being certified. And as bad as the attack in January 2021 turned out to be, we shudder to think how much worse things could get if future invaders break in with assault weapons and hand grenades and use those weapons. Even the South surrendered at the end of the Civil War and acknowledged the Confederacy had come to an end. Trump has vowed to never concede defeat and will no doubt claim to have the won the 2020 election for as long as he lives.

As an example of how to reject extremism, Barry Goldwater crit- icized Robert Welch—the head of the then-prominent radical-right group the John Birch Society—far more strenuously than Trump and many contemporary Republicans have ever criticized modern right-wing extremists such as followers of the QAnon conspiracy theory. Welch didn't use the term "Deep State" that Trump popularized, but he painted a similar dark conspiracy theory. The John Birch Society leader absurdly contended the U.S. government was "under operational control of the Communist Party" and called Republican president Dwight Eisenhower a "dedicated, conscious agent of the Communist conspiracy." While not criticizing the Birch Society itself, Goldwater said Welch should resign as head of the group because his views were "far removed from reality and common sense."[10]

On the Democratic side, George McGovern never called himself a socialist, as Senator Bernie Sanders did when he twice campaigned for the Democratic presidential nomination. In fact, when he was running for president, McGovern told *Business Week*: "It's hard for me to believe that Congress would pass a program that would wreck the free enterprise system.... I don't want to recommend things that I know have no chance of support."[11] In the 2020 presidential election campaign, the Democratic Socialists of America endorsed Sanders.[12] But when McGovern ran for president in 1972, prominent communist Angela Davis denounced him, saying "there is no fundamental difference between Nixon and McGovern" and calling McGovern "part of a vast system of exploitation."[13]

In the years since Goldwater and McGovern ran for president, extremism has grown within each political party as Democrats and Republicans have refused to take firm stands against it within their ranks. Both parties have welcomed all the votes, campaign contributions, and volunteer help they could get, with rare exceptions. As we have pointed out, activist Democrats tend to be further left than most supporters of the party and activist Republicans tend to be further right. As a result, the need to win the support and campaign contributions of the activists has pushed each party away from the political center. The

Center for Responsive Politics reported that in the 2020 campaign cycle only about 2 percent of U.S. adults made political campaign contributions of $200 or more.[14] This tiny fraction of voters has influence within each party far out of proportion to its size.

HOW EXTREMISTS OPERATE TODAY

The media are an important factor contributing to the growth of extremism. The internet, social media, cable TV news, and talk radio have given political extremists new ways to organize, build strength, gain attention, and gain followers. Fox News, Newsmax, and One America News Network reinforce the beliefs of those on the right, while CNN and MSNBC do the same for those on the left. Before these modern communications tools existed, it was much harder for extremist groups to get off the ground and grow. Today, extremists on the left and right can meet virtually with like-minded individuals anywhere in the nation and even internationally, and live in their own information ecosystems that fan the flames of division.

Far-left anarchist groups communicate with supporters and recruit new ones on Facebook, Twitter, Instagram, and Reddit, while right-wing extremist groups are often forced to retreat to platforms like Discord and Parler, the "free speech" forum, because many have been barred from the major social media platforms because they called for violence. Many of these extremist groups and both ends of the political spectrum now employ marketing and public relations techniques to play down their extremism in order to appeal to a broader swath of Americans. According to counterinsurgency expert David Kilcullen—a retired Australian Army officer and former adviser to the U.S. State Department and to U.S. and allied forces in Iraq—"Antifa groups have websites, Facebook pages, and social media tools; study the tactics of other groups; host training events; and have thought-leaders."[15] And Kilcullen says extremist groups attempt to downplay any violent intentions they have, to protect themselves from criminal charges. "For the most part, in fact, U.S. armed groups do not advocate armed overthrow of the state," Kilcullen writes. "Left-wing militias describe themselves as community self-defense organizations or above-ground militant formations engaged in 'active resistance'— resisting, rather than overthrowing the state. On the right, militias call themselves 'constitutionalists' and 'patriots' who, far from advocating the overthrow of the government, pledge to uphold the law and the Constitution."

Right-wing extremists and terrorists have been forced out of mainstream social media sites and found other ways to connect online. According to the Center for Strategic and International Studies: "Right-wing terrorists have used various combinations of Facebook, Twitter, YouTube, Gab, Reddit, 4Chan, 8kun (formerly 8Chan), Endchan, Telegram, Vkontakte, MeWe, Discord, Wire, Twitch, and other online communication platforms." In fact, right-wing extremists have even recruited via computer games.[16]

Beyond recruiting supporters and coordinating their events, the internet has allowed extremist groups and domestic terrorists to create an effective "leaderless resistance." This structure, which many groups have adopted, rejects a highly centralized, organized hierarchy in favor of a widely decentralized, smaller network of actors. Small cells across the nation execute their own agendas and acts of violence or terrorism. The internet connects these individual cells, often through untraceable and unobservable virtual private networks or encryption services like Signal. University of Chicago assistant professor of history Kathleen Belew wrote in her 2018 book, *Bring the War Home: The White Power Movement and Paramilitary America*, that the purpose of this decentralization is to "prevent the infiltration of groups, and the prosecution of organizations and individuals, by formally dissociating activists from each other and by eliminating official orders."[17] This makes it hard for law enforcement to monitor these groups and prosecute members when crimes are committed.

For all these reasons, extremism is a much more potent force in the United States and in both the Republican and Democratic Parties today than arguably any time since Reconstruction after the Civil War. A report issued in March 2021 by the Office of the Director of National Intelligence said that "domestic violent extremists . . . who are motivated by a range of ideologies and galvanized by recent political and societal events in the United States pose an elevated threat to the Homeland in 2021."[18] The report predicted that violent domestic extremists "will almost certainly" attack again before 2022 and said the "most lethal" threat comes from extremists motivated by racial and ethnic hatred.

The *Washington Post* reported in April 2021: "Domestic terrorism incidents have soared to new highs in the United States, driven chiefly by white-supremacist, anti-Muslim and anti-government extremists on the far right, according to a *Washington Post* analysis of data compiled by the Center for Strategic and International Studies. The surge reflects a growing threat from homegrown terrorism not seen in a quarter-century, with right-wing extremist attacks and plots greatly eclipsing those from the far left and causing more deaths, the analysis shows."[19]

In another illustration of the problem of extremism, the Anti-Defamation League reported in March 2021 that White supremacist propaganda reached its highest level in at least a decade in 2020. According to the Associated Press, "There were 5,125 cases of racist, anti-Semitic, anti-LGBTQ and other hateful messages spread through physical flyers, stickers, banners and posters, according to Wednesday's report. That's nearly double the 2,724 instances reported in 2019. Online propaganda is much harder to quantify, and it's likely those cases reached into the millions, the anti-hate organization said."[20]

But while elected officials in both parties are quick to attack extremists aligned with the other party, they are often reluctant to attack violent extremists on their own side. Some on the left are too quick to demonize all police officers for the misconduct of a minority of officers toward Black Americans—while some on the right are reluctant to condemn pro-Trump rioters and other lawbreakers engaging in violence against police. This double standard must end for the good of our country.

RESPONDING TO VIOLENT EXTREMISTS

In the 2020 urban riots, we saw many Democrats stress that most pro-testers demonstrating against racism and police misconduct were peaceful and didn't riot. That was true, but it didn't erase the destruction caused by the rioting. Think about the impact of this in the real world. Imagine you owned a convenience store or a consumer electronics store looted and burned to the ground by a few rioters. The fact that hundreds of other people protested peacefully for hours before your store was destroyed wouldn't lessen the pain inflicted by rioters.

On the other side of the political spectrum, many Republicans stressed that the rioters who broke into the Capitol to overturn the 2020 presidential election were just a tiny minority of Trump supporters—as if this lessened the seriousness of the insurrection against our elected government. Senator Ron Johnson (R-WI) went even further when he engaged in revisionist history and said he didn't feel threatened by the pro-Trump mob that invaded the Capitol.

"I know those are people that love this country, that truly respect law enforcement, would never do anything to break the law so I wasn't concerned," Johnson said of the Capitol rioters in a nationally syndicated radio interview with talk show host Joe Pagliarulo in March 2021. This absurd claim was disproven by the suicides of police officers Jeffrey Smith, Howard Liebengood, Gunther Hashida, and Kyle DeFreytag, who took their own lives after the trauma of being attacked in the Capitol insurrection. Five people died in the attack and about 140 police officers were injured by the rioters who Johnson said "truly respect law enforcement" and "would never break the law." Additionally, one of the most seriously injured officers "lost an eye, another suffered two cracked ribs and two smashed spinal discs" and many "officers suffered concussions and other bodily injures from being beaten with flagpoles, sprayed with bear spray, punched, dragged and trampled," the *Washington Post* reported.[21]

Johnson added in the same radio interview: "Now, had the tables been turned—now, Joe, this will get me in trouble—had the tables been turned and President Trump won the election and those were tens of thousands of Black Lives Matter and Antifa protesters, I might have been a little concerned."[22] Democrats and columnists called on Johnson to resign after the interview was aired, calling his comments racist. In a *Washington Post* column headlined "Ron Johnson's Racism Is Breathtaking," Eugene Robinson wrote: "It has become perfectly acceptable in the Republican Party to just go ahead and say the racism out loud—and to do so with apparent pride, and with no fear of consequences....Johnson should have been pilloried by his GOP colleagues in the Senate, but none spoke up in outrage—or even mild disagreement."[23]

Washington Post columnist Michael Gerson, who was the chief speechwriter for Republican president George W. Bush, also criticized Republicans for not repudiating Johnson, writing: "A political movement will either police its extremes or be defined by them. Disapproval from opponents is easy to dismiss as mere partisanship. It is through self-criticism that a political party defines and patrols the boundaries of its ideological sanity."[24]

Johnson denied he is a racist and defended himself in a *Wall Street Journal* op-ed, writing, "Leftists who want to memory hole last summer's political violence immediately started lecturing me that the 2020 protests were mostly peaceful. Apparently they've forgotten that, according to the Armed Conflict Location & Event Data Project, 570 leftist protests became riots last year. Twenty-five people lost their lives and 700 law enforcement officers were injured. Braying about 'peaceful protests' offers no comfort to those victims or the other innocent Americans whose homes, businesses, and property were destroyed."[25]

THE THREAT OF POLITICAL EXTREMISM

Later in March 2021, Trump joined Johnson in falsely describing the attack on the Capitol by his supporters. "Right from the start, it was zero threat," Trump told Laura Ingraham on Fox News. "Look, they went in—they shouldn't have done it—some of them went in, and they're hugging and kissing the police and the guards, you know? They had great relationships. A lot of the people were waved in, and then they walked in, and they walked out." In response, Representative Adam Kinzinger (R-IL), one of only ten House Republicans who joined Democrats to vote to impeach Trump for "incitement of insurrection," tweeted that Trump's comment was "quite honestly sick and disgusting."[26]

Yet most Republicans believed Trump's and Johnson's lies about the 2020 election and the Capitol riot, according to a Reuters-Ipsos poll released in April 2021—while independents and Democrats did not. The poll found that 55 percent of Republicans believed at least somewhat that "the Jan. 6 riot at the Capitol was led by violent left-wing protestors trying to make Trump look bad"—but only 25 percent of independents and just 19 percent of Democrats believed that. And 51 percent of Republicans said they agreed at least somewhat that the rioters who attacked the Capitol were "mostly peaceful law-abiding Americans" protesting the election results—while only 25 percent of independents and 16 percent of Democrats held that view.[27]

What has America come to when violent attacks on police officers aren't condemned by everyone—regardless of who the attackers are and regardless of what cause they espouse? Twelve Republican House members even voted against a resolution to award Congressional Gold Medals to the members of the Capitol Police, Washington Metropolitan Police, and the Smithsonian Institution law enforcement agency who protected them and their fellow lawmakers when the Capitol was attacked. Many of the twelve objected to the use of the term "insurrectionists" to describe the attackers who sought to overturn Joe Biden's election.[28]

And as mentioned previously, Republican senators used the filibuster at the end of May 2021 to block the creation of a bipartisan independent commission to investigate the insurrection at the Capitol. The Senate voted 54–35 to debate the bill, but needed 60 votes to overcome the GOP filibuster. Only six Republicans voted in favor of allowing a debate on the commission, which would have been modeled after the commission created to investigate the 9/11 terrorist attacks. The House voted 252–175 earlier in the month in favor of the commission, with the support of only 35 Republicans.[29] Many GOP lawmakers argued that the commission was unnecessary. They expressed concern that the commission would hurt them in the 2022 midterm election and that former president Trump would attack any Republican who voted for it.

While a House select committee was created to investigate the insurrection, an independent commission would have been a better vehicle for conducting a nonpartisan probe of the events leading up to and during the rioting. Republicans were wrong to oppose it. Peggy Noonan, a former speechwriter for President Reagan, wrote in her *Wall Street Journal* column in June 2021 that a commission is needed because former president Trump continues to tell his followers the Big Lie that he actually won the 2020 election. She called the lie "an untreated cancer" and added that "the only thing that can stop it is true facts independently developed and presented with respect."[30] We agree.

It should be obvious to everyone that we don't have Republican police and Democratic police in America—just nonpartisan police forces funded by taxpayers to defend us all against lawbreakers, regardless of their race, ethnicity, and political beliefs. The Capitol Police and other responding law enforcement officers who were attacked by rioters risked their lives to protect Republican and Democratic lawmakers alike, along with their staffs. The people the officers protected included Senator Johnson and Democratic representative Alexandria Ocasio-Cortez, a staunch advocate of defunding the police. In addition, many of the police officers in cities around the country who were attacked by rioters in 2020 were Black, and many of the businesses attacked by rioters were owned by Black people. Why are their attackers not condemned as loudly by all Democrats as they condemn the rioters who attacked the Capitol? And why can't all Republicans condemn the Capitol rioters with the same fervor they express when condemning the urban rioters?

A tragedy arising out of extremist rioting was the murder of David Dorn, a seventy-seven-year-old retired St. Louis police captain who was fatally shot in June 2020 while protecting a friend's pawnshop from looters.[31] Dorn's widow, Ann Dorn, cried as she spoke about his killing on a video played at the Republican National Convention in August 2020. "Violence and destruction are not legitimate forms of protest. They do not safeguard Black lives. They destroy them," Mrs. Dorn said. "As I slept, looters were ransacking the shop. They shot and killed Dave in cold blood and live-streamed the execution and his last moments on this Earth.... Dave's grandson was watching the video on Facebook in real time, not realizing he was watching his own grandfather dying on the sidewalk."[32]

Let's be clear: America has a long history of demonstrations and non-violent civil disobedience as forms of protest. Dr. Martin Luther King Jr. was jailed twenty-nine times for his protests of segregation in the civil rights struggle in the 1950s and 1960s, and many other civil rights campaigners were arrested as well—and sometimes beaten by police with no justification.[33] But Dr. King was a firm believer in nonviolence. He courageously campaigned against the evil of racism by appealing peacefully to the conscience of America. He never led an attack or a riot on the Capitol or anywhere else. There is no question that peaceful protests—whether against racial injustice, in support of Trump's claims of election fraud, or on other topics—are protected by the First Amendment to the Constitution. However, the violent lawbreakers who invaded the Capitol and the violent lawbreakers who burned and looted stores and government buildings in many cities after George Floyd was murdered were extremist criminals—not protesters. Both groups should be prosecuted for their crimes.

It's time for the left and right to come to a commonsense consensus that we need the police to protect us all, and to agree that the majority

246 / AMERICA: UNITE OR DIE

of police are neither racists nor members of a mythical Deep State conspiracy—just as the vast majority of protesters for racial justice are not rioters and looters. As we said earlier in this book, there is no question that some police engage in brutality and criminal conduct. They need to be fired and prosecuted to the full extent of the law. But we have to stop tarring all the good cops with the same brush as the bad ones. In addition, we need to dispense with the idea of defunding the police. As we have pointed out, far more Black lives are saved by police than are taken by police each year. Cities should reform and improve police departments, give officers better training, bar racial profiling, and do everything possible to minimize the use of deadly force unless there is no alternative to protect their own lives or the lives of others. However, improving police departments will require that we spend more on them, not less. Defunding police departments weakens them, strengthens criminals, and endangers the law-abiding majority of citizens—regardless of their race, ethnicity, or political affiliation.

If police departments in Georgia and Colorado had been defunded they might not have been able to respond so quickly and effectively in March 2021 to arrest the men charged with murdering eight people (including six Asian American women) in the Atlanta area and ten people in Boulder.[34] Boulder police officer Eric Talley was tragically shot and killed when he stopped the gunman in the mass murder there in a supermarket. A father of seven, he was rightly praised as a hero for sacrificing his life to save others. Had his job been eliminated by defunding the police, he would likely still be alive today, but more innocent victims might have been killed by the gunman as a smaller police force took longer to respond with fewer officers.[35]

INCREASING NUMBERS OF EXTREMISTS

As an example of extremism on the right, millions of Americans and many Republican elected officials have accepted former president Trump's Big Lie that he won the 2020 election. By continuing to spread this lie, Trump is placing his own political interest ahead of America's national interest. In addition, Trump has refused to denounce QAnon, the right-wing extremist group that embraces crazy and baseless conspiracy theories about Democrats running a Deep State of Satan-worshipping pedophiles. While QAnon's absurd conspiracy theories are different than those embraced by Robert Welch and the John Birch Society in the 1950s and 1960s, they are even more dangerous. That's because the conspiracy theories are spread on right-wing social media, websites, talk radio, and TV channels that didn't exist when Barry Goldwater was a presidential candidate.

The FBI issued a bulletin in May 2019 labeling QAnon a domestic terrorism threat that was "very likely" to commit violent crimes, but Trump claimed in October 2020—more than a year later— that he didn't know anything about the group's beliefs and refused to say its conspiracy theories were false.[36] Given that the president of the United States has access to intelligence reports from the FBI and all other federal law enforcement and intelligence agencies, and is offered daily intelligence briefings, Trump's statement is not believable.

In addition, in a debate with Joe Biden, then-president Trump refused to condemn White supremacist groups for their involvement in sometimes violent counter-protests during the 2020 urban riots. "Almost everything I see is from the left wing, not the right wing," Trump said. When asked specifically if he would condemn the Proud Boys, a far-right extremist group that has engaged in violence, Trump said: "Proud Boys, stand back and stand by"— a comment that the Proud Boys took as an endorsement. Joe Biggs, a Proud Boys organizer in Florida, posted a message on Parler—an online safe haven for extremist groups—saying:

"President Trump told the Proud Boys to stand by because someone needs to deal with antifa . . . well sir! we're ready!!"[37]

The next day, Trump said: "I don't know who the Proud Boys are." Yet just a week earlier, FBI Director Christopher Wray—who was appointed by Trump—told a congressional panel that most of the recent deadly attacks in the U.S. by extremist groups were committed by anti-government extremists and White supremacists. And according to the Southern Poverty Law Center: "Rank-and-file Proud Boys and leaders regularly spout white nationalist memes and maintain affiliations with known extremists. They are known for anti-Muslim and misogynistic rhetoric. Proud Boys have appeared alongside other hate groups at extremist gatherings such as the "Unite the Right" rally in Charlottesville, Virginia . . . which brought together a broad coalition of extremists including Neo-Nazis, antisemites and militias."[38]

The Anti-Defamation League describes the Proud Boys as "Misogynistic, Islamophobic, transphobic and anti-immigration. Some members espouse white supremacist and anti-Semitic ideologies and/or engage with White supremacist groups . . . members are regulars at far-right demonstrations and Trump rallies. After several years of forging alliances with members of the Republican political establishment, the Proud Boys have carved out a niche for themselves as both a right-wing fight club and a volunteer security force for the GOP. Despite their associations with mainstream politicians, Proud Boys' actions and statements repeatedly land them in the company of white supremacists and right-wing extremists. . . . Events held in the aftermath of the murder of George Floyd allowed the Proud Boys to brand themselves as 'law and order' counterpoint to Black Lives Matter protesters, although the Proud Boys themselves generally precipitated the most egregious acts of violence and intimidation against protesters. . . . The Proud Boys have also been embraced by a number of Fox News hosts."[39] Federal prosecutors later said that Proud Boys were among the rioters who broke into the U.S. Capitol on January 6, 2021. Nearly twenty Proud Boys or associates were arrested after the insurrection.[40]

As we have said, the riot at the Capitol created a more serious crisis than the urban riots following the killing of George Floyd by Minneapolis police because the attack on the Capitol threatened our democracy by attempting to overturn Trump's defeat in a democratic election. But the urban riots were a threat to our democracy as well, because they included looting, arson, and other lawbreaking that can't be tolerated in a nation where violence must not be part of political protest by the left or the right. In any society, the only way to avoid chaos is give just two institutions—law enforcement and the military—the right to resort to violence, and then only in order to protect the American people. If others can freely turn to violence to achieve political aims or any other goals and get away with it—no matter how righteous they believe their cause to be—our democracy may be replaced by an authoritarian form of government to restore order.

On the left, Biden and many other Democrats supported peaceful protests following George Floyd's murder that were led by the group Black Lives Matters and others, but denounced riots that erupted during those protests. Biden issued a statement six days after Floyd was killed that said: "Every person of conscience can understand the rawness of the trauma people of color experience in this country, from the daily indignities to the extreme violence, like the horrific killing of George Floyd. Protesting such brutality is right and necessary. It's an utterly American response. But burning down communities and needless destruction is not. Violence that endangers lives is not. Violence that guts and shutters businesses that serve the community is not."[41]

Biden's statement set the right tone, but his critics justifiably complained that he and other Democrats did not forcefully condemn the groups behind the riots. In his column in the *Wall Street Journal* on a Trump-Biden debate, James Freeman wrote: "In Tuesday night's presidential debate in Cleveland, former Vice President Joe Biden said that violence is never 'appropriate' but he did not condemn people who have been perpetrating it in cities across America. Taking the opportunity to address directly the antifa movement, Mr. Biden simply described its lack of centralized structure....Could Mr. Biden possibly be unaware of the street violence in U.S. cities inflicted for months by leftist radicals? Antifa is not the only really bad idea. Similar groups go by different names and Mr. Biden didn't choose to condemn any of them....Why is Mr. Biden not making more of an effort to distance himself from violent leftist radicals?"[42]

Former New York City Police Commissioner Bernard Kerik, who supported President Trump's reelection and who received a pardon from Trump for his felony convictions of tax fraud and making false statements, wrote an op-ed in the *Hill* in August 2020 to criticize speakers at the Democratic National Convention for their reaction to the urban riots. He wrote: "They chose to ignore antifa and Black Lives Matter–affiliated militants even as they burned police stations, tore down monuments to our war dead and Founding Fathers, assaulted police officers, looted hundreds of stores, blocked highways, declared a section of downtown Seattle separate from American law, and—yes—killed innocent people.... Washington, D.C., Mayor Muriel Bowser waxed poetic about how she rewarded the 'protesters' by creating 'Black Lives Matter Plaza' in front of the White House, with no mention of the widespread violence, vandalism of war memorials, attempts to pull down Andrew Jackson's statue, or even the fact that activists promptly augmented her taxpayer-funded Black Lives Matter street mural with an equally large 'Defund the Police' message."[43]

In another example of left-wing extremism out of control, Democratic Seattle mayor Jenny Durkan waited three weeks before ordering dozens of people arrested and evicted from an area in downtown they had occupied and declared to be an autonomous protest zone. Durkan originally praised the occupation as an expression of democracy and called it part of "a summer of love." She proposed a 5 percent cut in the police budget—but the occupiers demanded an even more reckless 50 percent cut. In an effort to appease the occupiers, Durkan even ordered police to abandon their precinct station in the occupation zone. When the mayor belatedly ordered the occupation zone cleared, following four shootings and two deaths, she said the city had "reasonably facilitated an ongoing exercise" of free speech, but would not "provide limitless sanctuary to occupy city property, damage city and property, obstruct the right of way, or foster dangerous conditions."[44] It should not have taken her three weeks to reach this obvious conclusion. When the Seattle city council voted in August 2020 to cut the police budget, forcing the layoff of up to a hundred officers, Carmen Best—the city's first Black police chief—resigned in protest.[45]

THE GROWTH OF EXTREMISM

The move by growing numbers of Democrats to accept extremism is also illustrated by the growing approval of socialism within the party. Senator Bernie Sanders (who is aligned with Democrats but not a member of the party) and Representatives Alexandria Ocasio-Cortez, Rashida Tlaib, Cori Bush, and Jamaal Bowman all call themselves democratic socialists—giving socialists more seats in Congress in 2021 than at any time in American history. The members of the Democratic Socialists of America holding elective office at the local, state, and federal level around the nation rose from 71 in 2020 to 101 in 2021 as a result of the 2020 elections, Occidental College politics professor Peter Dreier wrote in *Talking Points Memo* following the elections.[46] "Most of the socialists who have recently been elected to office represent safe blue areas, but they have also made inroads in purple areas, including Montana, Indiana, North Dakota, Texas and Tennessee," Drier wrote. "DSA [Democratic Socialists of America] . . . had only 6,000 members a few years ago but now it has over 87,000 dues-paying members with several hundred chapters in all 50 states. A much larger number of Americans embrace its ideas and its activities, too."

The record number of socialists in elected office, coupled with the increasing support for socialists by voters, especially young voters (which we discussed earlier in this book), are a strong indication that if current trends continue the leftward tilt of the Democratic Party could accelerate in coming years. That could result in growing numbers of Democratic candidates and officeholders openly and proudly calling themselves socialists. This is a troubling development that will drive Democrats and Republicans even further apart, making cooperation between the two parties even harder to achieve.

THE WIDENING DIVIDE BETWEEN LEFT AND RIGHT

If Republicans operate as a center-right party and Democrats operate as a center-left party, the two sides can bridge their differences to effectively govern. But if a sizable chunk or even a majority of Democrats embrace socialism in future years, and if a large faction or majority of Republicans embrace far-right extremist policies, it's hard to see how such vast differences can be bridged. A Zogby Analytics® poll taken in February 2021 reported that 46 percent of Americans said that it was likely that the United States will have another civil war.[47] We must act now to unite so we can avert such a frightening outcome.

As an example of the rise of extremist views in both major political parties, a 2019 paper titled "Lethal Mass Partisanship," written by two political scientists—Louisiana State University professor Nathan Kalmoe and University of Maryland professor Lilliana Mason—found that polling showed about 60 percent of both Republicans and Democrats think that the opposing party poses a "serious threat to the United States and its people."[48] Even more alarming, just over 42 percent of people identifying with each party agreed with the statement: "[Opposing party supporters] are not just worse for politics—they are downright evil." Further, nearly 20 percent of Republicans and Democrats agreed with the statement that their political opponents "lack the traits to be considered fully human—they behave like animals." And 16 percent of Republicans and 20 percent of Democrats think "we'd be better off as a country if large numbers of the opposing party in the public today just died." Writing about the study in the *New York Times*, columnist Thomas Edsall called the findings "startling, but maybe they shouldn't have been."[49]

According to a decennial study by the Pew Research Center published in 2014, since 1994 the proportion of Democrats and Republicans with centrist views significantly fell as extremist views rose. When giving ordinary voters the same ten-point questionnaire about their political values, the answers have radically changed in the past three decades. Growing numbers of Republicans have moved to the ideological right, while Democrats have moved to the left. The study found that "the overall share of Americans who express consistently conservative or consistently liberal opinions has doubled over the past two decades from 10 percent to 21 percent. And ideological thinking is now much more closely aligned with partisanship than in the past. As a result, ideological overlap between the two parties has diminished: Today, 92 percent of Republicans are to the right of the median Democrat, and 94 percent of Democrats are to the left of the median Republican."[50] We suspect that polarization has grown worse since this 2014 survey, with the rise of extremism during the Trump years in the White House. A more recent study shows extremist groups have grown and become bolder. According to a study by the Southern Poverty Law Center published in February 2021, the number of White nationalist groups has grown enormously—by 55 percent since 2017.[51] This includes "accelerationist" groups "that believe mass violence is necessary to bring about the collapse of our pluralistic society."[52]

Authorities said one important group of right-wing extremists is the Oath Keepers, which the *Washington Post* called "the most high-profile self-styled militia group in the country." The *Post* said the Oath Keepers and Proud Boys are major targets of the FBI investigation into the attack by Trump supporters on the U.S. Capitol.[53] As of April 2021, thirteen members of the Oath Keepers faced criminal charges in the January 6 attack among more than four hundred people charged in the riot so far.[54] The Oath Keepers' founder, former Army paratrooper Stewart Rhodes, told followers at a rally carried on the group's YouTube channel after Trump's election defeat: "You must declare that Joe Biden is not just not your president. He is not anybody's president. He will be a usurper, he will be a pretender, and everything that comes out of his mouth, and everything he signs into so-called legislation will be null and void from inception." In August 2020, before he was kicked off Twitter (where the Oath Keepers had 30,000 followers) and Facebook (where the group had hundreds of thousands of followers), Rhodes wrote that "Civil war is here right now" and predicted "open warfare with Marxist insurrectionists by Election Day."[55]

The fanaticism of Trump's extremist followers who attacked the U.S. Capitol to try to overturn his election loss and their lack of trust in our nation's system of government reminded CNN Chief National Security Correspondent Jim Sciutto of Islamist terrorists he covered in the Middle East. In an op-ed published by the *Washington Post* in February 2021, Sciutto said that in America, "domestic radicalism has deep parallels to jihadist terrorism: Both movements are driven by alienation from the political system and a resulting breakdown in social norms. For some groups and individuals, this breakdown leads to violence they see as justified to achieve political ends."[56]

All-out political combat is waged by Democrats as well as Republicans, and left-wing radicals have turned to violence just as have those on the right. In addition to seeing this in the urban riots following the killing of George Floyd, we saw it on June 14, 2017. On that day, James Hodgkinson—who had been a volunteer on Bernie Sanders's presidential campaign and expressed hostility to Republicans—opened fire on a baseball field where Republican members of Congress were practicing for the annual congressional charity baseball game. After first asking Rep. Jeff Duncan (R-SC) if Republicans or Democrats were on the field and being told the players were Republicans, Hodgkinson shot and wounded five people. The wounded included then-House Majority Whip Steve Scalise (R-LA), a Capitol Police special agent, two lobbyists, and a congressional staffer. Scalise was seriously injured and was unable to return to the House for over three months. Hodgkinson was killed in an exchange of gunfire with police.[57]

In an issue brief published by the Center for Strategic & International Studies in June 2020, Senior Vice President Seth Jones examined 893 terrorist attacks in the U.S. between January 1994 and May 2020 (a period ending shortly before the 2020 riots) and concluded that while right-wing extremist were responsible for most of the attacks, a significant number were carried out by left-wing extremists, as well as by religious extremists (with the most serious terrorist attacks by far being those carried out on September 11, 2001, by Islamists).

"The far-left includes a decentralized mix of actors," Jones wrote.[58] "Anarchists are fundamentally opposed to a centralized government and capitalism, and they have organized plots and attacks against government, capitalist, and globalization targets. Environmental and animal rights groups, such as the Earth Liberation Front and Animal Liberation Front, have conducted small-scale attacks against businesses they perceive as exploiting the environment. In addition, the far-left includes Antifa, which is a contraction of the phrase 'anti-fascist.' It refers to a decentralized network of far-left militants that oppose what they believe are fascist, racist, or otherwise right-wing extremists. While some consider Antifa a sub-set of anarchists, adherents frequently blend anarchist and communist views. One of the most common symbols used by Antifa combines the red flag of the 1917 Russian Revolution and the Black flag of nineteenth-century anarchists. Antifa groups frequently conduct counter-protests to disrupt far-right gatherings and rallies. They often organize in black blocs (ad hoc gatherings of individuals that wear black clothing, ski masks, scarves, sunglasses, and other material to conceal their faces), use improvised explosive devices and other homemade weapons, and resort to vandalism. In addition, Antifa members organize their activities through social media, encrypted peer-to-peer networks, and encrypted messaging services such as Signal."

Jones added, "Antifa groups have been increasingly active in protests and rallies over the past few years, especially ones that include far-right participants. In June 2016, for example, Antifa and other protestors confronted a neo-Nazi rally in Sacramento, California, where at least five people were stabbed. In February, March, and April 2017, Antifa members attacked alt-right demonstrators at the University of California, Berkeley, using bricks, pipes, hammers, and homemade incendiary devices. In July 2019, William Van Spronsen, a self-proclaimed Antifa, attempted to bomb the U.S. Immigration and Customs Enforcement detention facility in Tacoma, Washington, using a propane tank but was killed by police."

MEDIA COVERAGE OF EXTREMISTS

The news media give extremists an enormous amount of coverage, providing the public with a misleading impression of how much support the extremists enjoy and how much influence and power they wield. That's because fiery speeches and radical proposals—particularly if they lead to violence and rioting—make for compelling stories, especially on TV, where pictures are of paramount importance. In contrast, policy discussions about practical centrist compromise proposals are often boring, unless you're a policy wonk.

This explains why reality TV star Donald Trump received far more news coverage than any of his sixteen opponents for the Republican presidential nomination in 2016 and also received far more news coverage than Democratic presidential nominee Hillary Clinton. Trump put on quite a show at his rallies, regularly insulted his opponents to an unprecedented degree, and made extravagant and extremist promises—including saying he would make Mexico pay to build a wall along the U.S. southern border, would negotiate fantastic trade deals because he was the world's greatest dealmaker, would cut taxes, balance the budget, reduce crime, replace the Affordable Care Act with something far better and cheaper, and create a huge number of American manufacturing jobs and jobs in coal mining.

Trump received free media coverage that would have cost $5.6 billion if he bought the equivalent amount of advertising in the 2016 campaign, according to the media tracking firm mediaQuant. The firm said that's more than Hillary Clinton, her Democratic primary opponent Senator Bernie Sanders, and Republican candidates Senator Ted Cruz and Senator Marco Rubio *combined* received.[59] In just the final twelve months of the campaign Trump received over $800 million in free earned broadcast media, while Clinton received $666 million. Trump got $2.6 billion in free earned online news media, compared to $1.6 billion for Clinton. And on Twitter Trump received $402 million in free attention, dwarfing the $166 million Clinton received. Trump also received more newspaper coverage than Clinton, mediaQuant found.

Any president commands a huge amount of media attention. But Trump arguably got more round-the-clock media attention than any other president once he arrived in the White House. His conduct was outrageous, unpredictable, unprecedented, and extreme, acting like a magnet for journalists. In addition, he tweeted attacks and provocative statements incessantly until he was kicked off his favorite social media platform on January 8, 2021, following his inflammatory remarks to followers who attacked the Capitol two days earlier. As president, Trump worked hard to dominate the news every day and on most days succeeded. He frequently turned to Fox News opinion hosts who he could count on to give him softball interviews and let him say whatever he wanted and talk for long stretches of time without ever being challenged.

In an article headlined "How the Press Covered the Last Four Years of Trump," published in the *Columbia Journalism Review* in October 2020, Jon Allsop and Pete Vernon wrote: "The media's response to the Trump presidency has been marked, perhaps above all, by an obsession with Trump. His ability to act as the press's assignment editor—be it by design or accident of his erratic personality (and there are strong opinions on both sides of that debate)—remains undimmed...he routinely says and does things that would trigger a month of controversy under any other president, yet pass mostly without comment. For every outrage that got normalized, however, Trump served up a fresher, zanier controversy to chew on."[60]

On the left, the media fascination with extremists turned Representative Alexandria Ocasio-Cortez into a magnet for news coverage soon after she defeated a veteran incumbent in a primary for her New York congressional seat in 2018. An article published by the Axios political news website in February 2019 was headlined: "Alexandria Ocasio-Cortez Is the Democrats' Trump."[61] It said the democratic socialist attracted more media attention in her first month in the House than any other House Democrat except Speaker Nancy Pelosi. "The Ocasio-Cortez web traffic blitz, and cable-news cascade, is because she has introduced—and aggressively defended and promoted—progressive policies around income taxes and climate change on social media."

Two years later, in January 2021, the conservative Sinclair Broadcast Group found that Ocasio-Cortez was still getting enormous media attention. "In the annals of American politics, there is no precedent for the global fame of Rep. Alexandria Ocasio-Cortez," Sinclair reported. "At thirty-one, AOC, as the congresswoman is universally known, is already the subject of no fewer than four biographies, two volumes of her quotations, a coffee table book of photographs, a coloring book, several comic books, and magazine coverage that has placed her, often with dynamic photo shoots, on the covers of *Vanity Fair*, *Rolling Stone*, the *Hollywood Reporter*, and *TIME*, among other periodicals."[62]

But despite the huge amount of attention extremists command in news coverage, they don't represent the majority of the American people. According to a study by our firm, Schoen Cooperman Research—conducted shortly after Biden was elected president—62 percent of Americans viewed his victory as a mandate for centrist policies. Only 28 percent believed Biden's victory represented a mandate for progressive policies. We found that 39 percent of Americans believed the Democratic Party's agenda was too left-wing, and that two-thirds agreed with Democratic Rep. Abigail Spanberger's comment that "misguided talks of socialism hurt [the Democrats] in many races and even cost them many elections."[63] Yet despite the overwhelming evidence that most Americans do not support a progressive agenda, we see time and time again that congressional Democrats yield to the far-left wing of their party.

COUNTERING EXTREMISM

There is no quick and easy solution to counter extremism. But an important step will be for Democratic and Republican politicians to find the courage to speak out against extremism on their own side of the aisle and call for moderation. While many Democrats and Republicans have denounced violence by their supporters, far fewer have denounced the groups and individuals behind the violence. For example, only ten House Republicans voted to impeach President Trump for inciting the attack on the Capitol, and only seven GOP senators voted to convict Trump on that charge.[64] The Republicans who cast these votes exhibited profiles in courage, even though many are not seeking reelection or are not facing reelection to the Senate in 2022, because they knew Trump would viciously attack them for their votes—as he did.

"Our Constitution and our country is more important than any one person," said Senator Bill Cassidy (R-LA). "I voted to convict President Trump because he is guilty." Senator Susan Collins (R-ME), said: "In this situation, context was everything. Tossing a lit match into a pile of dry leaves is very different from tossing it into a pool of water, and on January 6 the atmosphere among the crowd outside the White House was highly combustible....Instead of preventing a dangerous situation, President Trump created one. And rather than defend the Constitutional transfer of power, he incited an insurrection with the purpose of preventing that transfer of power from occurring."[65] Both Cassidy and Collins were reelected in 2020, so their Senate seats will not be on the ballot until 2026.

Former Republican president George W. Bush strongly condemned the attack on the Capitol. "I was sick to my stomach . . . to see our nation's Capitol stormed by hostile forces," Bush said in an interview with the CEO of the *Texas Tribune* several weeks after the Capitol riot. "It undermines rule of law and the ability to express yourself in peaceful ways in the public square.... This was an expression that was not peaceful."[66] Importantly, in the interview Bush rejected Trump's Big Lie that Democrats stole the election. That rejection is vital, because the millions of Trump voters who sincerely believe he won the election bear a grudge against Biden that will be hard to erase. Their hostility to Biden—nurtured by Fox News and other right-wing media—resulted in Biden never having the traditional "honeymoon" period on Capitol Hill in his first months in office. Congressional Republicans didn't want to alienate their base and so made it clear they would oppose the Democratic president at every turn. We saw this when not a single GOP House member or senator voted in favor of Biden's $1.9 trillion coronavirus relief package, which passed both houses in March 2021 and was signed into law by Biden.[67]

On the Democratic side, there were few criticisms of the Black Lives Matter organization and Antifa, although there were plenty of denunciations of the violent riots sparked by the killing of George Floyd. For example, in addition to the criticism of urban rioting by Biden cited above, House Majority Whip James Clyburn (D-S.C.) said: "We have to make sure we do not allow ourselves to play the other person's game....Peaceful protest is our game. Violence is their game. Purposeful protest is our game. This looting and rioting, that's their game. We cannot allow ourselves to play their game....Setting a fire, throwing stones at police officers, that's destructive behavior, which will not contribute to anything that will make this a better country and make a better future for our children and our grandchildren."[68]

Republicans did not hesitate to strongly criticize Democratic city and state officials for failing to do enough to end the urban rioting and looting, pointing out that there were many Black victims of the lawlessness. A *Wall Street Journal* editorial published in June 2020 at the height of the riots and protests supported the Republican argument, stating: "Public officials let rioters exploiting the memory of George Floyd run wild in the streets...liberal Democratic cities let lawless radicals harass and plunder almost at will....This isn't merely about damage to property. It's about destroying the order required for city life. Non-criminals are afraid to go into these cities to make a living."[69]

In addition, Democrats who attacked then-president Trump for holding large campaign rallies and superspreader events at the White House at the height of the coronavirus pandemic came under fire from Republicans for defending the racial justice protests that brought thousands of people to gather in close proximity, where many did not wear masks. Representative Ken Buck (R-CO) expressed this view in an op-ed published by Fox News in June 2020: ". . . as thousands of looters and rioters ransack stores, burn churches and spread violence across our nation, where are these same Leftist politicians that chided faithful and freedom-loving Americans just weeks ago? . . . I have yet to hear any state or local leaders cry 'social distancing' and break up these mass gatherings out of coronavirus concerns. The Leftist media suddenly isn't concerned about the threat of coronavirus spreading among large crowds of angry protesters, when just weeks ago they lauded the arrest of hairdressers for reopening their shops."[70]

When Barry Goldwater uttered his famous line that "extremism in defense of liberty is no vice" there is no reason to believe he was thinking about rioters and domestic terrorists of either the right or left—much less endorsing such violent lawbreaking. In his commentary on the Goldwater speech for the Heritage Foundation mentioned at the beginning of this chapter, Lee Edwards also wrote that "Goldwater did not say 'Extremism is no vice' but, rather, 'Extremism in the defense of liberty is no vice.' The all-important qualifying phrase, 'in the defense of liberty,' was ignored or excised by Goldwater's opponents and the media. People only heard, or thought they heard, 'Extremism is no vice.'"[71] And Edwards pointed out that Martin Luther King Jr. responded to criticism by some clergy members that he was an extremist by writing in his "Letter from a Birmingham Jail": "Was not Jesus an extremist for love? . . . Was not Paul an extremist for the Christian gospel? . . . So the question is not whether we will be extremists, but what kind of extremists we will be."

Extremism occupies a far more prominent place in American society and politics today than in 1964 when Goldwater waged his unsuccessful presidential campaign. Goldwater moved the Republican Party rightward, as Democrats moved leftward beginning with George McGovern's unsuccessful presidential campaign in 1972. Political polarization has accelerated ever since as the American people have grown further and further apart, leaving our nation dangerously divided and leaving Republicans and Democrats in Congress arrayed against each other like opposing armies on a Civil War battlefield.

As *New York Times* columnist Ezra Klein points out in his 2020 book, *Why We're Polarized*: "It is easy to cast a quick glance backward and assume our present is a rough match for our past, that the complaints we have about politics today mirror the complaints past generations had of the politics of their day. But the Democratic and Republican Parties of today are not like the Democratic and Republican Parties of yesteryear. We are living through something genuinely new. Rewind to 1950. That was the year the American Political Science Association (APSA) Committee on Political Parties released a call to arms that sounds like satire to modern ears . . . the ninety-eight-page paper, coauthored by many of the country's most eminent political scientists . . . pleads for a more polarized political system. It laments that the parties . . . work together too easily, leaving voters confused about who to vote for and why. 'Unless the parties identify themselves with programs, the public is unable to make an intelligent choice between them,' warned the authors."[72]

Having the two political parties "work together too easily" is certainly not the problem our nation confronts today. Having two political parties is a good thing, of course, because having a one-party state is an invitation to dictatorship. And while we don't want the two parties to look like twins, we need them to operate like siblings—different from one another, having rivalries, but part of the same family and each caring about their common welfare. We need to go back to a time when the parties were adversaries rather than enemies, working together for the benefit of the American people at all levels of government. To accomplish this goal, the parties need to both move toward the sensible center and reject the polarization of their extremist fringes.

6 | RUSSIA, CHINA, AND THE NEW COLD WAR

The United States became a global power with its victory in the Spanish-American War in 1898 and has been the mightiest superpower in history since its victory in World War II. The vast majority of Americans now alive were born after that war ended in 1945, so we've never known a time when our country wasn't the most economically and militarily powerful nation on Earth. As a result, we tend to assume that American dominance is just the natural order of things, destined to continue for all time. However, that is a wrong and dangerous assumption.

Just because a nation is powerful and dominant at one point in time doesn't mean it will maintain that status. History is filled with examples of this, including the Roman Empire, imperial China, imperial Spain, the British Empire, the Ottoman Empire, and the Soviet Union until it broke up in 1991. Today, leaders of Russia and China are working hard to restore their past glory and add the U.S. to the list of former great powers. Their goal is to replace our model of democracy and individual freedom with their model of authoritarianism and individual subservience to the state. They hold themselves up to nations around the world as models of successful and efficient government, far better at solving problems and building better futures for their people than democracies. They tell other nations and their own people that America is a chaotic and deeply divided country, with a failed government and an unworkable democratic system crippled by endless debate and gridlock.

The most partisan members of the American political class—on both the right and left—are aiding Russia and China in their effort to throw democracy onto the ash heap of history. By doing everything they can to sabotage the opposing political party—regardless of how much harm they inflict on our nation and our people—American hyper-partisans give the Russian and Chinese dictatorships a priceless gift: evidence that democracies are doomed to internal strife and ideological civil war.

The fighting and feuding politicians in Washington act more like members of rival gangs or enemy combatants than patriots who put America first in all their actions. Witness the almost automatic opposition of congressional Republicans to everything President Obama proposed, which now continues with everything President Biden proposes. In the same way, when President Trump was in office, Democrats fought him at every turn as part of "the resistance." Compromises between the two parties on major legislation are rare. Biden's $1.9 trillion coronavirus economic stimulus legislation was narrowly passed by the House and Senate in March 2021 without a single Republican vote.[1] In 2017, President Trump's $1.5 trillion in tax cuts were passed in both chambers without a single Democratic vote.[2] In these and other instances, neither side was willing to compromise sufficiently to pass consensus legislation. It seems that many lawmakers would rather see the other party fail than see our nation succeed.

The urban riots following the horrific killing of George Floyd by a Minneapolis police officer and the deadly insurrection by rioters who stormed our Capitol were broadcast around the globe, looking like scenes from a film about a dystopian Third World failed state. They were a serious blow to America's global image—and great news for China and Russia. The disturbances, which all elicited police responses to restore order, enabled China and Russia to say their violent crackdowns on protests in their own countries are no different from the response of

U.S. authorities. Referring to America's urban riots, the editor of the Chinese state-owned *Global Times* newspaper, Hu Xijin, said he wanted to ask House Speaker Nancy Pelosi and Secretary of State Mike Pompeo: "Should Beijing support protests in the U.S., like you glorified rioters in Hong Kong?"[3]

Indeed, the leaders of Russia and China couldn't ask for better propaganda footage than riots in our cities and at the Capitol to illustrate their contention that democracy is a system of government that leads to violent disorder and widespread suffering. And George Floyd's murder fed perfectly into the claims by China and Russia that America is a racist nation, where Black people are brutalized and murdered by police. When Chinese president Xi Jinping and Russian president Vladimir Putin have been criticized for killing and trying to kill their own political opponents, they have pointed to the killing of Floyd and other Black Americans by police as evidence of blood on the hands of governments in the U.S.

For example, in a meeting between U.S. secretary of state Antony Blinken and top Chinese diplomat Yang Jiechi in Alaska in March 2021, Blinken quite rightly criticized China for violating human rights in Tibet, Hong Kong, and its Xinjiang region. More than 1 million Uyghur Muslims have been imprisoned and sentenced to forced labor in Xinjiang and women have been forcibly sterilized there to reduce the population of the ethnic minority, according to human rights groups. The U.S. and others have accused China of crimes against humanity and genocide for its persecution of the Uyghurs.[4]

Yang responded to Blinken's criticism by accusing America of failing to respect human right because it has "slaughtered" Black Americans such as George Floyd. "We believe that it is important for the United States to change its own image and to stop advancing its own democracy in the rest of the world," Yang said. "Many people within the United States actually have little confidence in the democracy of the United States and they have various views regarding the government of the

United States....On human rights, we hope that the United States will do better on human rights. China has made steady progress in human rights, and the fact is that there are many problems within the United States regarding human rights, which is admitted by the U.S. itself as well....And the challenges facing the United States in human rights are deep-seated. They did not just emerge over the past four years, such as Black Lives Matter...the United States does not have the qualification to say that it wants to speak to China from a position of strength."[5]

China–U.S. tensions rose even further a few days later. The Chinese government banned the chair and vice chair of the U.S. Commission on International Religious Freedom and several Canadian officials from entering China and doing business with any Chinese citizens and institutions because the U.S. and Canadian officials have criticized China's treatment of the Uyghurs in Xinjiang. The commission chair is Gayle Manchin, wife of Senator Joe Manchin (D-WV). The vice chair is Tony Perkins, president of the Family Research Council, a conservative Christian policy and lobbying organization.

Demonstrating China's intolerance of any criticism, the Chinese Foreign Ministry issued a statement about the banned American officials: "They must stop political manipulation on Xinjiang-related issues, stop interfering in China's internal affairs in any form, and refrain from going further down the wrong path. Otherwise, they will get their fingers burnt."[6] That brought a sharp response from Secretary of State Blinken, who said in a statement: "Beijing's attempts to intimidate and silence those speaking out for human rights and fundamental freedoms only contribute to the growing international scrutiny of the ongoing genocide and crimes against humanity in Xinjiang."[7]

Chinese state media then called for boycotts of foreign companies that had stopped buying cotton from Xinjiang because the companies feared the cotton may have been grown and harvested using forced labor. About 20 percent of the world's cotton is grown in Xinjiang, so sales of the crop are a major Chinese export.[8] The companies China wants boycotted include Nike and H&M (Hennes & Mauritz), a Swedish clothing retailer with over 5,000 stores in seventy-four countries. "When you swing the big stick of sanctions at Xinjiang companies, you will also hit yourself," Xu Guixiang, a spokesman for the Xinjiang region's government, said at a news conference. "We hope that more companies like H&M will keep their eyes open and distinguish right from wrong." China also drew attention to racism in the U.S. by posting cartoons on social media depicting pre–Civil War slavery in the U.S., when slaves were forced to pick cotton in the South.[9] The European Union, the U.S., Britain, and Canada all imposed economic sanctions on China in late March 2021 because of the nation's policies in Xinjiang regarding the Uyghurs. This followed action by the Trump administration in its last week in power banning imports of cotton and tomatoes from Xinjiang and all products made with those crops.[10]

China again sought to divert attention to problems in the U.S. following the March 2021 murders of eight people (including six Asian American women) in the Atlanta area, as Chinese state media accused the U.S. of fostering anti-Asian racism. "It is part of a broader strategy that the Chinese Communist Party is enacting to undermine our democracy," Representative Stephanie Murphy (D-FL) told the *Washington Post* in March 2021. "So when you see them creating that false equivalency . . . it is their way to sow discord in our society, because they understand when we are not united, we are weaker in leading the world in confronting their bad behavior." Murphy, who came to the U.S. as a refugee from Vietnam as a child, added: "We have to be able to make a very clear distinction that our adversary and competitor is the Chinese Communist Party, not the Chinese people, and certainly not the Asian Americans who live here and who have contributed so much to this country. . . . When we attack Americans of Asian descent, we attack ourselves."[11]

Tenzin Dorjee, a senior researcher at the Tibet Action Institute, agreed with Murphy. In an op-ed headlined "Anti-China Is Not

Anti-Asian" that was published in the *Washington Post* in April 2021, Dorjee wrote: "Some of Beijing's harshest critics are Asian Americans. Uyghur refugees, Hong Kong democrats, Chinese dissidents and Tibetan exiles such as myself, whose communities back home reel under Beijing's boot, are urging Congress to censure China for its crimes. Asking lawmakers of conscience to hold their tongue on Beijing's genocide to supposedly prevent racial violence here is to set up a false trade-off between Asian American safety and Uyghur lives, both of which should be treated as nonnegotiable."[12]

Like President Xi, President Putin has responded to U.S. criticism of his many human rights violations by accusing America of the same type of wrongful actions that he and Russia have engaged in. For example, in an interview with Russian state TV in the summer of 2020, Putin said the urban riots then raging in the U.S. were "a sign of some deep-seated internal crisis." He added: "I think the problem is that group interests, party interests are put higher than the interests of the whole of society and the interests of the people. The president says we need to do such-and-such but the governor somewhere tells him where to go." In contrast, Putin said that in Russia, he doubted "that anyone in government or the regions would say 'we're not going to do what the government says, what the president says, we think it's wrong.'"[13]

Putin is correct in saying the president of Russia does not get criticized the way the president of the United States does. But Putin conveniently neglected to say that criticizing the president in Russia could land someone in prison, a hospital bed, or an early grave. Just look at what happened to Russian opposition leader Alexei Navalny, who was poisoned with a chemical nerve agent in the summer of 2020, reportedly on orders of Putin (Putin denies involvement), and nearly died. Navalny was arrested when he returned to Russia from his hospitalization in Germany in January 2021 and is now in prison on trumped-up charges.[14]

Unlike Putin, we don't think automatic obedience to the president is a virtue. We're thankful that in the United States the government is the servant of the people—unlike in Russia and China, where the people are the servants of the government. And we firmly believe that the freedoms Americans enjoy under our Constitution and our ability to freely elect our leaders are our nation's strength—not a weakness. But America needs to find a midpoint between lockstep public agreement by government officials on everything—as we see in Russia, China, and other authoritarian states—and constant fighting and an inability to reach agreement on just about anything, as is now the case between Republicans and Democrats in our own dysfunctional government. The more Democrats and Republicans fight with each other in Congress, crippling our government, the more Presidents Putin and Xi celebrate. And lately we have given these two ruthless dictators a lot to celebrate.

Today, Americans are so deeply and dangerously divided—not just in Washington but in communities around the country—that we don't even agree on what basic American values should be, whether there is such a thing as American exceptionalism, and what makes our democracy and our nation distinctive. This lack of a coherent American vision is a major weakness that China and Russia are more than happy to exploit. Imagine if we had this kind of division in World War II—if one political party was determined to defeat fascism and the Axis powers of Germany, Japan, and Italy, while the other political party thought we should side with the Axis against Britain, France, and their allies. Congress would be paralyzed into inaction.

In another victory for Russia and China, former president Trump's incessant and blatantly false claims that he was the victim of a rigged and corrupt election have given the two authoritarian states the perfect response to criticism of their own elections, which actually are rigged and corrupt. Don't point fingers at us, they can say. What about the fraudulent American elections?

America once set the gold standard for the world for free and fair elections. But while the 2020 elections were free and fair—with presidential results validated by numerous state recounts, court decisions, and Republican and Democratic officials—Trump's Big Lie has disastrously undermined faith in American elections. For example, two Pew Research Center polls published in April 2021 showed a big divide between Democrats and Republicans on making it easy for Americans to vote, with Republicans far more suspicious of the voter fraud Trump so frequently complained about. Pew found that only 28 percent of Republicans but an overwhelming 85 percent of Democrats agreed with the statement: "Everything possible should be done to make it easy for every citizen to vote."[15]

The loss of faith in U.S. elections by millions of Americans has given Russia and China an enormous propaganda victory and has helped them to discredit our democracy and democracies in other nations. The more Democrats and Republicans fight over how we conduct elections, the more Russia and China benefit. An example of this took place when a bitter fight erupted between Democrats and Republicans in late March and April 2021 after the Republican legislature and governor in Georgia enacted a law changing the way elections are run in the state. President Biden called the Georgia law "Jim Crow of the twenty-first century" and said "it must end." He asked the Justice Department to see if the federal government can do anything to block it.[16] Democrats said the Georgia law amounted to voter suppression that would reduce turnout of reliably Democratic Black voters, and was a GOP attempt to boost the chances for Republicans to win elections. However, Republicans vehemently denied the law would suppress votes in Georgia and said it was needed to prevent voter fraud. They even argued that the law could actually make in-person voting easier.

The Georgia law outraged Democrats by making it harder to vote with mail ballots, reducing the number of drop boxes for mail ballots, giving the state legislature increased power over local election boards, banning mobile voting places, and making it a crime to give voters waiting in line anything to eat or drink. At the same time, the law expands the required days of early voting and adds another weekend of voting.

And the law requires precincts with many voters to add voting machines or staff, or split precincts in half—actions that could shorten voter lines on Election Day. An analysis of the law by *New York Times* reporter Nate Cohn concluded that "the law's voting provisions are unlikely to significantly affect turnout or Democratic chances. It could plausibly even increase turnout. In the final account, it will probably be hard to say whether it had any effect on turnout at all."[17]

Yet Democrats and voting rights groups quickly cast the fight against the Georgia voting law as a battle against a racist effort to keep Black Americans from voting. Major League Baseball acceded to pressure from civil rights groups and moved the All-Star Game out of suburban Atlanta in protest.[18] James Quincey, the CEO of Atlanta-based Coca-Cola Co., called the Georgia voting law "unacceptable" and "a step backward." Former president Trump accused the MLB of "interfering with free and fair elections" and called for a boycott of baseball, Coca-Cola, and other companies that complained about the law. A group of state legislators demanded that a Coca-Cola vending machine be removed from their office suite. Georgia-based Delta Airlines also criticized the law and the Georgia House responded by voting to cancel a tax break on jet fuel that could cost the airline tens of millions of dollars.[19] However, the state Senate adjourned until 2022 without voting on the measure.[20]

We can picture Presidents Putin and Xi laughing at all this and agreeing on the superiority of their own authoritarian systems. It's absurd that Democrats and Republicans in Georgia, around the nation, and in Washington can't agree on reasonable safeguards to ensure voters can verify their identities without restricting their right to vote. Just about all of us have a Social Security card with a number, and just about everyone sixty-five and older has a Medicare card with a number. These don't cost anyone anything. Why not have a card for voting that could be swiped like a credit card to indicate a person has voted in a particular election, or could have its number entered in a database if someone votes by mail? That's just one commonsense measure that both parties ought to be able to agree on to make voting twice in the same election or some other form of fraudulent voting extraordinarily difficult, if not impossible. But instead of turning to nonpartisan technical experts to make elections more secure, politicians on both sides of the aisle would rather do battle, undermining our stability and core values, and strengthening our adversaries. This makes no sense.

THE RUSSIA-CHINA AXIS

Today, the United States is engaged in a two-front Cold War with China and Russia to determine if dictatorships or democracies will triumph. The two authoritarian states are also challenging America's preeminence in the economic and military spheres. President Abraham Lincoln said in the Gettysburg Address in 1863 that "government of the people, by the people, for the people, shall not perish from the earth."[21] Will his prophecy prove true, or will authoritarian regimes like those in Russia and China spread across the world—even reaching the United States to end the bitter struggle between the left and right that is ripping our nation apart today? Right now democracy is not winning the battle against dictatorships.

As President Biden told reporters at his first White House news conference in March 2021, Presidents Xi and Putin think "autocracy is the wave of the future and democracy can't function in an ever—an ever-complex world....Look, I predict to you, your children or grandchildren are going to be doing their doctoral thesis on the issue of who succeeded: autocracy or democracy? Because that is what is at stake, not just with China. Look around the world. We're in the midst of a fourth industrial revolution of enormous consequence. Will there be middle class? How will people adjust to these significant changes in science and technology and the environment? How will they do that? And are democracies equipped—because all the people get to speak—to compete?... [T]his is a battle between the utility of democracies in the twenty-first century and autocracies. If you notice, you don't have Russia talking about communism anymore. It's about an autocracy.... We've got to prove democracy works."[22] At another event in the Rose Garden the same month, Biden made the danger of government gridlock clear in the struggle to preserve democracy. "It's critical to demonstrate that government can function—can function and deliver prosperity, security, and opportunity for the people in this country," the president said.[23]

For years, American elected officials in both political parties had hoped—naively it turns out—that the establishment of diplomatic and trade relations between China and the U.S. in 1979 and the breakup of the Soviet Union in 1991 would lead to a gradual liberalization in the two communist states over a period of years, moving both nations away from authoritarianism and toward democratic and free-market reforms and nonaggression against other nations. Some economic liberalization did indeed occur in both nations, leading to a limited form of capitalism subservient to government, but it was not followed by other lasting reforms. And Russia and China rejected the potential of the internet and modern communications tools to promote global connectivity, democracy, and freedom. Instead, the two nations used new technology to create Orwellian surveillance states, with greater powers than ever before to stifle efforts at democratic reforms.

In fact, both Russia and China became more aggressive in their efforts to undermine democracy in the U.S. and around the world during the terms of Presidents Obama and Trump. Obama's disastrous "lead from behind" strategy ceded the U.S. role as leader of the Free World and sought to win over Russia and China with gestures of friendship that Obama hoped would be reciprocated. But Russia and China saw Obama's gestures as signs of weakness that they could and did exploit.

Trump's erratic and unpredictable foreign policy—highlighted by his strange affinity for Putin and unwillingness to criticize the Russian leader—was marked by scattershot isolationism, along with frequent criticism and insults directed at America's European allies. While Trump's "America First" slogan excited his base voters, around the globe it was seen by many as an abandonment of America's post–World War II role as the world's indispensable nation in defending our friends against the aggression of authoritarian states. Although their policies were very different, together Obama and Trump weakened America's position as the global defender of democratic institutions. This was good news for Russia and China and they asserted themselves to fill the leadership void.

We can only hope that President Biden—with his decades of experience in foreign policy and in dealing with Russia and China in the Senate and as vice president—will do a better job than Obama and Trump standing with our allies and standing up to Russia and China. This is essential, because the survival of democracy requires strong backing from the United States in deeds as well as words. But Americans can't fight on behalf of democratic ideals when we are losing faith in those ideals ourselves. How can we hope to beat back authoritarianism, as earlier generations did in World Wars I and II, when some Americans have suggested that we would be better off with China's government-controlled economic system, or when 37 percent of Republicans in a 2016 poll said they have a favorable opinion of Putin?[24] We must reassert our position on the world stage as the guardian of liberty, equality, and opportunity—but first, it is essential to renew our own belief in our founding ideals.

Today most Democrats and Republicans are in agreement that Russia and China are threatening democracy in America and in nations around the world, and threatening America's place as the dominant global economic and military power. The two authoritarian states make no secret of their ambitions. Both nations have been expanding their militaries for years and have used the United Nations and other international organizations to protect themselves and allies from the consequences of their human rights violations. Both are brazen in their espionage and cyberwarfare operations against the U.S. and other nations. Both use military muscle to bully other nations in their spheres of influence. The 2018 U.S. National Defense Strategy correctly states: "China and Russia want to shape a world consistent with their authoritarian model."[25] We need to face up to a harsh reality: What we are seeing today is the most dramatic challenge to Western democracy since the end of the Cold War.

China and Russia don't have identical interests and objectives, but they have grown closer in recent years to confront their common major adversary: the United States. This is even truer today than it was in 2014, the year *The Russia-China Axis: The New Cold War and America's Crisis of Leadership*, by Douglas Schoen and Melik Kaylan, was published.[26] The book noted that Americans "do not defend and argue for the principles of freedom, liberty, and democracy as we once did. As a result, those ideals lack a global champion in an era of great social and economic dislocation, political violence, and technological change. In the meantime, the Chinese and Russians have put forward compelling alternative models—authoritarian, nationalistic, antidemocratic, and socially conservative—that have resonated with millions.... The United States, meanwhile, largely stays silent, conceding the rhetorical and even moral high ground to those despotic antidemocratic regimes."

At a 2019 conference in Moscow, Chinese president Xi called Russian president Putin "my best friend and colleague" and said "we will strengthen our mutual support on key issues." Putin joined the exchange of compliments and described the Russia-China relationship as "a global partnership and strategic cooperation."[27] This was not empty rhetoric. According to the Worldwide Threat Assessment released by the U.S. intelligence community in 2019, Russia and China "are more aligned than at any point since the mid-1950s."[28] It would be hard enough to defend democracy and the national security of America and our allies against one of these authoritarian powers. Defending against them both at the same time is an enormous challenge that cries out for a united and bipartisan effort, in the same way America responded to the challenge of fascism and imperialism in World War II. While we're not expecting Russia and China to launch World War III against the U.S. with conventional or nuclear forces, a war is already underway in cyberspace, in communications, in diplomacy, in trade, and in the struggle to preserve freedom and democracy. Defeating Russia and China on all these fronts, while maintaining the strongest military on Earth, will not be easy. However, the U.S. must accomplish this vital task to preserve democracy at home and abroad.

On the military front, both Russia and China have engaged in big buildups in this century, but still spend nowhere near what America spends on defense. Russian military spending grew 175 percent between 2000 and 2019, the Stockholm International Peace Research Institute reported, to hit $65.1 billion. The institute reported that China's military spending has also been growing, hitting $261 billion in 2019.[29] U.S. military spending is far higher than Russia and China combined, coming in at $740 billion for the 2021 fiscal year.[30] Some additional national security spending by all three countries is not included in their official defense budgets.

Russia and China cooperate closely militarily. Since 2015, the Russian and Chinese navies have held dozens of joint exercises in the Baltic Sea, the Mediterranean Sea, the Indian Ocean, and the South China Sea. In 2018, the two nations joined forces for the largest military exercise since the Cold War on Russia's shared border with China next to the Korean Peninsula, involving thousands of troops. Stephen Blank, a senior fellow with the American Foreign Policy Council, suggested that maneuvers "may have originally been intended as an exercise in anticipation of a U.S. attack on North Korea."[31]

In 2019, the Russian and Chinese navies participated in Operation Mosi, hosted by the South African Navy, which was designed to "enhance interoperability and maritime security."[32] China and Russia followed this up with another joint naval drill later that year in the Gulf of Oman, this time with virulently anti-American Iran. And in September 2020, Russia and China held joint military drills in southern Russia, despite the raging coronavirus pandemic. Most telling, however, were joint air and missile defense exercises held by Russia and China in 2017. These exercises, as Blank points out, required both nations to "put their cards on the table" and to reveal their four "C's"—command, control, communications, and computer capabilities—along with their intelligence and surveillance capabilities.[33] Together, the activities of Russia and China show that they are working together in a military alliance, even though they have not formalized the alliance with a signed agreement.

Russia and China also work as allies at the United Nations, where both have veto power as members of the Security Council. And both nations support rogue authoritarian states Iran, North Korea, and Syria against U.S. interests. Russian foreign minister Sergey Lavrov described their partnership this way: "As regards international issues, we feel—and our Chinese friends share this view—that our cooperation and coordination in the international arena are one of the most important stabilizing factors in the world system. We regularly coordinate our approaches to various conflicts, whether it is in the Middle East, North Africa, or the Korean peninsula. We have regular and frank and confidential consultations."[34]

In addition to their military alliance, China and Russia have strengthened their trade ties and cooperation on the economic front. The *Global Times*, a publication controlled by the Chinese Communist Party, reported in March 2021: "China and Russia are seeking to further bolster the security of their financial and trade relations to fend off threats posed by some 'unfriendly' countries . . . the US and a few Western countries that are imposing unilateral sanctions on China and Russia....The renewed commitment also offered a sobering reminder of the need to further boost cooperation in trade and investment, which, despite recent improvements, still lags behind and isn't reflective of the constantly rising strategic partnership between the two nations."[35] The Chinese government-controlled newspaper said that trade between

Russia and China was worth nearly $108 billion, down almost 3 percent from the previous year due primarily to the coronavirus pandemic. In 2020, China was Russia's top trading partner, and purchased 14.5 percent of Russia's exports.[36] However, in 2019 (the most recent year available), Russia ranked only number thirteen among China's trading partners, purchasing just 2 percent of Chinese exports.[37]

Russia primarily exports raw materials to China, while China primarily exports finished goods to Russia. Russia, which is rich in oil and natural gas reserves, is a vital energy supplier to China. In 2014, the two nations closed the biggest natural gas deal Russia has taken part in since the fall of the Soviet Union. Putin oversaw Russian firm Gazprom's signing of a thirty-year deal with the China National Petroleum Corporation, which is estimated to be worth over $400 billion and is routing 38 billion cubic meters of gas into China annually.[38] Russia is also China's largest arms supplier, providing about 70 percent of China's total arms imports between 2014 and 2018.[39]

THE CHINESE THREAT

A report issued by the U.S. intelligence community in April 2021 concluded that China is the top long-term threat to America and our allies. The intelligence community's Annual Threat Assessment said China wants to increase its influence around the world and weaken America's foreign alliances as part of a campaign to "foster new international norms that favor the authoritarian Chinese system." In addition, the report warned of China's growing military might, stating that the communist regime plans to at least double its number of nuclear weapons in the next decade and will seek to establish military bases in other countries. China also poses a serious threat to Taiwan and will pressure the independent nation "to move toward unification" and become part of China, the report said.[40]

China has made no secret of its belief in the superiority of its author-itarian system since communists came to power in 1949. More recently, President Xi Jinping's infamous Document No. 9—which he issued in 2013 for distribution to Communist Party cadres—makes his implaca-ble hostility to democracy clear. The document explicitly banned what it called seven core Western values from China, including: "Western constitutional democracy"; "universal values" of human rights, media independence, and civic participation; "neo-liberalism"; and criticism of the Communist Party's past. The *New York Times* quoted Cheng Xin-ping, deputy head of propaganda for the city of Hengyang, as saying at the time: "Promotion of Western constitutional democracy is an attempt to negate the party's leadership" and accusing human rights advocates of wanting to "ultimately to form a force for political confrontation."[41] Indeed, under Xi's repressive regime, human rights lawyers and activ-ists, feminists, journalists, religious leaders, ethnic minorities, scholars, and others have faced greater harassment and imprisonment since the issuance of Document No. 9. The document "put the Communist Party's paranoia and illiberalism on display in its own words," the *Washington Post* said in a 2015 editorial.[42]

President Trump seemed to believe that he could charm Xi with flattery and by being a charming host when the two dined at Trump's Mar-a-Lago estate in Florida in 2017, boasting in an interview with Fox Business that he gave the Chinese leader "the most beautiful piece of chocolate cake you've ever seen and President Xi was enjoying it" and saying that "I mean, we understand each other" and "we had great chemistry."[43] Other presidents of both parties who came before Trump—from Nixon onward—also thought they could win China's leaders over to become less authoritarian and less dangerous to their neighbors. That was a mistake. Xi—who serves as Communist Party general secretary, president of China, and chairman of the Central Military Commission—is installed as a dictator for life. This enables him to take a long view in working to advance what he sees as China's interest over the next fifty years and beyond, just as his communist predecessors did. He realizes full well that American elected officials are focused on looking good before they are up for reelection, putting them at a disadvantage.

There is no question that China is a major violator of human rights. The U.S. State Department's annual report on human right around the world in 2020, issued in March 2021, extensively documents these violations by China, including: "Arbitrary or unlawful killings by the government; forced disappearances by the government; torture by the government; harsh and life-threatening prison and detention conditions . . . political prisoners; politically motivated reprisal against individuals outside the country . . . arbitrary interference with privacy; pervasive and intrusive technical surveillance and monitoring; serious restrictions on free expression, the press, and the internet, including physical attacks on and criminal prosecution of journalists, lawyers, writers, bloggers, dissidents, petitioners, and others as well as their family members, and censorship and site blocking; . . . severe restrictions and suppression of religious freedom; substantial restrictions on freedom of movement;…forced labor and trafficking in persons; severe restrictions on labor rights, including a ban on workers organizing or joining unions of their own choosing; and child labor."[44]

China is the biggest foreign threat to America's democracy and economy. The People's Republic is using American dependence on Chinese imports and the desire of U.S. businesses to sell to the Chinese market of more than 1.4 billion people (the largest in the world) as leverage. In 2019, the U.S. imported goods and services from China valued at almost $472 billion, while America exported $163 billion in goods and services to China, the Office of the U.S. Trade Representative reported.[45] Loss of the Chinese import and export market would be devastating to many American retailers and businesses, as well as to many U.S. businesses and farmers reliant on selling to China. For example, General Motors has sold more cars in China than the company has sold in the U.S. every year since 2009—meaning GM would suffer enormously if it suddenly lost access to the Chinese market.[46] In sharp contrast, the U.S. imported only $24 billion in goods and services from Russia and exported nearly $11 billion worth of goods and services to Russia in 2019.[47] The value of U.S. imports from Russia was only about 5 percent of the value of U.S. imports from China, and U.S. exports to Russia were worth only about 7 percent of U.S. exports to China.

In a speech to leading U.S. business executives and former government officials in February 2021, top Chinese diplomat Yang Jiechi made it clear China won't have good business relations with any foreign companies that complain about Chinese human rights violations in Tibet, Hong Kong, Xinjiang, or elsewhere, or about China's demands that Taiwan come under control of the mainland communist government. He also pressured his audience to lobby the Biden administration to reverse Trump's tough-on-China policies and to oppose proposals to decouple the U.S. and Chinese economies.

Describing Yang's speech in a *Wall Street Journal* op-ed published in March 2021, former Trump administration deputy national security adviser Matt Pottinger wrote: "Beijing's message is unmistakable: You must choose. If you want to do business in China, it must be at the expense of American values. You will meticulously ignore the genocide of ethnic and religious minorities inside China's borders; you must disregard that Beijing has reneged on its major promises—including the international treaty guaranteeing a 'high degree of autonomy' for Hong Kong; and you must stop engaging with security-minded officials in your own capital unless it's to lobby them on Beijing's behalf. Another notable element of Beijing's approach is its explicit goal of making the world permanently dependent on China, and exploiting that dependency for political ends."[48]

President Trump sought to stand up to China for its unfair trading practices and theft of American intellectual property by imposing tariffs on some imports from China. That prompted Chinese retaliatory tariffs and brought Trump criticism at home and abroad for launching a trade war that raised prices of Chinese products for American consumers and reduced sales of U.S. farm products and other products to China. We tend to take a dim view of protectionism and barriers to free trade, but China has been pursuing unfair trading practices for years, so something must be done to stop it.

For example, China has consistently devalued its currency, the yuan, in the last two decades by buying large quantities of dollars and selling the yuan. By lowering demand for the yuan, Beijing artificially depresses its price in relation to other currencies. The other countries of the world, now with a more powerful currency compared to the yuan, can import Chinese goods more cheaply. On the other hand, while the erosion of the power of the yuan makes Chinese goods look more appealing to the rest of the world, it is more expensive for Chinese citizens to import goods from abroad. Essentially, this practice is equivalent to China imposing tariffs on imports while other countries lower their tariffs on China. As a result, "Made in China" has become one of the most recognizable labels in the world. Beijing sacrificed the quality of life of its citizens (who could not as easily afford foreign products) for a boost in its exports and a rapid shift to a manufacturing economy.

As Chinese imports make up more and more of the international economy, China has greater leverage to negotiate trade deals. In a world increasingly averse to free trade, China has been winning battles for trade agreements against the United States. In July 2019, fifty-four countries in Africa signed a free-trade agreement, the largest such agreement since the founding of the World Trade Organization in 1994. China brokered the deal, and has itself signed free-trade pacts with more than forty of the fifty-four signatories. In 2017, when President Trump pulled the United States out of the Trans-Pacific Partnership—a free-trade agreement with twelve Pacific Rim countries that was designed to act as a counterweight to China's expansionist ambitions—China negotiated an agreement called the Regional Comprehensive Economic Plan with the same twelve nations, essentially taking America's empty seat.

China's theft of American companies' intellectual property (such as trade secrets about how to manufacture a particular product) is a major component of its unfair economic policies. China requires foreign companies to give up valuable intellectual property to win permission to operate in the lucrative Chinese market. Chinese companies then use the knowledge they have gained from the foreign companies to manufacture copycat versions of the foreign products and sell them in China and later in other countries at a lower price. China reaps the profits and largely displaces the foreign products, many of which are made by American companies. No one knows exactly how much China's intellectual property theft costs U.S. companies, but estimates in 2020 ranged from $225 billion to $600 billion annually, the international law firm Crowell & Moring reported.[49]

To expand its influence with nations around the world and gain leverage over them, while also increasing trade, Xi Jinping launched the massive Belt and Road Initiative in 2013, scheduled for completion in 2049. The initiative is an infrastructure-building project that will span Asia, the Middle East, Africa, and Europe if completed. It will also put China at the center of a massive trading bloc. Also referred to as the New Silk Road, the plan is to include an overland and overseas component, and will build highways, railways, ports, and pipelines that will reach over sixty countries and two-thirds of the world's population. The first piece of the project is the land portion—what Xi calls the Silk Road Economic Belt—and is planned to connect China to the rest of Asia and to Europe. The second piece—the Maritime Silk Road—is supposed to tie port cities on the South China Sea to ports in the Indian Ocean and the Mediterranean. Plans call for ports and shipping lanes "that will connect Quanzhou to Venice, with prospective stops along the way in Malaysia, Ethiopia and Egypt," Ben Mauk wrote in the *New York Times* in 2019.[50] Beyond physical infrastructure, the Belt and Road Initiative is slated to expand the digital infrastructure in many countries. This will create new markets and deals for China's already massive state-sponsored telecom companies like Huawei and ZTE, and allow them to penetrate more deeply into the telecom infrastructure of developing countries.

The cost of the Belt and Road Initiative, financed in large part by loans made by China to other nations, is expected to reach $8 trillion, with China paying $1 trillion and other nations paying the remainder. However, some countries have told China they need to restructure billions of dollars in Chinese loans they have already received to fund their share of the project, because they can't make full payments due to the global economic downturn caused by the coronavirus pandemic.[51] If the Belt and Road Initiative goes forward to completion, nations around the world will wind up owing China trillions of dollars in total debt, putting China in a strong position to demand favorable treatment from these nations on an array of fronts in return for debt forgiveness or delayed repayment of the loans. Alternatively, China can foreclose on land, infrastructure, and mineral resource deposits in developing nations in the event of loan defaults.

For example, when a China-financed port project in Sri Lanka failed to meet its loan repayment schedule, China foreclosed on the loan. The Sri Lankan government then gave a Chinese-backed corporation a ninety-nine-year lease on the port and 15,000 acres around it in 2017. Sri Lanka still owed over $8 billion to Chinese government-controlled businesses for projects even after the foreclosure on the port.[52] "The case is one of the most vivid examples of China's ambitious use of loans and aid to gain influence around the world—and of its willingness to play hardball to collect," the *New York Times* reported in 2018. "The debt deal also intensified some of the harshest accusations about President Xi Jinping's signature Belt and Road Initiative: that the global investment and lending program amounts to a debt trap for vulnerable countries around the world, fueling corruption and autocratic behavior in struggling democracies." The same *Times* report found that Chinese loans have financed thirty-five ports on six continents.[53] While China rarely seizes property as it did in Sri Lanka, its harsh loan conditions create economic dependence on Beijing, which allows the Chinese government to gain greater access to developing economies and get special treatment for Chinese companies.

China uses its economic and diplomatic power to try to exempt itself from international rules, arrangements, and commitments and to withhold information about its activities. It works through the World Trade Organization, the United Nations, the World Health Organization, and other international organizations it belongs to in order to influence events around the world. China has become the second-largest contributor to the United Nations peacekeeping budget and the third-largest contributor to the overall U.N. budget. As the U.S. intelligence community pointed out in its 2019 Worldwide Threat Assessment, China "is using its influence to press the U.N. and member states to acquiesce in China's preferences on issues such as human rights and Taiwan."[54]

The Chinese government's greatest international impact in 2020 and 2021 was arguably in the area of global public health, arising out of its cover-up of vital information about the coronavirus pandemic that began in the Chinese city of Wuhan in late 2019. Full Chinese disclosure of everything it knew about the virus could have helped nations around the world act more quickly and effectively against COVID-19, which at this writing has killed more than 3 million people worldwide. The U.S. and thirteen other countries issued a statement in March 2021 criticizing China for "withholding access to complete, original data and samples" of the coronavirus at the beginning of the pandemic and for refusing to fully cooperate with an investigation of the origins of the pandemic carried out by the World Health Organization. WHO head Tedros Adhanom Ghebreyesus acknowledged that his organization's investigation of COVID-19 was "not extensive enough" because of the lack of Chinese cooperation.[55]

Jamie Metzl, a member of a WHO advisory committee who served on the National Security Council in the Clinton administration, agrees with Ghebreyesus. Metzl discussed the issue in an interview with

60 Minutes that was broadcast in March 2021. He said that a WHO team visited Wuhan to try to determine if COVID-19 was caused by a coronavirus that infected someone working at the Wuhan Institute of Virology or if the virus leaked in some other way from the institute. He said the institute has "probably the world's largest collection of bat viruses [believed to be the source of COVID-19], including bat coronaviruses." Chinese scientists actually conducted the WHO investigation and simply informed the WHO team of their findings clearing the lab of involvement with COVID-19, Metzl said. He said members of the WHO group spent only three hours at the Chinese lab and didn't get "access to records and samples and key personnel" and "weren't allowed to do their own primary investigation." Additionally, China had veto power over which foreign scientists were on the team and no one on the team was trained in how to formally investigate a lab leak, Metzl said.[56]

Additionally, Dr. Robert Redfield, a virologist who headed the Centers for Disease Control and Prevention during the Trump administration, told CNN in February 2021 that evidence suggests the virus causing COVID-19 escaped from the Wuhan Institute of Virology. He said a localized outbreak of the disease began in Wuhan in September or October 2019 and then spread throughout China over the next two months. However, China didn't notify U.S. officials of a "mysterious cluster of pneumonia patients" that turned out to be the previously unknown disease COVID-19 until December 31, 2019. Both Redfield and Dr. Anthony Fauci, director of the National Institute of Allergy and Infectious Diseases, told CNN that if the U.S. and countries around the world had known about the new disease earlier they could have responded far more effectively and saved lives. "I think it would have been a significant difference," said Fauci, who advised President Trump and now advises President Biden on the pandemic. "I think if we had sent our people into Wuhan and been able to talk to the Chinese scientists in a conversation that might have lasted an hour, you could have gotten so much information right from the get go. They would have told us, don't believe what you're reading. This is spread asymptomatically. It spreads highly efficiently and it's killing people." China originally downplayed the severity of COVID-19 and inaccurately stated the disease could not be transmitted by people, slowing the global response.[57]

After the severity of the pandemic became known, the Chinese government denied doing anything wrong regarding COVID-19 and falsely pointed to other nations as the source of the disease. In a story published in December 2020 headlined "China Peddles Falsehoods to Obscure Origin of Covid Pandemic," the *New York Times* reported: "Facing global anger over their initial mishandling of the outbreak, the Chinese authorities are now trying to rewrite the narrative of the pandemic by pushing theories that the virus originated outside China.... The campaign seems to reflect anxiety within the ruling Communist Party about the continuing damage to China's international reputation brought by the pandemic. Western officials have criticized Beijing for trying to conceal the outbreak when it first erupted."[58]

The secrecy and duplicity of China regarding the COVID-19 pandemic undoubtedly cost lives, slowing the response of scientists, doctors, and governments around the world to the pandemic. But the blame for this misconduct lies squarely on the shoulders of the Chinese government and Communist Party—not the Chinese people and certainly not Asian Americans. The rise in hate crimes against Asian Americans in the U.S. is an example of ugly racism that should be strongly condemned by every elected official and rejected by all Americans.

On the military front, China is no match for the U.S. today, but that may change. The *Washington Post* reported in April 2021: ". . . China could be within five years of surpassing the U.S. military....Since taking office, leaders in the Biden administration, like their predecessors under President Donald Trump, have identified China as the top threat to U.S. security. They have voiced concerns about America's eroding edge as Beijing showcases its growth in satellites, ballistic missiles, bombers, fighter aircraft, submarines, and naval vessels."[59]

China has also waged an aggressive cyberwarfare campaign against the United States. FBI Director Christopher Wray said in 2019 that Chinese hacks are "more challenging, more comprehensive and more concerning than any counterintelligence threat" that the U.S. faces. In 2020, Wray said that the FBI was opening a new China-related counterintelligence case every ten hours on average.[60] Beijing is focused on gaining access to government secrets, along with innovative technology and intellectual property from the private sector. In the process, China has invaded the privacy of millions of Americans. "It's the people of the United States who are the victims of what amounts to Chinese theft on a scale so massive that it represents one of the largest transfers of wealth in human history," Wray said. "If you are an American adult, it is more likely than not that China has stolen your personal data."[61]

THE RUSSIAN THREAT

Russia doesn't have the economic power to hurt the U.S. on the trade front in the same way China can. But Russia has used its military muscle to challenge the U.S. around the globe for many years, beginning at the end of World War II when the Soviet Union turned the neighboring Eastern European nations of Albania, Bulgaria, Czechoslovakia, East Germany, Hungary, Poland, Romania, and Yugoslavia into satellites with communist governments subservient to Moscow.[62]

In 1955, all these nations except Yugoslavia formed the Warsaw Pact as a military alliance headed by the Soviets to counter the NATO alliance of the U.S. and Western European nations, with the two sides facing off with armed forces ready for a war that thankfully never came. The Warsaw Pact broke up in 1991—the same year the Soviet Union broke up and East and West Germany reunified as a member of NATO.[63] The breakup split the Soviet Union into fifteen republics—Armenia, Azerbaijan, Belarus, Estonia, Georgia, Kazakhstan, Kyrgyzstan, Latvia,

Lithuania, Moldova, Russia, Tajikistan, Turkmenistan, Ukraine, and Uzbekistan. Russia is by far the most powerful, but is much diminished from the days when the fifteen republics were united as one nation.[64] By way of comparison, Russia remains the geographically largest nation on Earth, covering 6.6 million square miles.[65] But the Soviet Union covered 8.65 million square miles—over 2 million square miles more.[66] If you subtracted 2 million square miles from the total area of the United States (including Alaska and Hawaii), we would lose about 55 percent of our territory.

The Soviets worked against the interest of the U.S. and our allies around the world, supporting communist insurgencies, revolutions, and regimes in their Eastern European satellites and in China, North Korea, North Vietnam, Afghanistan, Cuba, and elsewhere. North Korea and North Vietnam benefited greatly from Soviet and Chinese support in their wars with the U.S. and allied forces. America and the Soviet Union nearly went to war in 1962 when the Soviets placed nuclear missiles in Cuba, but they agreed to withdraw the missiles after President John F. Kennedy promised not to invade Cuba and secretly agreed to remove U.S. missiles from Turkey.[67] Soviet forces invaded Afghanistan in 1979 to support a pro-Soviet communist government but withdrew in 1988 and 1989 when they were unable to defeat Muslim insurgents.[68] (The U.S. withdrew from Afghanistan for the same reason.)

In addition, the Soviet Union built a nuclear force unmatched by any nation except the U.S. According to Arms Control Association, Russia currently has an estimated 6,375 nuclear warheads, while the U.S. has 5,800. China is a distant third place in the number of nuclear warheads, with 320. Under the new Strategic Arms Reduction Treaty, Russia has 1,326 nuclear warheads deployed on 485 intercontinental ballistic missiles, submarine-launched ballistic missiles, and strategic bombers. The U.S. has 1,373 nuclear warheads deployed on 655 ICBMs, submarines, and bombers.[69]

Russia has continued its aggressive actions around the world since the breakup of the Soviet Union. To cite just some examples: Russia invaded the Republic of Georgia in 2008, waged a five-day war to support separatists in two regions of that nation, and still occupies 20 percent of Georgia in support of the separatists.[70] Russia invaded Ukraine in February 2014 and quickly annexed the Crimean Peninsula, marking the first time any nation had annexed territory in Europe since World War II.[71] And Russia continues to occupy two separatist republics in eastern Ukraine and has distributed Russian passports to residents of the occupied area since 2019.[72] In 2015, Russia launched its largest and longest military operation since the fall of the Soviet Union when it sent warplanes and ground troops to intervene in the Syrian Civil War. It has succeeded in keeping dictator Bashar Assad in power against what began as a popular uprising and turned into a struggle against the ISIS terrorist group and rebel forces, but the civil war continues.[73]

Along with China, Russia maintains trade, economic cooperation, and security ties with Iran, diluting the impact of U.S. sanctions reimposed by then-president Trump against the Islamic Republic. "China and Russia are now integrally involved in Iran's affairs, from its oil and port infrastructure to its defense capabilities," *Foreign Affairs* reported in November 2020.[74]

In addition, Russia is a strong supporter of Venezuela's anti-American socialist president Nicolas Maduro, who presides over a country plagued by a failing economy, hyperinflation, shortages of medicine and food, and electric power outages. While over fifty nations—including the U.S.—recognize National Assembly leader Juan Guaido as Venezuela's president, strong backing from Russia and China has helped Maduro retain power.[75]

In military action, Russia utilizes mercenary troops, including some trained by the Russian intelligence service SVR (successor to the Soviet Union's KGB) for many foreign operations. The mercenaries use Russian equipment and take orders from the Kremlin. The Wagner Group—a private military contractor with mercenaries that have been deployed in Ukraine, Libya, Sudan, Venezuela, Belarus, Syria, and elsewhere in service to Russia—has played a key role in Russian foreign military engagements, allowing Russia to deny it has deployed its army to do battle in these countries.

Describing the company in an article posted by the Center for Strategic and International Studies in September 2020, German Council on Foreign Relations Senior Fellow Andras Racz wrote: "The Russian private military company Wagner Group may appear to be a conventional business company. However, its management and operations are deeply intertwined with the Russian military and intelligence community. The Russian government has found Wagner and other private military companies to be useful as a way to extend its influence overseas without the visibility and intrusiveness of state military forces. As a result, Wagner should be considered a proxy organization of the Russian state rather than a private company selling services on the open market....Wagner Group is far from being the sole Russian private military company. Anna Maria Dyner lists several other Russian private military companies that have operated abroad, such as the E.N.O.T. Corporation in Syria and the Feraks group in Iraq, Afghanistan, Iraqi Kurdistan, and Sri Lanka, as well as the Antiterror-Orel Group and many others."[76]

Everywhere they go, the Russian mercenaries tilt the balance in favor of autocracy and away from democracy. For instance, in Belarus, the Wagner Group sent dozens of mercenaries to incite violent unrest before the July 2020 presidential election. In Syria, Russian paramilitary forces clashed with American-supported Kurdish troops and about forty U.S. Army Rangers and Delta Force operators in a four-hour battle in which about 250 mercenaries were killed.[77]

A significant portion of Russia's military spending goes toward the modernization of its nuclear arsenal. In an address to the Russian Federal Assembly in 2018, Putin said: "During all these years since the unilateral U.S. withdrawal [in 2001] from the ABM [Anti-Ballistic Missile]

Treaty, we have been working intensively on advanced equipment and arms, which allowed us to make a breakthrough in developing new models of strategic weapons.... These weapons form the backbone of our nuclear deterrence forces, just as of other members of the nuclear club." In the same speech, Putin said Russia was developing a nuclear-powered cruise missile. "It is a low-flying stealth missile carrying a nuclear warhead, with almost an unlimited range, unpredictable trajectory, and ability to bypass interception boundaries. It is invincible against all existing and prospective missile defense and counter-air defense systems," the Russian president said.[78]

Russia's military buildup in the last two decades has been part of a steady campaign to win back control of Putin's "near abroad," meaning the now-independent nations that were once joined with Russia in the Soviet Union. As Todd South wrote in *Military Times* in 2017: "Putin knows that Russia can't fight a conventional war or extend far from its border. But it can push incrementally to reclaim historical Russian territory and destabilize NATO."[79] Russia has perfected a form of "hybrid warfare" that seamlessly combines cyberwar, conventional war, and diplomatic and economic pressure. The playbook calls for disrupting a nation—socially, politically, and economically—and then taking advantage of the turmoil. With propaganda, espionage, and cyberwar, Moscow is targeting the U.S. more fiercely than any other country. Russia's cyber campaign has succeeded in contributing to division among Americans along party lines, the spread of false conspiracy theories, and the erosion of the common purpose and shared values that Americans hold.

Russia has been upgrading its cyberwar forces for years under Putin, enabling Russian hackers to exploit weaknesses in the political, infrastructure, government, and defense systems of the United States. For example, during the 2016 U.S. presidential campaign, Russian hackers were able to use a spearfishing email sent to the account of the assistant to Hillary Clinton campaign chairman John Podesta to access Podesta's email account. This allowed the Russians to collect passwords of other campaign staffers and leak 20,000 emails and other documents through the group WikiLeaks. These emails contained messages of high-ranking Democrats belittling Democratic presidential contender Senator Bernie Sanders and making clear their intention to coalesce the party behind Clinton. In 2018, indictments by Special Counsel Robert Mueller revealed that the leak was politically motivated and timed to coincide with the Democratic National Convention, where sowing disunity within the party would have its maximum effect.[80] The Russians achieved their goal. Sanders's appeals at the convention to support Clinton in the race against Donald Trump were booed by his supporters in the hall.

The goal of Russia's cyberattacks is to destabilize the U.S. and create disunity among Americans. President Putin wants to delegitimize American institutions, erode faith in the American democratic process, and foster doubt among the American people about the truthfulness or reliability of almost everything they are told by government, the media, and other institutions. He is succeeding spectacularly. To be sure, Putin would not mind stealing state secrets or exploiting our systemic vulnerabilities. However, his main goal is to foster exactly the kind of environment in which we now live, where there is wide disagreement on what constitutes objective truth and widespread distrust that serves as a breeding ground for false and divisive conspiracy theories.

In addition to working to influence the 2016 presidential election on behalf of Donald Trump, Russia did the same thing in 2020, believing he would pursue policies more favorable to Russia and hoping to undermine the faith of the American people in our democracy.[81] And on election night in 2020, the Associated Press—which counted votes in over 7,000 elections in the U.S. for about 12,000 news organizations around the world—was hit with thousands of cyberattacks "most especially from the Russian Federation" designed to disrupt the count, AP President and CEO Gary Pruitt said in March 2021. Pruitt said the AP fended off the attacks in 2020 and stopped a smaller number in 2016, when he received a call from Homeland Security Secretary Jeh Johnson, who told him that "President Obama was concerned that if AP were successfully hacked on election night, the confidence in American democracy would be shaken...people would wonder what's wrong with the United States, what's going on?"[82]

On top of this, in late 2020, in the final weeks of the Trump administration, U.S. officials acknowledged that a top Russian intelligence agency had hacked into computers used by businesses and by federal military, intelligence, and civilian agencies—including the Defense Department, State Department, Department of Homeland Security, Justice Department, Commerce Department, and Centers for Disease Control and Prevention—by compromising software made by the company SolarWinds.[83] Russia was not alone in targeting the U.S. for cyberattacks. In March 2021, Microsoft said that thousands of U.S. businesses and government agencies using a Microsoft email service had been victimized by a hacking campaign sponsored by the Chinese government.[84]

WHAT LIES AHEAD?

As we have said, Presidents Putin and Xi are undoubtedly delighted by the divisions tearing America apart. After all, the more Americans fight with each other, the less attention and energy we can devote to the very real threats to democracy and our national security that China and Russia pose.

Commenting on China–U.S. relations, *Wall Street Journal* columnist Gerard Baker wrote in March 2021 that "Chinese leadership understands that the greatest ideological weapon it now holds in its increasingly existential struggle with America is the gleeful enthusiasm for self-destruction that characterizes so much of elite opinion in the U.S." Baker wrote that the criticism China's top diplomat, Yang Jie-chi, directed at U.S. secretary of state Antony Blinken at their meeting in Alaska in early 2021 regarding America's record on human rights, treatment of minorities, and inequity in the U.S. "could have been lifted straight from the pages of the Democratic Party's presidential election platform, culled from Pulitzer Prize-winning newspaper stories, or jotted down in a student's notes from lectures delivered daily at America's top universities." Although he was writing about China, Baker's comments apply just as accurately to Russia and its criticism of the U.S.[85] Baker also sharply criticized "the fanatical insistence on the qualities that divide rather than unite Americans—race, sexual orientation, and multifarious 'gender'—as the principal characteristics of identity." His point was a good one. Rather than looking at ourselves as members of different demographic groups who happen to be Americans, we need to once again start looking at ourselves as Americans who happen to be members of different demographic groups. The erosion of faith among the American people and our leaders in our civic religion of democracy and our other institutions weakens the United States and empowers democracy's authoritarian adversaries. It blurs and minimizes the differences between authoritarianism and democracy that Americans in past generations saw clearly.

Syndicated columnist Victor Davis Hanson pointed out the sheer audacity and gall of China criticizing the U.S. record on human rights, and how the criticism feeds on America's internal divisions. Writing in March 2021, he said: "China may have destroyed the culture of Tibet, destroyed democracy in Hong Kong, put Muslim minorities in detention camps and systematically discriminated against African visitors, but the victimizer nonetheless plays the victim of supposed American racism. Each time prominent Americans damn the United States as racist, Chinese racists chime in, 'Amen!'"[86]

President Putin fired off his own criticism of America in March 2021 after President Biden was asked by George Stephanopoulos of ABC News if the American president knows Putin and thinks the Russian president is a killer. Biden responded: "Hmm, I do," clearly angering

Putin. As Masha Gessen wrote about Putin's response in the *New Yorker*: "Putin explained that the 'mentality of the American establishment' was shaped by a history of settler colonialism, the genocide of Native Americans, and slavery. He reminded his audience that the U.S. was the world's only country to have deployed nuclear weapons. Putin made these remarks at the end of a two-hour meeting with local officials in Crimea, which Russia began occupying seven years ago this week."[87]

The social unrest and the erosion of faith by Americans in our government and our fundamental institutions are powerful weapons for our adversaries. The champions of authoritarianism in Moscow and Beijing are determined to portray America as an oppressive and racist society that exploits the poor and middle class for the benefit of the rich and well connected. Under the Russian and Chinese narrative, America's commitment to justice, equality, and freedom is fraudulent. When Americans make this same argument, it is much easier for Russia and China to divert attention from their own grave violations of human rights and argue that their systems are indeed superior to democracy.

But democracy and authoritarianism are not equivalent. And despite our shortcomings since Europeans first arrived and took the land of Native Americans and enslaved Africans, America today is not in the same league as Russia and China when it comes to corruption, mistreatment of citizens, racism, and other vices. If America's founders (all White men) could magically come back to life today, they would no doubt be stunned to learn that a Black man has served as our president, that a higher percentage of women (who did not gain the right to vote until 1920) than men have voted in every presidential election since 1984, that a woman of African and South Asian descent is our current vice president, and that in a myriad of ways we are doing a much better job than they did living up to the lofty ideals they enshrined in the Declaration of Independence and Constitution. Certainly, much more progress is needed. But we have progressed very far over the course of our history. Yet Russia and China want us to believe this not the case.[88]

Despite all of America's shortcomings, it remains the world's best hope for the expansion of liberty, the protection of human rights, and the preservation of democracy. Russia and China pose the greatest threat to all these things and are waging a new Cold War against the rights we hold dear. The cause of America must be the cause of democracy. If it is not, authoritarian regimes will snuff out freedom wherever they can. Democracy is fragile. It only works when we have faith that it will. Only the United States can protect the world's faith in democracy—but we must start by believing in democracy ourselves.

7 / CENTRIST REFORMS TO REUNITE US

We have written this book to call attention to the urgent need to heal the serious divisions tearing America apart, turning us from the United States into divided states, divided communities, and even divided families. We have documented how these dangerous divisions—greater than at any time since America split in two during the Civil War—are threatening our democracy, our national security, our economic strength, and our status as a role model for other nations. And we have argued that the only way to heal these deep and disturbing rifts is to bring the American people together around a centrist, commonsense, bipartisan agenda—turning away from extremists on both the right and left, and settling our differences with compromises rather than confrontations that can paralyze government and sometimes spiral into violence.

As we have noted, Abraham Lincoln famously said in a speech in 1858 that "a house divided against itself cannot stand," quoting a line in the Gospels from Jesus.[1] Lincoln was talking about the divisions around the evil of slavery, saying: "I believe this government cannot endure, permanently half slave and half free." Importantly, Lincoln called for reconciliation and unity between the North and South to end our divisions once the Civil War had ended. He concluded his second Inaugural

Address in 1865 by saying: "With malice toward none, with charity for all, with firmness in the right as God gives us to see the right, let us strive on to finish the work we are in to bind up the nation's wounds, to care for him who shall have borne the battle and for his widow and his orphan—to do all which may achieve and cherish a just and lasting peace among ourselves and with all nations."[2]

Today we are divided by many issues and even by our perceptions of reality. Most frightening of all, our divisions are growing. Tens of millions of Americans believe that President Trump was reelected in 2020, but that the election was stolen from him by a vast conspiracy of Democratic and Republican state and local government officials throughout the nation. Trump continues to peddle this Big Lie, and we should believe him when he says he will never concede defeat and never acknowledge Joe Biden as the legitimate and lawfully elected president of the United States. Unlike Lincoln, Trump seeks to fan the flames of division with malice toward many. At the same time, some far-left Democrats want to use their bare majorities in the House and Senate (using a tiebreaking vote by Vice President Kamala Harris) to shove through far-reaching legislative change by abandoning the filibuster. They have attacked Senator Joe Manchin and other Democratic moderates for being unwilling to go along with their most progressive proposals.

Too many Americans today view those they disagree with politically not just as opponents but as enemies. Many of Trump's devoted followers believe Democrats are evil socialists who want to take away our freedoms and destroy our country. Millions of other Americans on the opposite end of the political spectrum believe Republicans are evil racists and fascists who don't care about America and our people, and are only interested in corruptly seeking power to enrich themselves and their rich and powerful political donors at the expense of everyone else.

We are under no illusions that we can come up with a set of policies that everyone will agree with to bring us together and deal with the many challenges America faces today. As the fifteenth-century monk and poet John Lydgate reportedly said: "You can please some of the people all of the time, you can please all of the people some of the time, but you can't please all of the people all of the time."[3] So we know that neither we nor anyone else can come up with policy prescriptions that will please all Americans—or even all readers of this book. Nevertheless, we don't want to let the perfect be the enemy of the good. So we are going to use this chapter to lay out compromise proposals that we believe can help unite the American people, strengthen and enhance our social fabric, help us better compete with foreign adversaries, and make the American Dream real again for millions of people in our country who now feel locked out of the gates to prosperity and opportunity. We want to restore the faith of the American people in democracy as our nation's secular religion, and help our democracy function efficiently, inclusively, and with the consent and support of the governed. We believe the best way to do this is to encourage the creation of a centrist coalition that will lessen polarization and enact incremental yet progressive change.

Right now, America's house is not just divided. It's on fire, consumed in the flames of hatred that too many of our citizens hold for each other. We saw this hatred erupt in the rioting and insurrection at our nation's Capitol on January 6, 2021. Earlier, we saw it erupt in cities across America when demonstrations for racial justice gave birth to riots in the spring and summer of 2020. We don't want to see violence break out again between our fellow Americans, although we fear it will. We don't want to see any of our fellow citizens killed or injured. Americans need to stop ceaselessly fighting with each other regarding just about everything and unite to put out the flames of hatred and division if we want our children, grandchildren, and generations to come to enjoy the blessings of liberty that we enjoy today. We hope the reforms outlined below will help extinguish the blaze.

ELECTION REFORM

Elections are common around the world, but their rules and fairness vary enormously. In the most repressive authoritarian states, the ruling regime decides who is eligible to run and results are predetermined. The incumbent party and the incumbent leader (assuming the leader seeks reelection) always win by a landslide. This is true, for example, in Russia, China, and North Korea. In a true democracy, of course, elections are free and fair—as was the case in the U.S. in 2020, despite the claims of former president Trump that the election was rigged in favor of his opponent, now-president Joe Biden. While there have been plenty of cases around the world where elections have been rigged to keep the incumbent or chosen successor in power, we've never before heard of one in which the rigging was done to defeat the incumbent—until Trump made his false victory claim.

Even when elections are free and fair, they can be structured in many different ways. In some countries leaders are elected directly by the people. In others they are elected by the legislative branch. In some countries multiple parties get seats in parliaments and form coalitions to determine which party rules and which leader takes office as the head of the government. In others, like the U.S., nearly all seats in the legislative branch are divided between two parties. And in non-parliamentary democracies like ours, the elected president's party doesn't always have a legislative majority.

One thing virtually all election systems have in common is that they change over time. For example, early in America's history, only White male property owners could vote. Voting was later expanded to include all White men and later Black men (officially soon after the Civil War, though not in practice until the 1960s in many places) and women in 1920. We believe changes are long overdue in the way American election campaigns are run and the way elections are conducted. The goal of these changes should be to create a level playing field for all candidates by increasing the disclosure of campaign contributions; giving candidates who aren't Democrats or Republicans a real chance of winning; reducing the outsize influence of extremists in party primaries so centrists have a better chance to be nominated; ending partisan redistricting of congressional and state legislative districts; and making it easy to vote to enable the most people possible to cast ballots, while safeguarding against election fraud.

The House voted 220–210 in March 2021 to approve a bill called the For the People Act that would accomplish many of these goals. A poll by Data for Progress and Vote Save America that gave likely voters a brief description of the bill in February 2021 found it was supported by 68 percent—including 70 percent of Democrats, 68 percent of independents, and 57 percent of Republicans.[4] Unfortunately, not a single Republican voted for the For the People Act in the House. It has virtually no chance of passing in the Senate if the filibuster rule stays in effect, because ten Republicans would need to join all fifty Democrats in the body to send it on to President Biden (who supports the bill) for his signature.

Among other provisions, the For the People Act would create national voting standards (standards now vary by state); set up commissions made up of five Democrats, five Republicans, and five independents to redraw congressional districts every ten years based on new census data, ending gerrymandering; require PACs, super PACs, and other groups donating to political candidates to publicly disclose their donors; create public financing of campaigns that would provide $6 in matching funds to candidates for every $1 raised in donations of up to $200, cutting the dependence of congressional and presidential candidates on big donors; guarantee all voters the right to cast ballots by mail; require at least fifteen days of early voting in federal elections; require states to automatically register citizens to vote based on government records; require the use of paper ballots (for documentation if recounts are needed); allow convicted felons who have completed their prison sentences to vote; and require presidential candidates to disclose their income tax returns (something Donald Trump never did). If the bill did pass, it would face challenges in court. The conservative Heritage Foundation, for example, contends many provisions in the bill are unconstitutional.[5]

The need for change in our electoral system is something that most Americans embrace. A Pew Research Center poll published in March 2021 found that 65 percent of Americans said our political system needs major changes or needs to be completely reformed. Another 28 percent said the system needs only minor changes, and only 7 percent said the system doesn't need to be changed at all.[6] The same poll found that 67 percent of Americans believe "most politicians are corrupt" and 56 percent believe elected officials don't care about what ordinary people think. And the poll found that 73 percent of Americans agree very much or somewhat that citizens, not members of Congress, ought to be able to vote directly to decide whether legislation involving certain key issues becomes law. An earlier Pew poll published in October 2019 found that 61 percent of Americans said the Democratic Party "is too extreme in its positions" and 63 percent said the same thing about the Republican Party.[7] Elected officials ought to take note of these numbers.

We agree with most of the For the People Act and believe it could give Senate Democrats and Republicans a platform to hammer out compromise legislation that could become law. Yet in today's dysfunctional Congress, that doesn't appear to be in the cards. On balance, if we were serving in the House or Senate we would vote for the bill. If we had the power to write and win passage of a centrist bill to restructure our elections, below is a list of what we would like to see in the legislation.

Disclose candidate tax records: Require all candidates for federal office—including the House and Senate, not just the presidency and vice presidency—to disclose their past five years of state and federal income tax returns and the returns of their spouses (if they file separately) at least sixty days before nominating contests (primaries, caucuses, or state conventions) are held. Then require those who are elected to release their state and federal income tax returns and the returns of their spouses every year they hold office. This is necessary so voters can know even before candidates are nominated if they have conflicts of interest and if officeholders are profiting from investments and business dealings because of the offices they hold. While the tax laws guarantee the privacy of our returns, it is reasonable to require candidates to give up that privacy (and the privacy of their spouses) to serve in elective office. No one is forced to run for elected office, so anyone can preserve the privacy of his or her returns by simply not running.

Nonpartisan redistricting: The boundaries of congressional and state legislative districts are redrawn every ten years to account for population shifts reported in the newest census. In most states, the legislature approves the new district boundaries. Lawmakers work hard to protect their own political parties. If one party controls both houses of a legislature it draws all the lines in its favor. If control of two houses is split, lawmakers have to reach a compromise. Most congressional and state legislative districts are drawn to favor one party or the other, depending on which party commands the allegiance of most voters in a particular district. This makes many elections noncompetitive. In such districts, winning the primary can virtually guarantee victory in the general election.

Nonpartisan redistricting is vital to give all voters, regardless of their political affiliation, fair representation. Congressional districts and state legislative districts should be contiguous and not split up municipal and country jurisdictions when possible, and pay no attention to the party affiliation of residents of a district. For example, rather than snaking through five counties to maximize or minimize the number of Democratic or Republican voters, a congressional district could cover one county and part of another without regard to the party preference of residents. Professional and nonpartisan demographers should draw up district maps. The maps could be approved by commissions as envisaged by the For the People Act, or by nonpartisan judges—such as each state's highest court, or a panel of judges appointed by the highest court.

Require top-two primaries: As we have discussed, in most states today the Democratic Party and the Republican Party each conduct primaries (or caucuses in a few states) to nominate candidates for elected office. Democrats on the far left and Republicans on the far right vote in disproportionate numbers because they tend to be the most politically involved, increasing the odds of extremist candidates being nominated. This often disenfranchises moderates because it frequently keeps moderate candidates off the general election ballot. It also discourages elected officials and those running against them from taking centrist and bipartisan positions, lest they lose nominating contests. In top-two primaries—also known as jungle primaries—Democrats, Republicans, third-party candidates, and independents all run in one primary. The top two vote-getters run against each other in the general election. Such primaries are held in California and Washington State. In Louisiana, candidates from all parties run on the general election ballot and if one candidate gets a majority he or she is elected; if not, the top-two finishers face off in a runoff six weeks later. In Nebraska, members of the unicameral legislature run on a nonpartisan basis, so all candidates compete in one primary. And in Alaska primaries bring all candidates together and the top four then run against each other in the general election.[8] Primaries where candidates from multiple parties run give centrist, independent, and third-party candidates a better chance of being nominated and elected. This promotes bipartisanship and more effective government. It would be a big improvement over today's partisan primaries.

Ranked-choice voting and instant runoff voting: Our current electoral system discourages third-party and independent candidates from running because it is extraordinarily difficult for them to win. Since either a Democrat or a Republican almost always wins the partisan elections, most voters understandably consider a vote for anyone who isn't a member of one of the two major parties a wasted protest vote. Yet we need more elected officials who are neither Democrats nor Republicans. Freed of pressure from their major party to automatically oppose just about everything the other major party proposes, third-party and independent officials are able to be more bipartisan and pragmatic, voting based on the issues and not in partisan lockstep. Ranked-choice voting encourages more than two candidates because it allows voters to cast ballots for more than one candidate for an office. They simply mark their ballots with who they favor with a number: 1, 2, 3, 4, etc. Where this method is used, a candidate is declared the winner if he or she gets a majority of the votes, or in some cases in primaries if a candidate gets a specified large percentage of the vote. If no candidate gets the required percentage of votes, a runoff is held.[9]

Traditionally, runoffs have been held at a later date after nominating contests—usually between the top-two finishers, as we just discussed above. However, ranked-choice voting enables runoffs to be held instantly, without requiring a second election to be held—saving governments the expense and eliminating the need for voters to cast ballots a second time. The instant runoff is held by counting first-choice votes first. If one candidate gets the required majority or required near-majority he or she is declared the winner. If not, the candidate with the fewest votes is knocked out of contention. Ballots cast for the dropped candidate are then counted and the second-choice candidate on those ballots gets those votes. If no candidate then has a majority, the process is repeated and the votes of the candidate with the fewest votes go to the third-ranked choice and so on until one candidate gets enough votes to win. Instant runoff voting also works where more than one candidate can win, such as on a school board where several positions are filled at once.

Ranked-choice voting and instant runoff voting may sound complicated to those unfamiliar with these types of balloting, but that's not the case. This type of voting is also fairer than a multicandidate primary, where a candidate can win less than a third of the vote but still be nominated in a large field. It also eliminates spoiler candidates. For example, Green Party candidate Ralph Nader was criticized for taking votes away from Al Gore in the 2000 presidential election and Jill Stein was criticized for taking votes away from Hillary Clinton in 2016. Had the presidential elections been conducted using ranked-choice voting and had enough Nader voters listed Gore as their second choice, and enough Stein voters listed Clinton as their second choice, Gore and Clinton could have been elected president. At the same time, more voters would have felt free to cast ballots for Nader and Stein if they knew their second-choice votes could have stopped George W. Bush and Donald Trump from being elected.

The group FairVote reports that ranked-choice voting has been used in some municipal primaries and elections and was used in Democratic presidential nominating contests in 2020 in Alaska, Hawaii, Kansas, Maine, Nevada, and Wyoming. Alaska will use it in state elections in 2022 and in the presidential election in 2024. New York City first used it in city primary and special elections starting in 2021.[10] Pew reported in March 2021: "Lawmakers in twenty-nine states are considering measures this year that would adopt ranked-choice voting in some form, in local, statewide, or presidential primary elections. Many of those bills have bipartisan support. Depending on the state and which party is in power, some bills are sponsored by just Republicans or just Democrats."[11] If ranked-choice voting and instant runoff voting were used in congressional and presidential elections nationally, they would have enormous positive impact.

Expand nonpartisan elections: As we have pointed out repeatedly, the feuding and fighting between Democrats and Republicans is a major cause of the division tearing America apart and a roadblock to bipartisanship. Electing officials on a nonpartisan basis can help promote cooperation over confrontation, since officials don't feel obligated to oppose colleagues from the other party. While nonpartisan elections are common in America's small and midsize cities, they are rare in big cities and for state offices. As of April 2021, sixty-three of the mayors of America's hundred largest cities by population were Democrats, twenty-six were Republican, four were independents, and just seven were nonpartisan.[12] As we have noted, Nebraska is the only state with a nonpartisan (as well as a unicameral) state legislature. Statewide and federal elections are all partisan. As of 2021, two U.S. senators—Angus King of Maine and Bernie Sanders of Vermont—were independent, but they caucused with the Democrats and gave Democrats control of the Senate. The election changes described above would open the way for more independent and third-party candidates to seek elective offices, and would help break the stranglehold of the two parties that has played a big part in creating the gridlock that afflicts Congress today.

Additional voting reforms: The 2020 election saw a dramatic decrease of in-person voting on Election Day, as many states made mail-in and early in-person voting easier in response to the coronavirus pandemic. The percentage of ballots cast in person on Election Day plummeted from 60 percent in 2016 to just 28 percent in 2020, according to a poll of 18,000 voters in every state by the MIT Election Lab and YouGov. The 2020 Survey on the Performance of American Elections showed a significant jump in early in-person voting, going from 19 percent of votes cast in 2016 to 26 percent in 2020. Mail-in voting more than doubled, going from 21 percent of ballots in 2016 to 46 percent in 2020.[13] Total voter turnout in the 2020 presidential election set a new record, with 159.6 million Americans casting ballots, marking the first time more than 140 million Americans voted in an election. In addition, 66.7 percent of Americans eligible to cast ballots voted—the highest percentage since 1900, when 73.7 percent voted. (The record voter turnout as a percentage of eligible voters took place in 1876, when turnout hit 82.6 percent.)[14]

High voter turnout is a very good thing and should be welcomed by every American. Voting is the responsibility of each of us living in our democracy and makes government more responsive to our needs. This is why Dr. Martin Luther King Jr. and so many others worked so hard to ensure that Black Americans could exercise their constitutional right to vote, why women waged a long battle to amend the Constitution to belatedly gain the right to vote in 1920, and why so many people successfully campaigned to amend the Constitution to lower the voting age to eighteen in 1971. It is why Democrats are continuing to fight GOP efforts they say will make voting harder, arguing that Republicans want to suppress votes—particularly of Black voters, who tend to overwhelming vote for Democrats.

We support most of the changes in the For the People Act to make voting easier, including making mail-in voting permanent in every state without requiring voters to give a reason for wanting to vote using this method. However, as we write this, it is clear that Senate Republicans are not going to go as far as Democrats want. That means the bill passed by the House has virtually no chance of passage in the Senate. A bill passed with only Democratic support can be repealed when Republicans gain control of both houses of Congress, as will happen inevitably at some point. So for the sake of enacting a law that will stay on the books far into the future and have widespread support from the American people, Democrats need to be willing to compromise to win some Republican support. One way they can do this is by agreeing to some reasonable requirement for voter identification for in-person and mail-in voting.

Unfortunately, former president Trump's repeated lies for months before and after the 2020 election falsely claiming that mail-in voting was corrupted by fraud clearly influenced his supporters. As we pointed out earlier, a Quinnipiac Poll released January 11, 2021, found that 73 percent of Republicans believed Trump's assertions that there was widespread voter fraud in the election, but only 36 percent of independents and a mere 5 percent of Democrats believed this claim.[15] Even though there is no evidence of widespread voter fraud, we can't have a successful democracy if over 70 percent of voters in one major party believe the other party stole the last election.

New York Times columnist Ross Douthat wrote in March 2021 that studies show that voter ID laws don't have any impact on reducing the insignificant amount of voter fraud that takes place in elections.[16] In addition, Douthat said no-excuse mail-in voting didn't increase turnout in states that allowed this compared with states that made mail-in voting more difficult, and didn't affect Democratic turnout more than Republican turnout. While many more Democrats than Republicans voted by mail in 2020, more Republicans voted in person, so turnout was high among both groups. "So rule changes favored by Democrats that make it modestly easier to vote probably didn't help Democrats win the 2020 elections, and rule changes favored by Republicans that make it modestly harder to vote probably haven't suppressed minority votes," Douthat wrote. The studies he cited were from the Stanford Institute for Economic Policy Research and from Kyle Raze, a Ph.D. candidate at the University of Oregon.[17] Douthat wrote that the Stanford University authors said record voter turnout was prompted by a high level of voter interest in the 2020 election, rather than any changes in voting rules.

Voter ID laws can operate without reducing voter turnout if voters are given many options regarding what form of identification they can provide. One of the criticisms Georgia's new voting law received in the spring of 2021 was that it requires voters to provide their driver's license number or state identification card number on their absentee ballot. Major League Baseball announced in April 2021 that it was moving the All-Star Game from Atlanta to Denver to protest against the Georgia voting law, which Democrats charged was designed to suppress Black votes.[18] Yet the Office of the Colorado Secretary of State says on its website: "All voters who vote at the polls must provide identification. If you are voting by mail for the first time, you may also need to provide a photocopy of your identification when you return your mail ballot."

The Colorado website goes on to say that any one of these forms of valid ID is acceptable as long as it shows the voter's Colorado address: a Colorado driver's license or identification card issued by the Colorado Department of Revenue; a U.S. passport; an employee identification card with a photo issued by any federal, Colorado state, or local Colorado government entity; a pilot's license; a U.S. military identification card with a photo; a copy of a utility bill, bank statement, government check, paycheck, or other government document issued in the past sixty days showing the name and address of the voter; "a Certificate of Degree of Indian or Alaskan Native Blood"; a valid Medicare or Medicaid card; a certified copy of a U.S. birth certificate; a certified documentation of naturalization; a student identification card with a photo of the voter issued by an institute of higher education in Colorado; a veteran photo identification card issued by the U.S. Department of Veterans Affairs; an identification card issued by a federally recognized tribal government certifying tribal membership; verification that a voter is a resident of a group residential facility; verification that a voter is a person committed to the Department of Human Services and confined and eligible to register and vote; and "written correspondence from the county sheriff or his or her designee to the county clerk indicating that a voter is confined in a county jail or detention facility."[19]

It's hard to see how anyone can get by in today's society without even a single one of the above forms of ID. So it seems reasonable that Democrats and Republicans ought to be able to agree on a similar broad list of identification documents that could be used as voter ID nationally, helping to allay Republican fears of voter fraud while allaying Democratic fears that eligible voters will be denied their right to cast ballots for lack of ID.

One needed and obvious change that Democrats and Republicans ought to be able to agree on is to require votes cast by mail to be counted beginning several weeks before Election Day. In some states, election officials were not allowed to begin the vote count until Election Day or even until polls closed on the night of the 2020 election. This created delays of several days in some states before the winners of the presidential race and some other races were determined, since there was a record number of absentee votes. Nearly twice as many Democrats as Republicans voted by mail in the election—59 percent of Democrats, compared with only 30 percent of Republicans, the MIT study found.[20] So it should have come as no surprise that Trump performed well when Election Day votes were counted, but lost ground dramatically when the heavily Democratic mail-in ballots were counted and sometimes recounted over the next few days.

When Trump's early leads in Election Day vote counts were reversed in some states as absentee votes were counted, Trump falsely claimed this was evidence of Democrats fraudulently adding votes for Biden that Biden didn't actually receive. By beginning the counting of mail-in ballots earlier, election results should become known election night or early the next morning in more states, avoiding the days-long delays in the 2020 vote count that left the nation and the world in limbo about who was elected, and seemed to lend support to Trump's wild conspiracy theories.

End winner-take-all in the Electoral College: Many Democrats and even some Republicans have advocated abolishing the Electoral College and electing the president by a popular vote. They point out that five presidents were elected by winning the Electoral College vote while losing the popular vote: John Quincy Adams in 1824, Rutherford B. Hayes in 1876, Benjamin Harrison in 1888, George W. Bush in 2000, and Donald Trump in 2016.[21] However, amending the Constitution to get rid of the Electoral College isn't going to happen, because it would need the support of legislatures in small states that now get more clout because of the Electoral College. If a president were elected by popular vote, candidates would focus their campaigns and proposals on large metropolitan areas where they could pick up the most votes. Low-population states and rural communities would get little attention, so state legislators representing those areas will never approve substituting the popular vote for the Electoral College.

In all states except Maine and Nebraska, Electoral College votes are awarded on a winner-take-all system. As a result, presidential candidates focus all their attention on swing states where they have a shot at winning a majority of the popular vote to give them all of the state's electoral votes. This has a distorting effect, so that even heavily populated states that are solidly red or blue get little attention from candidates and the candidates don't tailor their policies to benefit those states and win votes. The best of example of this is solidly Democratic California. As America's most populous state, California had 55 electoral votes in 2020—more than 10 percent of the 538 total votes in the Electoral College and just over 20 percent of the 270 electoral votes needed to be elected president. Yet presidential candidates largely ignore the state (except for fundraising) because they assume the Democratic nominee will win. By contrast, states where the outcome of the election is uncertain—known as swing states and battleground states—get far more attention even though they have fewer electoral votes than California. In 2020, these states and their number of electoral votes were Arizona (11), Florida (29), Georgia (16), Iowa (6), Michigan (16), Minnesota (10), Nevada (6), New Hampshire (4), North Carolina (15), Ohio (18), Pennsylvania (20), and Wisconsin (10).[22]

We'd like to see states adopt the systems used in Maine and Nebraska and award electoral votes by congressional district.[23] Both states allocate two electoral votes to the statewide winner, and then one vote to the winner of each congressional district. This formula would work in every state, because each state has the same number of electoral votes as it has members of Congress (two senators plus all its House members). In 2020, both Maine and Nebraska split their electoral votes, with Biden getting three in Maine and one in Nebraska, and Trump getting one in Maine and four in Nebraska. If other states could split their electoral votes by congressional district, they would get more attention from presidential candidates, and third-party, independent, and centrist candidates would get a much better chance at picking up electoral votes. For example, in 1992, H. Ross Perot captured almost 19 percent of the popular vote but didn't win a single electoral vote. If he could have focused on friendly congressional districts, there's a good chance he would have pulled in some electoral votes.

Encourage the creation of a centrist third party: President George Washington is the only president who was not a member of a political party. He opposed the creation of parties because he said he wanted to represent all Americans, not just those in one political faction. Washington warned in his Farewell Address in 1796 that a political party "serves always to distract the public councils and enfeeble public administration. It agitates the community with ill-founded jealousies and false alarms, kindles the animosity of one party against another, foments occasionally riot and insurrection."[24] A wise observation.

The earliest political parties to capture the presidency were the Federalists, the Democratic-Republicans, and the Whigs. Abraham Lincoln became the first Republican president in 1861 and Republicans briefly renamed themselves the National Union Party in 1864 to gain support of Democrats who supported the Union in the Civil War. Since 1868, every American president has been either a Democrat or a Republican.[25]

Realistically, we're not going to abolish political parties. But that doesn't mean no new political parties can arise to hold seats in the House and Senate and even to capture the White House. We just need to level the playing field for third-party and independent candidates. As we have discussed extensively in this book, Democrats have moved farther to the left and Republicans have moved farther to the right in recent years, exacerbating the divisions in our country and contributing to gridlock and dysfunction in Congress.

Millions of Americans in the sensible center feel that they no longer have a political home and would welcome a political party that embraces pragmatic solutions and rejects extremism to deal with the many challenges America faces. Coauthor Douglas Schoen dubbed these voters Restless and Anxious Moderates (RAMs) some years ago. They include most independents and a fair number of Democrats and Republicans as well. These voters are practical, non-ideological, and unabashedly results-oriented. They eschew partisanship and want the parties to come together to confront the difficult challenges America is facing. We believe the RAMs could become the Restless and Anxious Majority if a credible third-party candidate emerges.

The RAMs make up roughly 35 to 40 percent of the American electorate. RAMs are ordinary, average Americans. They go online and they watch the news, but they are not the political activists of the blogosphere or the evangelical right. They are practical people who believe in consensus solutions to problems. When they look at politics in Washington, they are aghast. Our nation would benefit enormously if a moderate party reflecting the views of the RAMs could have a role in governing. Yet our political system—especially the Electoral College—is tilted against any candidate not running on the Democratic or Republican Party line.

The reforms we have advocated above—nonpartisan redistricting, splitting up the electoral votes of states by congressional districts, ranked-choice voting, and instant runoff voting—could help third-party and independent congressional and presidential candidates start winning elections. The same reforms could also work on the state and local level. Many elected officials will oppose these changes because the reforms endanger their hold on power. But it's long past time for the American people to demand changes like these to open up our electoral system to wider participation and fresh ideas from outside the Democratic and Republican Parties.

A Gallup poll published in February 2021 found that almost a two-thirds majority of adult Americans—62 percent—said they believe "a third major party is needed" because the Democratic and Republican Parties do an inadequate job of representing the American people. The percentage of Americans holding this view is now higher than ever recorded by Gallup, and has risen substantially since the question was first asked 2003, when only 40 percent said a third party was needed. The 2021 poll also showed that 50 percent of Americans identified as political independents—the highest percentage ever measured by Gallup. And the poll found only 37 percent of Americans expressed a favorable opinion of the Republican Party, while 48 percent said they viewed the Democratic Party positively.[26]

In a column headlined "America Could Use a Liberal Party," *New York Times* conservative (but anti-Trump) columnist Bret Stephens wrote in March 2021 that a centrist party dedicated to "the tenets and spirit of liberal democracy"—not "big-state welfarism"—is needed. He called the political center "the place most Americans still are, temperamentally and morally, and might yet return to if given the choice." And he listed some centrist views that most Americans hold: "Respect for the outcome of elections, the rule of law, freedom of speech, and the principle (in courts of law and public opinion alike) of innocent until proven guilty. Respect for the free market, bracketed by sensible regulation and cushioned by social support.... A commitment to equality of opportunity, not 'equity' in outcomes. A well-grounded faith in the benefits of immigration, free trade, new technology, new ideas, experiments in living...."[27]

Stephens added: "All of this used to be the more-or-less common ground of American politics, inhabited by Ronald Reagan and the two Bushes as much as by Barack Obama and the two Clintons.... America needs a Liberal Party that represents what we used to be and what we desperately need to become again." We agree wholeheartedly.

A new third party called the SAM (Serve America Movement) Party was launched in 2020 to appeal to centrists. Former representative David Jolly of Florida, who was a Republican while in Congress from 2014 to 2017 but has since quit the party, is executive chairman. "The United States is in the minority among leading nations in having an entrenched political duopoly—just two major parties, insulated from accountability by a campaign finance system that rewards their mutual power and protected by election rules deliberately implemented to limit challenges by independent candidates or new parties," Jolly wrote in explaining why the SAM Party was created. "Conversely, many nations have rich multi-party democracies, and research continually affirms they produce more inclusive policy outcomes, greater voter engagement and satisfaction, and better participation of both political and demographic minorities....The problem—the fatal flaw in today's American political system—is that there is not a political party structured to accommodate our diverse ideologies. Which is why the next successful party will not be one that defines itself by claiming a spot on the ideological spectrum. It will have a big tent platform that welcomes progressives, conservatives, moderates and single-issue voters. It will coalesce these competing perspectives around shared values of problem solving, democracy protection, election reform, and accountability."[28]

In addition, in May 2021, a group of 150 prominent centrist Republicans (many of them former elected officials) and independents opposed to former president Trump announced they had formed a group called A Call for American Renewal with the goal of reforming the Republican Party or possibly starting a new party "to give voice to the millions of Americans who feel politically homeless," leaders of the group wrote in a *Washington Post* op-ed. The op-ed stated: "Tragically, the Republican Party has lost its way, perverted by fear, lies, and self-interest. What's more, GOP attacks on the integrity of our elections and our institutions pose a continuing and material threat to the nation."[29]

We don't know what will happen to the SAM Party and A Call for American Renewal. We expect more groups may try to launch new parties. We do know that America desperately needs a centrist third party along the lines of what Bret Stephens described to run candidates for president, the Senate and House, governorships, and other state offices, along with local offices. Such a party could go a long way to transforming

America from the divided states back into the United States. Enacting the reforms described above could give such a third party a much greater chance to appeal to moderate voters—the RAMs—and to elect candidates.

Expand participation in presidential debates: Millions of Americans rely on the televised presidential candidate debates to help them decide which candidate to support. And candidates who participate in the debates (usually just the Democratic nominee and the Republican nominee) garner heavy media coverage both before and afterward. However, the Commission on Presidential Debates requires a candidate to show at least 15 percent support in national polls in the September before Election Day to participate in the three debates usually held. The Democratic and Republican presidential nominees can always meet the 15 percent hurdle. Third-party and independent candidates seldom can. To enable voters to hear from more than the two major party candidates, we'd like to see the commission allow the top *three* presidential candidates to participate in the debates. Given the polling data cited above that shows most voters believe we need a third major political party, expanding debate participation would clearly be an appropriate response to the wishes of the electorate. It would also incentivize strong third-party and independent candidates to run for president. The commission has refused to change its 15 percent rule and the Supreme Court has refused to hear a challenge to the rule.

CONGRESSIONAL REFORM

Some far-left Democratic and far-right Republican members of the House and Senate appear more interested in keeping high profiles on Twitter and Facebook and in appearing on TV and radio than in legislating and solving problems. To generate maximum publicity for themselves, they take extreme positions that make news, refusing to compromise and demonizing those they disagree with. This has contributed to the gridlock that has paralyzed Congress.

Compromise—once considered a virtue among lawmakers—is now considered a vice, as many Democrats fear they will face primary challenges from the far left and many Republicans fear they will face primary challenges from the far right. And because campaigns have become so expensive, lobbyists and big donors now wield outsize influence. The needs and concerns of ordinary citizens often get scant attention.

Lawmakers are spending less time than ever before in Washington getting to know each other and developing relationships that could enable them to work together on a constructive and bipartisan basis. In 2020 and 2021, this was partly due to distancing requirements necessitated by the coronavirus pandemic, but the trend has been developing for years as senators and representatives devote increasing amounts of time to fundraising and to events in their home states and districts in preparation for their reelection campaigns. For House members, fundraising and campaigning never stop, since they are up for reelection every two years.

Here are reforms we would like to see implemented to help improve the functioning of Congress:

Encourage bipartisan efforts: The Problem Solvers Caucus is a group of twenty-six moderate Democrats and twenty-six moderate Republicans in the House—12 percent of total House membership—dedicated to doing exactly what their name says: solving problems. They have many differences on issues facing Congress, but they are dedicated to bridging their differences and reaching compromise solutions. The group's website lists proposals the caucus has advanced (including some that have been passed by the House) on recovery from the coronavirus pandemic, infrastructure improvements, health care, immigration reform, criminal justice, and House rule changes to promote bipartisanship.[30]

In the Senate, ten Republicans and ten Democrats get together most Wednesdays for lunch and talk about legislation, issues in the news, and their personal lives to get to know each other. Since Senate Democrats need ten Republican votes to end a GOP filibuster on legislation, the moderate Republicans in the lunch group could create the basis for compromise with Democrats if both sides are flexible. The group did not succeed in passing legislation in the first months of the Biden presidency but isn't giving up. "It's harder to demonize someone you've broken bread with," Senator Susan Collins (R-ME) told the *Washington Post*.[31]

As an example of a compromise that could be achieved, the *Post* reported that Collins suggested raising the current $7.25 hourly minimum wage to $10.50—far less than the $15 Democrats are seeking but still a significant boost that would help low-wage workers while being low enough to minimize the need for employers to eliminate jobs. While low-wage workers would obviously rather earn $15 an hour than $7.25, they would certainly be better off getting $10.50 than holding out for years waiting for the Senate to get 60 votes to approve a raise to $15.

More bipartisan outreach is needed by members in both the House and Senate. The nation would benefit if they focused far more on legislating and far less on tweeting and their next TV appearance. Democrats and Republicans will always have disagreements, but we are all better off if they can come together on some things than if they obstinately refuse to reach agreement on almost anything of significance. As the old proverb states: "Half a loaf is better than none."

Media coverage focusing on legislative achievements: We're strong believers in freedom of the press under the First Amendment and don't believe government should have a role in determining how the media cover the news about Congress or anything else. However, we'd welcome an effort by the news media to give more attention to lawmakers who actually get things done and less to those who make wild statements and proposals that will never become law. For example, the Problem Solvers Caucus gets little attention, because many journalists believe that in order to attract a large audience news stories and interviews need to deal with conflict and controversy. The actual work of hammering out legislation is slow, detail-oriented, and can be boring. Shouting matches and extremist proposals by Democrats and Republicans draw more eyeballs.

In contrast, Democratic representative Alexandria Ocasio-Cortez of New York gets enormous news coverage for her pie-in-the-sky proposals that will never become law. According to the Center for Effective Lawmaking (run by Vanderbilt University and the University of Virginia), Ocasio-Cortez introduced twenty-one substantive bills in the 2019–2020 House session but they were never voted on in committees—a necessary first step before the full House can even consider a bill in most cases. The Center for Effective Lawmaking ranked Ocasio-Cortez a dismal No. 230 out of 240 House Democrats in effectiveness.[32]

Ocasio-Cortez's emphasis on getting publicity without getting anything done is illustrated by her proposal for infrastructure spending. At this writing, President Biden is having a hard time picking up support from Republicans and even some Democrats for his massive $3.5 trillion infrastructure and jobs plan because it is so expensive and broad. Ocasio-Cortez's response to the high hurdles this legislation faces was to complain that Biden doesn't want to spend enough and to call for $10 trillion in infrastructure spending over ten years—over three times as much as Biden is asking for. That got the congresswoman a guest appearance on the highly rated *Rachel Maddow Show* on MSNBC and generated a flood of news stories in the U.S. and Europe.[33] But there is no chance that a Congress reluctant to spend $3.5 trillion on broadly defined infrastructure will spend $10 trillion.

On the Republican side, Representative Marjorie Taylor Greene (R-GA) said she did not mind being stripped of her House committee assignments in February 2021 in response to her racist, Islamophobic, and anti-Semitic comments and her support for false conspiracy theories. "Going forward, I've been freed," Greene said. "I have a lot of free time on my hands, which means I can talk to a whole lot more people all over this country and . . . make connections and build a huge amount of support that I've already got started with." She tweeted that Democrats were "a bunch of morons" because without having to spend time on committee work she would have more time to raise money and build public support for her positions and for former president Trump. Like Ocasio-Cortez, Greene has drawn heavy media coverage.[34] Why legislate when you can communicate and spend more time on TV and Twitter? Call us old-fashioned, but we'd like to see lawmakers devote most of their time and attention to making laws instead of making media appearances, fundraising, and boosting their social media profiles. And we'd like to see the media spend more time reporting on legislative accomplishments than on publicity stunts.

Preserve the filibuster: Many Democrats are calling on the Senate to get rid of the filibuster, a rule that allows senators to block passage of legislation that fails to get 60 votes in the 100-member chamber. Supporters of eliminating the filibuster argue that it is anti-democratic and obstructionist, and is responsible for gridlock that turns the Senate into a graveyard for legislation—even when a majority of senators favor a measure. In 2021, Democrats held 50 seats in the Senate, so if they voted as a bloc with a tiebreaking vote by Vice President Harris they could get rid of the filibuster. This would considerably increase the chances that legislation favored by President Biden and other Democrats that passed in the House could also pass in the Senate and become law.

As we wrote earlier in this book, opposition by Democratic senators Joe Manchin of West Virginia, Kyrsten Sinema of Arizona—and perhaps others—makes it impossible for Democrats to eliminate the filibuster in the 2021–2022 session unless these senators change their minds. This could change, of course, if Democrats pick up more seats in the 2022 election. We quoted Manchin earlier stating he will not change his mind on the filibuster under any circumstances. Sinema said the same thing in an interview with the *Wall Street Journal* in early April 2021. "When you have a place that's broken and not working, and many would say that's the Senate today, I don't think the solution is to erode the rules," Sinema said. "I think the solution is for senators to change their behavior and begin to work together, which is what the country wants us to do." She added that the Senate's job is "to craft bipartisan solutions to solve the challenges we face in our country."[35]

We agree with Manchin and Sinema that the filibuster rule should stay in force. The endless feuding and fighting that Democrats and Republicans engage in on Capitol Hill is not only divisive, it is destabilizing to our government and harmful to our nation. Lawmakers need to learn how to get along and work together for the benefit of the American people and compromise to pass legislation both Democrats and Republicans can accept. Those who refuse to do this deserve to be criticized by their opponents in their next reelection campaign and should pay a price at the polls.

Also, as a practical matter, there is a good chance Democrats could lose their bare majority in the 2022 Senate elections—Republicans would only need to pick up a single additional seat. And a Republican might be elected president in 2024. If one or both of these developments takes place, you can be sure Democrats will regret losing their power under the filibuster to put a brake on GOP measures that advance a conservative agenda. To his credit, when Republican Mitch McConnell was Senate majority leader he rejected requests from President Trump to get rid of the filibuster as Trump sought to win passage for his legislative agenda. McConnell understood that he could go from majority leader to minority leader, as happened in 2021, and then would need the filibuster.

We do believe that the filibuster should be modified so that senators seeking to hold up legislation would have to actually speak on the Senate floor in a marathon session. This is known as a "talking filibuster," which we discussed in greater detail earlier. Manchin has indicated he could support this (and has in the past) but Sinema told the *Wall Street Journal* she didn't want to discuss hypotheticals. Unless Democrats can pick up any Republican support, they could only require the talking filibuster if every Democrat in the Senate votes to do so. The advantage of requiring a talking filibuster would be to make it harder to filibuster and likely reduce the frequency of filibusters to just deal with major legislation.

Restrictions on elected officials: All members of Congress, the president, and vice president should be required to divest their ownership of stocks, bonds, and business, and place their assets into blind trusts to avoid conflicts of interests. President Trump came under justified criticism for not doing this, and many businesses, organizations, and powerful individuals patronized his hotel in Washington and paid to hold events at his resorts and hotels to curry his favor.

An article by Dan Alexander published in *Forbes* in September 2020 was headlined "Trump's Business Raked in $1.9 Billion of Revenue during His First Three Years in Office" and documented Trump's earnings in detail.[36] NPR reported in January 2021: "When Donald Trump took office four years ago, he did not divest himself of the businesses that made him rich, a move which his critics said would lead to countless conflicts of interest. Well, since then, U.S. taxpayers have paid Trump properties for security costs involved in hosting hundreds of presidential visits. Foreign and domestic politicians have paid for countless stops at his hotels and resorts."[37]

In an article published in October 2020, the *Washington Post* reported that the U.S. government had paid Trump's companies at least $2.5 million, and his election campaign fundraising committee paid his companies $5.6 million for holding events at his properties. For example, the *Post* reported that Trump had visited his hotels and clubs more than 280 times and charged Secret Service agents and White House staff to rent rooms at the properties. Rather than holding all his U.S. meetings with foreign leaders at the White House or Camp David, Trump held some at his resorts, further filling his coffers. For example, at his summit with Japanese prime minister Shinzo Abe at Trump's Mar-a-Lago resort in Florida in April 2018 the resort "billed the U.S. government $13,700 for guest rooms, $16,500 for food and wine, and $6,000 for the roses and other floral arrangements," and billed the government $3 per bottle of water it supplied, the *Post* reported.[38] No president should be allowed to profit off the presidency like this again.

Ethics and divestiture legislation shouldn't ignore the spouses of elected officials. It would be excessive to demand that spouses sell small and mid-size businesses they own and run. However, spouses should have to divest ownership of large companies with the potential to influence legislation, or to make large profits from the status of the elected official. Finding the dividing line for what spousal business ownership should be allowed and what should not would be tricky. It should be studied by a panel of outside experts that would acknowledge that spouses of elected officials have the right to make a living, but would impose reasonable restrictions.

New restrictions on lobbying: Realistically, lobbying will never be eliminated. Businesses, organizations, and individuals have the right to hire people to represent them to seek passage of legislation, changes in regulations, or other actions from government. Reforms are needed, however, to shine light on what lobbyists do and to avoid conflicts of interest. Needed reforms include:

- Greater disclosure by lobbyists of their contacts with members of Congress. Lobbyists should have to report the date of every phone call, meeting, and event they participate in with members of Congress and their staffs, and the topics discussed.
- Reporting by lobbyists of every dollar they spend trying to influence government in the legislative and executive branches, including on public relations and advertising, and on advocacy groups.
- A ban on all federal employees and elected officials going to work for lobbyists for at least two years after they leave federal service. This is needed to ensure federal employees don't improperly help lobbyists with the understanding that they will be rewarded with a

higher-paying job as soon as they leave government service. President Trump issued an executive order in 2017 prohibiting White House officials from jumping right into lobbying after federal service. But near the end of his term he rescinded the order, helping out members of his administration in their searches for new jobs.

Some people will argue that the reforms we have outlined are too weak. Others will argue that they are too harsh and will drive good people from running for office or serving as government staffers. We believe they strike a middle ground and will be effective without being unreasonable.

COURT REFORM

Our independent federal judiciary plays a vital role in preserving America's democracy. At a time when Democrats and Republicans are arguing about almost everything and agreeing about almost nothing, Americans need to have faith that nonpartisan federal judges will settle partisan disputes based on the facts, the law, and the Constitution.

John Roberts recognized this when he was nominated to serve on the Supreme Court. At his Senate confirmation hearing in 2005, the now–chief justice said in his opening statement: "Judges and Justices are servants of the law, not the other way around. Judges are like umpires. Umpires don't make the rules, they apply them. The role of an umpire and a judge is critical. They make sure everybody plays by the rules, but it is a limited role. Nobody ever went to a ball game to see the umpire . . . we are a Government of laws and not of men. It is that rule of law that protects the rights and liberties of all Americans. It is the envy of the world, because without the rule of law, any rights are meaningless.... If I am confirmed, I will confront every case with an open mind. I will fully and fairly analyze the legal arguments that are presented. I will be open to the considered views of my colleagues on the bench, and I will decide every case based on the record, according to the rule of law, without fear or favor, to the best of my ability, and I will remember that it's my job to call balls and strikes, and not to pitch or bat."[39]

Supreme Court Justice Stephen Breyer said in a lecture at Harvard Law School in April 2021 that he fears many Americans view Supreme Court justices as "primarily political officials or 'junior league' politicians themselves rather than jurists."[40] "If the public sees judges as politicians in robes, its confidence in the courts—and in the rule of law itself—can only diminish, diminishing the court's power, including its power to act as a check on other branches," the justice said.[41] In addition, Breyer said people who support expanding the size of the Supreme Court to change the current ideological balance on the court—which now has six conservatives and three liberals (he among them)—should "think long and hard" before increasing the size of the high court. Such a move risks lessening public confidence in the court and making more people view it as a political institution, he said.

We agree with Breyer and others who have criticized Democrats calling for enlarging the nation's highest courts by "court-packing." If every president starts viewing expanding the size of the Supreme Court as an option to ensure a friendly reception for his or her policy views, where would court-packing end? There is no telling how large and unwieldly the high court would get. We could eventually get to a Supreme Court with several dozen members, which would be absurd. In addition, many more Americans would start looking at the Supreme Court like the president's Cabinet—an institution made up of presidential appointees who follow the president's orders, rather than an independent branch of government that makes judgments based on the law and the Constitution.

The Supreme Court has consisted of nine justices since Congress set that number in 1869. Democratic president Franklin Delano Roosevelt proposed increasing the number of justices to as many as fifteen in 1937 after the Supreme Court struck down key laws creating his New Deal programs, but his court-packing proposal met strong bipartisan opposition in Congress and from the American public. "Congress and the people viewed FDR's ill-considered proposal as an undemocratic power grab," said Barbara A. Perry, director of presidential studies at the Miller Center at the University of Virginia.[42]

Acting to fulfill one of his campaign promises, President Biden issued an executive order in April 2021 creating a thirty-six-member bipartisan commission to produce a report examining proposals to restructure the Supreme Court, including adding justices and setting term limits.[43]

Biden refused to say during the presidential campaign if he supported expanding the high court, kicking the can down the road on the hot-button issue by saying he would create a study commission. However, he was much less reticent in 1983, when as a senator he called packing the Supreme Court "a bonehead idea" by President Roosevelt. "It was a terrible, terrible mistake to make, and it put in question, for an entire decade, the independence of the most significant body . . . the Supreme Court of the United States of America."[44] In 2019, Biden said that adding justices to the court would destroy "any credibility the court has at all."[45] We believe he was right in his past comments, and would be wise to follow his earlier advice now.

Days after Biden ordered the creation of his court study commission, four liberal Democrats introduced legislation in the House and Senate to expand the Supreme Court from nine to thirteen members. The proposal received a cool reception from Democratic congressional leaders, who said they had no plans to bring up the court expansion legislation in their chambers before they see the report from Biden's commission.[46] The sponsors of court expansion legislation said they wouldn't have introduced their bill if Senator Mitch McConnell (R-KY), who was then Senate majority leader, had not refused to even hold hearings in 2016 on President Obama's nomination of Judge Merrick Garland to the Supreme Court and then rushed through the confirmation of now-Justice Amy Coney Barrett just days before the 2020 election. In 2016, McConnell said it was improper to confirm a Supreme Court justice in an election year, even though Obama had nine months left in his term in office. Yet McConnell had no problem confirming Barrett to the high court when Trump had just four months left in his term, saying the difference was that the presidency and the Senate majority were both in the hands of the same political party.[47]

In addition to holding open a Supreme Court seat until Obama's term was over, McConnell blocked over a hundred Obama nominees to district and appellate courts, enabling President Trump to fill the vacancies with conservative judges after he took office.[48] We believe that McConnell was wrong to politicize the judiciary by refusing to confirm Garland (who became attorney general in 2021) and the lower court judges. But Democrats would be equally wrong to further politicize the Supreme Court by court-packing to add liberal justices. Chief Justice Roberts and Justice Breyer were right to raise alarm bells about the harmful effects of turning our nation's highest court into another political institution where justices decide cases based on their political party affiliation.

The best way to depoliticize the Supreme Court and the rest of the federal judiciary would be to amend the Constitution. This is a drastic but necessary step. We don't amend the Constitution very often, since it takes approval by a two-thirds vote in both houses of Congress and ratification by three-fourths of state legislatures (or by a convention if two-thirds of states request one—something that has never happened). We'd like to see the Constitution amended to do the following to reform our court system:

- Require the full Senate to hold confirmation votes on nominations to the Supreme Court, appellate courts, and district courts within ninety days after they are made by the president. While the Senate could still reject nominees, it could not just refuse to act on them, as McConnell did with so many Obama nominees. McConnell set a terrible precedent for obstructionism on court nominations that must not become the norm whenever the Senate and the White House are controlled by different political parties.

- Set the size of the Supreme Court at its current composition of nine justices. This would make it very difficult to use court-packing in the future to change the ideological composition of the high court. A change would require another constitutional amendment, not just legislation passed by Congress.

- End lifetime appointments to the Supreme Court. Justices should be limited to serving eighteen or twenty years. Justices have served an average of sixteen years on the high court since it began hearing cases in 1790, meaning that many justices would not be affected by this limit.[49] One positive effect would be to reduce pressure on presidents to appoint justices as young as possible, to maximize their time on the bench. Another would be to reduce the political pressure involved with the selection of justices, since they would not continue on the high court for more than two decades, as happened with Justice William O. Douglas, who served for thirty-six years. A third positive effect would be to ease pressure on justices to continue serving even when old age and ill health have reduced their effectiveness, as they stay on the bench waiting until a president aligned with them ideologically assumes office to select their replacement. The most recent example of this was

Justice Ruther Bader Ginsburg, who was eighty-seven
when she died in office in 2020. The ten oldest Supreme
Court justices have ranged in age from eighty-two
to almost ninety-one when they left the court due to
retirement or death.[50]

An Ipsos poll conducted for Reuters and published in April 2021
found that 63 percent of U.S. adults supported age- or term limits for
Supreme Court justices, but only 38 percent supported adding four or
more justices to the high court. Reuters reported: "The poll found that
only 49 percent of Americans have a 'great deal' or a 'fair amount' of
confidence in decisions made by Supreme Court justices. In comparison,
43 percent of respondents expressed a similar amount of trust in decisions made by the White House and 32 percent said the same of decisions made by Congress."[51] Some people will always distrust our court
system, of course, claiming it is politicized. But the amendment we are
proposing would be a positive step to increase trust in our federal courts.

CRIMINAL JUSTICE REFORM

The video of the excruciating death of George Floyd after then-
Minneapolis police officer Derek Chauvin knelt on his neck for over
nine minutes while Floyd lay helpless and handcuffed on the street trau-
matized America. It should have. The racial justice protests by millions
of Americans and rioting that followed by far fewer in cities across the
nation were a wake-up call to the systemic racism that has victimized
African Americans like Floyd for over four hundred years. Justice was
served when, almost a year after Floyd's death, a jury found Chauvin
guilty of murdering him.

Tragically, as Chauvin stood trial, another Black man—twenty-year-
old Daunte Wright—was shot and killed by a police officer just ten miles

away in the Minneapolis suburb of Brooklyn Center. Officer Kim Potter, a twenty-six-year veteran of the suburban police department, was shown on video firing the fatal shot during a traffic stop after yelling that she was about to fire a Taser at Wright. Potter resigned and was charged with second-degree murder. She said the shooting was a terrible accident, caused by her mistaking her pistol for her Taser.[52] The shooting sparked nights of protests by hundreds of people, including looting by some. The Brooklyn Center police chief resigned and the city manager was fired.

There is no question that police brutality exists and that police have mistreated and even in some cases killed African Americans as well as others without justification. Thanks to police body cameras, smartphone cameras, and security cameras, we are now seeing examples of these injustices on video, unlike in years past. We can't ignore them. But as we pointed out earlier in this book, the overwhelming majority of police officers are not racists and do not assault and kill Black Americans or anyone else unless they feel their lives or the lives of others are threatened. Criminals pose a far greater danger to Black lives. While Black people made up about 13 percent of the U.S. population in 2019, they accounted for 53 percent of murder victims in the nation that year. A total of 7,484 of the 13,987 people murdered in the nation were Black in 2019.[53] Writing in *USA Today* in July 2020, Heather Mac Donald of the Manhattan Institute pointed out that less than half of 1 percent of the Black Americans killed in 2019 were unarmed people fatally shot by police.[54]

These disturbing statistics about the loss of so many Black lives to criminals should make it clear that we must not overreact to the grave misconduct by a relatively small number of police officers and defund or otherwise weaken police departments. If we do, Black Americans will suffer most and more will die. This is why the Defund the Police movement and calls to abolish the police are so harmful.

Following the Daunte Wright killing, far-left Democratic representative Rashida Tlaib of Michigan tweeted: "It wasn't an accident.

Policing in our country is inherently & intentionally racist. Daunte Wright was met with aggression & violence. I am done with those who condone government funded murder. No more policing, incarceration, and militarization. It can't be reformed."[55] We understand the anger at the unjustified deaths of Black people at the hands of police, but many thousands more Americans of every race and ethnicity would become victims of crimes, including murder, if we followed Tlaib's irresponsible advice and actually abolished police and abolished jails and prisons.

Detroit Police Chief James Craig, who is Black, responded to Tlaib by saying the congresswoman tweeted "a disgusting knee-jerk response," the *Detroit News* reported. "This [fatal shooting of Wright] was a tragic incident, and it should've never happened. But when these tragedies happen, you shouldn't just broad-bush the entire profession," Craig said. "To say policing should be abolished gives no consideration to the people who live in our neighborhoods who rely on police to provide service. What happens to those folks? What about the victims?" Police Chief John Blair of the Detroit suburb of Taylor made the same point about the grave harm that would be caused by abolishing the police. "It would hurt our minority communities the hardest," Blair said. "We should tread lightly. What happened [with the shooting death of Wright] was a tragic error. It was an unfathomable mistake. But you're dealing with human beings, and human beings are not infallible. [Former officer Kim Potter] does need to be dealt with criminally and civilly, and she'll get her day in court. But when you paint an entire group of people with a broad brush, that doesn't help society."[56]

The American people would never accept the nightmare of a lawless nation with no police and no prisons, where criminals could rob, rape, and murder without fear of arrest or imprisonment. No one on Earth would want to live in a country like this. Abolishing the police makes as much sense as abolishing hospitals and doctors because some people die as the result of medical malpractice, abolishing motor vehicles because some people die in traffic accidents, or abolishing swimming because some people drown. Interestingly, we did not hear Tlaib demand the abolition of police and imprisonment in April 2019 when a Florida man who was a Trump supporter was arrested and accused of threatening to kill her and other Democratic members of Congress.[57] Nor did Tlaib call for disbanding police departments and shutting down jails and prisons when she broke into tears on the House floor in February 2021 discussing the attack on the Capitol by Trump supporters and earlier death threats against her. "On my very first day of orientation, I got my first death threat," Tlaib said. "It was a serious one. They took me aside. The FBI had to go to the gentleman's home. I didn't even get sworn in yet, and someone wanted me dead for just existing."[58]

Don't get us wrong. Death threats to Rep. Tlaib were a crime and she and her staff were absolutely right to report the threats to law enforcement. No one should have to endure the fear sparked by death threats. But if no law enforcement agencies existed and no jails and prisons existed, there would be no one to arrest the man who threatened Tlaib, and he could not be punished for death threats or even for carrying them out. Tlaib, who was not in the Capitol when Trump supporters rioted, also spoke of the horror of watching the attack on TV. Her comments were clearly heartfelt and the rioters deserved the condemnation she leveled against them. But if police departments ceased to exist, no law enforcement officers would be in the Capitol to protect lawmakers. And if there were no jails and prisons, armed rioters could have invaded the Capitol without worrying about punishment. Even if they murdered hundreds of people, they would not have been arrested and could not have been jailed.

Tlaib's absurd position is not reflective of the Democratic Party. In fact, President Biden has called for an additional $300 million in federal funding for local law enforcement departments around the country to fund community policing programs.[59] That's the right course, because reforming police departments to make them more responsive to communities and to reduce the use of force—especially deadly force—will require more money going to police departments, not less.

Many solutions have been offered to improve policing. For example, the U.S. House passed the George Floyd Justice in Policing Act in March 2021 by a vote of 220–212, with no Republican support. As we wrote earlier, the bill would create a national database to track police misconduct, ban some types of no-knock search warrants, ban police chokeholds, ban religious and racial profiling, and make it easier to hold police officers accountable in civil and criminal court for misconduct.[60] President Biden supports the legislation, but the House bill is unlikely to win approval in the Senate because it would need 60 votes to overcome a Republican filibuster. The best course of action would be for the House and President Biden to try to work with South Carolina Republican senator Tim Scott, who is sponsoring police reform legislation that doesn't go as far as the House bill, to try to reach a compromise that can pass both houses and become law. Negotiations to do this began just days after the guilty verdict was handed down against Chauvin. We hope they are successful.

In another example of a response to the killing of George Floyd, the Maryland legislature overrode a veto by Republican governor Larry Hogan in April 2021 to enact three police accountability measures. Among other provisions, the bills impose the strictest restrictions in the U.S. on when police are authorized to use force, require police to use de-escalation techniques to try to defuse potentially violent situations, impose a criminal penalty on law enforcement officers who use excessive force, require officers to wear body cameras, give civilians a role in police disciplinary actions, and limit no-knock search warrants. "Maryland is leading the nation in transforming our broken policing system," said Maryland's Democratic House Speaker Adrienne A. Jones. "I am proud to lead the House in overriding the governor's veto and showing the nation exactly where we stand as a state." In vetoing the three bills, Governor Hogan said the measures would "erode police morale, community relationships, and public confidence" and "will result in great damage to police recruitment and retention, posing significant risks to public safety throughout our state."

We're not experts in policing and don't presume to know all the answers regarding what needs to be done to reform police departments while still protecting the safety of the American people. But the results of the changes in Maryland law should be studied after a year or two to determine their impact. If the changes are a plus, they could be replicated in other states or nationally. If they cause more harm than good, other states will know not to adopt them.

Regrettably, every society on Earth has experienced crime as far back as recorded history goes, and it's unrealistic to expect anything we do can abolish crime entirely. So police and prisons will always be necessary. If the House and Senate deadlock and can't agree on police reform legislation—or if legislation is enacted and Democrats believe it doesn't go far enough—a bipartisan commission should be appointed to launch a serious review of policing, similar to the Kerner Commission that examined riots in 160 American cities in the summer of 1967. President Biden and Senate and House Republican and Democratic leaders should all appoint members of this commission. It should hear from experts in policing and from groups and individuals that have raised complaints about police misconduct. The commission should also examine the serious issue of gun violence and make recommendations to reduce its deadly toll, while still preserving the rights of law-abiding gun owners.

America needs to find a midpoint between defunding or abolishing the police and the status quo, and find a way to deal with gun violence as well. A commission won't find magic solutions that please everyone, but it could be the first step in reforming and improving policing and making American communities safer and more just. It's not inconsistent to work to stop crime while also working to stop police misconduct. And if any challenge requires bipartisanship, it is this one.

INFRASTRUCTURE IMPROVEMENTS

America is crisscrossed with over 4 million miles of paved roads, 617,000 bridges, 140,000 miles of freight railroad track, 21,400 miles of passenger rail track, and 9,277 miles of commuter and hybrid rail. In addition, the nation has about 520 commercial airports and more than 300 ports, according to the American Society of Civil Engineers. Collectively, this accounts for our transportation infrastructure. The ASCE says much of this transportation infrastructure is in bad shape. The group's "2021 Report Card for America's Infrastructure" gives mass transit a grade of D–, roads a grade of D, airports a grade of D+, bridges a grade of C, ports a grade of B–, and railroads a grade of B.[61]

Part of the reason that roads, bridges, and mass transit get such low grades is that they rely on federal funding generated by the 18.4 cents-per-gallon federal excise tax on gasoline and the 24.4 cents-a-gallon federal excise tax on diesel fuel. Those taxes haven't been raised by Congress since 1993 because lawmakers are reluctant to face political criticism for raising taxes that hit almost everyone in the wallet. Consequently, the buying power of the fuel tax revenue has been eroded considerably by inflation. The taxes would need to jump to 33 cents-per-gallon on gasoline and 44 cents-per-gallon on diesel to have the same buying power in 2021 that they had in 1993. In addition, cars get much better fuel mileage today than they did in 1993, reducing the amount of fuel purchased. And a small but growing number of hybrid and all-electric vehicles are on the roads, further reducing fuel tax collections.[62]

The biggest infrastructure project in American history was the plan signed into law by Republican president Dwight Eisenhower in 1956 to build the Interstate Highway System, now stretching across 46,876 miles. But that was a long time ago. Democratic and Republican elected officials have long supported programs to maintain, expand, and improve our transportation infrastructure. However, they haven't always been able to reach agreement on exactly what to do and how to pay for it.[63] President Trump talked about holding a themed "Infrastructure Week" so often it became a running joke among the White House press corps, but he ultimately was unable to reach agreement with Congress on legislation.

The World Economic Forum has a broader definition of infrastructure beyond transportation. In addition to spending on roads, bridges, railroads, mass transit, airports, and ports, the international organization counts electricity grids and broadband internet as infrastructure.[64] That makes sense. But in legislation submitted to Congress in 2021, President Biden broadened his definition of infrastructure even further, to include trillions of dollars in spending on other things, including: clean drinking water (arguably qualifying as infrastructure because it includes replacing lead pipes and water lines); renovating public housing and school buildings, childcare facilities, hospitals for veterans, and federal buildings; universal pre-kindergaten; two years of free community college; paid family leave; "domestic manufacturing, research & development, and job training initiatives"; and expanding "home care services and providing additional support for care workers."[65] These programs all have merit and would create jobs, and certainly deserve serious congressional consideration. But if you want to call them infrastructure, you might as well call everything infrastructure. Congress could just as well be asked to approve military infrastructure, space exploration infrastructure, farm infrastructure, national park infrastructure, federal employee infrastructure, museum infrastructure, and on and on. The term becomes meaningless if it covers everything.

Polling showed that the Biden infrastructure and jobs plan was popular overall, but not with Republicans. A poll by the firm SurveyMonkey for the *New York Times* published in mid-April 2021 said the president's plan enjoyed the approval of 64 percent of Americans as a whole. That included near-unanimous approval from 97 percent of Democrats, strong majority approval from 72 percent of independents, but only minority approval from 29 percent of Republicans.[66] Writing in the *Wall Street*

Journal, Republican political consultant Karl Rove said compromise was needed. "If Mr. Biden genuinely wants bipartisanship…he can show it by agreeing to traditional infrastructure spending paid for with unspent Covid-19 money and other sources Republicans can accept," Rove wrote. "It could be bundled into a bill and passed with huge bipartisan margins in both chambers."[67] Biden could then seek separate legislation funding other programs he included in his big infrastructure package, Rove wrote. Republican lawmakers agreed with Rove. They told Biden they'd be receptive to spending more on traditional infrastructure but not on other things that Biden has mislabeled as infrastructure.

Biden took the advice of Rove and Republicans and supported a bill calling for spending $1 trillion on traditional infrastructure, while also supporting legislation calling for spending an additional $3.5 trillion on what he called "human infrastructure," including the items mentioned above. In a rare victory for bipartisanship, the Senate voted 69-30 in August 2021 to pass the $1 trillion bill.[68]

Senate passage of the $1 trillion traditional infrastructure spending measure should have counted as a victory for Biden, Democrats, Republicans and the American people. There is no such thing as a Democratic or Republican road or bridge—we all travel over them and don't want them falling apart. The Senate action cleared the path for the House to pass the $1 trillion bill to send to Biden for his signature to become law. Senate Democrats could then move on seek to approve the $3.5 trillion in other appropriations Biden supported via a procedure known as "budget reconciliation" that would have prevented a Republican filibuster in the Senate, as long as all 50 Democrats could agree to debate the same legislation.

But progressive Democrats in the House managed to snatch defeat from the jaws of victory. They insisted they would only vote in favor of the $1 trillion infrastructure bill in the Senate first passed the far more expensive and wide-ranging $3.5 trillion spending bill. In other words, to turn an old saying on its head, no loaf was better than half a loaf. While Senate Democrats stuck together to approve a budget resolution to clear the way for a vote on the $3.5 trillion bill, passage of the spending measure in the Senate without changes seems unlikely at this writing, Democratic Senators Joe Manchin and Kyrsten Sinema have both said they want to cut the amount being spent.

We have an alternate idea. First, House Democrats should pass the $1 trillion traditional infrastructure bill, rather than holding it hostage until the Senate passes the $3.5 trillion bill. Getting $1 trillion in infrastructure spending is hardly small change. It's certainly better than getting zero spending on infrastructure by refusing to compromise. Second, rather than bundling together a very expensive wish list of progressive programs in the $3.5 trillion bill, Democrats should split up the gigantic spending bill into smaller measures—for example, one to fund free community college, another to fund childcare programs, and so on—and work to win passage of each one by reaching out to more fiscally moderate Democrats along with Republicans and negotiating agreements on how much a majority of senators and representatives can agree to spend on each. Some of the programs would likely fail to pass and some would likely be approved with less funding. But putting some fiscal restraint in place is particularly important because according to the nonpartisan and nonprofit Committee for a Responsible Federal Budget the true cost of the $3.5 trillion bill could actually exceed $5 trillion. Even if every program in the giant spending bill is worthwhile and would benefit many people, there has to be a limit on how much the U.S. government can spend by raising taxes or (more likely) by increasing the federal deficit. Otherwise, why not follow the suggestion of Alexandria Ocasio-Cortez and spend $10 trillion, or do even better and spend $100 trillion or $900 trillion or even more?

We also believe that Biden ought to negotiate with Republicans who have expressed interest in raising fuel taxes to pay for some infrastructure improvements, even though the White House has said he will not consider such a tax increase because he pledged during the presidential campaign not to raise taxes on families making less than $400,000 a year.[69] Due to inflation, Americans are actually seeing their fuel taxes decrease slightly every year and have seen them decrease by a great deal since 1993. In addition, as more and more Americans switch to electric vehicles in coming years, another tax will need to be instituted based on miles driven or on something else to help fund improvements and maintenance to the roads and bridges motorists rely on.

REGULATORY AND TAX REFORM, AND JOB CREATION

Congressional Democrats and Republicans were united in 2021 in agreeing that America needed to revive its economy and create millions of jobs following the economic devastation that struck in March 2020 as the result of the coronavirus pandemic. But they were deeply divided as to what should be done to achieve their common goal.

In addition to tragically killing more than 620,000 Americans and infecting nearly 37 million by August 2021, the pandemic initially sent the U.S. unemployment rate soaring to the highest levels since the Great Depression, before our economy started improving in 2021.[70] While millions of white-collar workers were able to work from home on their computers, millions of people with jobs in health care, grocery stores, food processing plants, farms, factories, and other fields where remote work is impossible risked their health and lives by going to work. Millions of others—such as restaurant workers, barbers and beauticians, employees at theaters and other entertainment venues, and airline employees—were laid off. The American economy contracted by a record 31.4 percent in the second quarter of 2020—more than three times worse than any quarter since recordkeeping began in 1947. In early April 2020, unemployment peaked at 14.8 percent, as 43 percent of U.S. businesses remained shut to avoid the spread of the deadly virus. By

September 2020, Chapter 11 bankruptcies were up 78 percent over September 2019.[71] The Federal Reserve estimated in April 2021 that about 200,000 business locations above the typical annual level of 600,000 business closures permanently ceased operations during the first year of the pandemic.[72]

Vaccinations against COVID-19 increased rapidly in the winter and early spring of 2021, but slowed in summer, even though there was plentiful supply of coronavirus vaccines. The CDC reported that 169 million people in the U.S. had been fully vaccinated against COVID-19 by mid-August, accounting for 51 percent of the nation's population. However, the new more lethal and more infectious delta variant was creating a new surge in infections among Americans who disregarded science and medical advice and refused to get vaccinated. The July 2021 unemployment rate dropped to 5.4 percent, the lowest since the pandemic began, but that was still far above the 3.5 percent pre-pandemic rate in February 2020. While increased vaccinations are the key to ending the pandemic, America needs a bipartisan and centrist approach to recover from the economic damage caused by COVID-19 and build back better for the future. Below are some reforms that deserve support from Democrats and Republicans—if only they will move away from their far-left and far-right extremes.

Regulatory reform: Government regulations are vital to protect the health and safety of the American people, our environment, and our finances. Regulations bar fraud and monopolistic practices, protect Americans from illegal discrimination, and much more. However, the benefits of regulations need to be weighed against their costs on a case-by-case basis. Overregulation can add years and millions of dollars to the time and cost it takes to build a factory or other facility that could create hundreds or thousands of jobs, or to the time and cost of building a highway or mass transit line needed to ease traffic congestion. Overregulation can even stop projects from even being built, or businesses from even being opened, by adding enormously to their costs. Just as

Republicans have to accept that some regulations are needed, Democrats need to accept that other regulations amount to overkill.

In the 2020 edition of its report "Ten Thousand Commandments: An Annual Snapshot of the Federal Regulatory State," the business-supported Competitive Enterprise Institute said its "intentionally conservative estimate" was that American businesses, organizations, and individuals spend *$1.9 trillion* annually complying with federal regulations. The group called this a "hidden tax." CEI said federal agencies in the Trump administration published 2,964 final regulations in 2019—the lowest number since recordkeeping began in 1976.[73] Obviously, many of the regulations listed by CEI are necessary. But we need to ask: How many are unnecessary? How many do more harm than good? Which ones?

The Trump administration eliminated many regulations. We're not endorsing every regulatory change the administration made, but some regulations clearly deserved to be ditched and getting rid of them contributed to the booming economy America enjoyed before the pandemic hit. In addition, federal agencies suspended some regulations in 2020 to allow a speedier response to COVID-19. We need to find out if it makes sense to restore those regulations or if the government should make their suspension permanent.

Writing in *Forbes* magazine in May 2020, Susan E. Dudley said eliminating unneeded government regulations could play an important part in speeding America's recovery from the pandemic. "Now, more than ever, it is essential that policy officials pay serious attention to the effects of their actions on businesses, workers, and consumers," she wrote. "Government relief packages will not be enough to stave off an economic downturn. Actions that unleash innovation and encourage dynamism and virtuous competition are needed to bring the country, indeed the world, out from the economic recession caused by the pandemic." Dudley called for the creation of an independent federal commission—or a new executive branch agency or congressional agency—to review regulations suspended due to the pandemic and to later review other regulations to determine if they are really needed.⁷⁴ That makes sense to us. We believe such an entity ought to issue reports on its findings, and either Congress or federal agencies should then be able to eliminate or modify regulations when justified based on the findings of the reports.

Another useful reform would be to give all federal regulations expiration dates. Times and conditions change, so a regulation that makes sense in one year might be unneeded in five or ten years. Setting an expiration date, also known as a sunset date, on all regulations and requiring them to be reviewed at least every ten years would be beneficial. This would allow a federal commission, agency, or Congress to get rid of regulations that have outlived their usefulness or modify them. Regulations that were still needed could be renewed for up to another ten years.

Tax reform: Government spending is popular among those who benefit. Taxes are unpopular among those who get stuck with the bill. But the federal government can't just print money without collecting enough tax revenue. Our government can and does borrow, of course, but at some point borrowing has its limits. After emergency government spending to respond to the coronavirus pandemic, the national debt stood at over $28 trillion in the summer of 2021. If you split the bill for that debt equally among the American people it would amount to over $218,000 per household, or over $85,000 for every man, woman, and child in the United States. The Peter G. Peterson Foundation calculated that our $28 trillion national debt is greater than the size of the economies of China, Japan, Germany, and India *combined.*⁷⁵ Interest on the debt amounts to $800 million a day, the foundation found. That works out to $33.3 million per hour and $555,000 per minute.

Many left-wing Democrats seem to believe there is no limit to how much they can tax the rich and big businesses without hurting our economy and wiping out jobs. And many right-wing Republicans seem to believe that tax cuts will pay for themselves by sparking economic growth and that no taxes must ever be increased for any reason. Both views are wrong and neither is supported by evidence. For the good of our nation, both parties need to move toward the sensible center and figure out a way to have tax revenues and government spending match up.

No agreement to raise taxes and cut spending will pass in Congress without strong bipartisan backing and a pledge by each party not to attack the other for supporting such a deal. Many lawmakers will fear that voting in favor of tax increases or spending cuts will open them up to attack on the campaign trail. Right now, with the heightened animosity between the parties, getting an agreement like this between Democrats and Republicans doesn't seem likely.

As we write this, the possible tax increase drawing the most attention is a proposal by President Biden to raise the corporate income tax rate from the current 21 percent to 28 percent to fund his proposed infrastructure and jobs bill. The increase is exactly halfway between the current corporate tax rate and the 35 percent rate that was in effect before President Trump's 2017 tax cuts took effect. However, Democratic senator Joe Manchin of West Virginia has said he will not vote for a tax increase above 25 percent, and his vote is crucial for Democrats to pass anything in the equally divided Senate.[76] As we have written earlier in this chapter, we believe Biden defines infrastructure too broadly and he should come up with a less-costly version of his $3.5 trillion bill. If he shrinks his spending request for the measure, the president should be able to fund it with the 25 percent corporate rate Manchin supports, as long as Democrats remain united in support of a tax increase of that size.

A corporate tax increase, assuming it is enacted, should be just the beginning of tax reform and not the end. The Congressional Budget Office reports that when measured relative to the size of the economy, tax collections from corporations now amount to less than 25 percent of what they were in 1967. In addition to depriving the federal government of needed funds, this drop in the value of corporate tax collections has reduced the faith of the American people in the fairness of our tax system. In recent years polling by Gallup has shown that about 70 percent of Americans believe corporations aren't paying enough in federal taxes.[77]

President Biden has proposed closing a giant tax loophole that allows corporations to dodge U.S. taxes by shifting profits they earn in America to other nations with lower tax rates. As the *New York Times* explained in an editorial published in April 2021: "American companies and companies that make money in the United States are not paying enough money in taxes. . . . Fifty-five of the nation's largest corporations—including FedEx, Nike and the agribusiness giant Archer Daniels Midland—paid nothing in federal income taxes in 2020, despite collectively reporting more than $40 billion in profits, according to the Institute on Taxation and Economic Policy. The federal government lets companies avoid taxes by shifting profits earned in the United States to countries with lower tax rates."[78]

Biden's proposal makes sense. Closing loopholes like the one the president has identified enables the government to raise more money without raising tax rates as high as would otherwise be necessary to pay for programs and can limit borrowing. We can't blame corporations for taking advantage of loopholes that are legal. But Congress needs to close many loopholes to ensure the fairness of our tax system. It's outrageous that a middle-income family struggling to pay its bills pays more in taxes than a giant corporation earning billions of dollars annually. This unfairness feeds public distrust of our tax system and validates the view of millions of Americans that the rich and powerful get special treatment from government, while ordinary citizens get screwed. We understand Republican opposition to tax increases. However, closing loopholes through proposals like Biden's should be something both parties can agree on to fund critical programs.

Both parties also ought to be able to support cracking down on tax cheats to increase the amount of money the federal government collects in taxes. Internal Revenue Service Commissioner Charles Rettig testified in April 2021 before the Senate Finance Committee that *$1 trillion* or more in federal taxes may be going unpaid each year because the IRS does not have enough employees to detect a vast amount of taxpayer fraud and errors. That's a huge amount and senators on the panel were surprised it was so high. The IRS collected just over $3.5 trillion in taxes in the 2019 fiscal year, so recovering a chunk of the unpaid taxes could have a big impact. Rettig said that the IRS faces a huge manpower shortage because of inadequate funding from Congress in the past. "We're down 17,000 enforcement personnel over the last decade," he said. "That has to have an effect." The commissioner said the IRS has "about 6,500 frontline revenue agents who handle the most complex, sophisticated individual and corporate matters. Substantially, every one of them are dedicated to either high-income individuals, the most egregious cases or their largest corporations."[79]

The IRS has estimated in the past that it could bring in $5 to $7 more in tax collections for each additional dollar it spends on enforcement. If that estimate is accurate it would argue for an even greater IRS budget increase than the 10 percent President Biden has requested for the agency. Encouragingly, both Senate Finance Committee Chairman Ron Wyden (D-OR) and ranking member Mike Crapo (R-ID) agreed at their committee hearing that more should be done to collect taxes that are owed but not collected. A rare case of bipartisan agreement!

Job creation and a "living wage": As the recovery from the economic damage of the coronavirus pandemic continues, we can expect unemployment to fall for Americans in every demographic group. But beyond programs to decrease the jobless rate and speed the overall economy recover from the pandemic, it's vital that the federal government make a special effort to lower the unemployment rate among people of color and people without college educations.

The federal government should also do more to help minorities and people from low-income families get the education and training needed to qualify for good-paying jobs. In July 2021, the White unemployment rate was 4.8 percent, the Asian American rate was slightly higher at 5.3 percent, the Hispanic rate was 6.6 percent, and the Black unemployment rate was 8.2 percent. All these rates were higher than they were in March 2020 when the pandemic hit, but at that time people of color also had higher unemployment rates than Whites, the U.S. Bureau of Labor Statistics reported.[80]

Education is the ticket to reducing unemployment and to getting higher paychecks. For example, the Bureau of Labor Statistics reported that in March 2021 the unemployment rate for people with a bachelor's degree or higher was 3.7 percent, for those with some college or an associate degree it was 5.9 percent, for those with only a high school diploma it was 6.7 percent, and for those without a high school diploma it was 8.2 percent.[81] We'll discuss our ideas for increasing educational opportunities for all Americans in the next section of this chapter. But at the same time we work to expand educational opportunities, action is needed to provide more employment opportunities for those without a higher education and to train them for better-paying jobs.

In an example of effective bipartisanship, Congress and the Trump administration created Economic Opportunity Zones around the country that offer tax breaks for job-creating investments in low-income communities. The program was part of the 2017 tax cut legislation signed into law by President Trump. In just one of many responses to the zones, JPMorgan Chase announced that it would increase its lending program to small businesses by $4 billion.[82]

Senators Tim Scott (R-SC) and Cory Booker (D-NJ) sponsored the Opportunity Zones legislation in the Senate. Representatives Pat Tiberi (R-OH, who is no longer in office) and Ron Kind (D-WI) sponsored the legislation in the House. More than 8,600 Economic Opportunity Zones now exist across the U.S., with zones in every state and territory.[83] The first zones created by the program were designated in April 2018, so it's still relatively new, but the program shows promise for our post-pandemic future.[84] A similar program known as Empowerment Zones was created in 1993. While both these programs are helpful, more must be done. We hope that Senators Scott and Booker can work together again and bring Democrats and Republicans together in the House and Senate to pursue bipartisan ideas to open the doors to employment and opportunity to more Americans of color and more low-income communities. As we discussed earlier in this chapter, eliminating some unnecessary regulations could also help create jobs throughout the nation, including for people of color, those without a higher education, and in low-income communities.

In another initiative, Democrats are seeking an increase in the minimum wage to help low-wage employees earn enough to escape poverty. The Democrats argue that the current hourly minimum wage of $7.25 and the subminimum wage of $2.13 an hour that goes primarily to tipped restaurant workers is too low to constitute a living wage. We agree, and there is widespread bipartisan agreement that the minimum wage needs to increase. However, Republicans and some Democrats oppose the effort led by democratic socialist senator Bernie Sanders of Vermont to boost the minimum wage to $15 an hour in stages by 2025 for most workers and by 2027 for tipped workers. While more than doubling the $7.25 hourly minimum wage would boost the incomes of an estimated 32 million workers, it would also wipe out 1.4 million jobs, according to the Congressional Budget Office.[85] Many small-business owners—especially restaurant owners hit hard by the loss of business during the pandemic—have said such a big increase in such a short time could force them out of business.

The basis for a bipartisan compromise on the minimum wage is obvious: raise the minimum wage and subminimum wage above $7.25 an hour but below $15; or alternatively, raise the minimum wage to $15 over more years. In either case, the minimum wage should be indexed to inflation and raised annually after the initial raises, so it never again remains unchanged for years and loses so much purchasing power as the result of inflation. The minimum wage was last raised in 2009 and the subminimum wage was last raised in 1991. Since Democrats have said so many times that they want to see the minimum hit $15, we'd like to stick with that goal. But we'd like to see the $15 phased in to fully take effect after ten years, or even twelve years if necessary to get enough Republican votes to become law. This would be less disruptive to businesses, eliminate fewer jobs, and still significantly boost the minimum wage.

We've only touched on a few ideas here to create more jobs and boost the pay of the lowest-paid workers. Since creating jobs is a priority of both Democrats and Republicans, it is an area that offers many opportunities for bipartisan compromise if lawmakers are willing to do so. Voters need to make it clear that they want action and not just continued arguments from their elected representatives on this critical issue.

EDUCATION REFORM

We have extensively discussed the benefits of an improved education system and higher educational attainment for individuals and for our country earlier in this book. Here are needed reforms to achieve these goals.

Increase federal education funding: Wealthy and middle-class families are able to send their children to private schools or good public schools in affluent suburban districts. In contrast, poor and working-class families often have no option but to send their children to poorly funded public schools, with crowded classrooms, aging and run-down buildings, shortages of computers and up-to-date textbooks, and a lack of enrichment and advanced-level programs. The private and good suburban schools often attract many of the best teachers as well, giving their students yet another advantage. Children from poor and working-class families often grow up with a single parent and their parents frequently lack higher educations and sometimes are not proficient in English. In contrast, more affluent students often have college-educated parents who can help them with their studies and planning for college, and who are well positioned to advocate for the needs of their children in school. These and other factors combine to stack the deck against disadvantaged children from the time they first enter school.

The federal government needs to play a larger role in leveling the playing field to help students from low-income and working-class families achieve their full educational potential. We understand there is stiff competition for federal dollars among many worthwhile programs. But education spending needs to be high on the nation's priority list if America is to have the educated population we need to strengthen our economy and to break the cycle of poverty that traps millions of Americans.

President Biden clearly recognizes this need and has asked Congress for an extraordinary 41 percent increase in the Education Department budget for the 2022 fiscal year, bringing the department budget to $103 billion. This is a bold step that would benefit America's children and deserves bipartisan support. The Biden budget proposal would more than double funding for Title I—the program that aids school districts with many low-income K–12 students—from $17.1 billion in 2021 to $36.5 billion in 2022. In addition, the budget request included $1.5 billion in increased funding for the Child Care and Development Block Grant and a $1.2 billion increase in funding for Head Start. Both these programs provide early education and care for low-income children. These increases come on top of $100 billion for schools in the president's infrastructure proposal.

In higher education, Biden has requested a $3 billion increase in funding for Pell Grants to raise the maximum tuition assistance for each low-income college student in the program by $400. The president's budget request also seeks a $600 billion increase in funding for historically Black colleges and universities and community colleges that serve large numbers of minority students.[86]

We recommend the following additional actions.

Send more state and local school aid to low-income communities: Many suburban districts collect large amounts of property taxes to fund their schools, thanks to expensive homes and business located in the districts. However, many school districts with large numbers of low-income and working-class students collect lower amounts of property tax revenue on a per student basis, because homes and businesses in these districts on average have lower property valuations.

Most school districts in the U.S. get almost half of their funding from local sources—primarily property taxes. A nonprofit group called EdBuild issued a report in 2020 proposing that property tax revenue be distributed to schools at the county or state level, to reduce wide disparities between the level of per pupil funding between wealthy and low-income school districts. The EdBuild report said 13 states currently distribute school aid this way. The group found that the smallest disparities in school funding on a per pupil basis exist in Southeast states, where districts tend to be countywide. Districts in the rest of the country tend to be geographically smaller in most cases, so they have a greater mix of areas with high and low property valuations. This creates a dramatic gap in per pupil funding in many areas. For example, the difference in local property tax funding on a per student basis from the highest- and lowest-wealth school districts in Georgia (where most school districts cover an entire county) is $186 per year, the study found. In New York State, where most school districts are geographically smaller, the difference is $22,006 per student.[87]

EdBuild said its study of school funding nationwide found that 69 percent of all K–12 students and 76 percent of low-income students would benefit by this redistribution of school aid, with their school districts gaining an average of $1,000 in property tax revenue per student annually. However, because 31 percent of students would go to schools getting *less* property tax revenue on a per pupil basis under this change, the redistribution of property taxes faces opposition from those districts, the EdBuild study found. When Michigan adopted statewide distribution of property tax revenue in 1994, it added revenue from sales taxes and cigarette taxes as a source of school funding to lessen the impact of such cuts, the study found.[88]

Decisions on how property tax revenues are distributed to schools are up to each state. Congress and the president don't have any decisionmaking role on this issue. We believe it's in the best interest of the nation and America's schoolchildren for each state to move to a state-wide or at least countywide distribution of this money. Affluent communities should be allowed to impose additional taxes on themselves to boost funding for their schools. But a mechanism is needed to lessen the gap in available funding on a per-student basis between wealthy and low-income school districts.

Allow more charter schools to operate: Charter schools are publicly funded with tax revenue but are privately run. Since first appearing in Minnesota in 1992, they have spread to forty-three states and Washington, D.C. Most select students by random lotteries, because many more students apply than the schools can accommodate. The charter schools are exempted for many of the regulations that apply to traditional public schools, allowing them more freedom to try new and innovative approaches to education. Some charters require students to take more academically rigorous courses; for example, BASIS charter schools operating in Arizona, Louisiana, Texas, and the District of Columbia require students to take Advanced Placement courses and tests in at least six subjects to graduate from high school.

Other charters focus on technology, the arts, educating students with disabilities, or other areas. *Washington Post* education columnist Jay Mathews, who has written nine books about education topics—including charter schools—said in a column in January 2021: "I think charter schools are one of the most beneficial reforms in public education in the last two decades. That is particularly true for charters that have raised achievement rates among low-income students through longer school days and more support for teachers."[89]

However, teacher unions have raised strong objections to charter schools. In the 2015–16 school year (the most recent for which statistics are available) only about 24 percent of charter school teachers belonged to unions, because in most states the charters are exempted from having collective bargaining contracts. In contrast, about 73 percent of teachers in traditional public schools belong to unions.[90]

The National Education Association is a union for active and retired school staff members that has over 3 million members in 14,000 communities across the nation.[91] On its website, the NEA states: "Too frequently, charters are operated expressly for profit, or are nominally non-profit but managed or operated by for-profit entities. The growth of charters has undermined local public schools and communities without producing any overall increase in student learning and growth....Charter schools, by their very nature, drain funding from local public schools, which enroll over 90 percent of K-12 students....Governments at all levels have failed to implement systems that proactively monitor charter schools and hold them accountable. Several reports have documented millions of taxpayer dollars wasted by fraud, abuse, and mismanagement."[92]

Most school districts limit the number of charter schools allowed, so that the vast majority of students remain in traditional public schools. Because charter schools vary widely, it's impossible to make a blanket judgment about all of them. Some elected officials and candidates for office praise them and some criticize them. For example, in New York City—the nation's most populous school district—nearly 120,000 of the more than 1.1 million public school students attend charters.[93] Four candidates for New York City mayor in the June 2021 primary told a teacher union forum that they support existing limits on the number of charter schools allowed to operate, while another candidate said he would expand the number of charter schools allowed.[94]

In our view, charter schools have had a positive impact overall. As long as testing of students and school district monitoring of the charters show they are doing an effective job, they should be allowed to increase in numbers and have freedom and flexibility to operate. Charters that do a poor job should be shut down. Providing an alternative to poorly performing traditional public schools that are not serving the needs of their students makes sense, creates a competition that can spur the traditional public schools to do better, and benefits students.

Scholarships to private elementary and secondary schools: Scholarship programs to enable low-income students to pay for tuition and other costs at private K–12 schools are another way to help such students get a better education. Perhaps the best-known such program is the D.C. Opportunity Scholarship Program that operates in the nation's capital. Between its launch in the 2004–2005 school year through the 2020–2021 school year, the program has awarded 10,608 scholarships to students who have attended forty-two private schools. The average annual income of families with students receiving scholarships in 2020–2021 was just under $24,000. In 2020–2021, 82 percent of scholarship recipients were Black and 10 percent were Hispanic.[95] Many organizations and private schools provide scholarships like this. We'd like to see more of them to help low-income students get the same quality education as the children of affluent parents. While the vast majority of students will remain in public schools, more federal and state funds ought to be dedicated to giving an increased number of low-income students around the country the opportunity for a high-quality private school education.

Eliminating tuition at public community colleges: Some 46 percent of students enrolled in U.S. colleges are in two-year community colleges.[96] In the 2018–2019 academic year, 8.2 million students were enrolled in community colleges, including 5.6 million in public community colleges, according to the National Center for Education Statistics.[97] The Obama administration supported legislation titled America's College Promise Act in 2015 to provide for two years of free tuition at public community colleges, but Congress never acted on the legislation. The Democratic Party's 2020 platform calls for passage of the legislation and candidate Biden said during the election campaign that he supported it. President Biden made two years of tuition-free community college part of the American Families Plan that he proposed at the end of April

2021. We agree that this would be a positive step. Community college students need and deserve this extra financial assistance. An analysis by the Center of American Progress published in October 2020 found that "community colleges receive $8,800 less in education revenue per student enrolled than four year institutions.... That translates into a total gap of $78 billion between the two sectors."[98]

Making college more affordable: The 2020 Democratic Party platform calls for making four years of public college and university tuition-free for families with incomes of less than $125,000 a year, with funding coming from the federal government and states. The Republican Party didn't adopt a 2020 platform and simply endorsed President Trump's positions, which opposed free public college tuition.[99] Private colleges have criticized proposals for free tuition at public colleges, arguing that this would hurt all but the most sought-after private colleges by prompting fewer students to go to the private schools, which already charge significantly higher tuitions. Many private colleges have instead advocated for increased government financial aid to go to students so the students would have the freedom to choose whether to use the money (equivalent to the cost of public college tuition) at either public or private institutions of higher education. We like this approach, because it gives students a wider choice of colleges. As graduates of private universities ourselves, it would be hypocritical not to hold this view.

Of course, there are many other college costs besides tuition—chiefly room and board, books, and fees. We'd like to see these financial aid programs enacted to help students at both public and private schools cover the rising costs of college attendance:

- Interest-free loans to be repaid over thirty years, like a home mortgage. Eliminating interest costs would save graduates substantial amounts of money and spreading payments over thirty years would ease the annual repayment amount.

- Forgiveness of a portion of the interest-free loans for students who enter public service after graduation, including serving in the U.S. military, the Peace Corps, the anti-poverty program AmeriCorps VISTA, law enforcement and fire departments; teaching in low-income areas; and working in health care in underserved communities. Graduates could erase 10 percent of their outstanding loan balance for each year they spend working in these areas, so that if they stay in these jobs for ten years their entire loan would be forgiven.

- Provide similar incentives to students who enter the STEM (science, technology, engineering, and math) fields. Also, focus on improving STEM education from elementary school through graduate school. The U.S. currently has a shortage of workers in these important fields.

We've outlined an ambitious and expensive list of education programs, on top of the big increases in education funding President Biden has already asked Congress to approve. Enacting all these in one year may not be possible, but these ideas could serve as an education agenda for the Biden administration during his first term. In the short run, it's in the interest of both Democrats and Republicans to support these or similar programs because they make good political sense. Since millions of students—along with their parents—would benefit, elected officials supporting the programs could pick up votes. At the same time, lawmakers voting against the programs could lose votes. In the long run, this increased investment in education would strengthen our economy, make the U.S. more competitive with other nations, and help many young people escape poverty and build better futures.

The big question, of course, is whether both parties are willing to work together to reach bipartisan compromises to accomplish something. There's no question that Democrats will want to spend more than Republicans, and some on the far left will likely complain that whatever Biden seeks will not be enough. And there's no question that many Republicans will oppose tax increases to pay for education funding and oppose increased borrowing as well. America's young people and their parents are counting on lawmakers to reach some agreement and not simply attack each other and complain about the opposite party.

PROTECTING OUR HEALTH

The distrust of America's health care system, health care professionals, scientists, and coronavirus vaccines that we discussed earlier is dangerous, frightening, and deadly in the face of the growing toll from the pandemic. And on top of this, the partisan split between Democrats and Republicans on these issues is particularly disturbing.

Many Republicans and GOP elected officials have criticized mask mandates, social distancing, and business and school closures designed to combat the spread of COVID-19—and some Republican governors lifted those restrictions prematurely. Polls showed that many Republicans also said they didn't plan to get vaccinated against the killer disease. As we wrote earlier in this book, a Monmouth University poll in April 2021 found that only 5 percent of Democrats said they likely will never get a coronavirus vaccine, but that number rose to 22 percent for independents and soared to 43 percent of Republicans.[100]

Dr. Anthony Fauci, President Biden's chief medical adviser and an adviser to President Trump when he was in office, told CNN in April 2021 that it was "paradoxical" for the same people who complain about coronavirus restrictions to also reject vaccinations. "The fact that one may not want to get vaccinated, in this case a disturbingly large proportion of Republicans, only actually works against where they want to be," Fauci said. "They want to be able to say these restrictions that are put on by public health recommendations are things that they're very concerned about. But the way you get rid of those restrictions is to get as many people vaccinated as quickly and as efficiently as possible."[101]

Fauci bemoaned the partisan sniping in the battle against COVID-19 in another CNN interview broadcast a month earlier. "This is a war. So if you're going to fight a war, you better start shooting at the enemy instead of at each other," Fauci said. "I'm nervous about the intensity of the divisiveness in the country right now."[102] The divisiveness was so bad that Fauci admitted in April 2020 that in response to numerous death threats he was being protected around-the-clock by bodyguards. CNN said police were stationed outside his home in Washington.[103]

There was a similar partisan split over whether government officials should issue documents to people verifying they had been vaccinated against COVID-19. These have been referred to as vaccine passports, vaccine certificates, and by other names. A HarrisX-Hill poll published in April 2021 showed that 70 percent of Democrats favored such a government-issued document, but 60 percent of Republicans opposed it. Independents were evenly split, with 50 percent favoring such a document and 50 percent opposing it. Three Republican governors quickly came out against vaccine verification documents: Greg Abbott of Texas (who tested positive for COVID-19 in August 2021) banned government agencies and organizations that get public funding from utilizing verification documents, Ron DeSantis of Florida banned even private businesses in his state from using such documents, and Spencer Cox of Utah signed a bill into law blocking state government from creating or mandating such a document.[104]

In addition, Texas, Florida Tennessee Iowa, Oklahoma, South Carolina, Arizona and Utah banned schools from imposing mask mandates on their students and staff at the beginning of the 2021 fall semester, under either laws or executive orders by governors. All the above states had Republican governors in 2021.[105] Worcester State University assistant professor of Political Science Anthony D. Dell'Aera told CNBC in April

2021 that more Republicans than Democrats have had a higher level of distrust of government for years. He said that because of this, there was similar vaccine resistance among Republicans in 2009 when the swine flu pandemic hit, long before Donald Trump began campaigning for the 2016 Republican presidential nomination.[106]

We recommend the following actions to increase vaccine acceptance, increase trust in America's health care system, and be better prepared for the next pandemic.

Understand that public health isn't a civil liberties issue: UCLA history professor Peter Baldwin, who has written a book about how nations around the world responded to the coronavirus pandemic, has made a powerful case for rejecting claims that adhering to public health measures like mask-wearing, social distancing, and vaccinations violate our civil liberties. We agree with him.

In an op-ed published on the CNN website in April 2021, Baldwin wrote: "The claim that mask-wearing in public violates civil rights is too ludicrous to discuss. . . . The same libertarians who are resigned to seat belts, cycle helmets and condoms have resisted the single most effective personal protection against a respiratory contagion. That refusal to follow simple protective guidelines has only helped to spread the virus and prolong the pandemic."[107]

China already has unveiled a digital vaccine passport and Japan is developing one. The European Union has come out in favor of a "Digital Green Certificate" that would allow citizens who have been vaccinated, recovered from COVID-19, or tested negative for the coronavirus to travel anywhere in the twenty-seven nations belonging to the EU.[108] We understand the objections to the federal government requiring every American to be vaccinated and to have a document verifying this. But that shouldn't stop businesses such as restaurants, entertainment venues, cruise ships, airlines, and retail stores from requiring patrons to show proof of vaccination once everyone including young children can be vaccinated. Tech companies, business groups such as the U.S.

Chamber of Commerce and the Business Roundtable, and Democrats and Republicans at the federal, state, and local government level need to come together to figure out how to protect the American people without creating a permanent national ID card that civil libertarians could say would threaten our privacy and freedoms.

Depoliticize public health: The fact that President Trump was hospitalized with a serious case of COVID-19 ought to convince even his most ardent supporters that the disease is real and strikes people of every political persuasion. The former president can rightfully claim credit for pushing government to work with the private sector to develop safe and effective coronavirus vaccines in record time on his watch. Trump ought to become one of the biggest boosters of the vaccines and appear in public service announcements strongly endorsing vaccinations and urging his supporters to follow his example and get vaccinated. Instead, he has tepidly endorsed vaccinations in a few interviews. Other Republicans should also urge their supporters and constituents to get vaccinated.

Rely on trusted people to urge vaccinations: The Biden administration has launched an advertising campaign to boost public acceptance of coronavirus vaccinations, funded through a $250 million contract the Trump administration signed with the Fors Marsh Group, the *Washington Post* reported.[109] The Biden administration has created a network of "more than 275 member organizations, a diverse mix of advocacy organizations, sports leagues, faith leaders, and other prominent voices" to urge Americans to be vaccinated. "Participants include the American Medical Association, the NAACP, the National Association of Evangelicals, and the NFL." This is an important and welcome step. TV and radio stations and networks, newspapers and websites should also step up and run additional pro-vaccine ads as a public service at no charge.

In addition, trusted people such as family doctors, clergy members, and teachers should do everything possible to urge every American to be vaccinated. Since it appears that booster shots will be needed for the coronavirus vaccines over time, it's important that Americans understand and accept that vaccinations are essential and need to be repeated as health experts determine it is necessary. This is no different than the way millions of Americans get an annual flu shot. Schools should make vaccine education part of the curriculum to educate students from elementary school on up about the importance and safety of vaccines. Once coronavirus vaccines are approved for children, new parents should be instructed by pediatricians on the need to vaccinate their children, and schools should require children to be vaccinated against COVID-19 just as they are now required to be vaccinated against other diseases. According to the Centers for Disease Control and Prevention, by the age of two, just over 90 percent of American children are vaccinated against polio, measles, mumps, rubella, hepatitis B, and chickenpox.[110]

Prepare for the next pandemic: The 1918–1919 flu pandemic is believed to have infected about 500 million people—one-third of the world's population at the time—and killed at least 50 million people globally, including about 675,000 in the U.S.[111] Health experts agree that COVID-19 will not be the last pandemic to strike, and we could someday face a pandemic even worse.

In an article published by Kaiser Health News and The Daily Beast, Jim Robbins wrote that the average death rate of people infected with the coronavirus that causes COVID-19 is less than 1 percent. But the death rate of Middle East Respiratory Syndrome (MERS), which spread from camels to humans, is 35 percent. Even worse, he wrote that other viruses that have been transmitted from animals to humans, such as bat-borne Nipah, have a death rate as high as 75 percent. Fortunately, these far more deadly viruses are not as transmissible as the one that causes COVID-19 at this time, but that could change. "'What keeps me up at night is that another coronavirus like MERS, which has a much, much higher mortality rate, becomes as transmissible as COVID,' said Christian Walzer, executive director of health at the Wildlife Conservation Society. 'The logistics and the psychological trauma of that would be unbearable.'"[112]

Our point in citing this nightmarish scenario is that the federal government needs to do a better job preparing for the next pandemic, whether it comes in a year, ten years, or a hundred years. There is no way of knowing *when* another killer virus will strike, but we can be sure it will. This is not a political issue—it is a scientific, health, and national security issue. A report by the Government Accountability Office published in April 2021 after a thirteen-month investigation criticized the Department of Health and Human Services for management failures in the early days of the coronavirus pandemic, including jurisdictional disputes within the department about which of the several offices would handle different aspects of the evacuation of Americans from the scene of the original COVID-19 outbreak in China.[113] Just as the federal government prepares to anticipate and respond to hurricanes, earthquakes, forest fires, terrorist attacks, wars around the world, and even a nuclear strike against our nation, it needs to do more to prepare for the next pandemic.

Launch a global vaccination program: In July 2020, President Trump notified the World Health Organization—a United Nations agency—that the U.S. planned to withdraw. He later stopped paying dues to the organization. Because a one-year notification is required to withdraw, the U.S. had not completed cutting ties with the WHO when Trump left office. Trump was right to criticize the organization for its initial handling of COVID-19 when the disease first surfaced in China. However, his move to withdraw from the organization and halt payment of about $419 million in annual dues—about 20 percent of the WHO budget—weakened the agency's ability to combat the pandemic. President Biden wisely rejoined the WHO soon after he took office.[114]

Only about 4 percent of the people on Earth live in the U.S. That means even if every single American is vaccinated against COVID-19—something that won't happen—we couldn't wipe out the deadly disease, couldn't stop new variants from arising that might be more resistant to vaccines, and couldn't always keep infected people from other countries from entering the U.S. So, on top of the moral imperative to help save lives and protect people around the world from COVID-19, stamping out the disease in every nation in the world is in our national interest and will save American lives.

With 194 member nations and a history dating back to 1948, the WHO is ideally suited to be a vehicle for the world's wealthiest nations to lend a hand to poor nations to help them vaccinate as many of their citizens as possible. U.S. participation in an ambitious program to eventually vaccinate the vast majority of the over 7.7 billion people on the planet can save lives, build goodwill with nations around the world, and help to bring about a return to normalcy sooner by putting the pandemic behind us. In an important step, Moderna announced in May 2021 that it will sell up to 500 million doses of its coronavirus vaccine at the "lowest tiered price" to be used in a WHO campaign that will vaccinate people in poor nations around the world. However, most of the vaccine doses won't be available until 2022.[115]

President Biden told a joint session of Congress at the end of April 2021: "As our own vaccine supply grows to meet our needs—and we are meeting them—we will become an arsenal of vaccines for other countries, just as America was the arsenal of democracy in World War II." The president made good on that pledge when he announced in June 2021 that the U.S. will buy 500 million doses of the Pfizer coronavirus vaccine and donate them to ninety-two low- and moderate-income nations and the African Union.[116] At their summit in England in the same month, the other six countries in the Group of Seven industrialized nations (Canada, France, Germany, Italy, Japan, and the United Kingdom) pledged to donate an additional 500 million vaccine doses to COVAX, the global vaccine buying system run by the WHO, and Gavi, the Vaccine Alliance. White House officials said earlier that the U.S. will donate up to 60 million doses of the AstraZeneca COVID-19 vaccine to other nations, once the vaccine (already approved for use by some nations) is approved by the U.S. Food and Drug Administration.[117] All this is a strong start, but even more than the over 1 billion vaccine doses now pledged will be needed from the U.S. and other wealthy nations.

Biden's World War II analogy is a good one. Democrats and Republicans should support a global war on the coronavirus with the same united front that they supported the war against the Axis powers in the 1940s. They need to do this for the most obvious of reasons. Only by eradicating the coronavirus around the world can we be truly secure here at home, and avoid the development of more dangerous and potentially more deadly variants that could continue to put us at risk here at home, notwithstanding a relative high level of vaccination in the U.S. The only way to have the political will and economic commitment to get this done around the world is through bipartisanship here at home.

Create a stand-alone health department: The U.S. Department of Health, Education, and Welfare was created in 1953, bringing together agencies with vastly different functions. In 1980, the department was split into a Department of Education to focus on that important area and what is now the Department of Health and Human Services.[118] We'd like to see the department divided again into a Department of Health, headed by a physician, and a separate Department of Human Services. This would allow one department to focus on health alone, because it is such an important topic. Freed of responsibility from overseeing offices dealing with human services, the secretary of the new Department of Health could focus all his or her attention on protecting the health of the American people.

If there was ever an issue that cries out for bipartisan cooperation, health care is it. There isn't a single disease that attacks only members of one political party. Democrats and Republicans will certainly have legitimate differences on what health care policies to pursue, how much to spend, and how to fund programs. But in the war against COVID-19 and other diseases, we need to be united to protect each other and win the fight.

ENERGY REFORM

One of the most divisive issues splitting Democrats and Republicans today involves how to provide America with the enormous quantities of energy we need to heat and light our homes and businesses, manufacture products, grow crops, fuel our vehicles, and power all the appliances and devices that make modern life possible. Many Democrats want to quickly and drastically reduce the use of fossil fuels (coal, oil, and natural gas) as energy sources. Many Republicans argue that the U.S. should take advantage of the abundant quantities of valuable fossil fuels buried under our feet and move much more gradually toward other forms of energy as they become more affordable, reliable, efficient, and competitive with fossil fuels.

While the U.S. has just 4.2 percent of the world's population, we consume about 17 percent of the world's energy, according to the U.S. Energy Information Administration.[119] America also produces a disproportionate share of emissions of carbon dioxide, the greenhouse gas that accelerates climate change. According to the Union of Concerned Scientists, the U.S. produced 15 percent of the world's carbon dioxide emissions in 2018 (the most recent year available) from coal, natural gas, oil, and other fuels. The only nation that emitted more carbon dioxide was China. With about 18.5 percent of the world's population, China accounted for 28 percent of global carbon dioxide emissions. That was followed by India (with 17.7 percent of the world's population) producing 7 percent of carbon dioxide emissions; Russia (with 1.9 percent of global population) producing 5 percent; and Japan (with 1.6 percent of global population) producing 3 percent. No other nation produced more than 2 percent of global carbon dioxide emissions.[120]

Republicans have sharply attacked the Green New Deal, a plan proposed by Representative Alexandria Ocasio-Cortez of New York and Senator Ed Markey of Massachusetts designed to dramatically reduce carbon dioxide emissions; guarantee clean air, clean water, and healthy food as basic human rights; create jobs; and make major changes to America's economy. Among other provisions, the Green New Deal calls for producing all of America's electricity from renewable and zero-emissions power sources in ten years, upgrading every building in the nation to be more energy-efficient, and investing in electric vehicles.[121] The American Action Forum, a conservative think tank, estimates that implementing six key elements of the plan would cost between $52 trillion and $93 trillion over 10 years.[122] Ocasio-Cortez has estimated the Green New Deal would cost at least $10 trillion.[123] With such enormous variances, it's impossible to know how much the plan would cost other than to say it would definitely be a multitrillion-dollar initiative—a very heavy lift.

President Biden has not endorsed going as far as the Green New Deal. However, speaking at a virtual climate summit with leaders from thirty-nine other nations in late April 2021, Biden set a goal for 2030 of cutting U.S. greenhouse gas emissions to between 50 and 52 percent below what they were in 2005. This is a big increase from the target of a 26 to 28 percent cut in emissions by 2025 set by President Obama. In 2019 (the most recent year in which statistics are available), U.S. emissions were already 13 percent below 2005 levels. However, reaching Biden's target will be impossible without action by Congress, which would need to overcome objections by Republicans and likely some Democrats from states that produce fossil fuels (such as Senator Joe Manchin of coal-rich West Virginia) concerned that such rapid cuts in emissions could harm the economy and cause job losses in their states and elsewhere in the nation.[124]

Senate Minority Leader Mitch McConnell tweeted criticism of Biden's announcement on emissions cuts while the virtual climate summit was in progress. "This Administration's zeal for costly climate policy at home is not matched by our biggest competitors. China's share of emissions is nearly double ours. The Paris Agreement is largely toothless. Democrats can kill U.S. jobs & industries with no real impact on global emissions," McConnell said on Twitter.[125] McConnell made a valid point about China. Although China is an economic powerhouse and has the second-largest economy in the world (topped only by the U.S.), Chinese president Xi Jinping wants his nation to be treated as a developing nation and not held to the same standards as the U.S. and other industrialized nations. This is absurd. Writing about the virtual energy summit, the *Washington Post* reported: "Although the United States, Japan, and Canada on Thursday unveiled tighter new greenhouse gas emissions targets for 2030, Xi—as well as another key figure, Indian Prime Minister Narendra Modi—refrained from new commitments. After Xi's speech, Chinese officials tasked with briefing reporters and Chinese state media repeated longstanding lines that developed countries must do more to cut their emissions while developing economies should be allowed more slack. Environmental groups say they were disappointed because Xi has staked out significant long-term goals to reach carbon neutrality by 2060 but has not presented clarity about how to get there."

As for Biden's pledge on reducing U.S. emissions, the *Washington Post* correctly stated in an editorial published as the virtual summit was underway: "Such promises are easy. Making good on them, and on this one in particular, is hard.... Still, ramping up renewables while maintaining grid reliability is a major challenge. Huge amounts of new wind, solar and, potentially, nuclear and hydropower infrastructure must be built in a short time, and fossil fuel plants must be forced offline before their natural retirement dates."[126]

In his proposed budget for the 2022 fiscal year, President Biden asked Congress to approve $14 billion to fight climate change. The budget included $11.1 billion for the Environmental Protection Agency, which amounts to a hefty 21.3 percent increase. The budget request also called for $10.2 billion for the National Science Foundation—a 20 percent increase—including $500 million for research on clean energy and climate. In addition, Biden asked for a 10.2 percent increase in the Energy Department budget to $46 billion, including $1.9 billion to help electric power plants switch from fossil fuels to other energy sources by 2035.[127]

Biden has returned America to the Paris Climate Agreement (Trump withdrew from the pact) and wants to cut greenhouse gas emissions enough to make the U.S. carbon-neutral by 2050—meaning only as much carbon dioxide could be emitted as could be absorbed by the atmosphere. On his first day in office he ordered federal agencies to review and replace over 100 Trump administration environmental policies. In addition, Biden wants to install at least 500,000 new charging stations for electric vehicles around the nation and replace the current fleet of vehicles owned by the federal government with electric vehicles. Achieving Biden's goals would require a major reduction in the use of fossil fuels—especially coal—and a big increase in the use of renewable energy. Former secretary of state John Kerry, who Biden appointed to a new position of special envoy for climate, said: "We need to increase tree cover five times faster than we are. We need to ramp up renewable energy six times faster. And the transition to electric vehicles needs to take place at a rate 22 times faster."[128]

We agree with Democrats that fossil fuels need to eventually be phased out. But we agree with Republicans that the fuels can't be replaced quickly without incurring enormous costs and causing economic dislocation, big increases in unemployment in the domestic energy sector, possible power shortages, and an increased reliance on imported energy for at least the first few years of a rapid transition. As a result, we want to reach the goals Democrats have set, but at a slower pace. This creates a basis for centrist and bipartisan compromises that won't give either side all it wants, but could move America forward on energy while combating climate change. Here is what we propose.

Phase out coal: Coal is the dirtiest and most polluting fossil fuel. Its use needs to be phased out to make progress in the fight against climate change and air pollution. The Energy Information Administration states that burning coal to generate power emits: "Sulfur dioxide (SO2), which contributes to acid rain and respiratory illnesses; Nitrogen oxides (NOx), which contribute to smog and respiratory illnesses; Particulates, which contribute to smog, haze, and respiratory illnesses and lung disease; Carbon dioxide (CO_2), which is the primary greenhouse gas produced from burning fossil fuels (coal, oil, and natural gas); Mercury and other heavy metals, which have been linked to both neurological and developmental damage in humans and other animals; Fly ash and bottom ash, which are residues created when power plants burn coal."[129]

Depending on the type of coal burned, it emits almost twice as much or just over twice as much carbon dioxide as does natural gas. When coal is burned to generate 1 million Btu (British thermal units) of energy, it emits between about 206 and 229 pounds of carbon dioxide, depending on the type of coal used. Generating the same amount of energy from natural gas emits 117 pounds of carbon dioxide, while doing so from gasoline without ethanol generates about 157 pounds of carbon dioxide, and doing so from diesel fuel and heating oil generates about 161 pounds of carbon dioxide.[130] This makes it obvious that ending the use of coal for energy would have a significant impact on not only carbon dioxide pollution, but other forms of pollution as well.

Coal production in the U.S. has been falling for years, due to increased production of natural gas. The downside of ending coal use and production entirely, of course, would be that everyone in the coal industry would lose their jobs and coal mining communities would suffer economically. Total coal mining employment in the U.S. was nearly 92,000 in 2011 but fell to 44,100 by December 2020, according to the United Mine Workers union. However, many more people are economically dependent on the coal industry—the families of coal miners, along with businesses in coal country that sell them products and services, and government entities funded in part with taxes paid by coal companies and miners. The United Mine Workers recognizes that the days of coal mining are numbered. The union issued a report in April 2021 calling for "a true energy transition that will enhance opportunities for miners, their families, and their communities." In other words, programs to help coal industry employees get the education and training for new jobs, along with programs to attract different types of jobs and protect the economic health of the country. The union also called for programs to expand carbon capture and storage to reduce pollution from burning coal.[131]

To give employees and communities time to plan for the end of coal mining, we propose allowing new coal mining permits to be issued for another ten years, after which mining would be allowed to continue for as long as existing mines were productive. Coal company employees should be offered full scholarships for colleges and training programs to prepare them for new careers and other transitional assistance. In addition, wherever possible, new non-fossil fuel energy plants should be located in coal mining communities, with federal subsidies and tax breaks to incentivize these plants as well as other employers to locate where coal had been mined. Hardworking coal miners and support and supervisory employees in the industry, along with others in coal communities, should be protected to the extent practicable from economic harm.

Tax credits for electric vehicle manufacturers and non-fossil-fuel energy power plants: We agree with the proposals President Biden has already made to encourage electric vehicle production and the construction of non-fossil-fuel energy power plants. However, these proposals face an uncertain future due to Republican opposition. Whether or not these proposals become law, we would like to see tax credits for these businesses enacted, which might get a better reception from Republicans in Congress. We propose that Congress enact tax credits under which the first ten years of profits from the manufacture and sale of electric vehicles and from the sale of electricity produced at non-fossil-fuel plants would be entirely free of federal taxation. Over the next nine years, the tax credits would be phased out, so that vehicle manufacturers and energy companies would pay a growing share of taxes normally due: 10 percent the first year, 20 percent the second, 30 percent the third, and so on. These ten years of zero taxes and nine years of reduced taxes would give companies a huge incentive to build and sell electric vehicles and to shift power generation from fossil fuels to solar, hydroelectric, wave, wind, biomass, geothermal, and nuclear power.

The tax credits would also allow vehicle manufacturing and energy companies not dependent on fossil fuels to competitively price the vehicles and energy they produce, accelerating the move away from fossil fuels. Yes, this would deprive the federal government of huge amounts of tax revenue. But tax credits wouldn't require a big government bureaucracy to manage, as would loans or other payments to vehicle manufacturers and energy companies. Federal loans can wind up going to companies that fail, as happened with Solyndra, a solar panel manufacturing company that defaulted on a $535 million clean energy loan it obtained in 2009 from the U.S. Energy Department. A federal investigation later determined the company had engaged in "a pattern of false and misleading assertions" to get the loan it never repaid.[132] In contrast to loans, tax credits only go to companies that earn taxable profits. Factories manufacturing electric vehicles and energy plants that never make any money would have no taxable income that needs to be forgiven.

An alternate way of accomplishing this same goal regarding electric vehicles would be to give big refundable tax credits to people who buy such vehicles, staying level for ten years and then phasing out over the following nine years. We're not advocating refundable consumer tax credits for the full purchase price of vehicles—that would amount to giving free vehicles to every American driver, and the cost would be prohibitive. However, Congress could increase the current federal income tax credit for people who buy electric vehicles, and have a big impact as a result. The current federal tax credit for electric vehicle buyers is worth up to $7,500, based on the capacity of the battery used to power the vehicle. The *Washington Post* reports that the cheapest electric cars now have a suggested sale price of $30,000 to $40,000.[133] We recommend increasing the tax credit for electric vehicle purchases to $15,000 for 10 years, and then phasing it out by cutting it by $1,000 annually for the next 15 years. With the tax credit, the cost of the least-expensive electric cars would drop to $15,000 to $25,000, making them competitive with the lowest-price gasoline- and diesel-powered vehicles.

General Motors has said it will only make electric vehicles by 2035, and it's only a matter of time before all automakers follow suit, so there is no need for a permanent tax credit for electric vehicle buyers. But a short-term increased consumer tax credit like the one we are proposing would accelerate the demise of gasoline- and diesel-powered vehicles. The Environmental Protection Agency reports that the transportation sector accounts for 28 percent of annual greenhouse gas emissions in the U.S. Most of the emissions within the transportation sector—82 percent—come from cars and trucks.[134] So tax credits for either vehicle buyers or manufacturers to get more electric vehicles on the road quickly could have a big impact. Giving tax credits directly to consumers rather than vehicle manufacturers might be more politically attractive, because voters might see it as a benefit more directly going to them.

One note of caution on electric vehicles: It's important to remember that electric vehicles only provide maximum benefit in terms of emissions reductions when the electricity they use is generated with as little carbon dioxide production as possible. Cars that run on electricity produced by coal-fired power plants, for example, don't emit carbon dioxide and other pollutants from their tailpipes, but the coal plants emit large amounts of pollutants when they produce the electricity. So it's important to cut fossil fuel use at electric power plants in addition to getting more electric cars on the road.

Use tax credits to encourage the expansion of nuclear power: Some people might wonder why we are recommending that nuclear power plants qualify for the tax credits we want to also go to producers of renewable energy. According to the Nuclear Energy Institute, which represents the nuclear energy industry, ninety-four nuclear reactors in twenty-eight states already generate about 20 percent of the electricity produced in the United States—enough to power 75 million homes. Nuclear energy produces no carbon dioxide and no other harmful pollutants such as sulfur dioxide, nitrogen oxide, mercury, and particulate matter. And nuclear plants operate 24/7, unlike renewable energy sources. Existing nuclear plants already produce 55 percent of the carbon-free electricity in the U.S. each year.[135]

The 1979 meltdown at the nuclear plant at Three Mile Island in Pennsylvania was a tremendous setback for the nuclear power industry and generated understandable safety fears. However, as the *New Yorker* reported in a February 2021 article by Rebecca Tuhus-Dubrow: "Most epidemiological studies would eventually determine that the accident had no detectable health consequences." In addition, the 1979 film *The China Syndrome*—about a *fictional* meltdown at a corruptly operated nuclear plant—also helped turn public opinion against nuclear power.[136] Opposition grew even stronger with the Chernobyl nuclear meltdown in the Soviet Union in 1986, when a flawed nuclear reactor design, lax safety standards nowhere near as strict as those in the U.S., and poorly trained workers were responsible for a steam explosion that sent radioactive material across much of Europe and resulted in the deaths of twenty-eight people in several weeks, and fifteen more later from thyroid cancer.[137] Plans for building sixty-seven nuclear power plants in the U.S. were canceled between 1979 and 1988. Another meltdown took place at the Fukushima Daiichi nuclear plant in Japan in 2011. That prompted Japan and Germany to shut down nuclear plants, making the two nations more dependent on coal to generate electricity. "However, studies have found few health risks in connection to radiation exposure in Japan in the wake of the accident," Tuhus-Dubrow wrote.[138]

Tuhus-Dubrow reported in her *New Yorker* article that growing numbers of environmentalists are coming out in favor of building more nuclear power plants and renewing operating licenses of existing plants. They say

U.S. nuclear plants must meet strict standards for safety and American plants have a good safety record, with the exception of Three Mile Island. For example, James Hansen—the NASA scientist who first raised alarms about global warming in 1988—"has long advocated a vast expansion of nuclear power to replace fossil fuels," Tuhus-Dubrow wrote. She added: "Pro-nuclear environmentalists . . . see nuclear power not as something that could destroy the world but as something that could save it."[139]

Keep producing domestic oil and natural gas: The U.S. gets 37 percent of its total energy consumption from oil, 32 percent from natural gas, 11 percent from renewable sources, 11 percent from coal, and 8 percent from nuclear power, the Energy Information Administration reported in 2020.[140] Phasing out coal relatively rapidly, as we have proposed, will be difficult enough. We can't simply flip a switch and convert to 100 percent renewable energy in just a few years. This is why we advocate continued oil and natural gas production in the U.S.— including by using fracking on both private and federal lands—while we gradually move away from fossil fuels. The move can be accelerated by President Biden's proposals and the incentives we have described above to encourage expanded production of renewable and nuclear energy. If we halt U.S. oil and natural gas production before we no longer need these energy sources, we would simply have to import the fossil fuels, adding to our trade deficit and increasing greenhouse gas emissions due to emissions that take place when oil and natural gas have to travel to the U.S. from other nations. U.S. oil and natural gas extraction earned $375.2 billion in 2019.[141] This was used to employ workers, pay taxes, and strengthen the U.S. economy.

Develop the Keystone XL Pipeline: Bowing to pressure from environmentalists, on his first day in office President Biden canceled a permit for the Keystone XL pipeline to cross into the U.S. from Canada. This had symbolic value as a way of stating the U.S. was moving away from fossil fuels. It also scored political points for Biden with his party's left-wing. TC Energy, owner of the pipeline, canceled plans in June 2021 to complete it due to Biden's action.[142] We believe the president won't reverse his position, but a future president should consider reviving the project if a company is still interested in completing the pipeline. Completion of the pipeline would have sent a powerful message to the world about the enduring importance of fossil fuels, America's commitment to economic development and job creation, and the need to avoid appearing to defer to the political agenda of the extreme left.

The pipeline would have carried up to 830,000 barrels per day of Canadian crude oil extracted from tar sands in Alberta 1,200 miles to Nebraska, where it would join with an existing oil pipeline and go to U.S. oil refineries on the Gulf Coast. President Obama blocked development of the pipeline in 2015 but President Trump approved it. However, construction on the link from Canada to the U.S. was not completed in time to open the pipeline while Trump was in office.[143]

Pipelines have a long record of safely carrying oil long distances, although on rare occasions, spills have occurred. The safety record of pipelines is superior to the safety record of railroad cars, which now carry some Canadian oil into the U.S. Another oil pipeline called Keystone already operates from Alberta into the U.S. Biden's cancellation of Keystone XL hurt U.S. relations with our close ally Canada, which wants to export the Alberta oil. If Canada decides to ship the oil to Asia, it will generate far more pollution and deprive the U.S. of a valuable energy supply. The Canadian oil would have benefited U.S. national security as well, because Canada is a close ally with a stable government. We would never have to worry that the flow of Canadian oil would be disrupted by a military coup, a war, a blockage of the Suez Canal (as happened in 2021 with Middle East oil), or a dispute with oil-exporting nations. Such a dispute occurred in 1973–1974, when Arab nations belonging to the Organization of Petroleum Exporting Countries imposed on oil embargo on the U.S. and other nations supporting Israel in the 1973 Arab-Israeli war. Gasoline shortages hit drivers across the U.S. and the American economy suffered.[144]

Increase the federal solar tax credit: The federal solar investment credit, which was enacted in 2006, currently allows homeowners to get an income tax credit worth 26 percent of the cost of solar power they install. However, under current laws, this tax credit will be reduced, falling to 22 percent in 2023 and ending for homeowners in 2024. (The tax credit will continue indefinitely at a 10 percent level for businesses that install, develop, and/or finance solar power.) According to the Solar Energy Industries Association, since the tax credit was enacted "the U.S. solar industry has grown by more than 10,000 percent—creating hundreds of thousands of jobs and investing billions of dollars in the U.S. economy in the process." But since the solar industry was tiny in 2006, despite the huge percentage growth it only accounts for 2.5 percent of energy production in the U.S. today.[145]

Given that Republicans typically like tax cuts and tax credits more than they like programs that hand out money to businesses and individuals, we believe that increasing the federal solar tax credit and continuing it at a high level beyond 2024 would give a major boost to solar power use across the U.S., thereby decreasing fossil fuel consumption. We would increase the tax credit to 50 percent from the current 26 percent, keep it there for ten years, and then start phasing it out by reducing it by 5 percent annually.

Raise gasoline and diesel fuel taxes: As we wrote earlier, federal taxes on gasoline and diesel fuel have been frozen at 18.4 cents per gallon for gasoline and 23.4 cents per gallon for diesel since 1993. They should be raised to make up for inflation, which would require boosting the taxes to 33 cents for a gallon of gasoline and 44 cents for a gallon of diesel, and then indexed to inflation so they rise slightly each year. In addition to providing money for federal transportation spending, these increases would incentivize motorists to get electric vehicles more quickly. We don't expect Democrats and Republicans to agree to do this, however, since raising a broad-based tax like the one on motor fuels would be very unpopular with voters. In the long term, a new way to raise tax revenue for roads, bridges, and mass transit will be needed, as growing numbers of cars move to electric power.

IMMIGRATION REFORM

One of the most dramatic differences between President Trump and challenger Joe Biden during the 2020 presidential campaign was their attitude toward unauthorized immigration.

Trump cast illegal immigration as a major scourge and portrayed himself as the candidate best able to protect the American people from dangerous foreigners crossing the border. A *USA Today* analysis of Trump's remarks and tweets about illegal immigrants found that in hundreds of references by mid-2019 he described their entry into the U.S. as an "invasion" and characterized many of them by using the words "alien," "killer," "criminal," "animal," and "predator," among other pejoratives. He often told them to get "the hell out of our country."[146] When he announced his candidacy in his first presidential campaign in 2015, he said: "When Mexico sends its people, they're not sending their best.... They're sending people that have lots of problems.... They're bringing drugs. They're bringing crime. They're rapists. And some, I assume, are good people."[147]

Perhaps most famously, in the same campaign announcement speech, Trump promised to build a wall along the U.S.–Mexico border and said, "I will have Mexico pay for the wall, mark my words." Mexico never paid for the wall and leaders of that nation said it never would. Trump continued to criticize illegal immigration throughout his presidency and while he campaigned against Biden in 2020. By the time he left office, Trump had built 453 miles of "border wall system," according to the U.S. Customs and Border Protection agency, but the vast majority of that replaced portions of 654 miles of existing fencing that had been built before he took office. At the end of his term, "the

Trump administration has built just 47 miles of border wall where none existed before," NBC News reported in January 2021.[148] Trump also took numerous actions to tighten security along the southern border and to send unauthorized immigrants back to Mexico.

Biden campaigned on a pledge to quickly reverse most of Trump's immigration policies, although at this writing he has only reversed some by executive orders, since Congress has not acted on his proposed immigration reform legislation. Candidate Biden said he would lay out "a clear roadmap to citizenship" for the roughly 11 million unauthorized immigrants now living in the U.S., including approximately 654,000 immigrants brought to the U.S. as children and now temporarily protected from deportation under the DACA (Deferred Action for Childhood Arrivals) program; halt construction of Trump's border wall; make it easier for migrants to apply for asylum in the U.S. and not send them back to Mexico to await hearings; raise the annual cap for refugees settled in the U.S. from 15,000 set by Trump to the previous level of 125,000; reunify parents and children separated at the border; and end Trump's ban on people from twelve predominantly Muslim majority nations entering the U.S.[149] President Biden has listed the coronavirus pandemic and other reasons for slowing his ability to act as swiftly as he had hoped.

But while Biden issued executive orders beginning on Inauguration Day to accomplish some of his goals, he can't remake our immigration system to the extent he wants without new laws—meaning Congress would need to pass legislation. That will be a tall order, given that Democrats and Republicans look at immigration very differently. Biden proposed the U.S. Citizenship Act of 2021 on the day he took office to fulfill many of his campaign promises regarding immigration. The bill would create a road map for unauthorized immigrants to stay in the U.S. and eventually become citizens; make changes in the family-based immigration system to clear a backlog of cases and keep immigrant families together; bar discrimination against immigrants based on their religion;

bar discrimination against LGBTQ immigrants and their families; make it easier for foreign workers to get permission to say in the U.S.; protect immigrant workers from discrimination and improve the verification process for employment eligibility; provide more funds to deploy high-tech technology to enhance border security and reduce the flow of illegal drugs into the U.S.; crack down on criminal organizations; authorize a study of the need for additional barriers and roads on the border with Mexico; increase foreign aid to El Salvador, Guatemala, and Honduras to improve conditions there so fewer people would leave to come to the U.S.; and improve immigration courts.[150]

Since Biden took office, unauthorized immigration has increased sharply. "Now, the Biden administration is scrambling to control the biggest surge in twenty years, with the nation on pace for as many as 2 million migrants at the southern border this year—the outcome Biden said he wanted to avoid," the *Washington Post* reported in late March 2021. "There are now more than 10,000 unaccompanied migrant children in the care of the Department of Health and Human Services, and 5,000 more in the care of Customs and Border Protection, nearly twice the previous record."[151] The newspaper reported at the end of April 2021 that "unauthorized crossings along the Mexico border have remained near twenty-year-highs" during the month "with slightly fewer unaccompanied minors and family members taken into custody by U.S. agents but more adults arriving than in March." Customs and Border Protection reported that the number of arrests and detentions on the border in April rose to 178,622—up from 172,331 people a month earlier.[152]

The Biden White House claimed the sharp increase in illegal immigrants coming to the U.S. border was being primarily caused by problems in Guatemala, El Salvador, and Honduras—including a high rate of violence and other crime, poor economic conditions, and government corruption. However, Yahoo News reported in late April 2021: "A surge in large groups of people crossing the border illegally—particularly those that include families and unaccompanied minors—is being driven in part by the belief that the Biden administration's policies will allow migrants to stay in the U.S., according to an intelligence alert issued by U.S. Customs and Border Protection....A current Department of Homeland Security official, who asked for anonymity because of not being authorized to speak to the press, expressed frustration at the Biden administration's policies. The official said the rush to reverse Trump-era policies was done too quickly and without enough thought about what would happen next."[153] Representative Vincente Gonzalez (D-TX), who represents a district near the border, told the *Washington Post*: "When you create a system that incentivizes people to come across, and they are released, that immediately sends a message to Central America that if you come across you can stay....It incentivizes droves of people to come, and the only way to slow it down is by changing policy at our doorstep. If they don't change the policy, the flow of continued migration traffic isn't going to stop or slow down."[154]

So where do we go from here? Is there any way Democrats who believe immigration is a plus and Republicans who believe it is a minus can ever reconcile? The two parties have come close to reaching an agreement several times in recent years, but weren't able to close the deal. Yet the parties did come together in 1986, when President Ronald Reagan—a revered figure among many Republicans to this day—signed a far-reaching immigration law that granted amnesty to nearly 3 million immigrants in the U.S. illegally.[155] We believe there is a path for a bipartisan centrist compromise on immigration now. Here's what we recommend to reform our clearly broken immigration system.

Admit more legal immigrants: President Trump said while he was in office: "I want people to come into our country in the largest numbers ever, but they have to come in legally."[156]

That's a good point. We shouldn't encourage anyone to violate U.S. laws, and such violations promote disrespect for the law. When laws are widely violated, the government has two options: Crack down harder to enforce the laws (as Trump did with immigration laws), or change the laws. The federal government has often taken the latter approach.

For example, the Eighteenth Amendment to the Constitution went into effect in 1920 to ban the sale of most alcoholic beverages. However, Prohibition was very unpopular, widely violated, and spawned organized crime gangs—resulting in the repeal of the amendment in 1933. Similarly, growing numbers of states are now legalizing marijuana for medical or recreational use. And casino gambling is becoming legal in more and more states and Native American reservations. So a simple way to reduce illegal immigration would be to change our immigration laws to allow more legal immigration.

The Department of Homeland Security keeps records of the number of foreigners obtaining legal permanent resident status in the U.S. going back to 1820. The number peaked in 1991 at 1.82 million. In 2019 (the most recent year available), there were slightly over 1 million. Every year since 2005 (except for 2013) has experienced more legal immigrants than America had in 2019.[157] We'd like to see the number of foreigners legally permitted to enter the U.S. each year rise to about 3 million (including people seeking asylum and refugees). The increased number would enable many of the people who now come to the U.S. illegally to do so legally, reducing the number of people trying to enter without legal permission. Legal immigrants can be screened to ensure we are not admitting criminals or terrorists. Admitting immigrants who have been screened and approved is obviously a more secure system than having large numbers of migrants crossing the border illegally.

The first results of the 2020 Census provided evidence of the need for increased legal immigration. The report released in April 2021 showed that America's population grew in the previous decade at the slowest rate since the 1930s, hitting 331.5 million people as of April 1, 2020. This 7.4 percent growth was the second-slowest percentage rate of growth since the first U.S. Census in 1790. The Census Bureau attributed the low population growth rate to America's aging White population, lower fertility rates, and a slowdown in immigration.[158] Of these three factors, the only one the federal government has any power to control is immigration. In making the case for increased legal immigration, the *Washington Post* said in an editorial shortly after the Census Bureau report was released: "The 2020 census offers a powerful argument for immigration....Demographic stagnation, and the resulting possibility of anemic economic growth, threaten American vitality. The census numbers give the lie, again, to the idea that this country is "full," as President Donald Trump said, by way of justifying his assault on legal and illegal immigration, or that it has somehow reached the limits of its absorptive capacity. In fact, without robust population growth, and a steady supply of working-age strivers, there is no prospect of repairing the fraying social safety net that supports an aging population of retired Americans. Simply, lagging births and slowing immigration mean fewer workers, less production and the specter of languid economic growth, or none."[159]

The Associated Press reported in 2019 that immigration benefits the U.S. in many ways: "In general, the entire immigrant population is increasingly better educated than native-born Americans. They're more likely to have jobs. They're less likely to commit violent crimes. They help fuel economic growth. And as a group over time, they're no more a drain on taxpayers than native-born citizens....Economists say that restricting immigration would probably weaken economic growth."[160]

With more immigrants admitted legally to the U.S. each year, we should be able to allow in significantly more college-educated immigrants to ease the shortage of American-born scientists and engineers. Many strong foreign students who graduate from American colleges and universities would like to remain in the U.S., but are not allowed to. The American economy and the American people would benefit by allowing some of these new graduates who want to stay in the U.S. to do so.

The Pew Research Center reported in 2020 that the U.S. is home to more immigrants than any nation in the world. We ought to consider it a compliment and a vote of confidence in our democracy that so many people are uprooting themselves to come here. In 2018, there were 44.8 million immigrants living in the U.S., amounting to 13.7 percent of our population. That was almost triple the 4.8 percent of the U.S. population that was made up of immigrants in 1970. Pew estimates that in 2017, 45 percent of immigrants in the U.S. were naturalized citizens, 27 percent were legal permanent residents, 5 percent were temporary residents, and the remaining 23 percent were in America in violation of U.S. law. Pew said that in 2017 that there were about 10.5 million unauthorized immigrants in the U.S., making up 3.2 percent of America's population. Among the entire immigrant population living in the U.S. in 2018, 25 percent were born in Mexico, 6 percent were born in China, 6 percent were born in India, 4 percent were born in the Philippines, and 3 percent were born in El Salvador.[161] The federal government estimated the number of unauthorized immigrants in the U.S. in 2018 at 11.4 million—900,000 higher than the Pew estimate for 2017.[162]

Create a path to citizenship for immigrants: Unauthorized immigrants who have lived in the U.S. for at least one year, DACA recipients, and other immigrants protected from deportation under different programs should be given the opportunity to seek citizenship under an amnesty program. No one benefits if these people have to spend their lives in the shadows, unable to get good jobs or qualify for financial aid to attend college, and not paying taxes. We won't try to work out all the details, but in general these immigrants should have to pay any back taxes owed with penalties and interest, pay a fine of several thousand dollars for entering the U.S. illegally, have a clean criminal record (other than immigration and tax law violations), be living in a household with an income sufficient to be self-supporting, and wait five years after being granted amnesty to apply for citizenship. We understand that some people will criticize this as a reward for lawbreakers. But realistically, the federal government is not going to round up and deport the roughly 11 million people living in the U.S. in violation of the law. Most have jobs that benefit the nation, many have children born in the U.S., and many are married to American citizens. So, like it or not, these people are not going anywhere.

Secure the border: The only way Democrats will ever get Republicans on board behind immigration reform legislation will be to take action to better secure the border against illegal entry of new migrants. Trump and many Republicans in Congress have warned of the danger of open borders, saying we can't simply let an unlimited number of people who want to enter the U.S. come in. Many Republicans are calling on Biden to add to the 701 miles of border wall and fencing now existing to cover at least 1,000 miles of the nearly 2,000-mile-long U.S.-Mexico border. Some Democrats and environmentalists are calling on Biden to tear down all of the existing wall and fencing system.

Biden halted construction on the border barrier as soon as he took office. We don't favor tearing down the wall and fencing already built. That would be expensive, make the border less secure, and require the hiring of more Border Patrol agents to hold down illegal immigration. And what if the next Republican president decides he or she wants a wall? Will that new president spend billions of dollars to build a new barrier, only to have the next Democratic president spend billions of dollars to tear it down, only to have the next Republican president build the wall again, and on and on far into the future? That would be ridiculous.

We also don't favor building the wall and fencing system along the entire border with Mexico. There is no possibility Biden would agree to finish the entire barrier—Democrats, immigration advocates, and environmentalists who are part of his coalition would become apoplectic and denounce him. In fact, at the end of April 2021, Biden canceled contracts to complete some parts of the border barrier that were under construction with $3.3 billion in Defense Department funds when he took office. What remained undetermined was whether $5 billion in Department of Homeland Security funds approved by Congress for border barrier construction would be used for that purpose. Republicans contend that Biden is legally required to use the money to extend the border barrier, while Democrats want the funds used for other projects to improve and better secure the border.[163] A reasonable compromise would be to use a portion of the $5 billion to add to the border barrier in return for Republican support of other parts of Biden's immigration reform agenda.

Reduce the backlog in immigration courts: The Justice Department operates sixty-seven immigration courts around the nation, staffed by about 460 immigration judges.[164] The courts hear appeals from foreigners seeking asylum or refugee status in the U.S. by claiming they have been persecuted or have well-founded fears of being persecuted in their home countries based on either their race, religion, nationality, political opinions, or membership in a particular group.[165]

As of March 2021, there was a huge backlog of 1.3 million cases in the immigration courts, according to the Transactional Records Access Clearinghouse (TRAC), operated by Syracuse University. The backlog has grown enormously from just under 130,000 cases in fiscal 1998, and has skyrocketed since President Trump took office. In fiscal 2016, the backlog stood at about 516,000 cases, jumped to about 629,000 cases in fiscal 2017, and has kept on rising.[166] According to TRAC, at the start of President Biden's term of office the average wait for a hearing in immigration court was four years and five months between the time someone gets a notice to appear and his or her next scheduled hearing.[167] Such a long delay is intolerable.

"The backlog grew under Trump despite the former president adding hundreds of immigration judges," the *Texas Tribune* reported in February 2021. "But that wasn't enough to contain the 'tsunami of new cases filed in court' under the Trump administration's enforcement-heavy approach, a TRAC report states."[168] Gregory Chen, director of government affairs for the American Immigration Lawyers Association, told the *Texas Tribune* that in addition to hiring more immigration judges, the federal government needs to give judges more freedom to dismiss cases involving migrants who are not a security or flight risk.

During the Trump administration, about 68,000 asylum seekers were sent back to Mexico to await their immigration court hearings, under a program officially called the Migrant Protection Protocols but informally known as Remain in Mexico. Asylum seekers waited in crowded camps in squalid conditions south of the border, and many were not allowed to reenter the U.S. for hearings when the coronavirus pandemic hit. Some 28,000 asylum cases for migrants sent back to Mexico were closed because they did not return to the border for scheduled hearings. But in many cases that was because the migrants were kidnapped and held for ransom by criminals in Mexico or detained by government officials there, the *Washington Post* reported. President Biden ended the Remain in Mexico policy in February 2021 and immigrants began being allowed to slowly enter the U.S. to await their hearings.[169] Homeland Security Secretary Alejandro Mayorkas said the U.S. could not quickly accept asylum seekers because of the pandemic and urged would-be migrants to apply for asylum while remaining in their home countries.[170]

Clearly, the backlog in our immigration courts has created a nightmare situation that cannot be allowed to continue. We propose a major expansion of immigration courts through the hiring of new judges and streamlined and expedited hearings. In addition to hiring more judges for the courts, the Biden administration should appoint attorneys and retired judges to serve on immigration courts for one year to help clear the backlog. This would be similar to an administration request that was sent to employees in several federal agencies in April asking them to take a four-month paid leave from their positions to help care for over 20,000 migrant children being held in shelters filled beyond their capacity.[171]

It's obvious that America's immigration system is in crisis, even though President Biden and officials in his administration have shied away from using the word. It's not possible to listen to the extreme left and throw our borders open without any enforcement of our immigration laws. Nor is it possible to listen to the extreme right and seal our land and sea borders and our airports to keep all unauthorized immigrants out. According to a Department of Homeland Security report issued during the Trump administration, about 676,000 people who violated U.S. immigration laws in 2019 were foreign visitors who arrived by air or sea and overstayed their visas. An estimated 79 million foreign visitors entered the U.S. in 2019. Unless we are prepared to make it illegal for any foreign tourist, student, or business traveler to set foot in the U.S. for any reasons— and no one is seriously suggesting that—we will never be able to shut off visa overstays as a source of unauthorized immigrants.[172]

America cannot cut itself off from the rest of the world as if we inhabited our own planet. Nor should we try. Democrats and Republicans need to come together and acknowledge immigration has both plusses and minuses, and then figure out the best way to expand legal immigration and reduce illegal immigration. If they could do it during the Reagan presidency, they should be able to do it now.

RESPONDING TO THREATS FROM CHINA AND RUSSIA

The world we live in is not *Mister Rogers' Neighborhood*. Unlike the imaginary neighborhood in the children's TV show that aired from the 1960s to 2001, where kindness ruled the day and people and puppets all got along and amicably resolved their little disputes, the real world has more than its share of dangerous characters and irreconcilable differences. Chinese president Xi Jinping and Russian president Vladimir Putin are ruthless and dangerous dictators. They do not reciprocate gestures of friendship and kindness from the U.S. or any other country. Instead, they have only contempt for democracy and for the freedoms and rights Americans enjoy under our Constitution. They see America and other Western democracies as their enemies and they want to defeat us—not in war, because we are too strong, but in just about every other sphere.

Democratic and Republican U.S. presidents, their advisers, and members of Congress have too often taken the Mister Rogers approach to dealing with Russia and China. Offering gestures of friendship, trying to establish a personal rapport, expanding trade, engaging in cultural exchanges—our leaders have tried all these things and more. President Franklin Roosevelt successfully established an alliance with the tyrannical and murderous leader of the Soviet Union, Josef Stalin, to respond to the aggression of the even worse tyrant and mass murderer Adolf Hitler. But other than the World War II years battling Nazi Germany, we have been at odds with the Soviet Union and its successor state Russia since communists came to power in 1917, and with China since communists seized power there in 1949.

Xi and Putin don't have to worry about elections or term limits. Unless they are overthrown in coups, they will likely be able to stay in office until they die or choose to retire. They understand that U.S. presidents operate with short timelines geared to the next election, and so cannot continue unpopular military actions indefinitely. This is why U.S. presidents withdrew all troops from South Vietnam and Iraq (only to send them back again) and why President Biden will soon do so from Afghanistan. Xi and Putin also understand that American presidents are reluctant to confront them militarily. This no doubt entered Putin's calculations when Russia occupied part of Georgia in 2008, annexed Crimea in 2014 by seizing it from Ukraine, and interfered in our 2016 and 2020 presidential elections to help Donald Trump win. It is also why China is claiming vast portions of the South China Sea and saber-rattling against some of its neighbors—most ominously, Taiwan.

We devoted chapter 6 of this book to an in-depth discussion of the military, economic, cyber, and espionage threats we and the rest of the world face from the Chinese and Russian dictatorships, so we won't repeat that assessment. Here is our best advice on how to respond.

Work with other nations: Past Democratic and Republican American presidents formed alliances around the world to confront threats from the Soviet Union and later Russia, and from China. The North Atlantic Treaty Organization (NATO) in 1949 is our most well-known military alliance. In addition to the U.S., the original NATO members were Belgium, Canada, Denmark, France, Iceland, Italy, Luxembourg, the Netherlands, Norway, Portugal, and the United Kingdom. The alliance has since expanded to include thirty nations by adding Greece and Turkey (1952), Germany (1955), Spain (1982), the Czech Republic (1999), Hungary and Poland (1999), Bulgaria, Estonia, Latvia, Lithuania, Romania, Slovakia, and Slovenia (2004), Albania and Croatia (2009), Montenegro (2017), and North Macedonia (2020).[173] The nations that joined NATO since 1999 had all been either part of the Soviet Union, or Soviet allies in the Warsaw Pact (including some formerly joined together in Yugoslavia).[174] Other U.S. alliances include the Inter-American Treaty of Reciprocal Assistance in 1947, the North American Aerospace Defense Command (formed with Canada) in 1958, and ANZUS (the Australia, New Zealand, and U.S. Security Treaty) in 1951. In addition, America has trade and non-military cooperation agreements with many nations and is a member of the United Nations.

While the U.S. remains the most powerful military and economic power on Earth, we are strengthened in our competition against China and Russia by working with other nations. Unfortunately, President Trump frequently criticized and insulted our allies, touting his "America First" policy. This weakened our ability to stand up to Russia and China. Trump also was reluctant to criticize Putin and Russia on almost any topic. This was a dramatic reversal from past U.S. presidents of both parties, who had been sharp critics of Russia and the Soviet Union for most of the previous hundred years. It was clear early in President Biden's term that he will take a stronger stand than Trump against Russia. He imposed sanctions on Russia in April 2021 for Russia's interference in U.S. elections, "malicious cyber activities against the United States and its allies and partners," "transnational corruption to influence foreign governments," "extraterritorial activities targeting dissidents or journalists," and other actions that "violate well-established principles of international law," the White House said in a statement.[175]

Just days after he was inaugurated, Biden started repairing the damage Trump did to U.S. relations with allied nations and making clear he would stand up to Russia and China. This was a welcome change. Speaking to State Department employees in February 2021, Biden said: "America is back. Diplomacy is back at the center of our foreign policy. As I said in my inaugural address, we will repair our alliances and engage with the world once again, not to meet yesterday's challenges, but today's and tomorrow's. American leadership must meet this new moment of advancing authoritarianism, including the growing ambitions of China to rival the United States and the determination of Russia to damage and disrupt our democracy. We must meet the new moment accelerating global challenges—from the pandemic to the climate crisis to nuclear proliferation—challenging the will only to be solved by nations working together and in common. We can't do it alone . . . we must start with diplomacy rooted in America's most cherished democratic values: defending freedom, championing opportunity, upholding universal rights, respecting the rule of law, and treating every person with dignity....Over the past two weeks, I've spoken with the leaders of many of our closest friends—Canada, Mexico, the UK, Germany, France, NATO, Japan, South Korea, Australia—to [begin] reforming the habits of cooperation and rebuilding the muscle of democratic alliances that have atrophied over the past few years of neglect and, I would argue, abuse. America's alliances are our greatest asset, and leading with diplomacy means standing shoulder-to-shoulder with our allies and key partners once again. By leading with diplomacy, we must also mean engaging our adversaries and our competitors diplomatically, where it's in our interest, and advance the security of the American people....At the same time, I made it clear to President Putin, in a manner very different from my predecessor, that the days of the United States rolling over in the face of Russia's aggressive actions—interfering with our elections, cyberattacks, poisoning its citizens—are over. We will not hesitate to raise the cost on Russia and defend our vital interests and our people. And we will be more effective in dealing with Russia when we work in coalition and coordination with other like-minded partners."[176]

One of the worst mistakes made by Trump under his "America First" policy was his decision to pull the U.S. out of the Trans-Pacific Partnership, which would have been the world's largest free-trade agreement. The Obama administration reached the agreement with the Pacific Rim countries of Canada, Mexico, Peru, Chile, Japan, Malaysia, Vietnam, Singapore, Brunei, Australia, and New Zealand, but the deal was never ratified by Congress. Trump withdrew from the TPP on the day he was inaugurated in 2017, contending the agreement would lead to job losses in the U.S. and increase America's trade deficit. President Obama and other supporters of the TPP said it would have reduced prices of many products for U.S. consumers, enabled American companies to boost exports to other TPP nations, and created new jobs in the U.S.

Had the U.S. stayed in the TPP, it would have covered 40 percent of the world's trade and created consistent rules for investment and a fully integrated international economic area. Obama said the deal would ensure that "the United States—and not China—is the one writing this century's rules for the world's economy." China took advantage of Trump's withdrawal from the TPP by negotiating a trade agreement called the Regional Comprehensive Economic Partnership, made up of fifteen Asia-Pacific nations, and began its Belt and Road Initiative infrastructure program in partnership with nations from East Asia to Europe.[177] Although Secretary of State Hillary Clinton had been an enthusiastic supporter of the TPP when she was part of the Obama administration, she came out against the pact during her 2016 presidential campaign, probably in response to Trump's criticism of the deal.[178]

Confront Chinese and Russian aggression: The U.S. must step up efforts to guard against Russian and Chinese cyberattacks, spying, and election interference. This is a nonpartisan issue of national security. Republicans should join Democrats in making this a priority.

Russia shows no signs of giving up the Crimean Peninsula and its strategic Black Sea ports after seizing the area from Ukraine in 2014, while President Obama was in office. Russia massed about 110,000 troops near its border with the Eastern Ukraine region known as Donbas in April 2021, leading to fears of an invasion. Russian defense minister Sergei Shoigu announced late in the month that the troops would withdraw by May 1 after staging what he called a training exercise, but tensions remained high. Russia said it planned to leave hundreds of trucks and tanks at a base about a hundred miles from the Ukrainian border. Since 2014, Russian-backed separatists have been battling Ukrainian forces in a war that has killed more than 13,000 people, but has drawn too little worldwide attention.

Realistically, it is probably too late to get Russia to ever give up Crimea. But America and our NATO allies need to stand firm in support of Ukraine and provide the Ukrainian government with the modern sophisticated arms needed to respond effectively to a Russian invasion if one takes place. We don't want American troops to get into a shooting war with Russian forces in Ukraine, but Biden and our NATO partners need to make it crystal clear that invading Eastern Ukraine will be a costly move for Russia both militarily and with further economic sanctions by all NATO nations.

Similarly, Biden and our allies need to made it clear to China that if it invades Taiwan—which China considers to be a rebellious province within China—we will impose harsh economic sanctions on China that will cripple the Chinese economy. To prepare for the possibility of this, America should ramp up manufacturing within the U.S. of crucial products—or, if that is not possible, look for other nations to supply these products—to reduce our dependence on crucial Chinese goods such as pharmaceuticals. We must also stand firm with allies against abusive Chinese trade practices and theft of intellectual property, along with the genocide of the Uyghurs. And President Biden should see if he can negotiate some changes in the Trans-Pacific Partnership that will allow him to claim credit for improving the agreement (to reduce political opposition) and then work to bring the U.S. back into the agreement. Republicans have traditionally favored free-trade agreements and only turned against TPP because Trump did. With Trump out of office, business groups that have traditionally backed the GOP should try to get the party to return to its previous support of expanded global trade.

Involve Congress in foreign policy: We don't expect Republicans and Democrats (or even lawmakers within the same party) to always have identical foreign policy views when it comes to Russia and China— or any other parts of the world. But if other nations believe any agreement they reach with the U.S. president of one party will be likely be broken when a president from the other party is elected, they will be reluctant to agree to anything. This is harmful to America's national interests. Presidents of both parties understandably want as much freedom as possible to act in the realm of foreign and military policy, and so have increasingly bypassed Congress since the end of World War II (the last war declared by Congress). But involving Congress in major foreign policy and military actions helps avoid wild gyrations in foreign policy when administrations change.

For example, President Obama never submitted three major international agreements to Congress for approval—the Trans-Pacific Partnership, the Paris Climate Agreement, and the Iran nuclear deal that was designed to prevent that nation from developing nuclear weapons. If Obama had called these agreements treaties and submitted them to the Senate they could not have gone into effect without approval of two-thirds of senators. Treaties approved by the Senate have the force of federal law and are binding agreements between nations.[179] Realizing he had no chance of mustering a two-thirds vote in the Senate on the controversial agreements, Obama chose to call the Paris Climate Agreement and the Iran nuclear deal "executive agreements" so they would not need Senate approval as treaties. Obama was preparing to submit the Trans-Pacific Partnership to Congress as a trade agreement, but didn't do so after Trump was elected. It was clear at that point that the strong opposition by Trump, Senate Republicans following his lead, and several Democrats would make it impossible to win congressional approval.[180]

A *Harvard Law Review* article published in 2020, based on information the authors obtained from the federal government in a Freedom of
Information Act lawsuit, said the Constitution only talks about treaties
between nations, not executive agreements. But the authors—Curtis
A. Bradley, Jack A. Goldsmith, and Oona A. Hathaway—wrote that the
"treaty process has long been on a path to obsolescence.... Since the
late 1930s, well over 90 percent of all international agreements concluded on behalf of the United States have been executive agreements
rather than treaties. Many of these agreements involve minor or routine
commitments, but some are quite consequential.... The main reason
for the heavy reliance on executive agreements is that they are much
easier to make than treaties." The authors found that "executive agreements are only rarely publicized by the executive branch before they are
concluded. This means that the public cannot consider the merits and
potential effects of such an agreement before it becomes law." These
executive agreements are far from rare. In response to their lawsuit,
the authors received 5,689 cover memos for executive agreements made
from January 20, 1989, to January 20, 2017, covering the administrations of President George H. W. Bush, Bill Clinton, George W. Bush, and
Barack Obama.[181]

President Trump withdrew the U.S. from the Trans-Pacific Partnership on his first day in office—without having federal agencies analyze the agreement and without trying to negotiate changes to what he
considered its worst provisions. That sent a signal to nations around
the world that any agreement reached by the Obama administration
with other nations might now be thrown out. And sure enough, Trump
pulled out of the Paris Climate Agreement and the Iran nuclear deal,
after denouncing both and repeatedly criticizing Obama for agreeing
to them. We're not advocating that every executive agreement go to the
Senate as a proposed treaty. However, we believe the major ones should.
Yes, this would slow things down and some treaties would fail to get
Senate approval. Democracy is less efficient and speedy than one-person

rule. But the treaties that were approved by the Senate would be more likely to endure and not be thrown out by the next president, since they would have the backing of a two-thirds majority of senators (almost certainly including some senators from outside the president's party.) The requirement for Senate approval could also strengthen the president's negotiating hand. He or she could say that big concessions sought by other nations would never win Senate approval, and so be able to negotiate more favorable terms.

Restore bipartisanship to relations with China and Russia: Polling shows both Democrats and Republicans hold unfavorable views of Russia and China. While the views of Americans in different parties are not identical, they are not as sharply divided as on many other issues. A Gallup poll published in March 2021 found that, overall, only 20 percent of Americans have a favorable opinion of China, while only 22 percent have a favorable opinion of Russia. When measured by political party, just 10 percent of Republicans had a favorable opinion of China, compared with 22 percent of independents and 27 percent of Democrats. As for Russia, only 16 percent of Democrats had a favorable view of that country, compared with 24 percent of independents and 25 percent of Republicans.

"In a year upended by a pandemic first discovered in China, and perhaps the most widespread cyber-attack in the U.S. attributed to Russia by the U.S. intelligence community, both China and Russia have reached new low points in Americans' views," Gallup News Editor in Chief Mohamed Younis wrote. "China and Russia are among the more challenging nations for U.S. foreign policy under the Biden administration, as they were for the prior Obama and Trump administrations. But Biden's task may be made a bit easier if the current low favorable ratings mean Americans are unified in their perceptions of the challenges each country presents."

Younis is right. Because China and Russia are unpopular with Democrats, Republicans, and independents, there is no political benefit right now for any candidate to come to the defense of those dictatorial governments. As a result, this could be one of the most promising areas for lawmakers to come together in bipartisan agreement. That would be an important sign of progress.[182]

Hold defense spending steady: Some Democrats want to make big cuts in military spending in the 2022 fiscal year, while many Republicans want to keep giving the Pentagon significant budget increases, as Trump did. Senator Bernie Sanders, who chairs the Senate Budget Committee, has said he wants the defense budget cut by 10 percent. "Military spending, now higher than the next eleven nations combined, represents more than half of all federal discretionary spending," Sanders said. "If the horrific pandemic we are now experiencing has taught us anything, it is that national security means a lot more than building bombs, missiles, jet fighters, tanks, submarines, nuclear warheads, and other weapons of mass destruction." Fifty House Democrats wrote a letter to Biden asking for Defense Department budget cuts. Republicans are taking the opposite position, calling for increases in Pentagon spending of 3 to 5 percent above inflation. Biden has staked out a middle ground that ought to be the basis for a bipartisan centrist compromise. The president has asked Congress to approve $753 billion in defense-related spending, which is a 1.7 percent increase. We need a strong military to stand up to Russia, China, and other threats, but we also need investment in domestic programs underfunded in the Trump years.[183]

Of course the solutions in this chapter don't deal with every problem facing America. And we know they won't be universally embraced. But they are a starting point for the parties to come together and reach bipartisan agreements of the kind our country so desperately needs.

8 | CONCLUSION

W e have all heard the line: "United we stand, divided we fall." It's been said countless times, with its earliest use attributed to the ancient Greek storyteller Aesop.[1] It's as true today as it was when he lived some 2,500 years ago. Our nation's very name—the United States of America—tells us how important unity was to our founders. Yet today, millions of Americans have forgotten this important truth. Unity is sorely absent from our nation, as Democrats and Republicans all too often face off like enemy combatants, not believing or trusting each other, abandoning their faith in the institutions that are the pillars of our society, even embracing different versions of reality. Disunity, disagreement, and discord are tearing away at America and splitting the American people into warring camps, threatening our future as a democracy.

We have written this book to shine a spotlight on these danger-ous divisions and to offer a way to bring the American people closer together: the embrace of sensible, centrist, pragmatic, and bipartisan solutions to the many problems confronting our nation. If left and right dig in with nonnegotiable demands we will never agree on anything of significance. Rancor and discord will only grow, congressional gridlock will paralyze our government into inaction, and America will become a failed state. We fear authoritarianism may then replace our great democracy, as ordinary citizens demand a strong leader to bring order to the chaos enveloping our nation.

If Democrats keep moving further to the left and Republicans keep moving further to the right we will never come together. Instead, both sides need to move from the fringes to the moderate middle-of-the-road positions that millions of Americans embrace. As any married person knows, compromise is the key to getting along when disagreements arise. If you demand that you always get your way and refuse to give an inch you are likely headed for divorce. The same is true on a national level. Our partisan differences are not irreconcilable. But all of us need to confront these differences and work in partnership with our fellow Americans in a spirit of goodwill to find a way to bridge them.

We have filled this book with data documenting how differently Democrats and Republicans see the state of our union. We won't repeat all those poll results, but we want to call attention to an additional set of findings from two polls in late April 2021 to give a dramatic illustration of America's divisions. A *Washington Post*–ABC News poll found that 52 percent of American adults said they approved of the job President Biden is doing and 42 percent said they disapproved. An NBC News poll came up with a virtually identical approval rate for the president (and within the margin of error) of 53 percent and a disapproval rate of 39 percent.

Look at those results alone and you might think our divisions on Biden's performance are not all that deep. But look at the results when broken down by political party affiliation and you see the divisions are immense. In the *Post* poll, an impressive 90 percent of Democrats said they approved of the way Biden is handling his job as president, but his approval rating dropped to 47 percent of independents and plummeted to just 13 percent of Republicans.[2] The NBC poll result was very similar: 90 percent of Democrats said they approved of Biden's job performance, as did 61 percent of independents, but only 9 percent of Republicans.[3] It's certainly not surprising that more Democrats than Republicans approve of the job a Democratic president is doing. But the enormity of the difference in the president's approval ratings testifies to how profoundly far apart Democrats and Republicans are.

One reason for the huge divide between supporters of the two parties is a fundamental difference in their views of the role of government. Most Republicans embrace the view championed by President Reagan that taxes should be kept relatively low and that government needs to be kept relatively small and not try to solve all of society's problems. In contrast, most Democrats favor government taking a bigger role and want to see higher taxes levied on corporations and the wealthy to help pay the bill. Asked in a 2019 Gallup poll if "government should take active steps in every area it can to try and improve the lives of its citizens," 62 percent of Democrats agreed, but only 40 percent of independents and just 22 percent of Republicans held that view.[4] Asked in April 2021 if they supported President Biden's proposals to fund his infrastructure and jobs plan with higher taxes on corporations and families making more than $400,000 annually, 73 percent of Democrats said they did, as did 52 percent of independents, but only 32 percent of Republicans, according to a Morning Consult poll published in March 2021.[5]

President Clinton took a centrist position when he said in his 1996 State of the Union Address: "We know big government does not have all the answers. We know there's not a program for every problem. We have worked to give the American people a smaller, less bureaucratic government in Washington. And we have to give the American people one that lives within its means. The era of big government is over. But we cannot go back to the time when our citizens were left to fend for themselves. Instead, we must go forward as one America, one nation working together to meet the challenges we face together. Self-reliance and teamwork are not opposing virtues; we must have both."[6] Clinton made headlines with this effort to appeal to moderate Republicans and independents as well as Democrats. This strategy became known as triangulation, and was a key part of Clinton's successful reelection campaign.

In his first address to a joint session of Congress on April 28, 2021, President Biden made little effort to tailor his legislative agenda to the majority of independent and Republican voters worried about government getting too big, raising taxes too high, and adding too much to the ballooning national debt. Instead, he said he wanted government to get even bigger—a lot bigger. While he didn't use the phrase, his message was clear: The era of big government is back. Biden asked Congress to approve what amounted to a Reagan counterrevolution, returning government to the major expansions it experienced under Presidents Franklin Roosevelt and Lyndon Johnson. Progressives were delighted. At this writing, Biden is seeking approval in the House of the $1 trillion traditional infrastructure spending bill passed by the Senate, and the broader $3.5 trillion "human infrastructure" bill discussed earlier in this chapter. The House and Senate approved his $1.9 trillion coronavirus economic stimulus legislation early in his term with only Democratic votes. This came on top of legislation President Trump signed into law spending $900 billion to respond to COVID-19 and its economic impact in December 2020, following a similar $1.76 trillion bill he approved in March 2020.[7] Combined, all these bills added up to over $9 trillion in government spending—a staggering amount. By way of comparison, the Congressional Budget Office reports that when adjusted for inflation, it cost the United States less than half as much—the equivalent of about $4.1 trillion in 2020 dollars—to fight World War II.[8]

Republicans dug in their heels and went on the attack immediately after Biden delivered his speech in the House chamber, reacting like the rapid response team on a political campaign rather than lawmakers interested in any sort of compromise. "It's like the most radical Washington Democrats have been handed the keys, and they are trying to speed as far left as they can possibly go before American voters ask for the car back," said Senate Republican Leader Mitch McConnell.

Former secretary of state Mike Pompeo, who served under President Trump and may run for the Republican presidential nomination in 2024, said Biden "outlined a radical, socialist agenda for the next four years. That should trouble every freedom-loving American." Senator Tim Scott (R-SC), who delivered the official televised GOP response to the Biden speech, criticized the president for seeking a "partisan wish list" and said: "Three months in, the actions of the president and his party are pulling us further and further apart." Then-House Republican Conference Chair Liz Cheney (R-WY) didn't even wait to hear the Biden speech before she tweeted that the president "has completely abandoned his promise to unify and commitment to bipartisanship" and was instead pursuing "dangerous and divisive policies to appease the far-left."[9]

Despite her criticism of Biden, Cheney exchanged a fist bump with the president as he entered the House chamber for his address to members of Congress. Illustrating the extraordinary bitterness of the partisan divide—and the deep divide within the political parties—Cheney was attacked by some fellow Republicans for the gesture. Many Republicans already had a grudge against her for voting to impeach President Trump for inciting the January 6, 2021, riot at the U.S. Capitol. Donald Trump Jr. tweeted sarcastically: "'Republican' warmonger Liz Cheney gives Sleepy Joe a fist bump after he delivered a radical socialist vision for the future of America. So glad she's in the GOP leadership, I guess they wanted to be more inclusive and put Democrats in there too?!?" Responding to criticism, Cheney tweeted: "I disagree strongly w/@JoeBiden policies, but when the President reaches out to greet me in the chamber of the US House of Representatives, I will always respond in a civil, respectful & dignified way. We're different political parties. We're not sworn enemies. We're Americans."[10] Even boxers usually touch gloves at the start of a match as a sign of respect for their opponent. It's sad that a simple fist bump with a president from the other political party would be the cause for an attack on a member of Congress. And Trump Jr.'s reference to "Sleepy Joe" is an insult to the president of the United States that we can't imagine the child of any other former president using.

We understand that exchanging political punches and counterpunches is inevitable during political campaign season. But our nation is suffering because the political campaign season has been extended to cover 365 days a year, every year. Far too many elected officials in both parties are now focused primarily on getting on TV to attack their opponents and fundraising to campaign against them. And as the decibel level of partisan attacks grows, lawmakers and people running against them must make their attacks more and more extreme in order to get airtime. It's as if the main reason politicians want to get elected is to raise their profile and get reelected, rather than to accomplish anything on behalf of the American people. We need workhorses in Washington who can get things done. Instead, we are getting show horses who prance around in circles under the spotlight without moving forward.

WHY WE ARE DIVIDED

We have identified the key reasons for the deep divisions that plague America today and the public's loss of faith in the institutions that are the pillars of our society and our democracy. Here is a summary, as explained in greater detail earlier in this book:

- The growing influence of far-left Democrats and far-right Republicans in their parties and their unwillingness to compromise with their opponents. These zealots look down their noses at moderation and bipartisanship as signs of weakness and insufficient ideological commitment. They look at their opponents not simply as political adversaries, but as evil enemies. They have brought extremist ideas into the mainstream, and a minority of their most fervent followers even justify violence to achieve their goals.

- The rise of different media ecosystems that offer viewers, listeners, and readers "alternative facts," to use a phrase made famous by Kellyanne Conway, a senior adviser to then-president Trump. Viewers of Fox News, Newsmax, and One America News Network see a very different version of reality than viewers of CNN, MSNBC, NBC, ABC, and CBS. Readers of Breitbart.com, the *New York Post* and the *Washington Times* see news coverage dramatically differently from readers of the *New York Times*, the *Washington Post*, and *USA Today*. And social media are a Wild West of information and misinformation, where it is often hard to know what to believe. In truth, the very concept of facts and reality has been thrown into question.

- A political class that has lost touch with mainstream America. Politicians too often display profiles in cowardice, fearful of standing on principle and instead doing whatever it takes to get elected and reelected. Lobbyists for special interests wield enormous influence. Ordinary citizens wield far too little. Partisan redistricting of the U.S. House and state legislatures, a primary process that tends to nominate Democrats who are farthest left and Republicans who are farthest right, and the Electoral College winner-take-all rule in most states combine to make it difficult for moderates to be nominated and for third-party and independent candidates to be elected to any office.

- The demonization of government itself by some politicians, most often Republicans, who argue that government is the cause of our problems, not the solution to them. Some far-right groups like QAnon have advanced absurd conspiracy theories about secret government cabals working against the U.S. from within. The Big Lie that government officials stole the presidential election from Donald Trump and rigged it in favor of Joe Biden is particularly harmful, shaking the faith of many Republicans in democracy itself.

- The demonization of the police by some Democrats, who have called for defunding and in a few cases even disbanding police departments altogether in reaction to disturbing incidents of police brutality directed against African Americans that galvanized the nation. The incident that sparked the largest nationwide demonstrations was the horrific torture and killing of George Floyd in 2020 by fired Minneapolis police officer Derek Chauvin. Justice was served when Chauvin was convicted in April 2021 of Floyd's murder.

- Inequality of opportunity has created a two-tiered society of haves and have-nots, with too many Black and Hispanic Americans stuck at the bottom rung of the economic ladder. The effects of four hundred years of racism directed against African Americans have not disappeared, despite great progress that has been made since the dawn of the Civil Rights Movement in the 1950s and the election of a Black president and a Black vice president.

- An education system that underfunds many public elementary and secondary schools in low-income neighborhoods—often with many students of color—and provides inadequate funding to enable many students to pursue a higher education without incurring enormous debt.

- Growing pessimism about America's future and a fading belief in the American Dream. Too many people have concluded that hard work and playing by the rules aren't enough to open the doors to the middle class.

- Anti-democratic regimes ruling China and Russia that are threatening freedom around the world, fanning the flames of division in the U.S., and seeking to show democracy is a failed system and that America is a failed state. The two dictatorships are allied and share the goal of replacing the U.S. as the world's preeminent military and economic power. Russia—much diminished since the fall of the Soviet Union—stands little chance of achieving this goal in the foreseeable future. But a rising China is making a serious bid to surpass the U.S. in coming decades.

HOW TO REUNITE US

We have proposed the following solutions to the challenges confronting the United States:

Election reforms to enhance the chances of honest centrist, third-party, and independent candidates getting on the ballot and getting elected. These include:

- Disclosing tax records of candidates and officeholders to guard against conflicts of interest.
- Nonpartisan redistricting of congressional and state legislative districts to end gerrymandering.
- Top-two primaries, in which candidates of multiple parties run and the top two then compete to be elected.

- Ranked-choice voting and instant runoff voting
  to encourage voters to support a wider variety of
  candidates without feeling their votes are "wasted" on
  dark-horse candidates.
- Expanding nonpartisan elections, to stop candidates
  and officials from reflexively opposing any proposal
  from the opposite party.
- Making voting easier via mail-in voting and other
  actions.
- Awarding some Electoral College votes by congressional
  district rather than statewide on a winner-take-all basis.
  This would make it much easier for third-party and
  independent presidential candidates to pick up electoral
  votes and would put many more states into play in
  presidential elections for all candidates.
- Encouraging the creation of a centrist third party that
  would represent Restless and Anxious Moderate voters
  (RAMs), so Democrats and Republicans do not occupy
  almost all elected offices.
- Expanding participation in televised presidential
  candidate debates to include the top three candidates.
  Currently candidates must show at least 15 percent
  support in national polls to qualify for the debates,
  which usually means only the Democratic and
  Republican candidates qualify.

Congressional reforms to help break the gridlock that has paralyzed Congress; we call for:

- Encouraging groups of moderates to meet and work
  together across party lines. Models for this are the
  Problem Solvers Caucus in the House, and a group of

moderate senators who gather most Wednesdays for lunch.

- Encouraging media coverage focusing on legislative achievements rather than extremist proposals and shouting matches.

- Preserving the filibuster in the Senate so Democrats and Republicans have to work together on compromise legislation, but requiring senators to actually talk for hours on the floor. This would make it likely the rule mandating a 60-vote supermajority to pass legislation would be invoked less frequently. Laws approved on a bipartisan basis are less likely to be overturned after the next election.

- Requiring all members of Congress, the president, and vice president to divest their ownership of stocks, bonds, and businesses, and place their assets into blind trusts to avoid conflicts of interests.

- Requiring greater disclosure by lobbyists of their contacts with members of Congress. Lobbyists should have to report the date of every phone call, meeting, and event they participate in with members of Congress and their staffs, and the topics discussed. Lobbyists should also have to report every dollar they spend trying to influence government in the legislative and executive branches, including on public relations, advertising, and advocacy groups.

- Barring all federal employees and elected officials from going to work for lobbyists for at least two years after they leave federal service. This is needed to ensure federal employees don't improperly help lobbyists with the understanding that they will be rewarded with a higher-paying job as soon as they leave government service.

Court reforms to strengthen the trust of the American people in a nonpartisan judiciary. The Constitution should be amended to do the following:

- Require the full Senate to hold confirmation votes on nominations to the Supreme Court, appellate courts, and district courts within ninety days after they are made by the president. This would prevent the Senate majority from refusing to consider judicial nominees by the president of the opposite political party.
- Set the size of the Supreme Court at its current composition of nine justices. This would make it very difficult to use court-packing in the future to change the ideological composition of the high court. A change would require another constitutional amendment, not just legislation passed by Congress.
- End lifetime appointments to the Supreme Court. Justices should be limited to serving eighteen or twenty years. One positive effect would be to reduce pressure on presidents to appoint justices as young as possible, to maximize their time on the bench. Another would be to reduce the political pressure involved with the selection of justices, since they would not continue on the high court for more than two decades.

Criminal justice reforms that are long overdue and urgently needed in the wake of the police killings of George Floyd and other Black Americans. The reforms should include:

- The enactment of comprehensive police reform legislation designed to reduce police misconduct and the use of deadly force. At this writing, House and

Senate negotiators are working to come up with a
compromise between the George Floyd Policing Act that
was passed by the House and a Republican Senate bill
that makes significant reforms but does not go as far as
House Democrats want.

- A rejection of calls to defund or disband police
departments. Police budgets need to be used to improve
police performance, limit the use of deadly force by
police unless there is no other way for officers to protect
their own lives and the lives of others, and improve
training and accountability measures to reduce police
misconduct.

- The appointment of a bipartisan national commission
to launch a serious review of policing to make
recommendations for further reforms.

Infrastructure improvements that are needed to upgrade America's roads, bridges, mass transit, rail system, broadband, electric grid, and water delivery system. There is broad bipartisan support for these improvements, already passed by the Senate and now awaiting action in the House. However, President Biden has proposed spending on many other projects that he has labeled as infrastructure, including renovating public housing and school buildings, as well as childcare facilities, hospitals for veterans, and federal buildings. The president has also labeled spending to increase manufacturing, research and development projects, and job training programs as infrastructure—along with an expansion of home care services. Congressional Republicans oppose this broader definition and the far more costly programs Biden has proposed under his expansive definition. The needed compromise here is obvious: The House should approve the $1 trillion in upgrades to traditional infrastructure approved by the Senate and then both houses should consider the president's other proposals separately.

Regulatory and tax reform, and job creation to boost the U.S. economy, limit the increase in the national debt, and reduce unemployment in the wake of the recession caused by the coronavirus pandemic. Unfortunately, Democrats and Republicans are far apart on what needs to be done. Our centrist proposals call for:

- Finding a reasonable balance between preserving worthwhile regulations—including reinstating some eliminated by the Trump administration—and overregulation that slows economic growth and eliminates jobs. This is easier said than done, because Republicans and Democrats are so far apart on what they think the right level of regulation should be. To the extent possible, decisions should be made by doing a cost-benefit analysis on the value of regulations.

- Giving all federal regulations expiration dates of no longer than every ten years. This would allow a federal commission, agency, or Congress to modify or get rid of regulations that have outlived their usefulness. Regulations that are still needed could be renewed for up to another ten years.

- Raising taxes to pay for a bigger chunk of federal spending because we can't keep running up the massive federal debt indefinitely. Republicans who contend that no tax can ever be raised are wrong to take such an extreme position. But Democrats who contend taxes on corporations and wealthy Americans can be raised sky-high are wrong as well. Corporations pass on tax increases to consumers by raising prices. In addition, many will ship jobs to other countries if necessary to avoid excessively high taxes. President Biden has proposed raising the corporate income tax from the current 21 percent to 28 percent—halfway between the current corporate tax rate and the 35 percent rate that was in effect before President Trump's 2017 tax cuts took effect. However, Senator Joe Manchin has said he will not vote for a tax increase above 25 percent. President Biden should seek an increase of that amount, because it's more reasonable and because he can't win approval of a larger tax increase without the support of Manchin, assuming all Senate Republicans vote against any tax hike.

- Approving President Biden's proposal to close a tax loophole that allows corporations to dodge U.S. taxes by shifting profits they earn in America to other nations with lower tax rates. Fifty-five of the nation's largest corporations paid nothing in federal income taxes in 2020, despite collectively reporting more than $40 billion in profits, according to the Institute on Taxation and Economic Policy. Corporations should not be allowed to continue avoiding taxes by shifting profits earned in the United States to countries with lower tax rates.[11]

- Cracking down on tax cheats to increase the amount of money the federal government collects in taxes. Internal Revenue Service Commissioner Charles Rettig testified in April 2021 before the Senate Finance Committee that nearly $1 trillion or more in federal taxes may be going unpaid each year because the IRS does not have enough employees to detect a vast amount of taxpayer fraud and errors. President Biden has requested a 10 percent budget increase for the IRS to hire more auditors and other staff to recover some of these unpaid taxes. This proposal—or an even higher

increase in IRS funding—deserves broad bipartisan
support.

◦ Boosting job creation by creating more Opportunity
Zones or a similar program to offer tax breaks for
job-creating investments in low-income communities.
The program was part of the 2017 tax cut legislation
signed into law by President Trump. More than 8,600
Economic Opportunity Zones now exist across the U.S.,
with zones in every state and territory.[12]

◦ Raising the minimum wage to $15, as Democrats want,
but doing so more slowly to reduce the impact on
businesses and limit job losses. Senator Bernie Sanders
of Vermont is seeking to boost the minimum wage to
$15 an hour in stages by 2025 for most workers and
by 2027 for tipped workers. Most Republicans and
some Democrats oppose such a big increase at such
a rapid pace. We'd like to see the $15 phased in to
fully take effect after ten years, or even twelve years if
necessary to get enough Republican votes to become
law, and then indexed to rise annually to keep up with
inflation. The current hourly minimum wage is $7.25.
The subminimum wage, which goes primarily to
tipped workers, is only $2.13. We would phase out the
subminimum wage over ten or twelve years.

Education reform to prepare the American workforce to fill
good-paying jobs and to lift millions of families out of poverty. We support these steps:

◦ Increasing federal funding for education, focused
on helping schools with many low-income students.
Black and Hispanic students are disproportionately

represented among such students. We support
President Biden's request for an extraordinary 41
percent increase in the Education Department budget
for the 2022 fiscal year, bringing the department budget
to $103 billion.

- Increasing funding for Pell Grants by $3 billion to raise
  the maximum tuition assistance for each low-income
  college student in the program by $400, as President
  Biden has proposed. We also support the president's
  budget request that seeks a $600 billion increase in
  funding for historically Black colleges and universities
  and community colleges that serve large numbers of
  minority students.[13]

- Distributing property tax revenue to school districts
  on a statewide or countywide basis, rather than only
  within each district. This is a decision to be made at the
  state level. It would provide more funds to low-income
  districts with the greatest needs, reducing funding
  for wealthy districts. Districts could raise their local
  property taxes to avoid cuts in aid if they wished.

- Allowing more charter schools to operate to encourage
  innovation and a better education for students. Charters
  and their students should be evaluated annually and
  poorly performing charter schools should be closed.

- Providing more scholarships for low-income students to
  enable them to attend private elementary and secondary
  schools. A program in Washington, D.C., has awarded
  more than 10,600 such scholarships since the 2004–
  2005 school year.

- Eliminating tuition at public community colleges,
  as President Biden has proposed. In the 2018–2019
  academic year, 8.2 million students were enrolled in

community colleges, including 5.6 million in public community colleges, according to the National Center for Education Statistics.[14]

- Offering students at both public and private colleges interest-free loans to be repaid over thirty years, like a home mortgage, to make college more affordable.

- Forgiving a portion of the interest-free loans for students who enter public service after graduation, including: serving in the U.S. military, the Peace Corps, the anti-poverty program AmeriCorps VISTA, law enforcement and fire departments; teaching in low-income areas; and working in health care in underserved communities.

- Providing similar incentives to students who enter the STEM (science, technology, engineering, and math) fields. Also, focusing on improving STEM education from elementary school through graduate school.

Health care improvements to deal with the coronavirus pandemic, future pandemics, and other issues. We recommend:

- Working to depoliticize the COVID-19 pandemic and making vaccinations, mask-wearing, and social distancing issues of public health, not of civil liberties. This is a major problem, because many Republicans both oppose vaccinations and oppose precautions against the spread of the deadly disease. We hope former president Trump can be persuaded to play a leading role in this campaign, but we are not optimistic that he will do so. More realistically, trusted people such as family doctors, clergy members, and teachers should do everything possible to urge every American to be vaccinated.

- Expanding a global program with other wealthy nations through the World Health Organization to help poor nations vaccinate their populations against COVID-19.
- Once COVID-19 vaccines are approved for children, new parents should be instructed by pediatricians on the need to vaccinate their children, and schools should require children to be vaccinated against COVID-19 just as they are now required to be vaccinated against other diseases. In addition, schools should make vaccine education part of the curriculum to educate students from elementary school on up about the importance and safety of vaccines.
- Steps should begin as soon as possible to prepare for the next pandemic, which will inevitably come at some point. Just as the federal government prepares to anticipate and respond to hurricanes, earthquakes, forest fires, terrorist attacks, wars around the world, and even a nuclear strike against our nation, it needs to do more to prepare for the next pandemic on a continuing basis.
- Breaking the U.S. Department of Health and Human Services into two departments. A physician should head the Department of Health to focus on this area of critical importance.

Energy reform to replace fossil fuels with renewable and nuclear energy, but at a slower rate than Democrats want in order to minimize disruptions and job losses, and gain some Republican support. We propose:

- Phasing out coal because it is the most polluting fossil fuel. We would stop the issuance of new coal mining permits in ten years and then let existing mines continue operating until they are no longer productive. Coal company employees should be offered full scholarships for colleges and training programs to prepare them for new careers and other transitional assistance. In addition, wherever possible, new non-fossil-fuel energy plants should be located in coal mining communities, with federal subsidies and tax breaks to incentivize these plants as well as other employers to locate where coal had been mined.

- Offering tax credits for electric vehicle manufacturers and non-fossil-fuel energy power plants to incentivize the move away from fossil fuels. We propose that Congress enact tax credits under which the first ten years of profits from the manufacture and sale of electric vehicles and from the sale of electricity produced by non-fossil-fuels plants would be entirely free of federal taxation. Over the following nine years, the tax credits would be phased out, so that vehicle manufacturers and energy companies would pay a growing share of taxes normally due: 10 percent the first year, 20 percent the second, 30 percent the third, and so on.

- Using tax credits to encourage the expansion of nuclear power, which already generates about 20 percent of the electricity produced in the United States and produces no carbon dioxide and no other harmful pollutants.

- Continuing to produce domestic oil and natural gas as the U.S. gradually transitions away from the use of fossil fuels. Oil and natural gas cannot be quickly replaced. If we abruptly halted domestic production, we would be forced to increase imports of these fossil fuels. We would also destroy many American jobs faster than they could be replaced by new energy jobs.

- Finishing the Keystone XL pipeline, which has now been canceled. This would be an important and reliable source of oil from our neighbor and close ally Canada that we could use as we transition away from fossil fuels. Canada will sell the oil elsewhere if we don't buy it and that would create greater pollution.

- Increasing the federal solar tax credit to encourage more homeowners and businesses owners to install solar power generation. This could have a major impact on our need to generate electricity from other sources.

- Raising federal gasoline and diesel fuel taxes, which have been frozen at 18.4 cents per gallon for gasoline and 23.4 cents per gallon for diesel since 1993, to make up for inflation. This would require boosting the taxes to 33 cents for a gallon of gasoline and 44 cents for a gallon of diesel. Then index the taxes to inflation so they rise slightly each year. In addition to providing money for federal transportation spending, these increases would incentivize motorists to get electric vehicles more quickly.

Immigration reform to create a pathway to citizenship for the roughly 11 million unauthorized immigrants now in the U.S., along with immigrants who came here as children and have been allowed to stay under the DACA (Deferred Action for Childhood Arrivals) program. We also recommend:

- Admitting more legal immigrants, raising admissions from just over 1 million in 2019 to about 3 million per year, including asylum seekers and refugees.

This should include increased admissions of college-educated immigrants, such as those who have graduated from U.S. colleges and universities.

- Improving security on the U.S.-Mexico border. The existing border barrier should remain in place. Republicans and Democrats should reach a compromise to use a portion of the $5 billion in Department of Homeland Security funds already approved for barrier construction to add to the barrier in return for Republican support of other parts of Biden's immigration reform agenda

- Reduce the backlog in immigration courts that totaled 1.3 million cases in March 2021 by hiring more judges, appointing attorneys and retired judges to serve for one year on the courts, allowing streamlined and expedited hearings, and giving judges more discretionary authority to dismiss cases.

Respond to threats from China and Russia by working with our allies in NATO and other nations, in contrast to President Trump's approach of criticizing and insulting our allies and cozying up to Russian president Vladimir Putin. Reject the mistakes of past Democratic and Republican presidents who believed that making concessions to develop closer relations with Russia and China would result in the two dictatorial regimes becoming less oppressive, more respectful of human rights, and less hostile and aggressive toward other nations. Needed actions the U.S. should take include:

- Joining the Trans-Pacific Partnership, a free-trade agreement of Pacific Rim countries, to make America more competitive with China and bring many economic benefits. We are not expecting this to happen, because

President Trump vehemently opposed the agreement and many congressional Republicans fear if they repudiate any of his policies he will support primary challenges against them. Until Trump began his campaign for the presidency, Republicans traditionally supported free-trade agreements.

- Confronting Chinese and Russian aggression by stepping up efforts to guard against Russian and Chinese cyberattacks, spying, and election interference. This is a nonpartisan issue of national security. Republicans should join Democrats in making this a priority.

- Involving Congress in foreign policy by submitting more major agreements with foreign nations to Congress for approval as treaties. This would result in more bipartisan agreements that are less likely to be repudiated by the next president of the opposite political party.

- Restoring bipartisanship to relations with China and Russia. Because China and Russia are unpopular with Democrats, Republicans, and independents, there is no political benefit right now for any candidate to come to the defense of those dictatorial governments.

- Holding defense spending steady by approving the 1.7 percent increase in defense-related spending President Biden has proposed to Congress, or something close to that. Some Democrats want to make big cuts in military spending in the 2022 fiscal year, while some Republicans want defense spending to increase by 3 to 5 percent above the rate of inflation. Biden has proposed a compromise that will allow the nation to maintain a strong military posture.

WHAT'S NEXT FOR AMERICA'S DEMOCRACY?

The American people are frustrated by the political dysfunction in Washington and in many of our state capitals, and the broader dysfunction of our dangerously divided society. This has helped bring about distrust in government and many of our bedrock institutions. Trust continues on a downward slide that we must not allow to continue. In order to regain the trust of the American people, we must make fundamental changes to our democratic system—we must make it work. As part of this, politicians must do what they hate the most: returning power to the people, and letting the average American back into the decision-making process.

Despite the criticism it has come under in recent years, we are believers in American exceptionalism. No country in the world boasts citizens with such an entrepreneurial spirit and desire to advance. Americans find solutions to problems without permission. We innovate without apology. Many of the greatest advances in medicine, technology, energy, governance, infrastructure, engineering, and science have been driven by Americans. Most Americans believe this as well.[15]

As the late Pulitzer Prize–winning columnist Charles Krauthammer wrote: "America is the only country ever founded on an idea. The only country that is not founded on race or even common history. It's founded on an idea, and the idea is liberty. That is probably the rarest phenomena in the political history of the world; this has never happened before. And not only has it happened, but it's worked. We are the most flourishing, the most powerful, most influential country on Earth with this system, invented by the greatest political geniuses probably in human history."[16] We agree. But building a nation on an idea is a high-risk endeavor; it relies solely and entirely on the faith of the citizenry in that idea. If belief in this idea disappears for the majority of a nation's citizens, a giant shadow is cast on their future. This is why American democracy is in such grave danger today.

As we said at the beginning of this book, in the 1730s and 1740s the British colonies that would later become the United States underwent a Great Awakening—a Christian evangelical movement that some historians call the first inter-colonial or national event—even before America existed as a nation.[17] The Great Awakening unified the growing colonies more than any other event before the Revolutionary War. It grounded colonists from Maine to Georgia in a foundation of shared values—the same values that would shape the founding documents of the United States just a few decades later. Historian Paul Johnson wrote in his *History of the American People* in 1999 that the Great Awakening was the "proto-revolutionary event, the formative event preceding the political drive for independence and making it possible."[18] We need a secular Great Awakening today—a collective renewal of faith in our democracy and a recommitment to America's other founding ideals as well. These ideals include a belief in liberty, equality (despite the failure of the founders to embrace this in practice), opportunity, free markets, freedom of speech, the rule of law, and self-government.

President Biden made an eloquent appeal for unity in his April 2021 speech to a joint session of Congress, echoing some of the same points we have made in this book. The president said: "The question of whether our democracy will long endure is both ancient and urgent, as old as our Republic—still vital today. Can our democracy deliver on its promise that all of us, created equal in the image of God, have a chance to lead lives of dignity, respect, and possibility? Can our democracy deliver the most—to the most pressing needs of our people? Can our democracy overcome the lies, anger, hate, and fears that have pulled us apart? America's adversaries—the autocrats of the world—are betting we can't. And I promise you, they're betting we can't. They believe we're too full of anger and division and rage. They look at the images of the mob that assaulted the Capitol as proof that the sun is setting on American democracy. But they are wrong. You know it; I know it. But we have to prove them wrong. We have to prove democracy still works—that our government still works and we can deliver for our people."[19]

We concur. But Biden needs to combine the eloquence of action with those eloquent words. Unfortunately, in the first few months of his term, he chose to embrace far-left Democratic priorities and not make a serious effort to compromise with Republicans. If he keeps doing this, he could live up to the pre-election prediction of Senator Bernie Sanders and become "the most progressive president" since Franklin Roosevelt.[20] While that would make Biden an iconic figure among progressives, it could prevent him from seeing much of his agenda enacted into law in the face of unified Republican opposition and could make him a one-term president.

There are many differences between Franklin Roosevelt and Joe Biden, but perhaps the most important is the strength of the mandate they had from the American people and their support in Congress. In 2021, Democrats held a razor-thin majority in the House and Senate— and were in danger of losing majority control of one or both chambers in the 2022 elections. In contrast, Franklin Roosevelt swept into power in 1933 with huge Democratic majorities in the House and Senate and kept them. As Nate Silver wrote in FiveThirtyEight in 2010: "When F.D.R. took over the Presidency in 1933, the Democrats controlled 64 percent of the Senate seats and 73 percent (!) of the House seats, counting independents who were sympathetic to the party. And those numbers only increased over the next couple of midterms—during their peak during 1937–38, the Democrats actually controlled about 80 percent (!) of the seats in both chambers."[21] The chances that Democrats will rack up gigantic majorities like that in 2022 are lower than our chances of winning millions of dollars in the lottery—twice.

The simple truth is that the only way anything will get done in Washington in the next few years is for Democrats and Republicans to compromise. Neither side has done this lately. Republicans certainly didn't show any willingness to work with Biden and Democrats in Congress when they ferociously attacked just about everything the new president proposed early in his term. Fearful of angering former president Trump and having him back challengers to them in primaries, many Republicans in Congress even refused to reject Trump's Big Lie that a Deep State conspiracy of Republican and Democratic officials across the country robbed Trump of victory in the 2020 presidential election. Many congressional Republicans seem to believe their main job is to stop Biden from claiming any successes that would benefit him, rather than to do anything to benefit the American people.

When complaining about a variety of things he found intolerable during his two unsuccessful campaigns for the Democratic presidential nomination, an exasperated Senator Bernie Sanders frequently said: "Enough is enough!" We'll end with that line to describe our view of the poisonous atmosphere far-left Democrats and far-right Republicans have created that is crippling our nation and leaving the American people so badly divided. It is long past time for our great people to focus far more on what unites us than what divides us. Long past time for us to focus on combating threats like China, Russia, and the coronavirus pandemic that has invaded our shores than on combating our fellow citizens. Earlier generations of Americans won independence from Britain, united after a horrific Civil War that abolished the evil of slavery, defeated the forces of fascism bent on global conquest in World War II, landed men on the moon, and much more. If they could do all this, we can defeat the forces of division threatening the democracy they bequeathed to us, and we can pass a democratic future down to our children, grandchildren, and generations beyond.

The De Beers Group, a company that mines diamonds and sells them around the world, has a famous slogan: "A diamond is forever."[22] Our democracy is far more precious than the most precious stone, but we can't say that democracy is forever. It will survive only as long as we rally behind it and support it. We believe the American people are up to this important task, so we are optimistic about democracy's future.

It's time now for all of us to get to work, heal our divisions with our fellow Americans, and ensure that our democracy remains strong and healthy far into the future. The old saying is true: "United we stand, divided we fall."

Notes

INTRODUCTION

1. Douglas E. Schoen, *The End of Democracy? Russia and China on the Rise, America in Retreat* (Regan Arts, 2020).
2. Patrick J. Kiger, "How Ben Franklin's Viral Political Cartoon United the 13 Colonies," History.com, October 23, 2018. Accessed at https://www.history.com/news/ben-franklin-join-or-die-cartoon-french-indian-war.
3. "History of the Motto," United We Stand. Accessed at https://www.unitedwestand.com/motto/.
4. Abraham Lincoln, "House Divided Speech," June 16, 1858. National Park Service. Accessed at https://www.nps.gov/liho/learn/historyculture/housedivided.htm.
5. Guy Gugliotta, "New Estimate Raises Civil War Death Toll," *New York Times*, April 2, 2012. Accessed at https://www.nytimes.com/2012/04/03/science/civil-war-toll-up-by-20-percent-in-new-estimate.html.
6. Aaron O'Neill, "Population of the United States in 1860, by Race and Gender," Statista, March 19, 2021. Accessed at https://www.statista.com/statistics/1010196/population-us-1860-race-and-gender/.
7. "Will the US Have Another Civil War?" The Zogby Poll®, February 4, 2021. Accessed at https://zogbyanalytics.com/news/997-the-zogby-poll-will-the-us-have-another-civil-war.
8. Lisa Mascaro, Mary Clare Jalonick, Jonathan Lemire, and Alan Fram, "Trump Impeached After Capitol Riot in Historic Second Charge," Associated Press, January 13, 2021. Accessed at https://apnews.com/article/trump-impeachment-vote-capitol-siege-0a6f2a348a6e43f27d5e1dc486027860.

9. Amy Gardner, Mike DeBonis, Seung Min Kim, and Karoun Demirjian, "Republicans Vote to Acquit Trump on Impeachment Charge of Inciting Deadly Attack on the Capitol," *Washington Post*, February 13, 2021. Accessed at https://www.washingtonpost.com/politics/trump-acquitted -impeachment-riot/2021/02/13/dbf6b172-6e12-11eb-ba56-d7e2c8defa31 _story.html.

10. Catie Edmonson, Nicholas Fandos, and Thomas Kaplan, "House Votes to Eject Marjorie Taylor Green From Committees," *New York Times*. February 4, 2021. Accessed at https://www.nytimes.com/2021/02/04/us/marjorie -taylor-greene-committee-assignments.html?searchResultPosition=3.

11. Marianna Sotomayor, "Rep. Greene's Fundraising Haul Alarms Detractors, Who Warn She Represents a Dangerous Side of American Politics," *Washington Post*, April 10, 2021. Accessed at https://www .washingtonpost.com/politics/marjorie-taylor-greene-fundraising- trump/2021/04/10/6bd53032-993f-11eb-b28d-bfa7bb5cb2a5_story.html.

12. Marianna Sotomayor, "Rep. Greene's Fundraising Haul Alarms Detractors, Who Warn She Represents a Dangerous Side of American Politics."

13. Dana Rubenstein and Jeffery C. Mays, "Nearly $1 Billion Is Shifted from Police in Budget That Pleases No One," *New York Times*, June 30, 2020. Updated August 10, 2020. Accessed at https://www.nytimes .com/2020/06/30/nyregion/nypd-budget.html?searchResultPosition=1.

14. "LAPD Budget to Be Cut by $150 Million; Decision Triggered by Widespread Protests," NBC Los Angeles, City News Service, November 7, 2020. Accessed at https://www.nbclosangeles.com/news/local/lapd -budget-to-be-cut-by-150-million-decision-triggered-by-widespread -protests/2456578/.

15. Fola Akinnibi, Sarah Holder, and Christopher Cannon, "Cities Say They Want to Defund the Police. Their Budgets Say Otherwise," Bloomberg News, January 12, 2021. Accessed at https://www.bloomberg.com /graphics/2021-city-budget-police-funding/.

16. Holly Bailey, "Ex-Minneapolis Police Officers Charged in George Floyd's Death to Be Tried Separately, Judge Rules," *Washington Post*, January 12, 2021. Accessed at https://www.washingtonpost.com/national /minneapolis-police-officers-charged-in-george-floyds-death-to-be -tried-separately-judge-rules/2021/01/12/23e2d288-54d0-11eb-a817 -e5e7f8a406d6_story.html.

17. "Minneapolis Approves 'Historic' $27 Million Settlement with George Floyd's Family," CBS News, March 13, 2021. Accessed at https://www .cbsnews.com/news/george-floyd-city-minneapolis-settlement-27 -million/.

18. Larry Buchanan, Quoctrung Bui, and Jugal K. Patel, "Black Lives Matter May Be the Largest Movement in U.S. History," *New York Times*, July 3,

2020. Accessed at https://www.nytimes.com/interactive/2020/07/03/us/george-floyd-protests-crowd-size.html.

19. Stephanie Pagones, "Protests, Riots That Gripped America in 2020," Fox News, December 29, 2020. Accessed at https://www.foxnews.com/us/protests-riots-nationwide-america-2020.

20. Devlin Barrett, "2020 Saw an Unprecedented Spike in Homicides from Big Cities to Small Towns," *Washington Post*, December 30, 2020. Accessed at https://www.washingtonpost.com/national-security/reoord-spike-murders-2020/2020/12/30/1dcb057c-4ae5-11eb-839a-cf4ba7b7c48c_story.html.

21. German Lopez, "2020's Historic Surge in Murders, Explained," Vox, March 21, 2021. Accessed at https://www.vox.com/22344713/murder-violent-crime-spike-surge-2020-covid-19-coronavirus.

22. Stephanie Pagones, "Police Defunded: Major Cities Feeling the Loss of Police Funding as Murders, Other Crimes Soar," Fox News, April 1, 2021. Accessed at https://www.foxnews.com/us/police-defunded-cities-murders-crime-budget.

23. Liz Navratil, "Minneapolis to Spend $6.4 Million to Hire More Police," *Minneapolis Star Tribune*, February 12, 2021. Accessed at https://www.startribune.com/minneapolis-to-spend-6-4-million-to-hire-more-police/600022400/.

24. Jolie McCullough, "Gov. Greg Abbott Maintains Hard Line Against Cuts to City Police Budgets, Remains Silent on Reform Proposals," *Texas Tribune*, January 21, 2021. Accessed at https://www.texastribune.org/2021/01/21/greg-abbott-police-funding-reforms/.

25. Matt Zapotosky, Ann E. Marimow, and Devlin Barrett: "Merrick Garland Tells Senators Capitol Riot Investigation Will Be His First Priority as Attorney General," *Washington Post*, February 22, 2021. Accessed at https://www.washingtonpost.com/national-security/merrick-garland-confirmation-hearing/2021/02/21/b4725878-7474-11eb-9537-496158cc5fd9_story.html.

26. "Number of Murder Victims in the United States in 2019, by Race/Ethnicity and Gender," Statista, February 2, 2021. Accessed at https://www.statista.com/statistics/251877/murder-victims-in-the-us-by-race-ethnicity-and-gender/.

27. Heather Mac Donald, "There Is No Epidemic of Fatal Police Shootings Against Unarmed Black Americans," *USA Today*, July 3, 2020, updated July 6, 2020. Accessed at https://www.usatoday.com/story/opinion/2020/07/03/police-black-killings-homicide-rates-race-injustice-column/3235072001/.

28. Jason L. Riley, "Progressives Put the Racial 'Equity' Squeeze on Biden," *Wall Street Journal*, February 2, 2021. Accessed at https://www.wsj

.com/articles/progressives-put-the-racial-equity-squeeze-on-biden
-11612307761?page=1

29. Julia Manchester, "Analyst Says US Is Most Divided Since Civil War," *Hill*, October 3, 2018. Accessed at https://thehill.com/hilltv/what -americas-thinking/409718-analyst-says-the-us-is-the-most-divided -since-the-civl-war.

30. "Transcript of Bill Clinton Speech to the Democratic National Convention," *New York Times*, September 5, 2012. Accessed at https:// www.nytimes.com/2012/09/05/us/politics/transcript-of-bill-clintons -speech-to-the-democratic-national-convention.html.

31. Nate Cohn, "Why Political Sectarianism Is a Growing Threat to American Democracy," *New York Times*, April 19, 2021. Accessed at https://www .nytimes.com/2021/04/19/us/democracy-gop-democrats-sectarianism .html?action=click&module=RelatedLinks&pgtype=Article.

32. "Henry Clay," Biography.com, updated June 7, 2019. Accessed at https:// www.biography.com/political-figure/henry-clay.

33. Jon Levine, "Study Declares AOC One of the Least Effective Members of Congress," *New York Post*, April 3, 2021. Accessed at https://nypost .com/2021/04/03/aoc-was-one-of-least-effective-members-of-congress -study/.

34. "Joe Biden's Executive Orders and Actions," Ballotpedia, June 9, 2021. Accessed at https://ballotpedia.org/Joe_Biden's_executive_orders_and _actions

35. Phillip Cooper, *By Order of the President: The Use and Abuse of Executive Direct Action* (University Press of Kansas, 2015).

36. "What Is an Executive Order?" The American Bar Association, January 25, 2021. Accessed at https://www.americanbar.org/groups/public_education /publications/teaching-legal-docs/what-is-an-executive-order-/.

37. Carl Hulse, "Senate Ruling Gives Democrats a Back Door Around the Filibuster," *New York Times*, April 6, 2021. Accessed at https://www .nytimes.com/2021/04/06/us/politics/senate-filibuster-reconciliation .html?action=click&module=RelatedLinks&pgtype=Article.

38. Morgan Watkins, "While Trump Calls Him 'Gutless,' Mitch McConnell Says Focus Is 100% on 'Stopping' Biden," *USA Today*, May 5, 2021. Accessed at https://www.usatoday.com/story/news/politics/2021/05/05 /mitch-mcconnell-dodges-questions-rep-liz-cheney-2020-election /4965035001/.

39. Elana Schor, "Schumer on Ending Filibuster: 'Nothing's Off the Table,'" Associated Press, July 16, 2019. Accessed at https://apnews.com /article/210b5d7948f943aa809276f868617a16.

40. Jacqueline Alemany, "Power Up: Only Roughly a Fifth of Senate Democrats Are Committed to Totally Scrapping the Filibuster,"

Washington Post, March 17, 2021. Accessed at https://www
.washingtonpost.com/politics/2021/03/17/power-up-only-roughly
-fifth-senate-democrats-are-committed-totally-scrapping-filibuster/.

41. Joe Manchin III, "Joe Manchin: I Will Not Vote to Eliminate or Weaken
the Filibuster," *Washington Post*, April 7, 2021. Accessed at https://www.
washingtonpost.com/opinions/joe-manchin-filibuster
-vote/2021/04/07/cdbd53c6-97da-11eb-a6d0-13d207aadb78_story.html.

42. Cameron Peters, "Joe Manchin Opens the Door to Filibuster Reform," Vox,
March 7, 2021. Accessed at https://www.vox.com/2021/3/7/22318145/joe
-manchin-filibuster-reform.

43. Joe Manchin, "West Virginians Deserve a Government That Works for
Them," news release, January 27, 2011. Accessed at https://www.manchin
.senate.gov/newsroom/press-releases/manchin-west-virginians-deserve
-a-government-that-works-for-them.

44. "Cloture Motions," United States Senate. Accessed at https://www.senate
.gov/legislative/cloture/clotureCounts.htm.

45. "How Politics Has Pulled the Country in Different Directions," *Wall Street
Journal*, November 10, 2020. Accessed at https://www.wsj.com/graphics
/polarized-presidential-elections/.

46. Aron Zitner and Dante Chinni, "Democrats and Republicans Live in
Different Worlds," *Wall Street Journal*, September 20, 2019. Accessed at
https://www.wsj.com/articles/democrats-and-republicans-live-in-different
-worlds-11568996171

47. Tovia Smith, "'Dude, I'm Done': When Politics Tears Families and
Friendships Apart," *All Things Considered*, NPR, October 27, 2020.
Accessed at https://www.npr.org/2020/10/27/928209548/dude-i-m
-done-when-politics-tears-families-and-friendships-apart.

48. Molly Langmuir, "Donald Trump Is Destroying My Marriage,"
Intelligencer, *New York* magazine, November 27, 2018. Accessed at https://
nymag.com/intelligencer/2018/11/donald-trump-is-destroying-my
-marriage.html.

49. "Fox News Bests CNN As 'Most Trusted Name in News,'" Media Research
Center. Accessed at https://www.mrc.org/biasalerts/fox-news-bests-cnn
-most-trusted-name-news.

50. Ben Smith and Katie Robertson, "Jeff Zucker, CNN's Longtime Leader,
Says He Expects to Leave at Year's End," *New York Times*, February 4,
2021. Accessed at https://www.nytimes.com/2021/02/04/business/media
/cnn-jeff-zucker.html?referringSource=articleShare.

51. Erica Chenoweth and Jeremy Pressman, "This Is What We Learned by
Counting the Women's Marches," *Washington Post*, February 7, 2017.
Accessed at https://www.washingtonpost.com/news/monkey-cage

/wp/2017/02/07/this-is-what-we-learned-by-counting-the-womens
-marches/.

52. Ian Millhiser, "Mitt Romney Just Did Something That Literally No
Senator Has Ever Done Before," Vox, February 5, 2020. Accessed at
https://www.vox.com/2020/2/5/21125118/mitt-romney-impeachment
-vote-history.

53. Christiano Lima, "Trump Hits 'Cryin' Chuck Schumer' Over Past
Opposition to Iran Deal," *Politico*, May 10, 2018. Accessed at https://www
.politico.com/story/2018/05/10/trump-criticize-crying-chuck-schumer
-579908.

54. Daniella Diaz, "Trump: I'm a 'Very Stable Genius,'" CNN, January 6, 2018.
Accessed at https://www.cnn.com/2018/01/06/politics/donald-trump
-white-house-fitness-very-stable-genius/index.html.

55. Rosalind S. Heiderman, Spencer S. Hsu, and Rachel Weiner, "'Trump Said
to Do So': Accounts of Rioters Who Say the President Spurred Them to
Rush the Capitol Could Be Pivotal Testimony," *Washington Post*, January
16, 2021. Accessed at https://www.washingtonpost.com/politics
/trump-rioters-testimony/2021/01/16/01b3d5c6-575b-11eb-a931
-5b162d0d033d_story.html.

56. Trump tweet, December 21, 2020. Accessed at https://mobile.twitter.com
/C55730933/status/1341151450001502214.

57. Charlotte Klein, "Watch Giuliani Demand 'Trial by Combat' to Settle the
Election," *New York* magazine, January 6, 2021. Accessed at https://nymag
.com/intelligencer/2021/01/watch-giuliani-demand-trial-by-combat-to
-settle-election.html.

58. Maggie Haberman, "Trump Told Crowd 'You Will Never Take Back Our
Country With Weakness,'" *New York Times*, January 6, 2021 (updated
January 15, 2021). Accessed at https://www.nytimes.com/2021/01/06/us
/politics/trump-speech-capitol.html.

59. Brian Naylor, "Read Trump's Jan. 6 Speech, A Key Part of Impeachment
Trial," NPR, February 10, 2021. Accessed at https://www.npr.org/2021
/02/10/966396848/read-trumps-jan-6-speech-a-key-part-of-impeachment
-trial.

60. "Twitter Locks Trump's Account for 12 Hours, Facebook Blocks Him from
Posting for 24 hours," Fox 5, Washington, D.C. Accessed at https://www
.fox5dc.com/news/twitter-locks-trumps-account-for-12-hours-facebook
-blocks-him-from-posting-for-24-hours.

61. Tom Jackman, "Police Union Says 140 Officers Injured in Capitol Riot,"
Washington Post, January 27, 2021. Accessed at https://www.washingtonpost
.com/local/public-safety/police-union-says-140-officers-injured-in-capitol
-riot/2021/01/27/60743642-60e2-11eb-9430-e7c77b5b0297_story.html.

62 Whitney Wild, Paul LeBlanc and Rashard Rose, "2 more DC police officers who responded to Capitol insurrection have died by suicide," CNN, updated August 3, 2021. Accessed at https://www.cnn.com/2021/08/02/politics/dc-metropolitan-police-officer-suicide-january-6-capitol-riot/index.html

63. Katie Benner, "Trump and Justice Dept. Lawyer Said to Have Plotted to Oust Acting Attorney General," *New York Times*, January 22, 2021. Accessed at https://www.nytimes.com/2021/01/22/us/politics/jeffrey-clark-trump-justice-department-election.html.

64. Adam Gabbatt, "Fox Lurches Further to the Right to Win Back Hard-Edge Trump Supporters," *Guardian*, February 5, 2001. Accessed at https://www.theguardian.com/media/2021/feb/05/fox-news-lunges-further-right-win-back-hard-edge-trump-supporters.

65. Alan Feuer, "Dominion Voting Systems Files Defamation Lawsuit Against Pro-Trump Attorney Sidney Powell," *New York Times*, January 8, 2021 (updated March 26, 2021). Accessed at https://www.nytimes.com/2021/01/08/us/politics/dominion-voting-systems-files-defamation-lawsuit-against-pro-trump-attorney-sidney-powell.html.

66. Nick Corasaniti, "Rudy Giuliani Sued by Dominion Voting Systems Over False Election Claims," *New York Times*, January 5, 2021 (updated May 4, 2021). Accessed at https://www.nytimes.com/2021/01/25/us/politics/rudy-giuliani-dominion-trump.html.

67. Oliver Darcy, "Dominion Voting Systems Files $1.6 Billion Lawsuit Against Fox News for 'Orchestrated Defamatory Campaign,'" CNN, March 26, 2021. Accessed at https://www.cnn.com/2021/03/26/media/dominion-voting-systems-fox-news-lawsuit.

68. Jan Wolfe, "Ex-Trump Lawyer Powell Asks Judge to Toss Voting Machine Company's $1.3 Billion Lawsuit," Reuters, March 22, 2021. Accessed at https://www.reuters.com/article/us-usa-election-dominion-idUSKBN2BE32S.

69. "Call for Bar Condemnation and Investigation of President Trump's Campaign Lawyers for Subverting American Democracy," Lawyers Defending Democracy, December 4, 2020. Accessed at https://lawyersdefendingdemocracy.org/call-for-bar-condemnation-and-investigation-of-president-trumps-campaign-lawyers-for-subverting-american-democracy/.

70. Jonah E. Bromwich and Ben Smith, "Fox News Is Sued by Election Technology Company for Over $2.7 Billion," *New York Times*, February 4, 2021 (updated April 27, 2021). Accessed at https://www.nytimes.com/2021/02/04/business/media/smartmatic-fox-news-lawsuit.html.

71. Declaration of Independence, National Archives, July 4, 1776. Accessed at https://www.archives.gov/founding-docs/declaratio-transcript.

72. Scott Rasmussen, "34% Believe Federal Government Supports Founding Ideals of Freedom, Equality, Self-Governance," March 28, 2021. Accessed at https://scottrasmussen.com/34-believe-federal-government-supports -founding-ideals-of-freedom-equality-self-governance/.

73. Zahra Ullah and Anna Chernova, "Putin Signs Law Allowing Him to Run for Two More Terms as Russian President," CNN. Updated April 6, 2021. Accessed at https://www.cnn.com/2021/04/05/europe/putin-russia -presidential-term-intl-hnk/index.html.

74. "Russia Election: Vladimir Putin Wins by a Big Margin," BBC News, March 19, 2018. Accessed at https://www.bbc.com/news/world -europe-43452449.

75. "China's Xi Allowed to Remain 'President for Life' as Term Limits Removed," BBC News, March 11, 2018. Accessed at https://www.bbc.com /news/world-asia-china-43361276.

76. "Donald Trump Unfazed by Georgia Setback, Tells Supporters at Washington Rally 'Will Never Concede,'" Yahoo News, January 6, 2021. Accessed at https://in.news.yahoo.com/donald-trump-unfazed-georgia -setback-175311118.html.

77. Abraham Lincoln, "Transcript of Gettysburg Address (1863)," Ourdocuments.gov. Accessed at https://www.ourdocuments.gov/doc .php?flash=false&doc=36&page=transcript.

78. Joe Biden, "Inaugural Address by President Joseph R. Biden, Jr.," The White House, January 20, 2021. Accessed at https://www.whitehouse.gov /briefing-room/speeches-remarks/2021/01/20/inaugural-address-by -president-joseph-r-biden-jr/.

79. Scott Rasmussen, "New Low: 17% Say U.S. Government Has Consent of the Governed," Rasmussen Reports, August 7, 2011. Accessed at https:// www.rasmussenreports.com/public_content/politics/general_politics /august_2011/new_low_17_say_u_s_government_has_consent_of_the _governed.

80. Justin McCarthy, "In U.S., 65% Dissatisfied With How Gov't System Works," Gallup, January 22, 2014. Accessed at https://news.gallup.com /poll/166985/dissatisfied-gov-system-works.aspx.

81. Quote from Henry Kissinger, as quoted in *New York Times*, October 28, 1973. Accessed at https://en.wikiquote.org/wiki/Henry_Kissinger.

82. "Election results, 2020: Incumbent win rates by state," Ballotpedia, December 22, 2020. Accessed at https://ballotpedia.org/Election _results,_2020:_Incumbent_win_rates_by_state.

83. Independence USA PAC website. Accessed at https://www .independenceusapac.org/.

84. Mark A. Uhlig, "Jesse Unruh, a California Political Power, Dies," *New York Times*, August 6, 1987. Accessed at https://www.nytimes

.com/1987/08/06/obituaries/jesse-unruh-a-california-political-power
-dies.html.

85. "2020 Election to Cost $14 Billion, Blowing Away Spending Records,"
    OpenSecrets.org, October 28, 2020. Accessed at https://www.opensecrets
    .org/news/2020/10/cost-of-2020-election-14billion-update/.

86. Rachel Siegel, Jeff Stein, and Mike DeBonis, "Here's What's in the $900
    Billion Stimulus Package," *Washington Post*, December 27, 2020. Accessed
    at https://www.washingtonpost.com/business/2020/12/20/stimulus
    -package-details/.

87. "Broad Public Support for Coronavirus Aid Package: Just a Third Say It
    Spends Too Much," Pew Research Center, March 9, 2021. Accessed at
    https://www.pewresearch.org/politics/2021/03/09/broad-public-support
    -for-coronavirus-aid-package-just-a-third-say-it-spends-too-much/.

88. "Public Trust in Government: 1958–2019," The Pew Research Center, April
    11, 2019. Accessed at https://www.pewresearch.org/politics/2021/05/17
    /public-trust-in-government-1958-2021/.

89. "State of Union Address: Jimmy Carter," Teaching American History,
    January 19, 1978. Accessed at https://teachingamericanhistory.org/library
    /document/state-of-the-union-address-166/.

90. "President Reagan's Inaugural Address," January 20, 1981, The Ronald
    Reagan Foundation. Accessed at https://www.reaganfoundation.org
    /media/128614/inaguration.pdf.

91. E. J. Dionne, "Hating the Government Won't Improve It," *Washington
    Post*, January 20, 2019. Accessed at https://www.washingtonpost.com
    /opinions/hating-the-government-wont-improve-it/2019/01/20/
    ff80944c-1b66-11e9-8813-cb9dec761e73_story.html.

92. "'The Era of Big Government Is Over': Clinton's 1996 State of the Union,"
    PBS *Washington Week*, January 26, 1996. Accessed at https://www.pbs
    .org/weta/washingtonweek/web-video/era-big-government-over-clintons
    -1996-state-union.

93. Charles S. Clark, "Reinventing Government—Two Decades Later,"
    Government Executive, April 26, 2013. Accessed at https://www.govexec
    .com/management/2013/04/what-reinvention-wrought/62836/.

94. Eyder Peralta, "Obama: It's Not Bigger Government We Need, It's a
    'Smarter' One," NPR, February 12, 2013. Accessed at https://www.npr.org
    /sections/itsallpolitics/2013/02/07/171410659/live-blog-president
    -obamas-state-of-the-union-address.

95. Douglas E. Schoen, "Doug Schoen: Amazon's Cancellation of Move to
    NYC is Catastrophic and Could Hurt Far-Left Dems at Polls," Fox News,
    February 14, 2019. Accessed at https://www.foxnews.com/opinion/doug
    -schoen-amazons-cancellation-of-a-move-to-nyc-is-bad-news-and-could-
    hurt-far-left-dems-at-polls.

96. Winston Churchill, "The Worst Form of Government," International Churchill Society. Accessed at https://winstonchurchill.org/resources /quotes/the-worst-form-of-government/.

97. Daniel Patrick Moynihan, "An American Original," *Vanity Fair*, October 6, 2010. Accessed at https://www.vanityfair.com/news/2010/11/moynihan -letters-201011.

98. Aaron Blake, "Kellyanne Conway Says Donald Trump's Team Has 'Alternative Facts.' Which Pretty Much Says It All," *Washington Post*, January 22, 2017. Accessed at https://www.washingtonpost.com/news /the-fix/wp/2017/01/22/kellyanne-conway-says-donald-trumps-team -has-alternate-facts-which-pretty-much-says-it-all/.

99. Tom Jones, "America Is Watching the Evening News Again. TV News Numbers Are Up. Way Up," The Poynter Institute, April 16, 2020. Accessed at https://www.poynter.org/newsletters/2020/america-is-watching-the -evening-news-again-tv-news-numbers-are-up-way-up/.

100. Amy Watson, "Number of Daily Newspapers in the U.S. 1970–2018," Statista, March 3, 2020. Accessed at https://www.statista.com /statistics/183408/number-of-us-daily-newspapers-since-1975/.

101. Quinnipiac Poll news release, "74% of Voters Say Democracy in the U.S. Is Under Threat, Quinnipiac University National Poll Finds; 52% Say President Trump Should Be Removed From Office," Quinnipiac University, January 11, 2021. Accessed at https://poll.qu.edu/images /polling/us/us01112021_usmk38.pdf.

102. Charles Dickens. *A Tale of Two Cities*, 1859.

103. Mario Cuomo, "Mario Cuomo's 1984 Convention Speech," YouTube, July 16, 1984. Accessed at https://www.youtube.com/watch?v=kOdIqKsv624.

104. Kriston McIntosh, Emily Moss, Ryan Nunn, and Jay Shambaugh, "Examining the Black-White Wealth Gap," The Brookings Institution, February 27, 2020. Accessed at https://www.brookings.edu/blog/up -front/2020/02/27/examining-the-black-white-wealth-gap/.

105. "66.2 Percent of 2019 High School Graduates Enrolled in College in October 2019," U.S. Bureau of Labor Statistics. May 22, 2020.

106. Dion Rabouin, "The Myth of Closing the Racial Wealth Gap Through Education," Axios, June 29, 2020. Accessed at https://www.axios.com/racial -wealth-gap-education-8c106518-2b20-484e-b166-9601e1b89305.html.

107. Langston Hughes, "Harlem," 1951. Accessed at https://www.sjsu.edu /faculty/harris/Eng101_Harlem.pdf.

108. Robert Burns, Lolita Baldor, and Howard Altman, "US to 2,500 Troopers Each in Afghanistan and Iraq, as Ordered by Trump," Associated Press, January 15, 2021. Accessed at https://www.militarytimes.com/news /your-military/2021/01/15/us-down-to-2500-troops-in-afghanistan -as-ordered-by-trump/.

109. Will Weissert, "DHS Report: China Hid Virus' Severity to Hoard Supplies," Associated Press, May 4, 2020. Accessed at https://apnews .com/article/us-news-ap-top-news-international-news-global-trade -virus-outbreak-bf685dcf52125be54e030834ab7062a8.

110. David Cyranoski, "What China's Coronavirus Response Can Teach the Rest of the World," *Nature*, March 17, 2020. Accessed at https://www .nature.com/articles/d41586-020-00741-x.

111. Raymond Zhong and Paul Mozur: "To Tame Coronavirus, Mao-Style Social Control Blankets China," *New York Times*, February 15, 2020. Updated February 20, 2020. Accessed at https://www.nytimes .com/2020/02/15/business/china-coronavirus-lockdown.html.

112. "Putin, Before Vote, Says He'd Reverse Soviet Collapse if He Could: Agencies," Reuters, March 2, 2018. Accessed at https://www.reuters.com /article/us-russia-election-putin/putin-before-vote-says-hed-reverse -soviet-collapse-if-he-could-agencies-idUSKCN1GE2TF.

113. "Reuters/Ipsos: Trump's Coattails," Ipsos news release, April 2, 2021. Accessed at https://www.ipsos.com/sites/default/files/ct/news /documents/2021-04/topline_write_up_reuters_ipsos_trump_coattails _poll_-_april_02_2021.pdf.

114. Doug Schoen and Carly Cooperman, "Schoen & Cooperman: Election 2020—Biden, Dems Hurt by This and Here's How They Can Bounce Back," Fox News, November 16, 2020. Accessed at https://www.foxnews .com/opinion/election-2020-biden-dems-hurt-bounce-back-doug-schoen -carly-cooperman.

CHAPTER 1

1. Darryl Fears, "Hearing for Haaland, First Native American Pick to Run Interior Dept., Focuses on Fossil Fuels," *Washington Post*, February 24, 2021. Accessed at https://www.washingtonpost.com/climate -environment/2021/02/23/deb-haaland-interior-secretary-hearing/.

2. Sarah Repucci and Amy Slipowitz, "Freedom in the World 2021: Democracy Under Siege," Freedom House, 2021. Accessed at https:// freedomhouse.org/sites/default/files/2021-02/FIW2021 _World_02252021_FINAL-web-upload.pdf.

3. Joe Biden, "Inaugural Address by President Joseph R. Biden, Jr."

4. Susan Page, "Americans Back Tougher Gun Laws, but GOP Support Plummets Even After Atlanta, Boulder Shootings, Exclusive e Poll Finds," *USA Today*, March 24, 2021. Accessed at https://www.usatoday.com /story/news/politics/2021/03/24/poll-views-gun-laws-after-atlanta -boulder-show-even-deeper-divide/6963810002/.

5. "In Depth: Guns," Gallup poll, 2020. Accessed at https://news.gallup.com /poll/1645/guns.aspx.

6. Annie Karni, "With Gun Control Measures Stalled in Congress, Biden Announces Actions on Gun Violence," *New York Times*, April 8, 2021. Accessed at https://www.nytimes.com/2021/04/08/us/biden-gun -control.html?searchResultPosition=1.

7. Zachary B. Wolf, "Here's What Congress Is Considering on Gun Rights (And Why Nothing Will Happen)," CNN, March 23, 2021. Accessed at https://www.cnn.com/2021/03/23/politics/us-gun-laws-congress -explainer/index.html.

8. "Second Amendment," National Constitution Center, Ratified December 15, 1791. Accessed at https://constitutioncenter.org/interactive -constitution/amendment/amendment-ii.

9. Brenda Erickson, "Amending the U.S. Constitution," National Conference of State Legislatures. August 2017. Accessed at https://www.ncsl.org /research/about-state-legislatures/amending-the-u-s-constitution.aspx.

10. "Gun Violence Archive 2020," Gun Violence Archive. Accessed at https:// www.gunviolencearchive.org/past-tolls.

11. Lisa Dunn, "How Many People in the U.S. Own Guns?" Guns & America, September 17, 2020. Accessed at https://gunsandamerica.org /story/20/09/17/how-many-gun-owners-united-states-explainer/.

12. "In Depth Topics: Guns," the Gallup poll, 2020. Accessed at https://news .gallup.com/poll/1645/guns.aspx.

13. Ruth Igielnik and Anna Brown, "Key Takeaways on Americans' Views of Guns and Gun Ownership," Pew Research Center, June 22, 2017. Accessed at https://www.pewresearch.org/fact-tank/2017/06/22/key-takeaways -on-americans-views-of-guns-and-gun-ownership/.

14. Susan Page and Sarah Elbeshbishi, "Exclusive: Defeated and Impeached, Trump Still Commands the Loyalty of the GOP's Voters," *USA Today*, February 21, 2021 (updated February 22, 2021). Accessed at https://www .usatoday.com/story/news/politics/2021/02/21/exclusive-trump-party-he -still-holds-loyalty-gop-voters/6765406002/.

15. "Reuters/Ipsos: Trump's Coattails," Ipsos news release, April 2, 2021.

16. Marina Pitofsky, "Ocasio-Cortez: 'No Consequences' in GOP for Violence, Racism," *Hill*, January 28, 2021. Accessed at https://thehill.com /homenews/news/536240-ocasio-cortez-no-consequences-in-gop-for -violence-racism.

17. Tim Hains, "Maxine Waters Warns Trump Cabinet: 'The People Are Going to Turn' on You," RealClear Politics, June 24, 2018. Accessed at https://www.realclearpolitics.com/video/2018/06/24/maxine_waters _the_people_are_going_to_turn_on_trump_enablers.html.

18. "Americans' Views of Government: Low Trust, but Some Positive Performance Ratings," Pew Research Center, U.S. Politics & Policy, September 14, 2020. Accessed at https://www.pewresearch.org/politics /2020/09/14/americans-views-of-government-low-trust-but-some -positive-performance-ratings/.

19. "Confidence in Institutions," Gallup. Accessed at https://news.gallup.com /poll/1597/Confidence-Institutions.aspx.

20. "Tracking Trust in U.S. Institutions," Morning Consult, April 1, 2021. Accessed at https://morningconsult.com/tracking-trust-in -institutions/%23section-10.

21. "Trust in Government," Gallup, 2020. Accessed at https://news.gallup .com/poll/5392/Trust-Government.aspx.

22. Ben Sasse, "Sen. Ben Sasse's Maiden Speech," Sasse website, November 3, 2015. Accessed at https://www.sasse.senate.gov/public/index .cfm/2015/11/senator-ben-sasse-s-maiden-speech.

23. "Americans' Views of Government: Low Trust, but Some Positive Performance Ratings," Pew Research Center, U.S. Politics & Policy, September 14, 2020. Accessed at https://www.pewresearch.org/ politics/2020/09/14/americans-views-of-government-low-trust-but -some-positive-performance-ratings/.

24. Marc Hetherington, "Trust in Trump Comes from Lack of Trust in Government," The Brookings Institute, November 30, 2015. Accessed at https://www.brookings.edu/blog/fixgov/2015/09/16/trust-in-trump -comes-from-lack-of-trust-in-government/.

25. Marty Finnegan: "An Effort to Break the Gridlock in Washington," Kenosha News, November 18, 2018. Accessed at https://www .kenoshanews.com/opinion/an-effort-to-break-the-gridlock-in -washington/article_44767590-d150-5afb-bd67-7c1c6e745ee1.html.

26. Patrick Caddell, Scott Perkins, and Bob Miller, "It's Candidate Smith by a Landslide," HuffPost, July 4, 2014. Accessed at https://www.huffpost.com /entry/its-candidate-smith-by-a-_b_5552229.

27. Janet Hook, "Newt Faces Some 'Raw' Questions: Television: Six Twentysomething Men and Women Shoot the Breeze with the Speaker of the House in an MTV Round-Table Discussion," *Los Angeles Times*, July 14, 1995. Accessed at https://www.latimes.com/archives/la-xpm-1995-07-14 -ca-23765-story.html.

28. "2020 Virtual Oratorical World Championships Press Release," Optimist International. Accessed at https://www.optimist.org/member /scholarships4.cfm.

29. "Dueling Realities: Amid Multiple Crises, Trump and Biden Supporters See Different Priorities and Futures for the Nation," Public Religion Research Institute, October 19, 2020. Accessed at https://www.prri

.org/research/amid-multiple-crises-trump-and-biden-supporters-see
-different-realities-and-futures-for-the-nation/.

30. John Gramlich, "Looking Ahead to 2050, Americans Are Pessimistic About Many Aspects of Life in U.S.," Pew Research Center, March 21, 2019. Accessed at https://www.pewresearch.org/fact-tank/2019/03/21/looking -ahead-to-2050-americans-are-pessimistic-about-many-aspects-of-life -in-u-s/.

31. "The Economist-YouGov Poll," February 13–16, 2021. Accessed at https:// docs.cdn.yougov.com/3at75tb28w/econTabReport.pdf.

32. Juliana Menasce Horowitz, Ruth Igielnik, and Rakesh Kochhar, "Trends in U.S. Income and Wealth Inequality," Pew Research Center, January 9, 2020. Accessed at https://www.pewresearch.org/social-trends/2020 /01/09/trends-in-income-and-wealth-inequality/.

33. Katherine Schaffer, "6 Facts About Economic Inequality in the U.S.," Pew Research Center, February 7, 2020. Accessed at https://www.pewresearch .org/fact-tank/2020/02/07/6-facts-about-economic-inequality-in-the -u-s/.

34. James Truslow Adams Papers, 1918–1949, Columbia University Libraries Archival Collections. Accessed at http://www.columbia.edu/cu/lweb /archival/collections/ldpd_4078384/.

35. Ballard, "Is the American Dream Still Attainable?" YouGov, July 18, 2020.

36. May Wong, "Today's Children Face Tough Prospects of Being Better Off Than Their Parents, Stanford Researchers Find," Stanford University news release, December 8, 2016. Accessed at https://news.stanford .edu/2016/12/08/todays-children-face-tough-prospects-better-off -parents/.

37. Binyamin Appelbaum: "Family Net Worth Drops to Level of Early '90s, Fed Says," *New York Times*, June 11, 2012. Accessed at https://www .nytimes.com/2012/06/12/business/economy/family-net-worth-drops-to -level-of-early-90s-fed-says.html.

38. Appelbaum, "Family Net Worth Drops to Level of Early '90s, Fed Says."

39. Juliana Menasce Horowitz, Ruth Igielnik, and Rakesh Kochhar, "Trends in U.S. Income and Wealth Inequality."

40. Aimee Picchi, "Is the American Dream Dying?" CBS News, February 26, 2015. Accessed at https://www.cbsnews.com/news/pew-study-the -american-dream-is-dying/.

41. "President Biden Announces American Rescue Plan," White House news release, January 20, 2021. Accessed at https://www.whitehouse.gov /briefing-room/legislation/2021/01/20/president-biden-announces -american-rescue-plan/.

42. Jeff Cox, "Raising Minimum Wage to $15 Would Cost 1.4 Million Jobs, CBO says," CNBC, February 8, 2021. Accessed at https://www.cnbc

.com/2021/02/08/raising-minimum-wage-to-15-would-cost-1point4
-million-jobs-cbo-says.html.

43. "Confidence in Institutions," Gallup. Accessed at https://news.gallup.com
/poll/1597/Confidence-Institutions.aspx.

44. Dropout Rates, National Center for Education Statistics. Accessed at
https://nces.ed.gov/fastfacts/display.asp?id=16.

45. "U.S. Census Bureau Releases New Educational Attainment Data," March
30, 2020. Accessed at https://www.census.gov/newsroom/press
-releases/2020/educational-attainment.html.

46. "The Income Gaps in Higher Education Enrollment and Completion,"
Association of American Colleges and Universities News, June/July 2018.
Accessed at https://www.aacu.org/aacu-news/newsletter/2018/june
/facts-figures.

47. Julia Kagan, "G.I. Bill," Investopedia, Updated February 8, 2021. Accessed
at https://www.investopedia.com/terms/g/gi-bill.asp.

48. "College Enrollment Linked to Vietnam War," Associated Press,
September 2, 1984. Accessed at https://www.nytimes.com/1984/09/02
/us/college-enrollment-linked-to-vietnam-war.html.

49. "Percentage of the U.S. Population Who Have Completed Four Years of
College or More from 1940 to 2018, by Gender," Statista, January 20, 2021.
Accessed at https://www.statista.com/statistics/184272/educational
-attainment-of-college-diploma-or-higher-by-gender/.

50. Branka Vuleta, "27 Fascinating Facts About the US College Dropout Rate,"
What to Become, November 25, 2020. Accessed at https://whattobecome
.com/blog/college-dropout-rate/.

51. "Graduation Rates," National Center for Education Statistics. 2020.
Accessed at https://nces.ed.gov/fastfacts/display.asp?id=40.

52. "Undergraduate Retention and Graduation Rates," National Center for
Education Statistics. April 2020. Accessed at https://nces.ed.gov
/programs/coe/.

53. Jaison R. Abel and Richard Deitz: "Despite Rising Costs, College Is Still
a Good Investment," Federal Reserve Bank of New York, Liberty Street
Economics, June 5, 2019. Accessed at https://libertystreeteconomics.
newyorkfed.org/2019/06/despite-rising-costs-college-is-still-a-good
-investment.html.

54. Danielle Moore, "Do Americans Still Believe That the American Dream Is
Attainable?" Digitalhub, November 12, 2020. Accessed at https://www
.swnsdigital.com/2020/11/do-americans-still-believe-that-the-the
-american-dream-is-attainable/.

55. "Student Loan Debt Statistics," EducationData, 2021. Accessed at https://
educationdata.org/student-loan-debt-statistics.

56. Josh Boak, "A Multigenerational Hit: Student Debt Traps Parents and Kids," Associated Press, October 5, 2015. Accessed at https://apnews.com/article/2ec9421a478648bf82f423d4617da043.

57. "How to Know If You're on Track for Buying a House," SoFi, May 20, 2019. Accessed at https://www.sofi.com/blog/average-age-to-buy-a-house/.

58. Danielle Moore, "Do Americans Still Believe That the American Dream Is Attainable?"

59. Ernie Tedeschi, "The Mystery of How Many Mothers Have Left Work Because of School Closings," *New York Times*, October 29, 2020. Accessed at https://www.nytimes.com/2020/10/29/upshot/mothers-leaving-jobs-pandemic.html.

60. Ellen Terrell, "When a Quote Is Not (Exactly) a Quote: The Business of America is Business Edition," Library of Congress blog, January 17, 2019. Accessed at https://blogs.loc.gov/inside_adams/2019/01/when-a-quote-is-not-exactly-a-quote-the-business-of-america-is-business-edition/.

61. "Labor Movement," History.com, Updated March 31, 2020. Accessed at https://www.history.com/topics/19th-century/labor.

62. Darcy Eveleigh, "The Struggle of Third-Party Candidates Through the Years," *New York Times*. August 4, 2016. Accessed at https://www.nytimes.com/2016/08/04/upshot/third-party-candidates-through-the-years.html.

63. "Samuel Gompers," US History.com. Accessed at https://www.u-s-history.com/pages/h1747.html.

64. Franklin Delano Roosevelt, "Franklin Roosevelt's Re-Nomination Acceptance Speech (1936)," The American Yawp Reader. Accessed at https://www.americanyawp.com/reader/23-the-great-depression/franklin-roosevelts-re-nomination-acceptance-speech-1936/.

65. Terence McArdle, "The Socialist Who Ran for President from Prison—and Won Nearly a Million Votes," *Washington Post*, September 22, 2019. Accessed at https://www.washingtonpost.com/dc-md-va/2019/09/22/socialist-who-ran-president-prison-won-nearly-million-votes/.

66. Lydia Saad, "Socialism as Popular as Capitalism Among Young Adults in U.S.," Gallup, November 26, 2019. Accessed at https://news.gallup.com/poll/268766/socialism-popular-capitalism-among-young-adults.aspx.

67. "Confidence in Institutions," Gallup. Accessed at https://news.gallup.com/poll/1597/Confidence-Institutions.aspx.

68. "Chart Book: Tracking the Post-Great Recession Economy," Center on Budget and Policy Priorities, February 10, 2021. Accessed at https://www.cbpp.org/research/economy/tracking-the-post-great-recession-economy.

69. "Confidence in Institutions," Gallup.

70. Hillary Hoffower, "How Millennials Could Fare If the Coronavirus Triggers Another Recession," *Business Insider*, April 8, 2020. Accessed at

https://www.businessinsider.com/millennials-great-recession-finances-coronavirus-triggers-financial-crisis-2020-4.

71. Mary Mazzoni, "Americans Trust Banks Less Than Ever: This CEO Offers a Fix," Triple Pundit, February 19, 2019. Accessed at https://www.triplepundit.com/story/2019/americans-trust-banks-less-ever-ceo-offers-fix/82506.

72. Erin Barry, "25% of US Households Are Either Unbanked or Underbanked," CNBC, March 9, 2019. Accessed at https://www.cnbc.com/2019/03/08/25percent-of-us-households-are-either-unbanked-or-underbanked.html.

73. David Remnick, "Trump and the Enemies of the People," *New Yorker*, August 15, 2018. Accessed at https://www.newyorker.com/news/daily-comment/trump-and-the-enemies-of-the-people.

74. Megan Brenan, "Americans Remain Distrustful of Mass Media," Gallup, September 30, 2020. Accessed at https://news.gallup.com/poll/321116/americans-remain-distrustful-mass-media.aspx.

75. "Tracking Trust in U.S. Institutions," Morning Consult, April 1, 2021. Accessed at https://morningconsult.com/tracking-trust-in-institutions/.

76. "Voters' Reflections on the 2020 Election," Pew Research Center, January 15, 2021. Accessed at https://www.pewresearch.org/politics/2021/01/15/voters-reflections-on-the-2020-election/.

77. "The American Press, 'Infamous' from Day One," interview on *Fresh Air*, NPR. March 1, 2006. Accessed at https://www.npr.org/templates/story/story.php?storyId=5239527.

78. Ryan Mattimore, "Presidential Feuds with the Media Are Nothing New," History.com, updated September 3, 2018. Accessed at https://www.history.com/news/presidents-relationship-with-press.

79. "Is the Letter on Display That Truman Wrote in Defense of His Daughter's Singing?" Harry S Truman Library and Museum, December 6, 1950. Accessed at https://www.trumanlibrary.gov/education/trivia/letter-truman-defends-daughter-singing.

80. Joe Lockhart, "Get Over It, the Media Isn't Going to Give Joe Biden a Free Ride," CNN, updated March 1, 2021. Accessed at https://www.cnn.com/2021/03/01/opinions/media-coverage-joe-biden-press-breifings-lockhart/index.html.

81. James Hohmann, "The Daily 202: Stepped-up Attacks on the Press Reflect Trump's Bunker Mentality," *Washington Post*, October 12, 2017. Accessed at https://www.washingtonpost.com/news/powerpost/paloma/daily-202/2017/10/12/daily-202-stepped-up-attacks-on-the-press-reflect-trump-s-bunker-mentality/59de6f3f30fb0468cea81e90/.

82. "Lesley Stahl: Trump Admitted Mission to 'Discredit' Press," CBS News, May 23, 2018. Accessed at https://www.cbsnews.com/news/lesley-stahl -donald-trump-said-attacking-press-to-discredit-negative-stories/.

83. Howard Kurtz, "Janet Cooke's Untold Story," *Washington Post*. May 9, 1996. Accessed at https://www.washingtonpost.com/archive /lifestyle/1996/05/09/janet-cookes-untold-story/23151d68-3abd-449a -a053-d72793939d85/.

84. Mark Jurkowitz, Amy Mitchell, Elisa Shearer, and Mason Walker, "U.S. Media Polarization and the 2020 Election: A Nation Divided. Appendix: Detailed Tables," Pew Research Center, January 24, 2020. Accessed at https://www.journalism.org/2020/01/24/media-polarization-appendix -detailed-tables/.

85. Elisa Shearer, "More Than Eight-in-Ten Americans Get News from Digital Devices," Pew Research Center, January 12, 2021. Accessed at https:// www.pewresearch.org/fact-tank/2021/01/12/more-than-eight-in-ten -americans-get-news-from-digital-devices/.

86. Amy Mitchell, Mark Jurkowitz, J. Baxter Oliphant, and Elisa Shearer, "Americans Who Mainly Get Their News on Social Media Are Less Engaged, Less Knowledgeable," Pew Research Center, July 30, 2020. Accessed at https://www.journalism.org/2020/07/30/americans -who-mainly-get-their-news-on-social-media-are-less-engaged-less -knowledgeable/.

87. Margaret Sullivan, "These Local Newspapers Say Facebook and Google Are Killing Them. Now They're Fighting Back," *Washington Post*, February 4, 2021. Accessed at https://www.washingtonpost .com/lifestyle/media/west-virginia-google-facebook-newspaper -lawsuit/2021/02/03/797631dc-657d-11eb-8468-21bc48f07fe5_story.html.

88. Elizabeth Grieco, "Fast Facts About the Newspaper Industry's Financial Struggles as McClatchy Files for Bankruptcy," Pew Research Center, February 14, 2020. Accessed at https://www.pewresearch.org/fact -tank/2020/02/14/fast-facts-about-the-newspaper-industrys-financial -struggles/.

89. "Final Job Cuts Report for 2020; Over 2.3 Million, Nearly Half Due to COVID," Challenger, Gray & Christmas, January 2021. Accessed at https:// www.challengergray.com/blog/job-cuts-dec-2020-over-2-3-million -nearly-half-due-to-covid/.

90. Simon Kemp, "Digital 2020: 3.8 billion People Use Social Media." We Are Social, January 30, 2020. Accessed at https://wearesocial.com /blog/2020/01/digital-2020-3-8-billion-people-use-social-media.

91. J. Clara Chan, "US Newsrooms Lost a Record 16,160 Jobs in 2020, Study Finds," The Wrap, January 7, 2021. Accessed at https://www.thewrap .com/2020-newsroom-layoffs-data/.

92. Aimee Ortiz, "Confidence in Police Is at Record Low, Gallup Survey Finds," *New York Times*, August 12, 2020. Accessed at https://www.nytimes.com/2020/08/12/us/gallup-poll-police.html.

93. "Confidence in Institutions," Gallup.

94. N'dea Yancey-Bragg, "George Floyd's Brutal Death Sparked a Racial Justice Reckoning. One Officer Involved Goes on Trial This Month. What You Should Know," *USA Today*, March 4, 2021. Accessed at https://www.usatoday.com/story/news/nation/2021/03/04/derek-chauvin-trial-george-floyd-death-how-watch-what-know/6889289002/; Nicholas Bogel-Burroughs, "Derek Chauvin Will Now Face a Third-Degree Murder Charge," *New York Times*, March 11, 2021. Accessed at https://www.nytimes.com/2021/03/11/us/third-degree-murder-charge-derek-chauvin.html.

95. "George Floyd: Pew Survey on US Attitudes to Police Reveals Changes," BBC News, July 9, 2020. Accessed at https://www.bbc.com/news/world-us-canada-53343551.

96. Scott Clement and Emily Guskin, "Most Americans Support Greater Scrutiny of Police as Discrimination Concerns Persist, Post-ABC Poll Finds," *Washington Post*, April 23, 2021. Accessed at https://www.washingtonpost.com/politics/2021/04/23/poll-police-bias-floyd/.

97. Felicia Sonmez and Colby Itkowitz, "House Passes Expansive Policing Overhaul Bill Named in Honor of George Floyd," *Washington Post*, March 3, 2021. Accessed at https://www.washingtonpost.com/politics/george-floyd-police-reform-bill-vote/2021/03/03/5ea9ba3a-7c6c-11eb-85cd-9b7fa90c8873_story.html.

98. Marc A. Thiessen, "Biden Says He Wants Unity. He Can Prove It by Supporting Tim Scott on Police Reform," *Washington Post*, April 21, 2021. Accessed at https://www.washingtonpost.com/opinions/2021/04/21/biden-says-he-wants-unity-he-can-prove-it-by-supporting-tim-scott-police-reform/.

99. Marianne Levine, "Dick Durbin Apologizes to Tim Scott After 'Token' Remark," *Politico*, June 17, 2020. Accessed at https://www.politico.com/news/2020/06/17/durbin-scott-apology-326538.

100. Tal Axelrod, "Pelosi Refuses to Apologize for Accusing GOP of 'Trying to Get Away With Murder' with Police Reform Bill," *Hill*, June 24, 2020. Accessed at https://thehill.com/homenews/house/504333-pelosi-says-she-wont-apologize-for-accusing-gop-of-trying-to-get-away-with.

101. Lisa Mascaro, "Talks Narrow on a Compromise to Changes in US Policing Laws," Associated Press, April 22, 2021. Accessed at https://apnews.com/article/joe-biden-violence-legislation-death-of-george-floyd-racial-injustice-f78756fe5d1c645d5f14b738dd6d349a.

102. "George Floyd: Pew Survey on US Attitudes to Police Reveals Changes," BBC News, July 9, 2020. Accessed at https://www.bbc.com/news/world-us-canada-53343551.

103. Steve Crabtree, "Most Americans Say Policing Needs 'Major Changes,'" Gallup, July 22, 2020. Accessed at https://news.gallup.com/poll/315962/americans-say-policing-needs-major-changes.aspx.

104. Sarah Elbeshbishi and Mabinty Quarshie, "Fewer Than 1 in 5 Support 'Defund the Police Movement, *USA Today*/Ipsos Poll finds," *USA Today*. Accessed at https://www.usatoday.com/story/news/politics/2021/03/07/usa-today-ipsos-poll-just-18-support-defund-police-movement/4599232001/.

105. Reid J. Epstein, "These Top Democrats Go Further Than Biden on Divesting Police Funds," *New York Times*, June 26, 2020. Accessed at https://www.nytimes.com/2020/06/26/us/politics/defund-police-protests-democrats.html.

106. Barack Obama, "Barack Obama's Race Speech at the Constitution Center," National Constitution Center, March 18, 2008. Accessed at https://constitutioncenter.org/amoreperfectunion/docs/Race_Speech_Transcript.pdf.

107. Martin Luther King Jr., "'I Have A Dream' Speech, in Its Entirety," NPR, January 18, 2010. Accessed at https://www.npr.org/2010/01/18/122701268/i-have-a-dream-speech-in-its-entirety.

108. John Gramlich, "Black Imprisonment Rate in the U.S. Has Fallen by a Third Since 2006," Pew Research Center, May 6, 2020. Accessed at https://www.pewresearch.org/fact-tank/2020/05/06/share-of-black-white-hispanic-americans-in-prison-2018-vs-2006/.

109. Clyde Haberman, "The 1968 Kerner Commission Report Still Echoes Across America," *New York Times*, June 23, 2020 (updated October 7, 2020). Accessed at https://www.nytimes.com/2020/06/23/us/kerner-commission-report.html.

110. Marcus Casey and Bradley Hardy, "50 Years After the Kerner Commission Report, the Nation Is Still Grappling with Many of the Same Issues," Brookings, September 25, 2018. Accessed at https://www.brookings.edu/blog/up-front/2018/09/25/50-years-after-the-kerner-commission-report-the-nation-is-still-grappling-with-many-of-the-same-issues/.

111. "Race Relations," Gallup, 2021. Accessed at https://news.gallup.com/poll/1687/race-relations.aspx.

112. "Poll: Americans' Views of Systemic Racism Divided by Race," University of Massachusetts Lowell, September 22, 2020. Accessed at https://www.uml.edu/News/press-releases/2020/SocialIssuesPoll092220.aspx.

113. Laura Bliss, "Presidents Have Always Talked About 'Equity.' But What Kind?" Bloomberg City Lab, February 15, 2021. Accessed at https://www

.bloomberg.com/news/articles/2021-02-15/what-presidents-mean-when
-they-talk-about-equity.

114. Robby Soave, "Kamala Harris Says Equal Outcomes Should be the Goal of
Public Policy," Reason, November 2, 2020. Accessed at https://reason
.com/2020/11/02/kamala-harris-equality-equity-outcomes/.

115. Roberta Kaplan and Deborah Lipstadt, "Three Years Later,
Charlottesville's Legacy of Neo-Nazi Hate Still Festers," CNN, August 12,
2020. Accessed at https://www.cnn.com/2020/08/11/opinions
/charlottesville-three-years-later-hate-festers-lipstadt-kaplan/index.html.

116. Emmanuel Felton, "Black Police Officers Describe the Racist Attacks They
Faced As They Protected the Capitol," BuzzFeed News, January 9, 2021.
Accessed at https://www.buzzfeednews.com/article
/emmanuelfelton/black-capitol-police-racism-mob.

117. William H. Frey, "The US Will Become 'Minority White' in 2045, Census
Projects," The Brookings Institute, March 14, 2018. Accessed at https://
www.brookings.edu/blog/the-avenue/2018/03/14/the-us-will-become
-minority-white-in-2045-census-projects/.

118. "Understanding the 2020 Electorate: AP VoteCast Survey," NPR, updated
November 4, 2020. Accessed at https://www.npr.org/2020/11/03
/929478378/understanding-the-2020-electorate-ap-votecast-survey.

119. Dana Milbank, "Republicans Aren't Fighting Democrats. They're Fighting
Democracy," Washington Post, March 5, 2021. Accessed at https://www
.washingtonpost.com/opinions/2021/03/05/republicans-arent-fighting
-democrats-theyre-fighting-democracy/?arc404=true.

120. Suzette Hackney, "Black Voters Steer America Toward Moral Clarity in
Presidential Race," USA Today, November 12, 2020. Accessed at https://
www.usatoday.com/story/opinion/voices/2020/11/12/americans-didnt
-repudiate-donald-trump-but-black-voters-did-column/6222692002/.

121. "Statement by President Joe Biden on the House of Representatives
Passage of H.R. 1," The White House, March 4, 2021. Accessed at https://
www.whitehouse.gov/briefing-room/statements-releases/2021/03/04
/statement-by-president-joe-biden-on-the-house-of-representatives
-passage-of-h-r-1/.

122. Christopher Caldwell, "Senator Joe Manchin Has a Point," New York
Times, June 10, 2021. Accessed at https://www.nytimes.com/2021/06/10
/opinion/joe-manchin-voting-reform.html?searchResultPosition=1.

123. J. Edward Moreno, "Ocasio-Cortez Dismisses Proposed $1B cut:
'Defunding Police Means Defunding Police,'" Hill, June 30, 2020. Accessed
at https://thehill.com/homenews/house/505307-ocasio-cortez
-dismisses-proposed-1b-cut-defunding-police-means-defunding.

124. Bill McCarthy, "Ask PolitiFact: Where Was Alexandria Ocasio-Cortez
During the Capitol Riot?" Tampa Bay Times, February 5, 2021. Accessed at

https://www.tampabay.com/news/florida-politics/2021/02/05/ask-politifact-where-was-alexandria-ocasio-cortez-during-the-capitol-riot/.

125. Heather Long, Alyssa Flowers, and Andrew Van Dam, "Biden Stimulus Showers Money on Americans, Sharply Cutting Poverty and Favoring Individuals Over Businesses," *Washington Post*, March 6, 2021. Accessed at https://www.washingtonpost.com/business/2021/03/06/biden-stimulus-poverty-checks/.

126. "Executive Order on Advancing Racial Equity and Support for Underserved Communities Through the Federal Government," The White House, January 20, 2021. Accessed at https://www.whitehouse.gov/briefing-room/presidential-actions/2021/01/20/executive-order-advancing-racial-equity-and-support-for-underserved-communities-through-the-federal-government/.

127. Mark Moore, "Ex-NBA Star Charles Barkley Rips Politicians for Creating Racial Division," *New York Post*, April 5, 2021. Accessed at https://nypost.com/2021/04/05/charles-barkley-rips-politicians-for-stirring-racial-division/.

128. Adam Nagourney, "Mario Cuomo, Ex-New York Governor and Liberal Beacon, Dies at 82," January 1, 2015. Accessed at https://www.nytimes.com/2015/01/02/nyregion/mario-cuomo-new-york-governor-and-liberal-beacon-dies-at-82.html.

129. Heather McGhee, *The Sum of Us: What Racism Costs Everyone and How We Can Prosper Together* (One World, 2021).

130. Dave Davies, "'Sum of Us' Examines the Hidden Cost of Racism—For Everyone," *Fresh Air*, NPR, February 17, 2001. Accessed at https://www.npr.org/2021/02/17/968638759/sum-of-us-examines-the-hidden-cost-of-racism-for-everyone.

131. Jeff Stein, "'This Is the Fight': Demos's Heather McGhee on the Upside to Trump's Racial Politics," Vox, June 29, 2016. Accessed at https://www.vox.com/2016/6/29/12055272/demos-heather-mcghee-trump.

132. David E. Rosenbaum, "A Passion for Ideas: Jack French Kemp," *New York Times*, August 11, 1996. Accessed at https://www.nytimes.com/1996/08/11/us/a-passion-for-ideas-jack-french-kemp.html.

133. Sam Tanenhaus, "Note to Republicans: Channel Jack Kemp," *New York Times*, April 5, 2014. Accessed at https://www.nytimes.com/2014/04/06/sunday-review/note-to-republicans-channel-jack-kemp.html.

134. Jason Deparle, "How Jack Kemp Lost the War on Poverty," *New York Times* magazine, February 28, 1993. Accessed at https://www.nytimes.com/1993/02/28/magazine/how-jack-kemp-lost-the-war-on-poverty.html?searchResultPosition=1.

135. "Reagan National Defense Survey," The Ronald Reagan Presidential Foundation and Institute, February 2021. Accessed at https://www.reaganfoundation.org/reagan-institute/centers/peace-through-strength/reagan-institute-national-defense-survey/.

136. Lolita C. Baldor, "Pentagon to Better Screen Recruits for Extremist Behavior," Associated Press. April 9, 2021. Accessed at https://apnews.com/article/lloyd-austin-hate-groups-veterans-516c840617fbb9d92e57d5618871f083.

137. Will Kenton, "Affordable Care Act (ACA)," Investopedia, updated March 13, 2021. Accessed at https://www.investopedia.com/terms/a/affordable-care-act.asp.

138. Jeffrey M. Jones, "Affordable Care Act Approval Tied for High," Gallup, December 9, 2020. Accessed at https://news.gallup.com/poll/327431/affordable-care-act-approval-tied-high.aspx.

139. Cary Funk, Brian Kennedy, and Courtney Johnson, "Trust in Medical Scientists Has Grown in U.S., but Mainly Among Democrats," Pew Research Center, May 21, 2020. Accessed at https://www.pewresearch.org/science/2020/05/21/trust-in-medical-scientists-has-grown-in-u-s-but-mainly-among-democrats/.

140. Claudia Deane, Kim Parker, and Joihn Gramlich, "A Year of U.S. Public Opinion on the Coronavirus Pandemic," Pew Research Center, March 5, 2021. Accessed at https://www.pewresearch.org/2021/03/05/a-year-of-u-s-public-opinion-on-the-coronavirus-pandemic/.

141. "One in Five Still Shun Vaccine," Monmouth University Polling Institute, April 14, 2021. Accessed at https://www.monmouth.edu/polling-institute/reports/monmouthpoll_us_041421/.

142. Cary Funk and Alec Tyson, "Growing Share of Americans Say They Plan to Get a COVID-19 Vaccine—or Already Have," Pew Research Center, March 5, 2021. Accessed at https://www.pewresearch.org/science/2021/03/05/growing-share-of-americans-say-they-plan-to-get-a-covid-19-vaccine-or-already-have/.

143. Annie Karni, "Barron Trump Tested Positive for Coronavirus, Melania Trump Says," New York Times, October 14, 2020. Accessed at https://www.nytimes.com/2020/10/14/us/politics/barron-trump-coronavirus.html.

144. Meredith McGraw, "Trump Encourages Americans to Get the Covid Vaccine," Politico, March 16, 2021. Accessed at https://www.politico.com/news/2021/03/16/trump-americans-covid-vaccine-476479.

145. Annie Karni, "Barron Trump Tested Positive for Coronavirus, Melania Trump Says."

146. Kevin Breuninger, "Herman Cain Was on Ventilator Before He Died from Covid-19," CNBC, August 4, 2020. Accessed at https://www.cnbc

.com/2020/08/04/herman-cain-was-on-a-ventilator-before-he-died
-from-covid-19-top-aide-says.html.

147. Larry Buchanan, Quoctrung Bui, and Jugal K. Patel, "Black Lives Matter
      May Be the Largest Movement in U.S. History," *New York Times*, July 3,
      2020. Accessed at https://www.nytimes.com/interactive/2020/07/03
      /us/george-floyd-protests-crowd-size.html.

148. Jordyn Phelps and Elizabeth Thomas, "Trump at Mount Rushmore:
      Controversy, Fireworks and Personal Fascination," ABC News, July 4, 2020.
      Accessed at https://abcnews.go.com/Politics/trump-mount
      -rushmore-controversy-fireworks-personal-fascination/story?id=71595321.

149. Joe Sneve, "As Noem Scores Points for Her Pro-liberty Approach to
      COVID-19, Here's a Look at What She's Done," *Sioux Falls Argus Leader*,
      March 2, 2021. Accessed at https://www.argusleader.com/story
      /news/2021/03/02/how-governor-kristi-noem-handled-covid-19-south
      -dakota/6876347002/.

150. Mackenzie Bean, "COVID-19 Death Rates by State," *Becker's Hospital
      Review*, April 7, 2021. Accessed at https://www.beckershospitalreview
      .com/public-health/us-coronavirus-deaths-by-state-july-1.html.

151. "Governor Abbott Lifts Mask Mandate, Opens Texas 100 Percent," Office of
      the Texas Governor, March 2, 2021. Accessed at https://gov.texas.gov
      /news/post/governor-abbott-lifts-mask-mandate-opens-texas-100-percent.

152. Giovanni Russonello, "The Rising Politicization of Covid Vaccines," *New
      York Times*, updated April 7, 2021. Accessed at https://www.nytimes
      .com/2021/04/06/us/politics/covid-vaccine-skepticism.html
      ?searchResultPosition=1.

153. Patrick Svitek, "President Joe Biden Says Texas Made 'Big Mistake' by
      Lifting Mask Mandate, Suggests 'Neanderthal Thinking,'" *Texas Tribune*,
      March 3, 2021. Accessed at https://www.texastribune.org/2021/03/03
      /biden-texas-mask-order/.

154. "COVID-19 Vaccinations in the United States," U.S. Centers for Disease
      Control and Prevention. Accessed at https://covid.cdc.gov/covid-data
      -tracker/#vaccinations_vacc-total-admin-rate-total

155. "COVID-19 Dashboard," Center for Systems Science and Engineering
      at Johns Hopkins University (updated daily). Accessed at https://
      coronavirus.jhu.edu/map.html

156. Jennifer Latson, "The Vaccine Everyone Wanted," *Time*, February 23,
      2015. Accessed at https://time.com/3714090/salk-vaccine-history/.

157. Jennifer Rothenberg Gritz, "The Anti-Vaccine Movement Is Forgetting the
      Polio Epidemic," *Atlantic*, October 28, 2014. Accessed at https://www
      .theatlantic.com/health/archive/2014/10/the-anti-vaccine-movement-is
      -forgetting-the-polio-epidemic/381986/.

158. David M. Oshinsky, *Polio: An American Story* (Oxford University Press, 2006).

159. "Research Starters: Worldwide Deaths in World War II," The National WWII Museum. Accessed at https://www.nationalww2museum.org /students-teachers/student-resources/research-starters/research -starters-worldwide-deaths-world-war.

160. "A Brief History of Harvard College," Harvard College Handbook for Students. 2020–2021. Accessed at https://handbook.fas.harvard.edu/ book/brief-history-harvard-college; Doug Chesney, "The Nine Colonial Colleges," Going Colonial, October 3, 2018. Accessed at https://www .goingcolonial.com/colonial-colleges/.

161. "Declaration of Independence: A Transcription," National Archives, July 4, 1776. Accessed at https://www.archives.gov/founding-docs/declaration -transcript.

162. John Fea, Laura Gifford, R. Marie Griffith, and Lerone A. Martin, "Evangelism and Politics," Organization of American Historians. Accessed at https://www.oah.org/tah/issues/2018/november/evangelicalism-and -politics/.

163. "Do unto others as you would have them do unto you," Dictonary.com. Accessed at https://www.dictionary.com/browse/do-unto-others-as-you -would-have-them-do-unto-you.

164. Megan Brenan, "Religiosity Largely Unaffected by Events of 2020 in U.S.," Gallup, March 29, 2021. Accessed at https://news.gallup.com/poll/341957/ religiosity-largely-unaffected-events-2020.aspx?utm_source=alert&utm _medium=email&utm_content=morelink&utm_campaign=syndication.

165. Sarah Pulliam Bailey, "Church Membership in the U.S. Has Fallen Below the Majority for the First Time in Nearly a Century," *Washington Post*, March 29, 2021. Accessed at https://www.washingtonpost.com /religion/2021/03/29/church-membership-fallen-below-majority/.

166. "Confidence in Institutions," Gallup, 2020. Accessed at https://news .gallup.com/poll/1597/Confidence-Institutions.aspx.

167. Joyce A. Martin, M.P.H., Brady E. Hamilton, Ph.D., Michelle J.K. Osterman, M.H.S., and Anne K. Driscoll, Ph.D., "Births: Final Data for 2018," National Vital Statistics Reports, Centers for Disease Control and Prevention. November 27, 2019. Accessed at https://www.cdc.gov/nchs /data/nvsr/nvsr68/nvsr68_13-508.pdf.

168. Larry Bilotta, "18 Shocking Children and Divorce Statistics," Marriage Success Secrets. Accessed at http://www.marriage-success-secrets.com /statistics-about-children-and-divorce.html.

CHAPTER 2

1. "Spring 2021 Harvard Youth Poll," The Institute of Politics at Harvard University. Accessed June 15, 2021. Accessed at https://iop.harvard.edu/youth-poll/spring-2021-harvard-youth-poll.

2. Steven Sloan, "AP-NORC Poll: Few in US Say Democracy Is Working Very Well," AP NEWS, Associated Press, February 8, 2021. Accessed at https://apnews.com/article/ap-norc-poll-us-democracy-403434c2e728e42a955c72a652a59318.

3. "UMass Amherst/WCVB Poll Finds Nearly Half of Americans Say the Federal Government Definitely Should Not Pay Reparations to the Descendants of Slaves," UMass Amherst. Accessed June 15, 2021, https://www.umass.edu/news/article/umass-amherstwcvb-poll-finds-nearly-half.

4. "Do You Support or Oppose the Black Lives Matter Movement?" Civiqs, n.d. Accessed at https://civiqs.com/results/black_lives_matter?annotations=true&uncertainty=true&zoomIn=true.

5. "Many Value Democratic Principles, but Few Think Democracy Is Working Well These Days - AP-NORC," AP, March 4, 2021. Accessed at https://apnorc.org/projects/many-value-democratic-principles-but-few-think-democracy-is-working-well-these-days/.

6. "Spring 2021 Harvard Youth Poll," The Institute of Politics at Harvard University. Accessed June 15, 2021, https://iop.harvard.edu/youth-poll/spring-2021-harvard-youth-poll.

CHAPTER 3

1. "Election Results," Fox News. Accessed at https://www.foxnews.com/elections/2020/general-results.

2. Joe Biden, "Inaugural Address by President Joseph R. Biden, Jr."

3. "List of U.S. Congress Incumbents Who Did Not Run for Re-election in 2020," Ballotpedia. Accessed at https://ballotpedia.org/List_of_U.S._Congress_incumbents_who_did_not_run_for_re-election_in_2020.

4. Colby Itkowitz, "Ohio GOP Sen. Rob Portman Announces He's Retiring, Creating an Open Seat in 2022," *Washington Post*, January 25, 2021. Accessed at https://www.washingtonpost.com/politics/portman-senate-republicans/2021/01/25/d329d28c-5f2a-11eb-9061-07abcc1f9229_story.html.

5. Michael Lind, "To Have and to Have Not," *Harper's* magazine, June 1995. Accessed at http://www.hartford-hwp.com/archives/45/006.html.

6. Douglas E. Schoen, *Hopelessly Divided: The New Crisis in American Politics and What It Means for 2012 and Beyond* (Rowman & Littlefield, 2012).

7. *"A Republic, if You Can Keep It,"* Podcast interview with Richard Gephardt, Tallberg Foundation, January 29, 2021. Accessed at https://tallbergfoundation.org/podcasts/a-republic-if-you-can-keep-it/.

8. Thomas B. Edsall, "How Far Left Is Too Far Left for 2020 Democrats?" *New York Times*, April 10, 2019. Accessed at https://www.nytimes.com/2019/04/10/opinion/democratic-candidates-primaries.html.

9. Gwen Ifill, "The 1992 Campaign: Democrats; Clinton Says Foes Sow Intolerance," *New York Times*, September 12, 1992. Accessed at https://www.nytimes.com/1992/09/12/us/the-1992-campaign-democrats-clinton-says-foes-sow-intolerance.html.

10. "President Clinton's Vision," Clinton Presidential Center. Accessed at https://www.clintonfoundation.org/clinton-presidential-center/about/president-clintons-vision.

11. Alison Mitchell, "Stung by Defeats in '94, Clinton Regrouped and Co-opted G.O.P. Strategies," *New York Times*, November 7, 1996. Accessed at https://www.nytimes.com/1996/11/07/us/stung-by-defeats-in-94-clinton-regrouped-and-co-opted-gop-strategies.html.

12. Groucho Marx, "I'm Against It," from the film *Horse Feathers*, 1932. Accessed at https://www.youtube.com/watch?v=xHash5takWU.

13. Estelle Sommeiller and Mark Price, "The New Gilded Age: Income Inequality in the U.S. by State, Metropolitan Area and County," Economic Policy Institute, July 19, 2018. Accessed at https://www.epi.org/publication/the-new-gilded-age-income-inequality-in-the-u-s-by-state-metropolitan-area-and-county/.

14. Karl Marx and Friedrich Engels, *The Communist Manifesto*, 1848.

15. James Traub, "What Should Drive Biden's Foreign Policy?" *New York Times*, January 29, 2021. Accessed at https://www.nytimes.com/2021/01/29/opinion/biden-foreign-policy.html.

16. Michael Kranish, "Before Riot, Trump Said 'We Got to Get Rid' of Rep. Liz Cheney. Now She Supports Impeaching Him," *Washington Post*, January 12, 2021. Accessed at https://www.washingtonpost.com/politics/cheney-trump-house-impeach/2021/01/12/648c677a-54d2-11eb-a08b-f1381ef3d207_story.html.

17. Matthew Choi, "Ignoring Calls to Pull Back, Gaetz Slams Cheney in Her Home State," *Politico*, January 28, 2021. Accessed at https://www.politico.com/news/2021/01/28/matt-gaetz-liz-cheney-rally-463582.

18. Catie Edmondson and Nicholas Fandos, "House Republicans Choose to Keep Liz Cheney in Vote to Impeach Trump," *New York Times*, February 3, 2021. Accessed at https://www.nytimes.com/2021/02/03/us/liz-cheney-vote.html.

19. Paul Kane, "The Fading GOP Establishment Moves to Support Cheney as Trump Attacks and McCarthy Keeps His Distance," *Washington Post*,

April 24, 2021. Accessed at https://www.washingtonpost.com/powerpost /cheney-trump-mccarthy-orlando/2021/04/23/0b41df94-a3a4-11eb-85fc -06664ff4489d_story.html.

20. Paul Kane, "McCarthy Pushes Out Liz Cheney, Then Pushes Bipartisanship at the White House," *Washington Post*, May 12, 2021. Accessed at https://www.washingtonpost.com/powerpost/mccarthy /2021/05/12/395cec52-b33f-11eb-a980-a60af976ed44_story.html.

21. Jonathan Karl, Benjamin Siegel, and Allison Pecorin, "Liz Cheney Says She Regrets Voting for Trump in 2020," ABC News, May 14, 2021. Accessed at https://abcnews.go.com/Politics/liz-cheney-regrets-voting -trump-2020/story?id=77695446.

22. Paul Steinhauser, "Gaetz Tells Kinzinger to 'Bring It' as GOP Feud Heats Up," Fox News, February 11, 2021. Accessed at https://www.foxnews.com /politics/gaetz-tells-kinzinger-to-bring-it-as-gop-feud-heats-up.

23. Evan Perez, Paula Reid, Scott Glover, and David Shortell, "Gaetz Probe Includes Scrutiny of Potential Corruption Tied to Medical Marijuana Industry," CNN, April 23, 2021. Accessed at https://www.cnn.com /2021/04/23/politics/gaetz-probe-public-corruption-medical-marijuana /index.html.

24. Chris Cillizza, "This Democratic Congresswoman Just Spoke Some Hard Truth to Her Party," CNN, November 6, 2020. Accessed at https://www .cnn.com/2020/11/06/politics/abigail-spanberger-house-democrats -2020-election/index.html; Rachael Bade and Erica Werner, "Centrist House Democrats Lash Out at Liberal Colleagues, Blame Far-Left Views for Costing the Party Seats," *Washington Post*, November 6, 2020. Accessed at https://www.washingtonpost.com/politics/house-democrats -pelosi-election/2020/11/05/1ddae5ca-1f6e-11eb-90dd-abd0f7086a91 _story.html.

25. Ian Anson, "Americans Distrusted U.S. Democracy Long Before Trump's Russia Problem," Government Executive, August 24, 2018. Accessed at https://www.govexec.com/management/2018/08/americans-distrusted -us-democracy-long-trumps-russia-problem/150795/.

26. Samuel P. Huntington, "Dead Souls: The Denationalization of the American Elite," National Interest, March 1, 2004. Accessed at https:// nationalinterest.org/article/dead-souls-the-denationalization-of-the -american-elite-620.

27. Betsy Jones, Daniel Cox, Rachel Cooper, and Robert P. Lienesch, "America's Future: 1950 or 2050? Findings from the 2016 American Values Survey," Public Religion Research Institute, October 15, 2016. Accessed at https:// www.prri.org/research/poll-1950s-2050-divided-nations-direction -post-election/.

28. Douglas E. Schoen, *Hopelessly Divided: The New Crisis in American Politics and What it Means for 2012 and Beyond*.

29. Jeffrey M. Jones, "Congress' Job Approval Rating Improved by 10 Points," Gallup, January 29, 2021. Accessed at https://news.gallup.com /poll/328958/congress-job-approval-rating-improved-points.aspx.

30. David E. Shi, "A War of Independence that Divided American Colonies," *Atlanta Journal-Constitution*, August 11, 2012. Accessed at https://www .ajc.com/news/opinion/war-independence-that-divided-american -colonies/QNyLHauR5rBprEGIAF630O/.

31. Steve Corbin, "Most Americans are Politically Exhausted. Here's How They Can Change Things," *Des Moines Register*, February 20, 2020. Accessed at https://www.desmoinesregister.com/story/opinion/columnists /iowa-view/2020/02/20/politically-exhausted-americans-majority -bipartisanship/4800603002/. See also the More in Common website at https://www.moreincommon.com/.

32. Al Gore, *The Future: Six Drivers of Global Change* (Random House, 2013).

33. Samantha Subin, "Capitol Riot Reaction: Corporations and the Future of Political Donations," CNBC, January 13, 2021. Accessed at https://www .cnbc.com/2021/01/13/capitol-riot-reaction-corporations-and-political -donations.html.

34. Richard H. Pildes, "Small Dollars, Big Changes," *Washington Post*, February 6, 2020. Accessed at https://www.washingtonpost.com/outlook /2020/02/06/small-dollars-big-changes/?arc404=true.

35. OpenSecrets.org.

36. Reid Wilson, "Georgia Senate Races Shatter Spending Records," *Hill*, January 5, 2021. Accessed at https://thehill.com/homenews/campaign /532749-georgia-senate-races-shatter-spending-records.

37. Michael Levy, "Political Action Committee," Britannica, October 5, 2011. Accessed at https://www.britannica.com/topic/political-action -committee.

38. "What is a PAC?" OpenSecrets.org. Accessed at https://www.opensecrets .org/political-action-committees-pacs/what-is-a-pac.

39. Independence USA PAC website. Accessed at https://www .independenceusapac.org/.

40. "2020 Election to Cost $14 billion, Blowing Away Spending Records," Opensecrets.org. October 28, 2020. Accessed at https://www.opensecrets .org/news/2020/10/cost-of-2020-election-14billion-update/.

41. Jacob S. Hacker and Paul Pierson, *Winner-Take-All Politics: How Washington Made the Rich Richer—and Turned Its Back on the Middle Class* (Simon & Schuster, 2011).

42. Lauren Feiner, "Facebook Spent More on Lobbying Than Any Other Big Tech Company in 2020," CNBC, January 22, 2021. Accessed at https://

www.cnbc.com/2021/01/22/facebook-spent-more-on-lobbying-than-any
-other-big-tech-company-in-2020.html.

43. "Lobbying Data Summary," OpenSecrets.org, Center for Responsive
Politics. Accessed at https://www.opensecrets.org/federal-lobbying.

44. Julie Bykowicz and Brody Mullins, "Washington Lobbyists Know Biden
Well—as Their Former Boss," *Wall Street Journal*, November 16, 2020.
Accessed at https://www.wsj.com/articles/washington-lobbyists-know
-biden-wellas-their-former-boss-11605522603.

45. Christina Wilkie, "What the Michael Cohen Scandal Reveals About
Corporate Lobbying in the Age of Trump," CNBC, May 13, 2018. Accessed
at https://finance.yahoo.com/news/michael-cohen-scandal-reveals
-corporate-130000727.html.

46. "Revolving Door," OpenSecrets.org. Accessed at https://www.opensecrets
.org/revolving/index.php.

47. Ted Barrett, Kate Bolduan, and Deirdre Walsh, "'Super Committee' Fails
to Reach Agreement," CNN, November 21, 2011. Accessed at https://www
.cnn.com/2011/11/21/politics/super-committee/index.html.

48. Jack Abramoff, *Capitol Punishment: The Hard Truth About Washington
Corruption From America's Most Notorious Lobbyist* (WND Books, 2011).

49. Nathaniel Popper, "Disgraced Lobbyist Jack Abramoff Headed Back to
Jail," *New York Times*, June 25, 2020. Accessed at https://www
.nytimes.com/2020/06/25/us/politics/jack-abramoff-marijuana
-cryptocurrency.html.

50. "2020 Census Apportionment Delivered to the President," U.S. Census
Bureau, April 26, 2021. Accessed at https://www.census.gov/newsroom
/press-releases/2021/2020-census-apportionment-results.html.

51. "Redistricting and the Supreme Court: The Most Significant Cases,"
National Conference of State Legislatures, April 25, 2019. Accessed at
https://www.ncsl.org/research/redistricting/redistricting-and-the
-supreme-court-the-most-significant-cases.aspx.

52. Adam Liptak, "Supreme Court Bars Challenges to Partisan
Gerrymandering," *New York Times*, June 27, 2019. Accessed at https://
www.nytimes.com/2019/06/27/us/politics/supreme-court
-gerrymandering.html.

53. Nick Reynolds, "Republican Parties in 10 Wyoming Counties Have Now
Censured Cheney for Her Impeachment Vote," *Casper Star Tribune*,
February 1, 2021. Accessed at https://trib.com/news/state-and-regional
/govt-and-politics/republican-parties-in-10-wyoming-counties-have-
now-censured-cheney-for-her-impeachment-vote/article_455804e5
-991d-5d64-ae94-ba10bf34ebf2.html.

54. "U.S. Political Conventions & Campaigns," Northeastern University.
Accessed at https://conventions.cps.neu.edu/history/1789-1832/.

55. Trip Gabriel, "Republicans Fear Flawed Candidates Could Imperil Key Senate Seats," *New York Times*, March 24, 2021. Accessed at https://www.nytimes.com/2021/03/24/us/politics/senate-races-missouri-alabama.html?action=click&module=News&pgtype=Homepage.

56. Dave Roos, "5 Presidents Who Lost the Popular Vote but Won the Election," History.com. July 23, 2020. Accessed at https://www.history.com/news/presidents-electoral-college-popular-vote.

57. Ben Smith, "Jeff Zucker Helped Create Donald Trump. That Show May Be Ending," *New York Times*, September 20, 2020 (updated February 4, 2021). Accessed at https://www.nytimes.com/2020/09/20/business/media/jeff-zucker-helped-create-donald-trump-that-show-may-be-ending.html.

58. "Alexandria Ocasio-Cortez," Ballotpedia. Accessed at https://ballotpedia.org/Alexandria_Ocasio-Cortez.

59. "Iowa Quick Facts," State Library of Iowa. Accessed at https://www.iowadatacenter.org/quickfacts.

60. "Inequities Between New Hampshire Racial and Ethnic Groups Impact Opportunities to Thrive," New Hampshire Fiscal Policy Institute, June 30, 2020. Accessed at https://nhfpi.org/resource/inequities-between-new-hampshire-racial-and-ethnic-groups-impact-opportunities-to-thrive/.

61. Maria Cramer, "Besides Iowa, These Are the States with Caucuses," *New York Times*, February 4, 2020 (updated February 13, 2020). Accessed at https://www.nytimes.com/2020/02/04/us/politics/what-states-caucus.html.

62. Allison Kopicki, "Five Years Later, Poll Finds Disapproval of Bailout," *New York Times*, September 26, 2013. Accessed at https://economix.blogs.nytimes.com/2013/09/26/five-years-later-poll-finds-disapproval-of-bailout/?searchResultPosition=1.

63. Eric Lipton and Raymond Hernandez, "A Champion of Wall Street Reaps Benefits," *New York Times*, December 13, 2008. Accessed at https://www.nytimes.com/2008/12/14/business/14schumer.html?searchResultPosition=1.

64. Bruce Edwards, "College Supports Lehman CEO," *Rutland Herald*, October 17, 2018. Accessed at https://www.rutlandherald.com/news/college-supports-lehman-ceo/article_e70c6157-64b0-5618-b7d8-921f758f88ef.html.

65. D'Angelo Gore, "Obama's 'Economic Advisers,'" FactCheck.org, October 9, 2018. Accessed at https://www.factcheck.org/2008/10/obamas-economic-advisers/.

66. Scott Rasmussen and Doug Schoen, *Mad as Hell: How the Tea Party Movement Is Fundamentally Remaking Our Two-Party System* (Harper, 2010).

67. Ashley Parker, Josh Dawsey, and Yasmeen Abutaleb, "Ten Days: After an Early Coronavirus Warning, Trump Is Distracted as He Downplays Threat," *Washington Post*, September 16, 2020. Accessed at https://www .washingtonpost.com/politics/trump-woodward-coronavirus-downplay -ten-days/2020/09/16/6529318c-f69e-11ea-a275-1a2c2d36e1f1_story.html.

68. Niv Elis, "CBO Projects CARES Act Will Cost $1.76 Trillion, Not $2.2 Trillion," *Hill*, April 16, 2020. Accessed at https://thehill.com/policy /finance/economy/493218-cbo-projects-cares-act-will-cost-176-trillion -not-22-trillion.

69. Allan Sloan: "The CARES Act Sent You a $1,200 Check but Gave Millionaires and Billionaires Far More," ProPublica, June 8, 2020. Accessed at https://www.propublica.org/article/the-cares-act-sent-you-a -1-200-check-but-gave-millionaires-and-billionaires-far-more.

70. Rachel Siegel, Jeff Stein, and Mike DeBonis, "Here's What's in the $900 Billion Stimulus Package," *Washington Post*, December 27, 2020. Accessed at https://www.washingtonpost.com/business/2020/12/20 /stimulus-package-details/.

71. Sam Rayburn quote from 1953, quoted in *Speak, Mr. Speaker* (1978). Accessed at https://en.wikiquote.org/wiki/Sam_Rayburn.

CHAPTER 4

1. Lois Beckett, "At least 25 Americans Were Killed During Protests and Political Unrest in 2020," *Guardian*, October 31, 2020. Accessed at https:// www.theguardian.com/world/2020/oct/31/americans-killed-protests -political-unrest-acled.

2. Scott Rasmussen and Doug Schoen, *Mad as Hell*.

3. Casse Mudde and Cristobal Rovira Kaltwasser, *Populism: A Very Short Introduction* (Oxford University Press, 2017).

4. Cas Mudde, "The Problem with Populism," *Guardian*, February 17, 2015. Accessed at https://www.theguardian.com/commentisfree/2015 /feb/17/problem-populism-syriza-podemos-dark-side-europe.

5. Geoffrey Kabaservice, "Wild Populism Has a Long History in US Politics, but Trump Is Surely Unique," *Guardian*, January 14, 2017. Accessed at https://www.theguardian.com/commentisfree/2017/jan/15/wild -populism-long-history-us-politics-trump-surely-unique.

6. Isaac Chotiner, "How Socialist Is Bernie Sanders?" *New Yorker*, March 2, 2020. Accessed at https://www.newyorker.com/news/q-and-a/how -socialist-is-bernie-sanders.

7. Paul Taggart, *Populism* (Open University Press, 2000).

8. Marc Fisher, "Eroding Trust, Spreading Fear: The Historical Ties Between Pandemics and Extremism," *Washington Post*, February 15, 2021. Accessed at https://www.washingtonpost.com/politics/pandemics-spawn-extremism/2021/02/14/d4f7195c-6b1f-11eb-ba56-d7e2c8defa31_story.html.

9. Mark Rice-Oxley and Ammar Kalia, "How to Spot a Populist," *Guardian*. December 3, 2018.

10. "Presidential Election Results," Fox News. 2020. Accessed at https://www.foxnews.com/elections/2020/general-results.

11. Steve Liesman, "A Large Share of Republicans Want Trump to Remain Head of the Party, CNBC Survey Shows," CNBC, February 12, 2021. Accessed at https://www.cnbc.com/2021/02/12/a-large-share-of-republicans-want-trump-to-remain-head-of-the-party-cnbc-survey.html.

12. David Barstow, Susanne Craig, and Russ Buettner: "Trump Engaged in Suspect Tax Schemes as He Reaped Riches From His Father," *New York Times*, October 2, 2018. Accessed at https://www.nytimes.com/interactive/2018/10/02/us/politics/donald-trump-tax-schemes-fred-trump.html.

13. Russ Buettner and Susanne Craig, "Decade in the Red: Trump Tax Figures Show over $1 Billion in Business Losses," *New York Times*, May 8, 2019. Accessed at https://www.nytimes.com/interactive/2019/05/07/us/politics/donald-trump-taxes.html.

14. "Bernie Sanders Net Worth," Celebrity Net Worth. 2020. Accessed at https://www.celebritynetworth.com/richest-politicians/democrats/bernie-sanders-net-worth/; "Elizabeth Warren Net Worth," Celebrity Net Worth. 2020. Accessed at https://www.celebritynetworth.com/richest-politicians/democrats/elizabeth-warren-net-worth/.

15. Grant Suneson, "The Net Worth of Every US President from George Washington to Donald Trump," *USA Today*, February 13, 2019. Accessed at https://www.usatoday.com/story/money/2019/02/13/donald-trump-george-washington-net-worth-us-presidents/39011559/.

16. "#339 Donald Trump," *Forbes*, February 13, 2021. Accessed at https://www.forbes.com/profile/donald-trump/?sh=7ee118df47bd.

17. Hannah Hutyra, "115 Thomas Jefferson Quotes on Life, Government, and Religion," KeepInspiring.me, July 14, 2017. Accessed at https://www.keepinspiring.me/thomas-jefferson-quotes/.

18. Hannah Hutyra, "115 Thomas Jefferson Quotes on Life, Government, and Religion."

19. "Declaration of Independence: A Transcription."

20. Frederic Austin Ogg, *The Reign of Andrew Jackson* (CreateSpace, 2016).

21. Harry Watson, "Andrew Jackson, America's Original Anti-Establishment Candidate," *Smithsonian Magazine*, March 31, 2016. Accessed at https://

www.smithsonianmag.com/history/andrew-jackson-americas-original
-anti-establishment-candidate-180958621/.

22. Susan B. Glasser, "The Man Who Put Andrew Jackson in Trump's Oval
     Office," *Politico*, January 22, 2018. Accessed at https://www.politico.com
     /magazine/story/2018/01/22/andrew-jackson-donald-trump-216493/.

23. Jenna Johnson and Karen Tumulty, "Trump Cites Andrew Jackson as
     His Hero—and a Reflection of Himself," *Washington Post*, March 15, 2017.
     Accessed at https://www.washingtonpost.com/politics/trump-cites
     -andrew-jackson-as-his-hero--and-a-reflection-of-himself/2017/03/15
     /4da8dc8c-0995-11e7-a15f-a58d4a988474_story.html.

24. Michael Barone, "A Short History of American Populism," *Wall Street
     Journal*, February 4, 2010. Accessed at https://www.wsj.com/articles/SB10
     0014240527487033890004575033281965244048.

25. William Jennings Bryan, "William Jennings Bryan's 'Cross of Gold'
     Speech," July 9, 1896, at the Democratic National Convention, Chicago.
     Accessed at https://www.mtholyoke.edu/acad/intrel/speech/goldcros
     .htm.

26. William Jennings Bryan, "'Cross of Gold' Speech."

27. "William Jennings Bryan," Britannica, Updated January 7, 2021. Accessed
     at https://www.britannica.com/biography/William-Jennings-Bryan.

28. Chris Stirewalt, "From Bryan to Bernie," Fox News, February 9, 2020.
     Accessed at https://www.foxnews.com/politics/from-bryan-to-bernie.

29. Arthur Levine, "Donald Trump vs. William Jennings Bryan: What the
     Election of 1896 Teaches Us About 2016," *New York Daily News*, November
     29, 2016. Accessed at https://www.nydailynews.com/opinion/donald
     -trump-william-jennings-bryan-article-1.2891467.

30. Alan Brinkley, "Railing Against the Rich: A Great American Tradition,"
     Wall Street Journal, February 7, 2009. Accessed at https://www.wsj
     .com/articles/SB123396621006159013.

31. Annika Neklason, "When Demagogic Populism Swings Left," *Atlantic*,
     March 3, 2019. Accessed at https://www.theatlantic.com/politics
     /archive/2019/03/huey-long-was-donald-trumps-left-wing-counterpart
     /583933/.

32. Steven M. Gillon, "Why Populism in America Is a Double-Edged Sword,"
     History.com, updated February 7, 2019. Accessed at https://www.history
     .com/news/why-populism-in-america-is-a-double-edged-sword.

33. "Joseph McCarthy," History.com, updated May 16, 2019. Accessed at
     https://www.history.com/topics/cold-war/joseph-mccarthy.

34. Geoffrey Kabaservice, "Wild Populism Has a Long History in US Politics,
     but Trump Is Surely Unique."

35. Howell Raines, "George Wallace, Segregation Symbol, Dies at 79," *New York Times*, September 14, 1998. Accessed at https://www.nytimes .com/1998/09/14/us/george-wallace-segregation-symbol-dies-at-79.html.

36. Richard Pearson, "Former Ala. Gov. George C. Wallace Dies," *Washington Post*, September 14, 1998. Accessed at https://www.washingtonpost.com /wp-srv/politics/daily/sept98/wallace.htm.

37. "California Proposition 13, Tax Limitations Initiative (1978)," Ballotpedia. Accessed at https://ballotpedia.org/California_Proposition_13,_Tax _Limitations_Initiative_(1978).

38. John Fensterwald, "Defeat of Prop. 15 to Raise Commercial Property Taxes Denies Schools More Revenue," EdSource, November 11, 2020. Accessed at https://edsource.org/2020/defeat-of-prop-15-to-raise -commercial-property-taxes-denies-schools-more-revenue/643574.

39. John Myers, "Proposition 13 Treats All California Property Taxes the Same. Voters Could Change That in 2020," *Los Angeles Times*, August 15, 2019. Accessed at https://www.latimes.com/california/story/2019 -08-14/california-proposition-13-business-taxes-split-roll.

40. Clyde Haberman, "The California Ballot Measure That Inspired a Tax Revolt," *New York Times*, October 16, 2016. Accessed at https://www .nytimes.com/2016/10/17/us/the-california-ballot-measure-that-inspired -a-tax-revolt.html.

41. "Ronald Reagan," Biography.com, April 27, 2017 (updated November 12, 2020). Accessed at https://www.biography.com/us-president/ronald -reagan.

42. Kimberly Amadeo, "US Debt by President by Dollar and Percentage," The Balance, updated November 5, 2020. Accessed at https://www.thebalance .com/us-debt-by-president-by-dollar-and-percent-3306296.

43. Suzanne McGee, "How Billionaire Ross Perot Brought Populism Back to Presidential Politics," History.com, October 6, 2020. Accessed at https:// www.history.com/news/ross-perot-populist-1992-election-changed -politics.

44. Lesley Kennedy, "The 1994 Midterms: When Newt Gingrich Helped Republicans Win Big," History.com, October 9, 2018. Accessed at https:// www.history.com/news/midterm-elections-1994-republican-revolution -gingrich-contract-with-america.

45. David Winston, "The Contact with America: The Power of a Positive Message," The Ripon Forum, Ripon Society, September 2014. Accessed at https://riponsociety.org/article/the-contract-with-america-the-power-of -a-positive-message/.

46. David Winston: "The Contract with America's Legacy," *Roll Call*, September 25, 2019. Accessed at https://www.rollcall.com/2019/09/25 /the-contract-with-americas-legacy/.

47. "Great Recession," History.com, updated October 11, 2019. Accessed at https://www.history.com/topics/21st-century/recession.

48. Brooke Niemeyer, "There Have Been 6.3 Million Foreclosures in the U.S. in the Last Decade," MarketWatch, May 31, 2016. Accessed at https://www.marketwatch.com/story/there-were-63-million-foreclosures-in-the-last-decade-2016-05-31.

49. "The Recession of 2007–2009: BLS Spotlight on Statistics," Bureau of Labor Statistics, February 2012. Accessed at https://www.bls.gov/spotlight/2012/recession/pdf/recession_bls_spotlight.pdf.

50. Sarah Childress, "How Much Did the Financial Crisis Cost?" *Frontline*, PBS, May 31, 2012. Accessed at https://www.pbs.org/wgbh/frontline/article/how-much-did-the-financial-crisis-cost/.

51. "Great Recession," History.com.

52. Michael Erman, "Five Years After Lehman, Americans Still Angry at Wall Street: Reuters/Ipsos Poll," Reuters, September 15, 2013. Accessed at https://www.reuters.com/article/us-wallstreet-crisis-idUSBRE98E06Q20130915.

53. Philip Stephens, "Populism Is the True Legacy of the Global Financial Crisis," *Financial Times*, August 30, 2018. Accessed at https://www.ft.com/content/687c0184-aaa6-11e8-94bd-cba20d67390c.

54. Ross Douthat, "The Great Bailout Backlash," *New York Times*, October 25, 2010. Accessed at https://www.nytimes.com/2010/10/25/opinion/25douthat.html.

55. "Boston Tea Party," History.com, updated September 25, 2020. Accessed at https://www.history.com/topics/american-revolution/boston-tea-party.

56. "CNBC's Rick Santelli's Chicago Tea Party," YouTube, February 19, 2009. Accessed at https://www.youtube.com/watch?v=zp-Jw-5Kx8k.

57. Steven Perlberg, "Rick Santelli Started the Tea Party With a Rant Exactly 5 Years Ago Today—Here's How He Feels About It Now," *Business Insider*, February 19, 2014. Accessed at https://www.businessinsider.com/rick-santelli-tea-party-rant-2014-2.

58. Kimberly Amadeo, "The Tea Party Movement, Its Economic Platform, and History," The Balance, December 3, 2020. Accessed at https://www.thebalance.com/tea-party-movement-economic-platform-3305571.

59. Jeremy W. Peters, "The Tea Party Didn't Get What It Wanted, but It Did Unleash the Politics of Anger," *New York Times*, August 28, 2019 (updated August 30, 2019). Accessed at https://www.nytimes.com/2019/08/28/us/politics/tea-party-trump.html.

60. Patrik Jonsson, "Amid Harsh Criticism, 'Tea Party' Slips into the Mainstream," *Christian Science Monitor*, April 3, 2010. Accessed at https://www.csmonitor.com/USA/Politics/2010/0403/Amid-harsh-criticisms-tea-party-slips-into-the-mainstream.

61. "45% See Gap Between Governed and Those Who Govern As Comparable to American Revolution," Rasmussen Reports, June 15, 2011. Accessed at https://www.rasmussenreports.com/public_content/politics/general _politics/june_2011/45_see_gap_between_governed_and_those_who _govern_as_comparable_to_american_revolution.

62. Sean J. Miller, "Survey: Four in 10 Tea Party Members Are Democrats or Independents," *Hill*, April 4, 2010. Accessed at https://thehill.com /blogs/ballot-box/polls/90541-survey-four-in-10-tea-party-members -dem-or-indie.

63. Aaron Blake, "Obama: The Man of Many Slogans," *Washington Post*, July 10, 2012. Accessed at https://www.washingtonpost.com/blogs /the-fix/post/president-obama-a-man-of-many-slogans/2012/07/10 /gJQAf8UlaW_blog.html.

64. Jeff Sommer, "The War Against Too Much of Everything," *New York Times*, December 22, 2012. Accessed at https://www.nytimes.com/2012/12/23 /business/adbusters-war-against-too-much-of-everything.html.

65. Scott Rasmussen and Doug Schoen, *Mad as Hell*.

66. "Donald J. Trump Republican Nomination Acceptance Speech," DonaldJTrump.com. July 2016. Accessed at https://assets.donaldjtrump .com/DJT_Acceptance_Speech.pdf.

67. Jeremy W. Peters, "The Tea Party Didn't Get What It Wanted, but It Did Unleash the Politics of Anger."

68. Brian Greene, "How 'Occupy Wall Street' Started and Spread," *U.S. News and World Report*, October 17, 2011. Accessed at https://www.usnews.com /news/washington-whispers/articles/2011/10/17/how-occupy-wall-street -started-and-spread.

69. Jeff Sommer, "The War Against Too Much of Everything."

70. Brian Greene, "How 'Occupy Wall Street' Started and Spread."

71. Emily Stewart, "We Are (Still) the 99 Percent," Vox, April 30, 2019. Accessed at https://www.vox.com/the-highlight/2019/4/23/18284303 /occupy-wall-street-bernie-sanders-dsa-socialism.

72. Fareed Zakaria, "Mainstream Republicans Have Tolerated Extremism for Years. Can They Finally Control It?" *Washington Post*, February 18, 2021. Accessed at https://www.washingtonpost.com/opinions/mainstream -republicans-have-tolerated-extremism-for-years-can-they -finally-control-it/2021/02/18/f3c2cd72-722c-11eb-85fa-e0ccb3660358 _story.html.

73. Justin Schweitzer, "Ending the Tipped Minimum Wage Will Reduce Poverty and Inequality," Center for American Progress, March 30, 2021. Accessed at https://www.americanprogress.org/issues/poverty/reports /2021/03/30/497673/ending-tipped-minimum-wage-will-reduce-poverty -inequality/.

74. Carmen Reinicke, "A $15 Minimum Wage Would Give 19 Million Women a Raise—But It Might Not Happen Anytime Soon," CNBC, March 2, 2021. Accessed at https://www.cnbc.com/2021/03/02/a-15-minimum-wage-would-give-19-million-women-a-raise-but-not-soon.html.

75. Michael Collins and Paul Davidson, "$15 Minimum Wage Would Boost Pay for Millions but Would Cost 1.4 Million Jobs, Report Says."

76. Ryan Cooper, "Biden Warms Up to the Green New Deal," *The Week*, February 12, 2021. Accessed at https://theweek.com/articles/966321/biden-warms-green-new-deal.

77. Brian Steinberg, "Fox News Lays Off Political Editor Stirewalt, Digital Employees Amid Reorganization," *Variety*, January 19, 2021. Accessed at https://variety.com/2021/tv/news/fox-news-layoffs-digital-employees-1234887929/; Jeremy Barr, "Fox News Overhauls Daily Schedule, Moving News Anchor Martha MacCallum to Make Way for Opinion Expansion," *Washington Post*, January 11, 2021. Accessed at https://www.washingtonpost.com/media/2021/01/11/fox-news-overhaul-news-opinion-cnn-tapper-blitzer/.

CHAPTER 5

1. Barry Goldwater, "Goldwater's 1964 Acceptance Speech," *Washington Post*. Accessed at https://www.washingtonpost.com/wp-srv/politics/daily/may98/goldwaterspeech.htm.

2. Lee Edwards, "Barry Goldwater—The Most Consequential Loser of the 20th Century," The Heritage Foundation, July 18, 2019. Accessed at https://www.heritage.org/conservatism/commentary/barry-goldwater-the-most-consequential-loser-the-20th-century.

3. John Dean, "Don't Compare Trump's Presidential Campaign to Barry Goldwater's," *Verdict*, May 27, 2016. Accessed at https://verdict.justia.com/2016/05/27/dont-compare-trumps-presidential-campaign-barry-goldwaters.

4. Will Wilkinson, "On the Saying That 'Extremism in Defense of Liberty Is No Vice," Niskayen Center, January 5, 2016. Accessed at https://www.niskanencenter.org/on-the-saying-that-extremism-in-defense-of-liberty-is-no-vice/.

5. "1964," The American Presidency Project, UC Santa Barbara. Accessed at https://www.presidency.ucsb.edu/statistics/elections/1964.

6. Don Gonyea, "McGovern Legacy Offers More Than a Lost Presidency," NPR, October 21, 2012. Accessed at https://www.npr.org/2012/10/21/163342166/mcgoverns-life-leaves-more-than-a-lost-presidency.

7. David E. Rosenbaum, "George McGovern Dies at 90, a Liberal Trounced but Never Silenced," October 21, 2012. Accessed at https://www.nytimes .com/2012/10/22/us/politics/george-mcgovern-a-democratic-presidential -nominee-and-liberal-stalwart-dies-at-90.html.

8. Max Frankel, "President Won 49 States and 521 Electoral Votes," *New York Times*, November 9, 1972. Accessed at https://www.nytimes.com/1972 /11/09/archives/new-jersey-pages-president-won-49-states-and-521 -electoral-votes.html.

9. "U.S.A: Barry Goldwater's Concession Speech, 1964," video, British Pathe, Reuter's Historical Collection. Accessed at https://www.britishpathe.com/ video/VLVAA9B1HFZXRDFA1DHCWDCO7UAOZ-USA-BARRY -GOLDWATERS-CONCESSION-SPEECH/query/Barrie.

10. William F. Buckley Jr., "Goldwater, the John Birch Society and Me," *Wall Street Journal*, February 27, 2008. Accessed at https://www.wsj.com /articles/SB120413132440097025.

11. Sarah Blaskey and Phil Gasper, "How McGovern Tamed the Anti-War Movement," CounterPunch, November 1, 2012. Accessed at https://www .counterpunch.org/2012/11/01/how-mcgovern-tamed-the-anti-war -movement/.

12. Adam Gabbatt, "Democratic Socialists of America Back Bernie: 'The Best Chance to Beat Trump,'" *Guardian*, March 21, 2019. Accessed at https:// www.theguardian.com/us-news/2019/mar/21/democratic-socialists-of -america-bernie-sanders-2020.

13. Henry W. Mcgee III, "Angela Davis Says McGovern and Nixon Present No Choice," *Harvard Crimson*, October 31, 1972. Accessed at https://www .thecrimson.com/article/1972/10/31/angela-davis-says-mcgovern-and -nixon/.

14. "Donor Demographics," The Center for Responsive Politics, 2021. Accessed at https://www.opensecrets.org/elections-overview/donor -demographics.

15. David Kilcullen, "America in 2020: 'Insurrection' or 'Incipient Insurgency'?'" Foundation for Defense of Democracies, June 23, 2020. Accessed at https://www.fdd.org/analysis/2020/06/23/us-insurrection -or-incipient-insurgency/.

16. Seth Jones, Catrina Doxsee, and Nicholas Harrington, "The Escalating Terrorism Problem in the United States," Center for Strategic & International Studies, June 17, 2020. Accessed at https://www.csis.org /analysis/escalating-terrorism-problem-united-states.

17. Kathleen Belew, *Bring the War Home: The White Power Movement and Paramilitary America* (Harvard University Press, 2018).

18. "Domestic Violent Extremism Poses Heightened Threat in 2021," Office of the Director of National Intelligence. March 1, 2021. Accessed at https://

www.dhs.gov/sites/default/files/publications/21_0301_odni_unclass
-summary-of-dve-assessment-17_march-final_508.pdf.

19. Robert Harrow, Andrew Ba Tran, and Derek Hawkins, "The Rise of
    Domestic Extremism in America," *Washington Post*, April 12, 2021.
    Accessed at https://www.washingtonpost.com/investigations
    /interactive/2021/domestic-terrorism-data/?itid=hp-top-table-main.

20. Aaron Morrison, "White Supremacist Propaganda Surged in 2020,
    Anti-Defamation League Report Says," Associated Press, March 17, 2020.
    Accessed at https://www.post-gazette.com/news/nation/2021/03/17
    /White-supremacist-propaganda-surged-in-2020-report-says/stories
    /202103170101.

21. Whitney Wild, Paul LeBlanc and Rashard Rose, "2 more DC police officers
    who responded to Capitol insurrection have died by suicide," CNN,
    updated August 3, 2021. Accessed at https://www.cnn.com/2021/08/02
    /politics/dc-metropolitan-police-officer-suicide-january-6-capitol-riot
    /index.html

22. Amy B. Wang, "GOP Sen. Johnson Says Capitol Rioters Didn't Scare Him—
    But Might Have Had They Been Black Lives Matter Protesters," *Washington
    Post*, March 14, 2021. Accessed at https://www.washingtonpost.com/politics
    /2021/03/13/gop-sen-johnson-says-capitol-rioters-didnt-scare-him-might
    -have-had-they-been-black-lives-matter-protesters/.

23. Eugene Robinson, "Ron Johnson's Racism Is Breathtaking," *Washington
    Post*. March 15, 2021. Accessed at https://www.washingtonpost.com
    /opinions/the-ron-johnsons-of-the-republican-party-seem-proud-to-be
    -racist/2021/03/15/1ad4c514-85b0-11eb-bfdf-4d36dab83a6d_story.html.

24. Michael Gerson, "Ron Johnson Isn't a Republican Outlier," *Washington
    Post*, March 22, 2021. Accessed at https://www.washingtonpost.com
    /opinions/ron-johnson-isnt-a-republican-outlier/2021/03/22/fde3d8da
    -8b3d-11eb-a730-1b4ed9656258_story.html.

25. Ron Johnson, "I Won't Be Silenced by the Left," *Wall Street Journal*,
    March 15, 2021. Accessed at https://www.wsj.com/articles/i-wont-be
    -silenced-by-the-left-11615848103?mod=hp_opin_pos_3.

26. Colby Itkowitz, "Trump Falsely Claims January 6 Rioters Were 'Hugging
    and Kissing' Police."

27. "Reuters/Ipsos: Trump's Coattails," Ipsos news release, April 2, 2021.
    Accessed at https://www.ipsos.com/sites/default/files/ct/news
    /documents/2021-04/topline_write_up_reuters_ipsos_trump_coattails
    poll-_april_02_2021.pdf.

28. Colby Itkowitz and Meagan Flynn: "12 Republicans Opposed
    Congressional Gold Medals for Police Who Protected Them on January
    6," *Washington Post*, March 17, 2021. Accessed at https://www

.washingtonpost.com/politics/2021/03/17/dozen-republicans-voted
-against-congressional-gold-medals-police-who-protected-them-jan-6/.

29. Nicholas Fandos, "Senate Republicans Filibuster Jan. 6 Inquiry Bill,
    Blocking an Investigation," *New York Times*, May 28, 2021. Accessed at
    https://www.nytimes.com/2021/05/28/us/politics/capitol-riot
    -commission-republicans.html.

30. Peggy Noonan, "Why We Can't Move on From Jan. 6," *Wall Street Journal*,
    June 10, 2021, Accessed at https://www.wsj.com/articles/why-we-cant
    -move-on-from-jan-6-11623363175.

31. Minyvonne Burke, "Retired St. Louis Police Captain Killed by Looters
    While Trying to Protect Friend's Shop," NBC News, June 3, 2020.
    Accessed at https://www.nbcnews.com/news/us-news/retired-st-louis
    -police-captain-killed-looters-while-trying-protect-n1223386.

32. Tamar Lapin, "Widow of Ex-Police Captain Killed by St. Louis Rioters
    Gives Emotional RNC Remarks," *New York Post*, August 27, 2020. Accessed
    at https://nypost.com/2020/08/27/rnc-2020-widow-of-ex-police-captain
    -killed-by-st-louis-rioters-speaks/.

33. Christopher Klein, "10 Things You May Not Know About Martin Luther
    King Jr.," History.com, updated January 20, 2021. Accessed at https://
    www.history.com/news/10-things-you-may-not-know-about-martin
    -luther-king-jr.

34. Donesha Aldridge, "Here's How Georgia Troopers Caught the Metro
    Atlanta Spa Shooting Suspect," WXIA-TV, March 22, 2021. Accessed at
    https://www.11alive.com/article/news/crime/georgia-state-patrol-report
    -robert-aaron-long-suspect-arrest-spa-shootings/85-e401e6fb-d699-4124
    -8b25-839d334dd108.

35. Andrea Salcedo and Paulina Firozi, "Eric Talley, Officer Killed in Boulder
    Shooting, Loved His Job and His Seven Children: 'That Was
    His Life,'" *Washington Post*, March 23, 2021. Accessed at https://www
    .washingtonpost.com/nation/2021/03/23/eric-talley-boulder-shooting
    -police/.

36. Michael Kunzelman, "AP Explains: What's Behind Trump's Town Hall
    Answer on QAnon," Associated Press, October 16, 2020. Accessed at
    https://apnews.com/article/trump-town-hall-qanon-explained
    -b4614edad1aae27a0cbcb9dfe0c0c44c.

37. Richard Read, "Proud Boys, Told by Trump to Stand Back and Stand By,
    'All But Guarantees Violence,'" *Los Angeles Times*, updated October 1,
    2020. Accessed at https://www.latimes.com/world-nation
    /story/2020-09-30/proud-boys-joe-biggs-portland.

38. "Proud Boys," Southern Poverty Law Center. Accessed at https://www
    .splcenter.org/fighting-hate/extremist-files/group/proud-boys.

39. "Proud Boys," Anti-Defamation League. Accessed at https://www.adl.org /proudboys.

40. Spencer S. Hsu: "U.S. Alleges Proud Boys Planned to Break into Capitol on January 6 From Many Different Points," *Washington Post*, March 2, 2021. Accessed at https://www.washingtonpost.com/local/legal-issues /proud-boys-leader-capitol-riot/2021/03/02/0ca15138-7aed-11eb-85cd -9b7fa90c8873_story.html.

41. Joe Biden, "We Are a Nation Furious at Injustice," Medium, May 31, 2020. Accessed at https://medium.com/@JoeBiden/we-are-a-nation-furious-at -injustice-9dcffd81978f.

42. James Freeman, "Why Didn't Biden Condemn Antifa and Bernie Sanders?" *Wall Street Journal*, October 1, 2020. Accessed at https://www .wsj.com/articles/why-didnt-biden-condemn-antifa-and-bernie -sanders-11601586778?page=1.

43. Bernard Kerik, "Democrats Desperately Push the 'Peaceful Protesters' Delusion," *Hill*, August 21, 2020. Accessed at https://thehill.com /opinion/criminal-justice/513063-democrats-desperately-push-the -peaceful-protesters-delusion.

44. "Seattle Police Clear Out Protester-Occupied Zone," BBC, July 2, 2020. Accessed at https://www.bbc.com/news/world-us-canada-53254221.

45. "Seattle Chief's Departure Highlights Council Failure," *Seattle Times*, August 11, 2020. Accessed at https://www.seattletimes.com/opinion /editorials/seattle-chiefs-departure-highlights-council-failure/.

46. Peter Dreier, "The Number of Democratic Socialists in the House Will Soon Double. But the Movement Scored Its Biggest Victories Down Ballot," *Talking Points Memo*, December 11, 2020. Accessed at https:// talkingpointsmemo.com/cafe/number-democratic-socialists-congress -soon-double-down-ballot-movement-scored-biggest-victories.

47. "Will the US Have Another Civil War?" The Zogby Poll®, February 4, 2021. Accessed at https://zogbyanalytics.com/news/997-the-zogby-poll-will -the-us-have-another-civil-war.

48. Nathan P. Kalmoe and Lilliana Mason, "Lethal Mass Partisanship," January 2019. Accessed at https://www.dannyhayes.org/uploads/6/9/8/5 /69858539/kalmoe__mason_ncapsa_2019_-_lethal_partisanship_-_final _lmedit.pdf.

49. Thomas B. Edsall, "No Hate Left Behind," *New York Times*, March 13, 2019. Accessed at https://www.nytimes.com/2019/03/13/opinion/hate -politics.html.

50. "Political Polarization in the American Public," Pew Research Center, June 12, 2014. Accessed at https://www.pewresearch.org/politics/2014/06/12 /political-polarization-in-the-american-public/.

51. "Executive Summary: 2019 Year in Hate," Southern Poverty Law Center, March 18, 2020. Accessed at https://www.splcenter.org/news/2020/03/18/executive-summary-2019-year-hate.

52. Jason Wilson, "White Nationalist Hate Groups Have Grown 55% in Trump Era, Report Finds," *Guardian*, March 18, 2020. Accessed at https://www.theguardian.com/world/2020/mar/18/white-nationalist-hate-groups-southern-poverty-law-center.

53. Devlin Barrett, Spencer S. Hsu, Aaron Davis, and Tom Jackman, "DOJ Seeks to Build Large Conspiracy Case Against Oath Keepers for January 6 Riot," *Washington Post*, March 12, 2021. Accessed at https://www.washingtonpost.com/national-security/oattkeepers-capitol-riots-conspiracy/2021/03/11/03c26114-8291-11eb-9ca6-54e187ee4939_story.html.

54. Alan Feuer, "Oath Keeper Pleads Guilty and Will Cooperate in January 6 Riot Inquiry," *New York Times*, April 16, 2021. Accessed at https://www.nytimes.com/2021/04/16/us/politics/oath-keeper-guilty-plea.html.

55. Devlin Barrett, Spencer S. Hsu, Aaron Davis, and Tom Jackman, "DOJ Seeks to Build Large Conspiracy Case Against Oath Keepers for January 6 Riot."

56. Jim Sciutto, "The Capitol Rioters Speak Just Like the Islamist Terrorists I Reported On," *Washington Post*, February 19, 2021. Accessed at https://www.washingtonpost.com/outlook/capitol-riot-terrorism-islam-violence/2021/02/19/6d4b499a-7222-11eb-85fa-e0ccb3660358_story.html.

57. "Five People Shot, Including Republican Congressman, at Charity Baseball Game," History.com, updated June 11, 2020. Accessed at https://www.history.com/this-day-in-history/james-hodgkinson-shooting-republicans-baseball-game.

58. Seth G. Jones and Catrina Doxsee, "The Escalating Terrorism Problem in the United States," Center for Strategic & International Studies, June 17, 2020. Accessed at https://www.csis.org/analysis/escalating-terrorism-problem-united-states.

59. Emily Stewart, "Donald Trump Rode $5 Billion in Free Media to the White House," *The Street*, November 20, 2016. Accessed at https://www.thestreet.com/politics/donald-trump-rode-5-billion-in-free-media-to-the-white-house-13896916.

60. Jon Allsop and Pete Vernon, "How the Press Covered the Last Four Years of Trump," *Columbia Journalism Review*, October 23, 2020. Accessed at https://www.cjr.org/special_report/coverage-trump-presidency-2020-election.php.

61. Sara Fischer, Neal Rothschild, and Stef W. Kight, "Alexandria Ocasio-Cortez Is the Democrats' Trump," Axios, Updated February 11, 2019.

Accessed at https://www.axios.com/alexandria-ocasio-cortez-social -media-donald-trump-ee71d6b7-3aef-44aa-afcb-4826f8782a51.html.

62. James Rosen, "Ocasio-Cortez, Progressive Titan and Media Celebrity, Urges Regulation of: The Media," Sinclair Broadcast Group, January 15, 2021. Accessed at https://13wham.com/news/connect-to-congress/rep -ocasio-cortez-progressive-titan-and-media-celebrity-urges-regulation -of-media.

63. Doug Schoen and Carly Cooperman, "Schoen & Cooperman: Election 2020—Biden, Dems Hurt by This and Here's How They Can Bounce Back," Fox News, November 16, 2020. Accessed at https://www.foxnews .com/opinion/election-2020-biden-dems-hurt-bounce-back-doug -schoen-carly-cooperman.

64. John Eligon and Thomas Kaplan, "These are the Republicans Who Supported Impeaching Trump," *New York Times*, February 16, 2021. Accessed at https://www.nytimes.com/article/republicans-impeaching -donald-trump.html.

65. Jane C. Timm, "7 Republicans Found Trump 'Guilty' of Inciting Capitol Riot. They Explain Their Vote," NBC News, February 18, 2021. Accessed at https://www.nbcnews.com/politics/donald-trump/7-republicans-found -trump-guilty-inciting-capitol-riot-they-explain-n1257896.

66. Abby Livingston, "George W. Bush on Capitol Insurrection: 'I Was Sick to My Stomach,'" *Texas Tribune*, updated March 18, 2021. Accessed at https://www.texastribune.org/2021/02/24/texas-tribune-george-w-bush/.

67. Jacob Pramuk, "Biden Signs $1.9 Trillion Covid Relief Bill, Clearing Way for Stimulus Checks, Vaccine Aid," CNBC, March 11, 2021. Accessed at https://www.cnbc.com/2021/03/11/biden-1point9-trillion-covid-relief -package-thursday-afternoon.html.

68. Camille Caldera, "Fact Check: Democrats Have Condemned Violence Linked to BLM, Anti-fascist Protests," *USA Today*, updated August 13, 2020. Accessed at https://www.usatoday.com/story/news/factcheck /2020/08/13/fact-check-democrats-have-condemned-violence-linked -protests/3317862001/.

69. "Liberal Cities, Radical Mayhem," *Wall Street Journal*, June 2, 2020. Accessed at https://www.wsj.com/articles/liberal-cities-radical -mayhem-11591140986.

70. Ken Buck, "First Lockdowns, Then Riots—Here's How Left's Hypocrisy Added Fuel to the Fire," Fox News, June 7, 2020. Accessed at https://www .foxnews.com/opinion/lockdowns-riots-lefts-hypocrisy-fuel-fire-rep-ken -buck.

71. Lee Edwards, "Barry Goldwater—The Most Consequential Loser of the 20th Century."

72. Ezra Klein, "'Why We're Polarized.' By Ezra Klein: An Excerpt," *New York Times*, January 26, 2020. Accessed at https://www.nytimes.com/2020/01/28/books/review/why-were-polarized-by-ezra-klein-an-excerpt.html.

CHAPTER 6

1. Jacob Pramuk, "House Passes $1.9 Trillion Covid Relief Bill, Sends It to Biden to Sign," CNBC, March 10, 2021. Accessed at https://www.cnbc.com/2021/03/10/stimulus-update-house-passes-1point9-trillion-covid-relief-bill-sends-to-biden.html.
2. "How the Trump Tax Law Passed: Bipartisanship Wasn't an Ingredient," *Hill*, September 27, 2018. Accessed at https://thehill.com/policy/finance/408631-how-the-trump-tax-cuts-passed-bipartisanship-wasnt-an-ingredient.
3. Danica Kirka, "World Alarmed by Violence in US; Thousands March in London," Associated Press, May 31, 2020. Accessed at https://am920theanswer.com/news/politics/world-uneasily-watches-us-protests-but-us-racism-seen-before.
4. "Who Are the Uighurs and Why Is China Being Accused of Genocide?" BBC News, March 26, 2021. Accessed at https://www.bbc.com/news/world-asia-china-22278037.
5. "How It Happened: Transcript of the US-China Opening Remarks in Alaska," Nikkei Asia, March 19, 2021. Accessed at https://asia.nikkei.com/Politics/International-relations/US-China-tensions/How-it-happened-Transcript-of-the-US-China-opening-remarks-in-Alaska.
6. Nathan Place, "China Sanctions Joe Manchin's Wife, Other US Officials," *Independent*, March 27, 2021. Accessed at https://www.independent.co.uk/news/world/americas/us-politics/china-sanction-joe-gayle-manchin-b1823451.html.
7. "Blinken Condemns China Sanctions on U.S. Officials," Associated Press, March 27, 2021. Accessed at https://www.politico.com/news/2021/03/27/china-sanctions-xinjiang-478243.
8. Vanessa Friedman and Elizabeth Paton, "What is Going On With China, Cotton and All of These Clothing Brands?" *New York Times*. March 29, 2021. Accessed at https://www.nytimes.com/2021/03/29/style/china-cotton-uyghur-hm-nike.html?searchResultPosition=1.
9. Eva Dou, "China's Propaganda Machine Kicks into High Gear Over Xinjiang Criticism," *Washington Post*, March 28, 2021. Accessed at https://www.washingtonpost.com/world/asia_pacific/china-xinjiang

-boycott-propaganda/2021/03/29/0e845244-904f-11eb-aadc
-af78701a30ca_story.html.

10. Ana Swanson, "U.S. Bans All Cotton and Tomatoes From Xinjiang Region of China," *New York Times*, January 13, 2021 (Updated January 19, 2021). Accessed at https://www.nytimes.com/2021/01/13/business /economy/xinjiang-cotton-tomato-ban.html?searchResultPosition=2.

11. Josh Rogin, "The United States Must Confront the . . Chinese Communist Party and Racism at the Same Time," *Washington Post*, March 25, 2021. Accessed at https://www.washingtonpost.com/opinions/global -opinions/the-united-states-must-confront-the-chinese-communist -party-and-racism-at-the-same-time/2021/03/25/63fe8308-8d9c-11eb -9423-04079921c915_story.html.

12. Tenzin Dorjee, "Anti-China Is Not Anti-Asian," *Washington Post*, April 6, 2021. Accessed at https://www.washingtonpost.com/opinions/2021/04 /06/anti-china-is-not-anti-asian/.

13. Douglas E. Schoen, *The End of Democracy? Russia and China on the Rise, America in Retreat* (Regan Arts, 2020).

14. Andrew E. Kramer, "Navalny, Putin's Nemesis, Ends Hunger Strike in Russia," *New York Times*, April 23, 2021. Accessed at https://www.nytimes. com/2021/04/23/world/europe/russia-navalny-putin-hunger-strike.html.

15. Hannah Hartig: "Share of Republicans Saying 'Everything Possible' Should Be Done to Make Voting Easy Declines Sharply," Pew Research Center, April 1, 2021. Accessed at https://www.pewresearch.org/fact -tank/2021/04/01/share-of-republicans-saying-everything-possible -should-be-done-to-make-voting-easy-declines-sharply/; "Republicans and Democrats Move Further Apart in Views of Voting Access," Pew Research Center, April 22, 2021. Accessed at https://www.pewresearch .org/politics/2021/04/22/republicans-and-democrats-move-further-apart -in-views-of-voting-access/.

16. Glenn Kessler, "Biden Falsely Claims the New Georgia Law 'Ends Voting Hours Early,'" *Washington Post*, March 30, 2021. Accessed at https://www .washingtonpost.com/politics/2021/03/30/biden-falsely-claims-new -georgia-law-ends-voting-hours-early/.

17. Nate Cohn, "Georgia's Election Law, and Why Turnout Isn't Easy to Turn Off," *New York Times*, April 3, 2021. Accessed at https://www.nytimes .com/2021/04/03/upshot/georgia-election-law-turnout.html ?searchResultPosition=1.

18. Kevin Draper, James Wagner, Reid J. Epstein, and Nick Corasaniti, "M.L.B Pulls All-Star Game From Georgia in Response to Voting Law," *New York Times*, April 2, 2021. Accessed at https://www.nytimes.com/2021 /04/02/us/politics/mlb-all-star-game-moved-atlanta-georgia.html.

19. Carlie Porterfield, "Georgia Lawmakers Demand Removal of Coca-Cola Drinks in Latest Boycott Over Voting Law," *Forbes*, April 4, 2021.

20. Fredreka Schouten, "Georgia House Threatens Delta Tax Break After CEO Slammed New Voting Restrictions," CNN, April 1, 2021. Accessed at https://www.cnn.com/2021/04/01/politics/georgia-voting-law-house-delta-tax-breaks.

21. Abraham Lincoln, "The Gettysburg Address," Abraham Lincoln Online, November 19, 1863. Accessed at http://www.abrahamlincolnonline.org/lincoln/speeches/gettysburg.htm.

22. "Remarks by President Biden in Press Conference," The White House, March 25, 2021. Accessed at https://www.whitehouse.gov/briefing-room/speeches-remarks/2021/03/25/remarks-by-president-biden-in-press-conference/.

23. Tony Romm, "Biden to Unveil Major New Spending Plans as Democrats Eye Bigger Role for Government," *Washington Post*, March 28, 2021. Accessed at https://www.washingtonpost.com/us-policy/2021/03/28/biden-budget-infrastructure/.

24. Aaron Zitner and Julia Wolfe, "Donald Trump and Hillary Clinton's Popularity Problem," *Wall Street Journal*, May 24, 2016. Accessed at https://graphics.wsj.com/elections/2016/donald-trump-and-hillary-clintons-popularity-problem/.

25. "Summary of the 2018 National Defense Strategy of the United States of America," U.S. Department of Defense, January 20, 2018. Accessed at https://www.realcleardefense.com/articles/2018/01/20/summary_of_the_2018_national_defense_strategy_112929.html.

26. Douglas E. Schoen and Melik Kaylan, *The Russia-China Axis: The New Cold War and America's Crisis of Leadership* (Encounter Books, 2014).

27. Scott Neuman, "As Relations With U.S. Sour, Xi Describes Putin as 'Best Friend' at Moscow Meeting," NPR.org, June 6, 2019. Accessed at https://www.npr.org/2019/06/06/730200317/as-relations-with-u-s-sour-xi-describes-putin-as-best-friend-at-moscow-meeting.

28. Daniel R. Coats, "Worldwide Threat Assessment of the US Intelligence Community," January 29, 2019. Accessed at https://www.dni.gov/files/ODNI/documents/2019-ATA-SFR---SSCI.pdf.

29. Siemon T. Wezeman, "Russia's Military Spending: Frequently Asked Questions," Stockholm International Peace Research Institute, April 27, 2020. Accessed at https://www.sipri.org/commentary/topical-backgrounder/2020/russias-military-spending-frequently-asked-questions.

30. Matthew Daly, "Congress Overrides Trump Veto of Defense Bill," Associated Press, January 1, 2021. Accessed at https://www.defensenews

.com/congress/budget/2021/01/01/congress-overrides-trump-veto-of
-defense-bill/.

31. Stephen Blank, "Russia, China and Collaborative Actions: An Alliance
in the Making," Second Line of Defense, January 19, 2019. Accessed at
https://sldinfo.com/2019/01/russia-china-and-collaborative-actions-an
-alliance-in-the-making/.

32. Oriana Skylar Mastro, "Russia and China Team up on the Indian
Ocean," *Interpreter*, December 16, 2020. Accessed at https://www
.lowyinstitute.org/the-interpreter/russia-and-china-team-indian-ocean.

33. Stephen Blank, "Russia, China and Collaborative Actions: An Alliance in
the Making."

34. Stephen Blank, "Russia, China and Collaborative Actions: An Alliance in
the Making."

35. Wang Cong, "With China-Russia Ties at 'Best in History' Trade Still Needs
a Boost to Ensure Security," *Global Times*, March 23, 2021. Accessed at
https://www.globaltimes.cn/page/202103/1219223.shtml.

36. Daniel Workman, "Russia's Top Trading Partners," World's Top Exports,
February 28, 2021. Accessed at https://www.worldstopexports.com
/russias-top-import-partners/.

37. Daniel Workman, "China's Top Trading Partners," World's Top Exports,
Accessed at https://www.worldstopexports.com/chinas-top-import
-partners/.

38. Alec Luhn and Terry Macalister, "Russia Signs 30-Year Deal Worth
$400bn to Deliver Gas to China," *Guardian*, May 21, 2014. Accessed at
https://www.theguardian.com/world/2014/may/21/russia-30-year
-400bn-gas-deal-china.

39. Jonathan E. Hillman, "China and Russia: Economic Unequals," Center for
Strategic & International Studies, July 15, 2020. Accessed at https://www
.csis.org/analysis/china-and-russia-economic-unequals.

40. Shane Harris, "China Maneuvering to Expand Global Influence, Undercut
U.S., Intelligence Report Finds," *Washington Post*, April 13, 2021. Accessed
at https://www.washingtonpost.com/national-security/iran-nuclear
-us-intelligence/2021/04/13/bed17026-9c63-11eb-b7a8-014b14aeb9e4
_story.html.

41. Chris Buckley, "China Takes Aim at Western Ideas," *New York Times*,
August 19, 2013. Accessed at https://www.nytimes.com/2013/08/20/world
/asia/chinas-new-leadership-takes-hard-line-in-secret-memo.html.

42. "China's Pathetic Crackdown on Civil Society," *Washington Post*, April 22,
2015. Accessed at https://www.washingtonpost.com/opinions/chinas
-pathetic-lockdown/2015/04/22/bddf8fdc-e548-11e4-905f-cc896d379a32
_story.html.

43. Petra Cahill and Eric Baculinao, "Donald Trump Shares Chocolate Cake and 'Great Chemistry' with China's Xi," NBC News, April 13, 2017. Accessed at https://www.nbcnews.com/news/world/donald-trump -shares-chocolate-cake-great-chemistry-china-s-xi-n745931.

44. "2020 Country Reports on Human Rights Practices: China (Includes Hong Kong, Macau, and Tibet)," U.S. State Department, March 30, 2021. Accessed at https://www.state.gov/reports/2020-country-reports-on -human-rights-practices/china/.

45. "The People's Republic of China: U.S.-China Trade Facts," Office of the United States Trade Representative. Accessed at https://ustr.gov /countries-regions/china-mongolia-taiwan/peoples-republic-china.

46. David J. Lynch, "Wall Street's March into China Increasingly at Odds with Biden's Tough Stance," *Washington Post*, March 23, 2021. Accessed at https://www.washingtonpost.com/business/2021/03/23/goldman-sachs -china-biden/.

47. "Russia: U.S.-Russia Trade Facts," Office of the United States Trade Representative. Accessed at https://ustr.gov/countries-regions/europe -middle-east/russia-and-eurasia/russia.

48. Matt Pottinger, "Beijing Targets American Business," *Wall Street Journal*, March 26, 2021. Accessed at https://www.wsj.com/articles/beijing -targets-american-business-11616783268?mod=opinion_lead_pos5.

49. Kate Growley, Gabriel Ramsey, and Suzanne Trivette, "Is Chinese IP Theft Coming to an End?" Lexology, February 25, 2020. Accessed at https:// www.lexology.com/library/detail.aspx?g=4a3d77df-92f1-48af-bb21 -bb279417869b.

50. Ben Mauk, "Can China Turn the Middle of Nowhere Into the Center of the World Economy?" *New York Times Magazine*, January 29, 2019. Accessed at https://www.nytimes.com/interactive/2019/01/29/magazine /china-globalization-kazakhstan.html.

51. Maria Abi-Habib and Keith Bradsher, "Poor Countries Borrowed Billions from China. They Can't Pay It Back," *New York Times*, May 18, 2020. Accessed at https://www.nytimes.com/2020/05/18/business/china-loans -coronavirus-belt-road.html.

52. Kai Schultz, "Sri Lanka, Struggling With Debt, Hands a Major Port to China," *New York Times*, December 12, 2017. Accessed at https://www .nytimes.com/2017/12/12/world/asia/sri-lanka-china-port.html.

53. Maria Abi-Habib, "How China Got Sri Lanka to Cough Up a Port," *New York Times*, June 25, 2018. Accessed at https://www.nytimes .com/2018/06/25/world/asia/china-sri-lanka-port.html.

54. Daniel R. Coats, "Worldwide Threat Assessment of the US Intelligence Community."

55. Peter Beaumont, "UK and US Criticise WHO's Covid Report and Accuse China of Withholding Data," *Guardian*, March 30, 2021. Accessed at https://www.theguardian.com/world/2021/mar/30/who-criticises-chinas-data-sharing-as-it-releases-covid-origins-report.

56. Leslie Stahl, "What Happened in Wuhan? Why Questions Still Linger on the Origin of the Coronavirus," *60 Minutes*, CBS News, March 28, 2021. Accessed at https://www.cbsnews.com/news/covid-19-wuhan-origins-60-minutes-2021-03-28/.

57. Sanjay Gupta, "Autopsy of a Pandemic: 6 Doctors at the Center of the US Covid-19 Response," CNN, Updated March 26, 2021. Accessed at https://www.cnn.com/2021/03/26/health/covid-war-doctors-sanjay-gupta/index.html.

58. Javier C. Hernández: "China Peddles Falsehoods to Obscure Origin of Covid Pandemic," *New York Times*, December 6, 2020. Accessed at https://www.nytimes.com/2020/12/06/world/asia/china-covid-origin-falsehoods.html.

59. Missy Ryan, "The U.S. System Created the World's Most Advanced Military. Can It Maintain an Edge?" *Washington Post*, April 1, 2021. Accessed at https://www.washingtonpost.com/national-security/china-us-military-technology/2021/03/31/acc2d9f4-866c-11eb-8a67-f314e5fcf88d_story.html.

60. Zlatica Hoke, "FBI Director: China Poses Biggest Counterintelligence Threat to US," П О Р О Х И (Russian website), July 24, 2019. Accessed at https://porohy.com/2019/07/fbi-director-china-poses-biggest-counterintelligence-threat-to-us.html.

61. Christopher Wray, "The Threat Posed by the Chinese Government and the Chinese Communist Party to the Economic and National Security of the United States," FBI, July 7, 2020. Accessed at https://www.fbi.gov/news/speeches/the-threat-posed-by-the-chinese-government-and-the-chinese-communist-party-to-the-economic-and-national-security-of-the-united-states.

62. "Soviet Satellite States," Schoolhistory.org.uk, 2021. Accessed at https://schoolshistory.org.uk/topics/world-history/cold-war-1945-1972/soviet-satellite-states/.

63. "The Warsaw Pact Is Formed," History.com, May 12, 2020. Accessed at https://www.history.com/this-day-in-history/the-warsaw-pact-is-formed.

64. Matt Rosenberg, "What Was the USSR and Which Countries Were in It?" ThoughtCo, updated August 2, 2019. Accessed at https://www.thoughtco.com/what-was-the-ussr-1434459.

65. "Largest Countries in the World (by area)," Worldometer. Accessed at https://www.worldometers.info/geography/largest-countries-in-the-world/.

66. "Soviet Union," Encyclopedia Britannica. Accessed at https://www
    .britannica.com/place/Soviet-Union/The-Russian-Revolution.
67. "Cuban Missile Crisis," History.com, updated June 10, 2019. Accessed at
    https://www.history.com/topics/cold-war/cuban-missile-crisis.
68. "Soviets Begin Withdrawal from Afghanistan," History.com, updated July
    27, 2019. Accessed at https://www.history.com/this-day-in-history
    /soviets-begin-withdrawal-from-afghanistan.
69. "Nuclear Weapons: Who Has What at a Glance," Arms Control
    Association, updated August 2020. Accessed at https://www.armscontrol
    .org/factsheets/Nuclearweaponswhohaswhat.
70. Sarah Pruitt, "How a Five-Day War With Georgia Allowed Russia to
    Reassert Its Military Might," History.com, updated September 4, 2018.
    Accessed at https://www.history.com/news/russia-georgia-war-military
    -nato; Holly Ellyat, "Russia Is Still Occupying 20% of Our Country,
    Georgia's Prime Minister Says," CNBC, January 22, 2019. Accessed at
    https://www.cnbc.com/2019/01/22/russia-is-still-occupying-20percent
    -of-our-country-georgias-leader-says.html.
71. Gerard Toal, John O'Loughlin, and Kristin Bakke, "Six Years and $20
    Billion in Russian Investment Later, Crimeans Are Happy with Russian
    Annexation," *Washington Post*, March 18, 2020. Accessed at https://www
    .washingtonpost.com/politics/2020/03/18/six-years-20-billion
    -russian-investment-later-crimeans-are-happy-with-russian-annexation/.
72. Peter Dickinson, "All Roads Lead to Ukraine in Putin's Global Hybrid
    War," The Atlantic Council, January 5, 2021. Accessed at https://www
    .atlanticcouncil.org/blogs/ukrainealert/all-roads-lead-to-ukraine-in
    -putins-global-hybrid-war/.
73. "Russia and the War in Syria: In for the Long Haul," Deutsche Welle,
    October 1, 2020. Accessed at https://www.dw.com/en/russia-and-the-war
    -in-syria-in-for-the-long-haul/a-55112506.
74. Jamsheed K. Choksy and Carol E. B. Choksy, "China and Russia Have Iran's
    Back," *Foreign Affairs*, November 17, 2020. Accessed at https://www
    .foreignaffairs.com/articles/united-states/2020-11-17/china-and-russia-have
    -irans-back.
75. "Venezuela Crisis: How the Political Situation Escalated," BBC News,
    December 3, 2020. Accessed at https://www.bbc.com/news/world-latin
    -america-36319877.
76. "Band of Brothers: The Wagner Group and the Russian State," Center for
    Strategic & International Studies, September 21, 2020. Accessed at https://
    www.csis.org/blogs/post-soviet-post/band-brothers-wagner-group-and
    -russian-state.
77. Thomas Gibbons-Neff, "How a 4-Hour Battle Between Russian Mercenaries
    and U.S. Commandos Unfolded in Syria," *New York Times*, May 24, 2018.

Accessed at https://www.nytimes.com/2018/05/24/world/middleeast /american-commandos-russian-mercenaries-syria.html.

78. Dave Majumdar, "Russia's Nuclear Weapons Buildup Is Aimed at Beating U.S. Missile Defenses," *National Interest*, March 1, 2018. Accessed at https://nationalinterest.org/blog/the-buzz/russias-nuclear-weapons -buildup-aimed-beating-us-missile-24716.

79. Todd South, "What's Putin up to? The Russian Military Buildup in Europe Raises Tension," *Military Times*, September 13, 2017. Accessed at https:// www.militarytimes.com/news/2017/09/13/whats-putin-up-to-the -russian-military-buildup-on-europes-border-raises-tension/.

80. Ella Nilson, "Mueller Indictments: The Timing of the DNC Leak Was Intentional," Vox, July 13, 2018. Accessed at https://www.vox .com/2018/7/13/17569030/mueller-indictments-russia-hackers-bernie -sanders-hillary-clinton-democratic-national-convention.

81. Dustin Volz and Warren P. Strobel, "Russia, Iran Acted to Influence 2020 Presidential Election, Report Says," *Wall Street Journal*, updated March 17, 2021. Accessed at https://www.wsj.com/articles/putin -authorized-influence-operations-to-hurt-bidens-2020-candidacy-report -says-11615918958.

82. Gary Pruitt, "Cyberattacks on AP Election Platforms Came in 'Withering Numbers' from All Over the World," Connecting, March 31, 2021. Accessed at https://myemail.constantcontact.com/Connecting---March-31--2021. html?soid=1116239949582&aid=R1kzHFaaBx8.

83. David E. Sanger, Nicole Perlroth, and Eric Schmitt, "Scope of Russian Hacking Becomes Clear: Multiple U.S. Agencies Were Hit," *New York Times*, December 14, 2020 (updated February 9, 2021). Accessed at https:// www.nytimes.com/2020/12/14/us/politics/russia-hack-nsa-homeland -security-pentagon.html.

84. Kate Conger and Sheera Frenkel, "Thousands of Microsoft Customers May Have Been Victims of Hack Tied to China," *New York Times*, March 6, 2021. Accessed at https://www.nytimes.com/2021/03/06/technology /microsoft-hack-china.html.

85. Gerard Baker, "Western Culture Elites Are Giving Away Lenin's Rope," *Wall Street Journal*, March 22, 2021. Accessed at https://www.wsj.com /articles/western-culture-elites-are-giving-away-lenins-rope-11616433858.

86. Victor Davis Hanson, "Victor Davis Hanson: China's Contempt for US— They Seek Global Hegemony and This Is How We're Helping Them," Tribune Media Services, March 28, 2021. Accessed at https://www .foxnews.com/opinion/china-contempt-usglobal-hegemony-victor-davis -hanson.

87. Masha Gessen, "How Biden Rattled Putin," *New Yorker*, March 19, 2021. Accessed at https://www.newyorker.com/news/our-columnists/how-joe-biden-rattled-vladimir-putin.

88. Ruth Igielnik, "Men and Women in the U.S. Continue to Differ in Voter Turnout Rate, Party Identification," Pew Research Center, August 18, 2020. Accessed at https://www.pewresearch.org/fact-tank/2020/08/18/men-and-women-in-the-u-s-continue-to-differ-in-voter-turnout-rate-party-identification/.

CHAPTER 7

1. Abraham Lincoln, "House Divided Speech," Abraham Lincoln Online, June 16, 1858. Accessed at http://www.abrahamlincolnonline.org/lincoln/speeches/house.htm.

2. Abraham Lincoln, "Lincoln's Second Inaugural Address," National Park Service. March 4, 1865. Accessed at https://www.nps.gov/linc/learn/historyculture/lincoln-second-inaugural.htm.

3. Graeme Gordon, "Pleasing All the People All the Time," Praxity, September 5, 2018. Accessed at https://www.praxity.com/insights/blogs/posts/2018/september/pleasing-all-the-people-all-the-time.

4. Evangel Penumaka, "The For the People Act Is Popular, Pass It Right Away," Crooked Media, February 25, 2021. Accessed at https://crooked.com/articles/for-the-people-act/.

5. Peter W. Stevenson, "Here's What H.R.1, the House-Passed Voting Rights Bill, Would Do," *Washington Post*, March 5, 2021. Accessed at https://www.washingtonpost.com/politics/2021/03/05/hr1-bill-what-is-it/.

6. Richard Wike, Laura Silver, Shannon Schumacher, and Aidan Connaughton, "Many in U.S., Western Europe Say Their Political System Needs Major Reform," Pew Research Center, March 31, 2021. Accessed at https://www.pewresearch.org/global/2021/03/31/many-in-us-western-europe-say-their-political-system-needs-major-reform/.

7. "Partisan Antipathy: More Intense, More Personal," Pew Research Center, October 10, 2019. Accessed at https://www.pewresearch.org/politics/2019/10/10/partisan-antipathy-more-intense-more-personal/.

8. "State Primary Election Types," National Conference of State Legislatures, January 5, 2021. Accessed at https://www.ncsl.org/research/elections-and-campaigns/primary-types.aspx.

9. "Instant Runoff Voting: How Does It Work?" FindLaw, March 17, 2020. Accessed at https://www.findlaw.com/voting/how-u-s--elections-work/instant-runoff-voting--how-does-it-work.html.

10. "Where Ranked Choice Voting is Used," FairVote. Accessed at https://www.fairvote.org/where_is_ranked_choice_voting_used.

11. Matt Vasilogambros, "Ranked-Choice Voting Gains Momentum Nationwide," Pew Stateline, March 12, 2021. Accessed at https://www.pewtrusts.org/en/research-and-analysis/blogs/stateline/2021/03/12/ranked-choice-voting-gains-momentum-nationwide.

12. "Party Affiliation of the Mayors of the 100 Largest Cities," Ballotpedia, April 2021. Accessed at https://ballotpedia.org/Party_affiliation_of_the_mayors_of_the_100_largest_cities.

13. Nathaniel Rakich and Jasmine Mithani, "What Absentee Voting Looked Like in All 50 States," FiveThirtyEight, February 9, 2021. Accessed at https://fivethirtyeight.com/features/what-absentee-voting-looked-like-in-all-50-states/; "A Summary of the 2020 Election: Survey on the Performance of American Elections," Medium, January 22, 2021. Accessed at https://medium.com/mit-election-lab/a-summary-of-the-2020-election-survey-on-the-performance-of-american-elections-7a8d3f7bb83.

14. James M. Lindsay, "The 2020 Election by the Numbers," Council on Foreign Relations, December 15, 2020. Accessed at https://www.cfr.org/blog/2020-election-numbers.

15. Quinnipiac Poll news release, "74% of Voters Say Democracy in the U.S. is Under Threat, Quinnipiac University National Poll finds; 52% Say President Trump Should Be Removed from Office," Quinnipiac University, January 11, 2021. Accessed at https://poll.qu.edu/images/polling/us/us01112021_usmk38.pdf.

16. Ross Douthat, "Can Anything End the Voting Wars?" *New York Times*, March 16, 2021. Accessed at https://www.nytimes.com/2021/03/16/opinion/voting-republicans-democrats.html.

17. Jesse Yoder, Cassandra Hadan-Nader, Andrew Myers, Tobias Nowacki, Daniel M. Thompson, Jennifer A. Wu, Chenoa Yorgason, and Andrew B. Hall, "How Did Absentee Voting Affect the 2020 U.S. Election?" Stanford Institute for Economic Policy Research. Accessed at https://siepr.stanford.edu/sites/default/files/publications/21-011.pdf; Kyle Raze, "Voting Rights and Resilience of Black Turnout," Paper by Ph.D. candidate in economics at the University of Oregon, February 7, 2021. Accessed at https://kyleraze.com/files/shelby_county_voting.pdf.

18. Nick Corasaniti and Reid J. Epstein, "What Georgia's Voting Law Really Does," *New York Times*, April 2, 2021. Accessed at https://www.nytimes.com/2021/04/02/us/politics/georgia-voting-law-annotated.html.

19. "Acceptable Forms of Identification," Website of the Office of the Colorado Secretary of State, revised September 12, 2018. Accessed at https://www.sos.state.co.us/pubs/elections/vote/acceptableFormsOfID.html.

20. Charles Stewart III, "How We Voted in 2020: A First Look at the Survey of the Performance of the American Elections," MIT Election Data Science Lab, December 15, 2020. Accessed at http://electionlab.mit.edu/sites /default/files/2020-12/How-we-voted-in-2020-v01.pdf.

21. Dave Roos, "5 Presidents Who Lost the Popular Vote But Won the Election."

22. "Presidential Battleground States, 2020," Ballotpedia. Accessed at https:// ballotpedia.org/Presidential_battleground_states,_2020.

23. "Split Electoral Votes in Maine and Nebraska," 270towin.com. Accessed at https://www.270towin.com/content/split-electoral-votes-maine-and -nebraska.

24. "Political Parties," George Washington's Mount Vernon. Accessed at https://www.mountvernon.org/george-washington/the-first-president /political-parties/.

25. "Every US President Listed," *Guardian*. Accessed at https://www .theguardian.com/news/datablog/2012/oct/15/us-presidents-listed.

26. Jeffrey M. Jones, "Support for Third U.S. Political Party at High Point," Gallup, February 15, 2021.

27. Bret Stephens, "America Could Use a Liberal Party," *New York Times*, March 15, 2021. Accessed at https://www.nytimes.com/2021/03/15 /opinion/us-third-party-liberals.html.

28. David Jolly, "Why I've Signed on to Run a New Political Party That Spans the Ideological Divide," The Fulcrum. Accessed at https://thefulcrum.us /serve-america-movement.

29. Charlie Dent, Mary Peters, Denver Riggleman, Michael Steele, and Christine Todd Whitman, "The GOP Has Lost Its Way. Fellow Americans, Join Our New Alliance." Accessed at https://www.washingtonpost.com /opinions/2021/05/13/new-gop-alliance-dent-peters-riggleman-steele -whitman/.

30. "About the Caucus," Problem Solves Caucus website. Accessed at https:// problemsolverscaucus.house.gov/about.

31. Paul Kane, "Bipartisan Senate Lunch Crew Hopes to Do More Than Just Break Bread Together," *Washington Post*, March 26, 2021. Accessed at https://www.washingtonpost.com/powerpost/senate-bipartisan-covid -infrastructure/2021/03/24/cc111ed0-8cdc-11eb-a6bd-0eb91c03305a _story.html.

32. Jon Levine, "Study Declares AOC One of the Least Effective Members of Congress."

33. "Thunder on the Left: AOC Wants $10 Trillion Over 10 Years for Infrastructure Plan," Axios, April 1, 2021. Accessed at https://www.axios .com/aoc-biden-infrastructure-f2cbe0df-099e-47f6-a358-3c0938d4f642 .html.

34. Mike DeBonis and Paul Kane, "After Losing Committee Assignments, Marjorie Taylor Greene Says She Has Been 'Freed' to Push the GOP Further Right," *Washington Post*, February 5, 2021. Accessed at https://www.washingtonpost.com/politics/greene-trump-republicans/2021/02/05/f3e0a7be-67cf-11eb-886d-5264d4ceb46d_story.html.

35. Eliza Collins, "Kyrsten Sinema Defends Filibuster as Pressure Mounts from Progressives," *Wall Street Journal*, April 6, 2021. Accessed at https://www.wsj.com/articles/kyrsten-sinema-defends-filibuster-as-pressure-mounts-from-progressives-11617714005.

36. Dan Alexander, "Trump's Businesses Raked In $1.9 Billion of Revenue During His First Three Years in Office," *Forbes*, September 11, 2020. Accessed at https://www.forbes.com/sites/danalexander/2020/09/11/trumps-businesses-raked-in-19-billion-of-revenue-during-his-first-three-years-in-office/?sh=5e013891e137.

37. "How Trump's Businesses Benefited During His Presidency," *All Things Considered*, NPR, January 19, 2021. Accessed at https://www.npr.org/2021/01/19/958472500/how-trumps-businesses-benefited-during-his-presidency.

38. David Fahrenthold, Josh Dawsey, Jonathan O'Connell, and Anu Narayanswamy, "Ballrooms, Candles and Luxury Cottages: During Trump's Term, Millions of Government and GOP Dollars Have Flowed to His Properties," *Washington Post*, October 27, 2020. Accessed at https://www.washingtonpost.com/politics/ballrooms-candles-and-luxury-cottages-during-trumps-term-millions-of-government-and-gop-dollars-have-flowed-to-his-propertiesmar-a-lago-charged-the-government-3-apiece-for-glasses-of-water-for-trump-and-the-japanese-leader/2020/10/27/186f20a2-1469-11eb-bc10-40b25382f1be_story.html.

39. "Chief Justice Roberts Statement—Nomination Process," Office of the U.S. Courts. Accessed at https://www.uscourts.gov/educational-resources/educational-activities/chief-justice-roberts-statement-nomination-process.

40. Joan Biskupic, "Stephen Breyer Worries About Supreme Court's Public Standing in Current Political Era," CNN, updated April 6, 2021. Accessed at https://www.cnn.com/2021/04/06/politics/stephen-breyer-harvard-speech/index.html.

41. Marianna Sotomayor, "Democratic Leaders Throw Cold Water on Proposal to Expand Supreme Court," *Washington Post*, April 15, 2021. Accessed at https://www.washingtonpost.com/politics/democratic-leaders-throw-cold-water-on-proposal-to-expand-the-supreme-court/2021/04/15/51b84556-9dfc-11eb-8005-bffc3a39f6d3_story.html.

42. Lesley Kennedy, "This Is How FDR Tried to Pack the Supreme Court," History.com. Updated September 18, 2020. Accessed at https://www .history.com/news/franklin-roosevelt-tried-packing-supreme-court.

43. Tyler Pager, "Biden Unveils Commission to Study Possible Expansion of Supreme Court," *Washington Post*, April 9, 2021. Accessed at https://www .washingtonpost.com/politics/biden-to-unveil-commission-to-study -possible-expansion-of-supreme-court/2021/04/09/f644552c-9944-11eb -962b-78c1d8228819_story.html.

44. Brent Scher, "Biden Called Court Packing a 'Bonehead Idea' During 1983 Hearing," *Washington Free Beacon*, March 20, 2019. Accessed at https:// freebeacon.com/politics/biden-called-court-packing-a-bonehead -idea-during-1983-hearing/.

45. Kathleen Parker, "Biden Should Remember That He Once Called Court-packing a 'Bonehead Idea,'" *Washington Post*, April 16, 2021. Accessed at https://www.washingtonpost.com/opinions/biden-should-remember -his-own-words-on-court-packing/2021/04/16/3a195934-9ef2-11eb-b7a8 -014b14aeb9e4_story.html.

46. Marianna Sotomayor, "Democratic Leaders Throw Cold Water on Proposal to Expand Supreme Court."

47. Roxanne Roberts, "Merrick Garland Was Historically Snubbed—but He's Emerged More Respected Than Ever," *Washington Post*, October 10, 2020. Accessed at https://www.washingtonpost.com/lifestyle/style/merrick -garland-supreme-court-nomination/2020/10/06/7098085a-0719-11eb -9be6-cf25fb429f1a_story.html.

48. Priyanka Boghani, "How McConnell's Bid to Reshape the Federal Judiciary Extends Beyond the Supreme Court," *Frontline*, PBS, updated October 16, 2020. Accessed at https://www.pbs.org/wgbh/frontline /article/how-mcconnell-and-the-senate-helped-trump-set-records-in -appointing-judges/.

49. "FAQs—Supreme Court Justices," Supreme Court website. Accessed at https://www.supremecourt.gov/about/faq_justices.aspx.

50. "10 Oldest United States Supreme Court Justices," Oldest.org. Accessed at https://www.oldest.org/politics/supreme-court-justices-usa/.

51. Chris Kahn, "Most Americans Want to End Lifetime Supreme Court Appointments," Reuters, April 18, 2021. Accessed at https://www.reuters .com/business/legal/most-americans-want-end-lifetime-supreme-court -appointments-2021-04-18/.

52. Jeff Wagner, "Daunte Wright Shooting: No Arrests in 5th Night Of Protests," WCCO TV, April 16, 2021. Accessed at https://minnesota .cbslocal.com/2021/04/16/daunte-wright-shooting-hundreds-gather -outside-brooklyn-center-pd-for-5th-night-of-protests/.

53. "Number of Murder Victims in the United States in 2019, by Race/ethnicity and Gender," Statista. February 2, 2021. Accessed at https://www.statista.com/statistics/251877/murder-victims-in-the-us-by-race-ethnicity-and-gender/.

54. Heather Mac Donald, "There Is No Epidemic of Fatal Police Shootings Against Unarmed Black Americans."

55. George Hunter, "Tlaib Calls US Policing 'Intentionally Racist,' Gets Pushback," *Detroit News*, April 13, 2021. Accessed at https://www.detroitnews.com/story/news/local/michigan/2021/04/13/tlaib-calls-us-policing-intentionally-racist-gets-pushback/7207266002/.

56. George Hunter, "Tlaib Calls US Policing 'Intentionally Racist,' Gets Pushback."

57. Christal Hayes, "Trump Supporter Threatens to Kill Democratic Lawmakers Over Rep. Omar's 9/11 Comments, Docs Say," *USA Today*, April 19, 2018. Accessed at https://www.usatoday.com/story/news/politics/2019/04/19/rep-ilhan-omar-rashida-tlaib-targeted-racist-death-threats-man-arrested/3522754002/.

58. Cassidy Johncox and Grant Hermes, "Rep. Rashida Tlaib Recounts Past Death Threats in Tearful Capitol Riot Speech on House Floor," WDIV-TV, February 5, 2021. Accessed at https://www.clickondetroit.com/news/politics/2021/02/05/us-rep-rashida-tlaib-recounts-past-death-threats-in-tearful-capitol-riot-speech-on-house-floor/.

59. David Nakamura, "Biden Pick for Top Civil Rights Post Spars with Republicans Over Police Funding," *Washington Post*, April 14, 2021. Accessed at https://www.washingtonpost.com/national-security/kristen-clarke-confirmation/2021/04/14/74de72d4-9d35-11eb-8005-bffc3a39f6d3_story.html.

60. Felicia Sonmez and Colby Itkowitz, "House Passes Expansive Policing Overhaul Bill Named in Honor of George Floyd," *Washington Post*, March 3, 2021. Accessed at https://www.washingtonpost.com/politics/george-floyd-police-reform-bill-vote/2021/03/03/5ea9ba3a-7c6c-11eb-85cd-9b7fa90c8873_story.html.

61. "2021 Report Card for America's Infrastructure," American Society of Civil Engineers, 2021. Accessed at https://infrastructurereportcard.org/wp-content/uploads/2020/12/2021-IRC-Executive-Summary.pdf.

62. "Key Elements of the U.S. Tax System," Tax Policy Center. Updated May 2020. Accessed at https://www.taxpolicycenter.org/briefing-book/what-highway-trust-fund-and-how-it-financed.

63. Frank Newport, "Infrastructure Action Should Be a No-Brainer," Gallup, December 11, 2020. Accessed at https://news.gallup.com/opinion/polling-matters/327587/infrastructure-action-no-brainer.aspx.

64. Karl Rove, "Why Biden Won't Build Bridges to the GOP," *Wall Street Journal*, April 14, 2021. Accessed at https://www.wsj.com/articles/why-biden-wont-build-bridges-to-the-gop-11618437451?mod=trending_now_opn_5.

65. Allison Pecorin and Trish Turner, "Universal pre-K, free community college tuition: What's in $3.5T budget bill," ABC News, August 9, 2021.

66. Jim Tankersley, Ben Casselman, and Emily Cochrane, "Voters Like Biden Infrastructure Plan; G.O.P. Still Sees an Opening on Taxes," *New York Times*, April 15, 2021. Accessed at https://www.nytimes.com/2021/04/15/business/economy/infrastructure-economy-biden.html?searchResult Position=13.

67. Karl Rove, "Why Biden Won't Build Bridges to the GOP."

68. Kelsey Snell, "The Senate Approves The $1 Trillion Bipartisan Infrastructure Bill In A Historic Vote," NPR, August 10, 2021. Accessed at https://www.npr.org/2021/08/10/1026081880/senate-passes-bipartisan-infrastructure-bill

69. Seung Min Kim and Tony Romm, "Biden Insists He's Willing to Negotiate with Republicans on Infrastructure," Washington Post, April 12, 2021. Accessed at https://www.washingtonpost.com/us-policy/2021/04/12/biden-infrastructure-congress/.

70. "COVID-19 Dashboard," Center for Systems Science and Engineering at Johns Hopkins University (updated daily). Accessed at https://coronavirus.jhu.edu/map.html

71. Kimberly Amadeo, "How COVID-19 Has Affected the U.S. Economy," The Balance, updated February 24, 2021. Accessed at https://www.thebalance.com/how-covid-19-has-affected-the-us-economy-5092445.

72. Ruth Simon, "Covid-19's Toll on U.S. Business? 200,000 Extra Closures in Pandemic's First Year," *Wall Street Journal*, April 16, 2021. Accessed at https://www.wsj.com/articles/covid-19s-toll-on-u-s-business-200-000-extra-closures-in-pandemics-first-year-11618580619.

73. "Federal Regulations Cost an Estimated $1.9 Trillion Per Year: Many Rules Hinder Virus Response, Economic Recovery," Competitive Enterprise Institute, May 28, 2020. Accessed at https://cei.org/citations/federal-regulations-cost-an-estimated-1-9-trillion-per-year-many-rules-hinder-virus-response-economic-recovery/.

74. Susan E. Dudley, "Regulatory Reform to Get the Economy Moving," *Forbes*, May 14, 2020. Accessed at https://www.forbes.com/sites/susandudley/2020/05/14/regulatory-reform-to-get-the-economy-moving/?sh=2d933d6a1681.

75. "The National Debt Is Now More Than $28 Trillion. What Does That Mean?" Peter G. Peterson Foundation. 2021. Accessed at https://www

.pgpf.org/infographic/the-national-debt-is-now-more-than-28-trillion
-what-does-that-mean.

76. Jeff Stein and Tony Romm, "Citing His 'Leverage,' Manchin Says White
House Tax Plan Must Change," *Washington Post*, April 5, 2021. Accessed at
https://www.washingtonpost.com/us-policy/2021/04/05/joe
-manchin-white-house-tax/.

77. David J. Lynch, "Biden Wants to Crack Down on Corporate Tax
Loopholes, Resuming a Battle His Predecessors Lost," *Washington Post*,
April 20, 2021. Accessed at https://www.washingtonpost.com/us
-policy/2021/04/20/corporate-tax-loopholes-biden/.

78. "Make Tax-Dodging Companies Pay for Biden's Infrastructure Plan,"
Editorial in the *New York Times*, April 17, 2021. Accessed at https://www
.nytimes.com/2021/04/17/opinion/sunday/biden-taxes-companies.html.

79. John McCormick, "IRS Chief Says $1 Trillion in Taxes May Go
Uncollected Each Year," *Wall Street Journal*. Updated April 13, 2021.
Accessed at https://www.wsj.com/articles/irs-chief-says-1-trillion-in
-taxes-may-go-uncollectedeach-year-11618337765.

80. "The Employment Situation—March 2021," U.S. Bureau of Labor Statistics
news release. Accessed at https://www.dol.gov/newsroom/economicdata
/empsit_04022021.pdf.

81. "The Employment Situation—March 2021."

82. "6 Companies Making a Big Investment in Their Communities," JUST
Capital, September 24, 2019. Accessed at https://justcapital.com/news
/companies-making-a-big-investment-in-their-communities/.

83. "Opportunity Zones," Economic Innovation Group. Accessed at https://
eig.org/opportunityzones/history.

84. "Opportunity Zones Frequently Asked Questions," Internal Revenue
Service, updated December 15, 2020. Accessed at https://www.irs.gov
/credits-deductions/opportunity-zones-frequently-asked-questions.

85. Carmen Reinicke, "A $15 Minimum Wage Would Give 19 Million Women a
Raise—But It Might Not Happen Anytime Soon"; Michael Collins and Paul
Davidson, "$15 Minimum Wage Would Boost Pay for Millions but Would
Cost 1.4 Million Jobs, Report Says."

86. Lauren Camera, "Biden's Budget Significantly Boosts K-12 Education
Spending," *U.S. News and World Report*, April 9, 2021. Accessed at https://
www.usnews.com/news/education-news/articles/2021-04-09/bidens
-budget-significantly-boosts-k-12-education-spending.

87. Cory Turner, "A Bold Pitch to Boost School Funding for the Nation's Most
Vulnerable Students," *All Things Considered*, NPR, May 27, 2020. Accessed
at https://www.npr.org/2020/05/27/861325304/a-bold-pitch-to-boost
-school-funding-for-the-nations-most-vulnerable-students.

88. Cory Turner, "A Bold Pitch to Boost School Funding for the Nation's Most Vulnerable Students."

89. Jay Mathews, "Can Charter Schools Pick the Best Students? No, but Many Believe the Myth," *Washington Post*, January 2, 2021. Accessed at https://www.washingtonpost.com/local/education/charter-schools-lotteries/2020/12/31/2816a31e-4aaf-11eb-839a-cf4ba7b7c48c_story.html.

90. "National Teacher and Principal Survey," National Center for Education Statistics, 2015–16. Accessed at https://nces.ed.gov/surveys/ntps/tables/Table_TeachersUnion.asp.

91. "About NEA: Purpose and Power in Community," National Education Association website. Accessed at https://www.nea.org/about-nea.

92. "Charter School Accountability," National Education Association website. Accessed at https://www.nea.org/student-success/smart-just-policies/funding-public-schools/charter-school-accountability.

93. "DOE Data at a Glance," New York City Department of Education website. Accessed at https://www.schools.nyc.gov/about-us/reports/doe-data-at-a-glance.

94. Carl Campanile and David Meyer, "NYC Mayoral Candidate Ray McGuire Supports Lifting Charter-School Cap," *New York Post*, April 18, 2021. Accessed at https://nypost.com/2021/04/18/nyc-mayoral-candidate-mcguire-supports-lifting-charter-school-cap/.

95. "Program Fact Sheet" for 2020–2021. D.C. Opportunity Scholarship Program, December 18, 2020. Accessed at https://servingourchildrendc.org/wp-content/uploads/2021/01/DC-OSP-Program-Fact-Sheet-SY-2020-21.pdf.

96. "A Quick Rundown of Community College Diversity Statistics," Everfi, updated December 1, 2020. Accessed at https://everfi.com/blog/colleges-universities/community-college-diversity-statistics/.

97. "Community College FAQs," Community College Research Center. Accessed at https://ccrc.tc.columbia.edu/Community-College-FAQs.html.

98. Victoria Yuen, "The $78 Billion Community College Funding Shortfall," Center for American Progress, October 7, 2020. Accessed at https://www.americanprogress.org/issues/education-postsecondary/reports/2020/10/07/491242/78-billion-community-college-funding-shortfall/.

99. Morley Winograd and Max Rubin, "Tuition-free College Is Critical to Our Economy," EdSource, November 2, 2020. Accessed at https://edsource.org/2020/tuition-free-college-is-critical-to-our-economy.

100. "One in Five Still Shun Vaccine," Monmouth University Polling Institute, April 14, 2021. Accessed at https://www.monmouth.edu/polling-institute/reports/monmouthpoll_us_041421/.

101. Richard Luscombe, "Fauci: Republican Vaccine Deniers Are Hurting Efforts to Lift Covid Restrictions," *Guardian*, April 18, 2021. Accessed at

https://www.theguardian.com/us-news/2021/apr/18/coronavirus
-anthony-fauci-republican-vaccine-deniers-restrictions.

102. Jacqueline Howard, "What Covid-19 War Was Really Like in Trump's White House," CNN. Updated March 28, 2021. Accessed at https://www.cnn.com/2021/03/28/health/covid-war-doctors-fauci-birx-hahn-redfield-gupta-bn/.

103. Kate Bennett and Evan Perez: "Nation's Top Coronavirus Expert Dr. Anthony Fauci Forced to Beef Up Security as Death Threats Increase," CNN, updated April 2, 2020. Accessed at https://www.cnn.com/2020/04/01/politics/anthony-fauci-security-detail/index.html.

104. Carlie Porterfield, "U.S. Voters Are Narrowly in Favor of Vaccine Passports, Poll Suggests," *Forbes*, April 7, 2021.

105. Alison Durkee, "Tennessee Becomes Latests State To Ban School Mask Mandates—Here's The Full List," Forbes August 17, 2021. Accessed at https://www.forbes.com/sites/alisondurkee/2021/08/17/tennessee-becomes-latest-state-to-ban-school-mask-mandates—heres-the-full-list/?sh=73fac10227e0

106. Berkeley Lovelace Jr., "Fauci Says It's 'Disturbing' That Some People Won't Take Covid Vaccine Because of Politics," CNBC, April 19, 2021. Accessed at https://www.cnbc.com/2021/04/19/fauci-disturbing-that-some-wont-take-covid-vaccine-because-of-politics.html.

107. Peter Baldwin, "Vaccine Passports—a Technical, Not An Ideological Issue," CNN, April 20, 2021. Accessed at https://www.cnn.com/2021/04/19/opinions/vaccine-passport-covid-19-baldwin/index.html.

108. Ashley Welch, "Vaccine Passports: What They Are and Why You May Need One Soon," Healthline, April 5, 2021. Accessed at https://www.healthline.com/health-news/vaccine-passports-what-they-are-and-why-you-may-need-one-soon.

109. Dan Diamond, "'We Can Do This': Biden Unveils Pro-vaccine TV Ads, Network of Grass-roots Leaders to Push Shots," *Washington Post*, April 1, 2021. Accessed at https://www.washingtonpost.com/health/2021/04/01/biden-pro-vaccine-tv-ads/.

110. "Percent of Children Vaccinated by Age 24 Months," National Center for Health Statistics, Centers for Disease Control and Prevention, March 29, 2021. Accessed at https://www.cdc.gov/nchs/fastats/immunize.htm.

111. "1918 Pandemic," Centers for Disease Control and Prevention, March 20, 2019. Accessed at https://www.cdc.gov/flu/pandemic-resources/1918-pandemic-h1n1.html.

112. Jim Robbins, "Heading Off the Next Pandemic," Kaiser Health News, January 4, 2021. Accessed at https://khn.org/news/infectious-disease-scientists-preventing-next-pandemic/.

113. Dan Diamond, "Federal Turf Wars over Coronavirus Rescues Created 'Health and Safety Issues,'" *Washington Post*, April 19, 2021. Accessed at https://www.washingtonpost.com/health/2021/04/19/coronavirus-response-wuhan-cruise-ship/.

114. Karen Weintraub, "Biden Administration Renewed Support for World Health Organization Is 'Good News for America and the World,' Scientists Say," *USA Today*, January 22. 2021. Accessed at https://www.usatoday.com/story/news/health/2021/01/22/scientists-applaud-biden-decision-rejoin-world-health-organization/4243377001/.

115. Emily Rauhala and Erin Cunningham, "Moderna to Supply 500 Million Vaccine Doses to WHO's Struggling Covax Initiative," *Washington Post*, May 3, 2021. Accessed at https://www.washingtonpost.com/world/moderna-vaccine-covax/2021/05/03/0837f4f4-ac0b-11eb-82c1-896aca955bb9_story.html.

116. "Fact Sheet: President Biden Announces Historic Vaccine Donation: Half a Billion Pfizer Vaccines to the World's Lowest-Income Nations," The White House, June 10, 2021. Accessed at https://www.whitehouse.gov/briefing-room/statements-releases/2021/06/10/fact-sheet-president-biden-announces-historic-vaccine-donation-half-a-billion-pfizer-vaccines-to-the-worlds-lowest-income-nations/.

117. Nathaniel Weixel, "Biden Vows US Will Be 'Arsenal of Vaccination' for Other Countries," *Hill*, April 28, 2021. Accessed at https://thehill.com/policy/healthcare/550854-biden-vows-us-will-be-arsenal-of-vaccination-for-other-countries.

118. "HHS Historical Highlights," U.S. Department of Health and Human Services, January 21, 2021. Accessed at https://www.hhs.gov/about/historical-highlights/index.html.

119. "What Is the United States' Share of World Energy Consumption?" U.S. Energy Information Administration. Accessed at https://www.eia.gov/tools/faqs/faq.php?id=87&t=1.

120. "Each Country's Share of CO2 Emissions," Union of Concerned Scientists, updated August 12, 2020. Accessed at https://www.ucsusa.org/resources/each-countrys-share-co2-emissions; "Countries in the World by Population (2021)," Worldometer. Accessed at https://www.worldometers.info/world-population/population-by-country/.

121. Lisa Friedman, "What Is the Green New Deal? A Climate Proposal, Explained," *New York Times*, February 21, 2019. Accessed at https://www.nytimes.com/2019/02/21/climate/green-new-deal-questions-answers.html.

122. Doug Holtz-Eakin, "How Much Will the Green New Deal Cost?" Aspen Institute, June 11, 2019. Accessed at https://www.aspeninstitute.org/blog-posts/how-much-will-the-green-new-deal-cost/.

123. Eliza Relman, "Alexandria Ocasio-Cortez Says Her Green New Deal Climate Plan Would Cost at Least $10 Trillion," *Business Insider*, June 5, 2019.

124. Andrew Puko and Timothy Restuccia, "At Earth Day Climate Summit, Biden Pushes for Sharp Cut to Greenhouse-Gas Emissions," *Wall Street Journal*, April 22, 2021. Accessed at https://www.wsj.com/articles /biden-to-urge-climate-action-at-world-leaders-summit-11619085614.

125. Sen. Mitch McConnell tweet, April 22, 2021. Accessed at https://twitter .com/LeaderMcConnell/status/1385291316008034313.

126. "Biden Promises Big on Climate Change. Delivering Will Be Much Harder," editorial in *Washington Post*, April 21, 2021. Accessed at https:// www.washingtonpost.com/opinions/biden-promises-big-on -climate-change-delivering-will-be-much-harder/2021/04/21/3392a908 -a154-11eb-a7ee-949c574a09ac_story.html.

127. Timothy Gardner and Valerie Volcovici, "Biden Budget's $14 Bln Hike for Climate Includes Big Boost for EPA, Science," Reuters, April 9, 2021. Accessed at https://www.reuters.com/world/us/biden-budgets-14-bln -hike-climate-includes-big-boosts-epa-science-2021-04-09/.

128. Lauren Sommer, "How Fast Will Biden Need to Move on Climate? Really, Really Fast," NPR, February 2, 2021. Accessed at https://www.npr.org /2021/02/02/963014373/how-fast-will-biden-need-to-move-on-climate -really-really-fast.

129. "Coal Explained," U.S. Energy Information Administration, updated December 1, 2020. Accessed at https://www.eia.gov/energyexplained /coal/coal-and-the-environment.php.

130. "How Much Carbon Dioxide Is Produced When Different Fuels Are Burned?" U.S. Energy Information Administration, updated June 17, 2020. Accessed at https://www.eia.gov/tools/faqs/faq.php?id=73&t=11.

131. "Preserving Coal Country," United Mine Workers, April 2021. Accessed at https://umwa.org/wp-content/uploads/2021/04/UMWA-Preserving -Coal-Country-2021.pdf.

132. Carol D. Leonning, "Top Leaders of Solyndra Solar Panel Company Repeatedly Misled Federal Officials, Investigation Finds," *Washington Post*, August 26, 2015. Accessed at https://www.washingtonpost.com /news/federal-eye/wp/2015/08/26/top-leaders-of-solyndra-solar-panel -company-repeatedly-misled-federal-officials-investigation-finds/.

133. Sarah Kaplan, "Thinking of Buying an Electric Vehicle? Read This First," *Washington Post*, March 30, 2021. Accessed at https://www .washingtonpost.com/climate-solutions/2021/03/30/climate-curious -electric-cars/.

134. "Fast Facts on Transportation Greenhouse Gas Emissions," U.S. Environmental Protection Agency, June 2020. Accessed at https://

www.epa.gov/greenvehicles/fast-facts-transportation-greenhouse-gas
-emissions.

135. "The Advantages of Nuclear Energy," Nuclear Energy Institute. Accessed
at https://nei.org/advantages.

136. Rebecca Tuhus-Dubrow, "The Activists Who Embrace Nuclear Power,"
New Yorker, February 19, 2021. Accessed at https://www.newyorker
.com/tech/annals-of-technology/the-activists-who-embrace-nuclear
-power.

137. "Chernobyl Accident 1986," World Nuclear Association, updated April
2020. Accessed at https://www.world-nuclear.org/information-library
/safety-and-security/safety-of-plants/chernobyl-accident.aspx.

138. Rebecca Tuhus-Dubrow, "The Activists Who Embrace Nuclear Power."

139. Rebecca Tuhus-Dubrow, "The Activists Who Embrace Nuclear Power."

140. "U.S. Energy Facts Explained," U.S. Energy Information Administration,
updated May 7, 2020. Accessed at https://www.eia.gov/energyexplained
/us-energy-facts/.

141. N. Sönnichsen, "Gross Output of the Oil and Gas Extraction Industry in
the United States from 1998 to 2019," Statista, November 6, 2020. Accessed
at https://www.statista.com/statistics/193418/gross-output-of-the-us-oil
-and-gas-extraction-industry-since-1998/.

142. "Keystone Pipeline Officially Canceled After Biden Revokes Key Permit,"
Reuters, June 9, 2021. Accessed at https://www.cnbc.com/2021/06/09/tc
-energy-terminates-keystone-xl-pipeline-project.html.

143. "Keystone XL Pipeline: Why Is It So Disputed?" BBC News, January 21,
2021. Accessed at https://www.bbc.com/news/world-us-canada
-30103078.

144. "Oil Embargo, 1973–1974," Office of the Historian, Foreign Service
Institute, U.S. State Department. Accessed at https://history.state.gov
/milestones/1969-1976/oil-embargo.

145. "Solar Investment Tax Credit (ITC)," Solar Energy Industries Association,
2021. Accessed at https://www.seia.org/initiatives/solar-investment-tax
-credit-itc.

146. John Fritze, "Trump Used Words Like 'Invasion' and 'Killer' to Discuss
Immigrants at Rallies 500 Times," *USA Today*, August 8, 2019. Accessed at
https://www.usatoday.com/story/news/politics/elections/2019/08
/08/trump-immigrants-rhetoric-criticized-el-paso-dayton-shootings
/1936742001/.

147. Jacqueline Thomsen, "Trump on Criticizing Mexican Immigrants:
'Peanuts' Compared to the Truth," *Hill*, August 2, 2018. Accessed at
https://thehill.com/homenews/administration/400196-trump-says
-calling-mexican-immigrants-rapists-was-peanuts-in.

148. Jane C. Timm, "Fact Check: Mexico Never Paid for It. But What About Trump's Other Border Wall Promises?" NBC News, January 12, 2021. Accessed at https://www.nbcnews.com/politics/donald-trump/fact -check-mexico-never-paid-it-what-about-trump-s-n1253983.

149. Mimi Dwyer, "Factbox: U.S. President-elect Biden Pledged to Change Immigration. Here's How," Reuters, January 15, 2021. Accessed at https:// www.reuters.com/article/us-usa-biden-immigration-promises-factbo /factbox-u-s-president-elect-biden-pledged-to-change-immigration -heres-how-idUSKBN29K1X1.

150. "Fact Sheet: President Biden Sends Immigration Bill to Congress as Part of His Commitment to Modernize Our Immigration System," The White House, January 20, 2021. Accessed at https://www.whitehouse.gov /briefing-room/statements-releases/2021/01/20/fact-sheet-president -biden-sends-immigration-bill-to-congress-as-part-of-his-commitment -to-modernize-our-immigration-system/.

151. Ashley Parker, Nick Miroff, Sean Sullivan, and Tyler Pager, "'No End in Sight.' Inside the Biden Administration's Failure to Contain the Border Surge," *Washington Post*, March 20, 2021. Accessed at https://www .washingtonpost.com/politics/biden-border-surge/2021/03/20/21824e94 -8818-11eb-8a8b-5cf82c3dffe4_story.html.

152. Nick Miroff, "Border Crossings Leveling Off but Remain Near 20-Year-High, Preliminary April Data Shows," *Washington Post*, April 23, 2021. Accessed at https://www.washingtonpost.com/national /mexico-border-crossings-april/2021/04/23/31206e82-a459-11eb-8a6d -f1b55f463112_story.html; Nick Miroff, "Border Arrests Rose Slightly in April, but Fewer Minors Crossing Without Parents Eases Pressure on Biden Administration," *Washington Post*, May 11, 2021. Accessed at https:// www.washingtonpost.com/national/border-arrests-rise -fewer-unaccompanied-minors/2021/05/11/c4c74d02-b1a8-11eb-a3b5 -f994536fe84a_story.html.

153. Jana Winter and Caitlin Dickson, "CBP: 'Perceptions of U.S. Immigration Policy Changes' Driving Border Surge," Yahoo News, April 23, 2021. Accessed at https://news.yahoo.com/cbp-perceptions-of-us-immigration -policy-changes-driving-border-surge-182555511.html.

154. Ashley Parker, Nick Miroff, Sean Sullivan, and Tyler Pager, "'No End in Sight.' Inside the Biden Administration's Failure to Contain the Border Surge."

155. "A Reagan Legacy: Amnesty for Illegal Immigrants," *All Things Considered*, NPR, July 4, 2010. Accessed at https://www.npr.org/templates/story /story.php?storyId=128303672.

156. Josh Boak, "AP Fact Check: Trump Plays on Immigration Myths," Associated Press, February 8, 2019. Accessed at https://www.pbs.org /newshour/politics/ap-fact-check-trump-plays-on-immigration-myths.

157. "Persons Obtaining Lawful Permanent Resident Status: Fiscal Years 1820 to 2019," The 2019 Yearbook of Immigration Statistics, U.S. Department of Homeland Security, October 27, 2020. Accessed at https://www.dhs.gov /immigration-statistics/yearbook/2019/table1.

158. Tara Bahrampour, Harry Stevens, Adrian Blanco, and Ted Mellnik, "2020 Census Shows U.S. Population Grew at Slowest Pace Since 1930s," *Washington Post*. Updated April 26, 2021. Accessed at https://www .washingtonpost.com/dc-md-va/interactive/2021/2020-census-us -population-results/?itid=lk_readmore_manual_6.

159. "The 2020 Census Offers a Powerful Argument for Immigration," editorial in *Washington Post*, April 29, 2021. Accessed at https://www.washingtonpost .com/opinions/the-2020-census-is-a-clarion-call-for-immigration/2021 /04/29/0c58df2e-a799-11eb-bca5-048b2759a489_story.html.

160. Josh Boak, "AP Fact Check: Trump Plays on Immigration Myths."

161. Abby Budiman, "Key Findings About U.S. Immigrants," The Pew Research Center, August 20, 2020. Accessed at https://www.pewresearch.org/fact -tank/2020/08/20/key-findings-about-u-s-immigrants/.

162. "How Many People are Coming to the US and Who is Immigrating to the US Today?" USA Facts. Accessed at https://usafacts.org/state-of-the -union/immigration/.

163. Nick Miroff, "Biden Cancels Border Wall Projects Trump Paid for with Diverted Military Funds," *Washington Post*, April 30, 2021. Accessed at https://www.washingtonpost.com/national/border-wall-cancelled /2021/04/30/98575af0-a9ec-11eb-b166-174b63ea6007_story.html.

164. "Office of the Chief Immigration Judge," U.S. Department of Justice. Updated December 7, 2020. Accessed at https://www.justice.gov/eoir /office-of-the-chief-immigration-judge.

165. "Who Is Eligible for Asylum of Refugee Protection in the U.S.?" Nolo.com. Accessed at https://www.alllaw.com/articles/nolo/us-immigration/who -eligible-asylum-refugee-protection.html.

166. "Immigration Court Backlog Tool," TRAC Immigration, March 2021. Accessed at https://trac.syr.edu/phptools/immigration/court_backlog/.

167. "The State of Immigration Courts: Trump Leaves Biden 1.3 Million Case Backlog in Immigration Courts," TRAC Immigration, January 19, 2021. Accessed at https://trac.syr.edu/immigration/reports/637/.

168. Julián Aguilar, "President Biden's Early Immigration Overhaul Has Overlooked One Growing Problem: A Massive Court Backlog," *Texas Tribune*, February 4, 2021. Accessed at https://www.texastribune .org/2021/02/04/joe-biden-immigraton-court-backlog/.

169. Kevin Sieff, "They Missed Their U.S. Court Dates Because They Were Kidnapped. Now They're Blocked from Applying for Asylum," *Washington Post*, April 24, 2021. Accessed at https://www.washingtonpost.com/world/2021/04/24/mexico-border-migrant-asylum-mpp/.

170. John Burnett, "Asylum-Seekers Are Entering the U.S. Again—But Many More Migrants Are Left Behind," NPR, March 6, 2021. Accessed at https://www.npr.org/2021/03/06/973824927/asylum-seekers-are-entering-the-u-s-again-but-many-more-migrants-are-left-behind.

171. Michael D. Shear, Zolan Kanno-Youngs, and Eileen Sullivan, "Young Migrants Crowd Shelters, Posting Test for Biden," *New York Times*, April 10, 2021. Accessed at https://www.nytimes.com/2021/04/10/us/politics/biden-immigration.html?action=click&module=Spotlight&pgtype=Homepage.

172. "Fiscal Year 2019 Entry/Exit Overstay Report," U.S. Department of Homeland Security, March 20, 2020. Accessed at https://www.dhs.gov/sites/default/files/publications/20_0513_fy19-entry-and-exit-overstay-report.pdf; S. Lock, "Number of Inbound International Visitors to the United States from 2011 to 2019," Statista, March 16, 2021. Accessed at https://www.statista.com/statistics/214686/number-of-international-visitors-to-the-us/.

173. "Member Countries," North Atlantic Treaty Organization, updated September 24, 2020. Accessed at https://www.nato.int/cps/en/natolive/topics_52044.htm.

174. "What Was the Warsaw Pact?" North Atlantic Treaty Organization. Accessed at https://www.nato.int/cps/us/natohq/declassified_138294.htm.

175. "Fact Sheet: Imposing Costs for Harmful Foreign Activities by the Russian Government," The White House, April 15, 2021. Accessed at https://www.whitehouse.gov/briefing-room/statements-releases/2021/04/15/fact-sheet-imposing-costs-for-harmful-foreign-activities-by-the-russian-government/.

176. "Remarks by President Biden on America's Place in the World," The White House, February 4, 2021. Accessed at https://www.whitehouse.gov/briefing-room/speeches-remarks/2021/02/04/remarks-by-president-biden-on-americas-place-in-the-world/.

177. James McBride, Andrew Chatzky, and Anshu Siripurapu, "What's Next for the Trans-Pacific Partnership (TPP)?" The Council on Foreign Relations. Updated February 1, 2021. Accessed at https://www.cfr.org/backgrounder/what-trans-pacific-partnership-tpp.

178. Doug Palmer, "Clinton Raved About Trans-Pacific Partnership Before She Rejected It," *Politico*, October 8, 2016. Accessed at https://www.politico.com/story/2016/10/hillary-clinton-trade-deal-229381.

179. "About Treaties," U.S. Senate. Accessed at https://www.senate.gov/about /powers-procedures/treaties.htm.

180. James McBride, Andrew Chatzky, and Anshu Siripurapu, "What's Next for the Trans-Pacific Partnership (TPP)?"; Alan Yuhas, "Congress Will Abandon Trans-Pacific Partnership Deal, White House Concedes," *Guardian*, November 12, 2016. Accessed at https://www.theguardian.com /business/2016/nov/12/tpp-trade-deal-congress-obama.

181. Curtis A. Bradley, Jack L. Goldsmith, and Oona A. Hathaway, "The Failed Transparency Regime for Executive Agreements: An Empirical and Normative Analysis," *Harvard Law Review*, 2020. Accessed at https:// harvardlawreview.org/2020/12/the-failed-transparency-regime-for -executive-agreements/.

182. Mohamed Younis, "China, Russia Images in U.S. Hit Historic Lows," Gallup, March 1, 2021. Accessed at https://news.gallup.com/poll/331082 /china-russia-images-hit-historic-lows.aspx.

183. Steve Beynon, "Biden's 1st Budget Request Sidelines Defense Spending in Favor of Massive Domestic Investments," Military.com, April 9, 2021. Accessed at https://www.military.com/daily-news/2021/04/09/bidens -1st-budget-request-includes-715-billion-dod-ignores-calls-slash-or-boost -military-spending.html.

CHAPTER 8

1. "Who coined the phrase 'United we stand, divided we fall'?" Quora, updated 2017. Accessed at https://www.quora.com/Who-coined-the -phrase-United-we-stand-divided-we-fall.

2. Dan Balz, Scott Clement, and Emily Guskin, "Americans Give Biden mostly Positive Marks for First 100 Days, Post-ABC Poll Finds," *Washington Post*, April 25, 2021. Accessed at https://www.washingtonpost .com/politics/2021/04/25/biden-100-days-poll/.

3. Mark Murray, "Poll: At 100 Days, Biden's Approval Remains Strong. Can the Honeymoon Last?" NBC News, April 25, 2021. Accessed at https:// www.nbcnews.com/politics/meet-the-press/poll-100-days-biden-s -approval-remains-strong-can-honeymoon-n1265199.

4. Jeffrey M. Jones and Lydia Saad, "U.S. Support for More Government Inches Up, but Not for Socialism," Gallup, November 18, 2019. Accessed at https://news.gallup.com/poll/268295/support-government-inches-not -socialism.aspx.

5. Claire Williams, "Raising Taxes on Wealthy Americans and Corporations to Fund Biden's Infrastructure Plan Is OK with over 1 in 2 Voters," Morning Consult, March 31, 2021. Accessed at https://morningconsult.

com/2021/03/31/biden-infrastructure-plan-raising-taxes-wealthy
-corporations/.

6. Bill Clinton, "President Clinton's 1996 State of the Union Address as delivered," Clinton White House Archives. January 23, 1996. Accessed at https://clintonwhitehouse4.archives.gov/WH/New/other/sotu.html.

7. Niv Elis, "CBO Projects CARES Act Will Cost $1.76 Trillion, Not $2.2 Trillion."

8. Doug Whiteman, "The Financial Facts You Never Learned About World War II," Moneywise, December 23, 2020. Accessed at https://moneywise.com/life/lifestyle/financial-facts-about-world-war-ii.

9. David Jackson, "Amid Fights over Donald Trump, Republicans Unite to Bash Joe Biden and His 100-Day Speech," *USA Today*, April 29, 2021. Accessed at https://www.usatoday.com/story/news/politics/2021/04/29/amid-infighting-republicans-unite-bash-joe-bidens-speech/7386489002/.

10. Lexi Lonas, "Cheney on Fist Bump with Biden: 'We're Not Sworn Enemies. We're Americans,'" *Hill*, April 29, 2021. Accessed at https://thehill.com/homenews/house/551096-cheney-on-fist-bump-with-biden-were-not-sworn-enemies-were-americans?rl=1.

11. "Make Tax-Dodging Companies Pay for Biden's Infrastructure Plan."

12. "Opportunity Zones," Economic Innovation Group. Accessed at https://eig.org/opportunityzones/history.

13. Lauren Camera, "Biden's Budget Significantly Boosts K-12 Education Spending."

14. "Community College FAQs," Community College Research Center.

15. Dave Lawler, "Belief in American Exceptionalism on the Decline: Poll," Axios, November 22, 2019. Accessed at https://www.axios.com/american-exceptionalism-poll-foreign-policy-ages-479fefc8-608b-4010-9c18-2c7e925ef4df.html..

16. Mark J. Perry, "Quotation of the Day on American Exceptionalism," American Enterprise Institute, June 22, 2018. Accessed at https://www.aei.org/carpe-diem/quotation-of-the-day-on-american-exceptionalism/.

17. "How the Great Awakening Impacted American Unity, Democracy, Freedom, & Revolution," *The Founding* (blog), April 27, 2018. Accessed at https://thefounding.net/effects-of-the-great-awakening-unity-democracy-freedom-revolution/.

18. Paul Johnson, *A History of the American People* (Harper Perennial, 1999).

19. Joe Biden, "Remarks by President Biden in Address to a Joint Session of Congress," The White House, April 28, 2021. Accessed at https://www.whitehouse.gov/briefing-room/speeches-remarks/2021/04/29/remarks-by-president-biden-in-address-to-a-joint-session-of-congress/.

20. Gregg Re, "Biden Could Be 'Most Progressive President Since FDR,' Sanders Predicts," Fox News, July 8, 2020. Accessed at https://www.foxnews.com/politics/biden-most-progressive-president-fdr-sanders.
21. Nate Silver, "Obama's No F.D.R.—Nor Does He Have F.D.R.'s Majority," FiveThirtyEight, March 1, 2010. Accessed at https://fivethirtyeight.com/features/obamas-no-fdr-nor-does-he-have-fdrs/.
22. "A Diamond Is Forever," De Beers Group. Accessed at https://www.debeersgroup.com/about-us/a-diamond-is-forever.

Afterword

August 31, 2021

The failure of the two parties to achieve any consensus on the withdrawal from Afghanistan, both before and after the deadly terrorist
attack which took thirteen American lives at the Kabul airport on
August 26, 2021, underscores the weakness that division creates in the
face of emboldened and unified autocratic and assertive adversaries.